INFANT and CHILD CARE

INFANT and CHILD CARE

A GUIDE to EDUCATION in GROUP SETTINGS

WILLIAM FOWLER

The Ontario Institute for Studies in Education

ALLYN and BACON, INC.

Boston London Sydney Toronto

To my first teachers, my children
Velia Mauri
Monique
and Josephine

Photo Chapter 1 by Jacqueline Roberts; all other photos by Ron Wood.
Illustrations by Helen Fox.

Library of Congress Cataloging in Publication Data

Fowler, William
    Infant and child care.

    Bibliography: p.
    Includes index.
      1. Child development—Study and teaching.
2. Domestic education—Study and teaching.
3. Play. I. Title.
HQ755.7.F68   372.21   79–10176
ISBN 0–205–06514–7

Printed in the United States of America.

CONTENTS

PREFACE

In *Infant and Child Care: A Guide to Education in Group Settings* I have tried to formulate a coherent approach to the problems of caring for children in groups through the application of principles of child development and learning. It is a system of early care and education designed to meet the socioemotional and intellectual needs of ordinary children from different cultural and home backgrounds. The book is both a theoretical statement and a detailed practical guide intended to serve a wide range of educational institutions and day care and preschool organizations.

The book consists of four parts, the first a theoretical chapter on human development and principles of early care and education (which are elaborated in Appendix A); and a series of three parts concerned with child care and development in relation to three basic types of experience characteristic of early development: basic care, play, and planned learning experience. Theory also serves as the conceptual framework for each of *three developmental interaction models* described for characteristic forms of early experience. A model for feeding, dressing, washing, and other *basic care routines* is discussed in Chapter 2; one concerning the *nature of play* and its relation to characteristics of materials in Chapters 6 and 7; and a model for *planned educational activity* (guided learning) in Chapter 10.

Each model chapter is followed by a series of chapters describing the use of space and materials, and teaching and care techniques appropriate for that activity. While these chapters concentrate on practical concerns and techniques in detail, they too are cast in an explanatory framework of principles. Two additional appendixes provide an evaluation guide for monitoring both children's development and the efforts of teachers to facilitate their development (Appendix B); and a chart of a toy curriculum (Appendix C) designed to supplement the discussion of how the design of materials affects their use that appears in Chapter 7. The overall plan of the book thus attempts to weave theory and practice together in a unified whole.

The book is rounded out by the addition of a short companion volume entitled *Curriculum and Assessment Guides for Infant and Child Care*. This book contains three age-graded, logically sequenced teaching programs. The first provides a comprehensive *curriculum on knowledge*, both of structures and processes, moving developmentally from the concrete toward the abstract. The second presents a sequenced series of *problem-solving tasks* and the third a detailed *program for fostering language development*. Each of the three programs includes detailed descriptions of techniques for teaching the various concepts.

These guides are completed by a comprehensive system (Environmental Profile) for evaluating the quality of early educational and group care environments and programs. The Environmental Profile provides for detailed ratings on the quality of a number of salient characteristics of several significant aspects of early care: physical space, toys and equipment, the child's socioemotional care, and the educational program. For convenience, the briefer child development-teacher monitoring guide presented in Appendix B and the toy curriculum presented in Appendix C of the main text are also included in the companion volume.

These twin books contain a number of unusual features. They present a theory and set of principles that are worked out in detailed techniques, point-by-point, for the care and education of infants and young children. Second, the principles and methods are comprehensive and are applied to all major aspects of cognitive learning, language, sensorimotor skills, and socioemotional development. Third, the entire approach is ecological in outlook, describing the care principles and characteristics of children and caregivers in terms of concrete relations with physical and social environments. The chapters on the physical and social environments, free play programs, the analysis of toys and materials, and the evaluation system all provide repeated testimony to this outlook. Fourth, theory is not only translated directly into specific techniques, but further spelled out in complete curriculum programs and assessment techniques. Fifth, the framework is written at once in terms of the universal needs and characteristics of children and child care, and in terms of the specific problems and needs of children from different cultures and home environments. It is interdisciplinary in scope and clinical as well as educational and developmental in orientation. Discussions of care problems of girls and boys and children from different culture, language, and emotional backgrounds are included. In general, the book is extensively supplied with examples of problems of care, education, and cognitive and socioemotional development, and ways of solving them.

The scope of the book and the extent of analysis and detail are intended to meet the needs and interests of many different educational levels and professional groups. The abundance of examples, the detailed account of methods and the way in which principles are constantly related to practice are designed to make the book particularly suitable for introductory courses in early education and child care both in general undergraduate programs and in community college and similar one and two year educational settings. The extent of descriptive detail, illustrations, and curriculum suggestions in the main text, as well as the curriculum and assessment guidebook, are likely to appeal to many practically focused preservice and inservice training programs. The division of the book into problem and activity topics, such as in Chapter 2, describing the basic routines of child care, in Chapter 7, describing the use of toys, or in Chapter 9, describing the specifics on organizing and supervising play groups, lends the book to selective use for highly specialized, practical training purposes, topic-by-topic. The two books are also in many ways manuals or reference guides equally intended to serve busy supervisors, teachers, day care workers, and other practitioners directly involved in day-to-day operation of centers and preschool programs of all kinds.

At the same time, the theoretical basis and scope of principles with which the book is developed would be useful for advanced undergraduates and specialized graduate courses at the M.Ed. level, where more use would be made of the theoretically oriented material presented in Chapters 1 and 6 and Appendix A. The book has in fact been used successfully in prepublication form with students ranging from the introductory community college level to the M.Ed. level, varying the theoretical and practical emphasis according to student interest. It is hoped that the attempted broad coverage and elaboration of concepts will make the published book similarly useful to teachers and users in the field in different ways at different times.

My own experience, as a researcher and teacher in early education and as a clinician and psychologist, has of course been a major influence on the book. The research embraces a variety of studies, many of which involve the design of total systems of care for fostering development in group settings. Within this framework, but also in the home and other settings, numerous small studies aimed more specifically at stimulating concept learning, problem solving, language (including second languages, such as Italian, French, Chinese, and Russian), early reading, and motor skills were undertaken. The interactive, play oriented model for guided learning, described in Chapter 10 and subsequent chapters, grew out of these studies. The larger framework on the total organization of the ecology of care, described in Parts II and III of the book, is founded in several longitudinal investigations, ranging from one to five years in length. These include an experimental nursery school for three year old identical twins and triplets, a comprehensive program developed while I was principal of the Laboratory Nursery School at the University of Chicago, a three year program of infant day care designed for a private agency, the Canadian Mothercraft Society, and a five year program on public day care developed for the first infant day care center established by the municipality of Metropolitan Toronto (see Bibliographies). In addition to designing programs, directing inservice teacher training and providing clinical guidance, I have taught full or part-time in several programs.

Many people have thus contributed to this book over a good many years. Aside from the many theorists and investigators to whom I owe much, I have learned most from teachers, supervisors, parents, and day care staff with whom I collaborated in the variety of nursery school, day care, and parent guidance programs I have undertaken. I would like to particularly thank the following people, who helped me in special ways: Nasim Khan and Karen Ogston for their important contributions to the Diagnostic-Developmental Monitoring and Environmental Profile assessment scales; Suzanne Gemmill-Freeman, Danda Humphreys, and Amy Swenson for their valuable editorial aid; Helen Fox for her painstaking illustrations; Jackie Roberts and Ronald Wood for their fine photography; Elisabeth Renko and the staff, parents, and children at the Woodbine day care center, and the supervisors, staff, parents, and children at the Wychwood day care center for kindly cooperating in the photography; Margot Videki, who typed the final manuscript so well, and many other typists who ably typed various portions of earlier drafts; Sandy Socolar, whose exceptional concern made publication possible at all; and former students and researchers too numerous to mention, who contributed many ideas and efforts to the projects through which much of the book was shaped.

And, as always, the children who were the touchstone of it all.

INTRODUCTION

The need for a comprehensive approach to the care of infants and young children in groups is a current matter of great concern. The trend for women to join the labor force has continued over many years and recently expanded until almost half of all adult women now work. Someone must care for their children while they work. How is it to be done? But it is not economics alone that pushes women to work and sparks the growth of institutionalized day care. The force and scope of the new movement for the emancipation of women has established the idea of day care as a permanent institution freely available for all women to use for their children at least some part of every day. The current rapid growth of parent co-op, storefront, agency, apartment, commercial, and other forms of day care, swelling the ranks of public day care and nursery schools, testifies to the power of this idea.

Actually, the practice of placing little children in the hands of "baby sitters" for substitute care during various periods of the day is as old as human society. In almost all folk societies, older sisters, aunts, grandmothers, and not infrequently many male members of the extended family routinely shared in the care of the young. Family life was embedded in a network of close relations in small communities. Work and home were seldom far apart and neighbor and family lived and worked side by side, dividing and co-operating in the care of the children as much as in the duties of preparing meals, making clothes, and growing or hunting for food. Duties were divided in different ways, following cultural practice, often by sex and age, but rarely were the mother and nuclear family alone left to care for the children. Methods were based on intuition and cultural practices, whose reasons were lost in the mist of history.

With the rise of the city as an accompaniment of advances in technology, the neighborly, shared work communities disappeared or evolved in different ways. Servants, slaves, and tutors performed the child care tasks for the people of means, while the bulk of the people continued to rely on the extended family and neighbors. In recent centuries, however, with the rise of industrial societies that have drawn women to work away from home, babysitters of one kind or another came into being, though they were not always known by that name. In English tradition, during the sixteenth century, village women began to take in the children of women who were beginning to work in factories or mines. Crowded in a poor kitchen with a curriculum of the switch and perhaps an ABC hornbook, the 'dame schools' were forerunners of both public and nursery schools and modern day care centers, especially of family day care.

While the public school has long been an established institution in industrialized societies, and the nursery school dates to the turn of the century, the day care center has a shorter history. Early day care is widespread in all socialist countries, such as China, the USSR, and Eastern Europe, is fairly common in Western Europe and Israel, but has only recently taken root in Canada and the United States. Public and professional acceptance of group care for children before the ordinary school age of five to seven has stumbled on the traditional concern for the young child's supposed need for full-time mothering at home. Yet generations of mainly middle class three and four year olds attending nursery schools have been shown in the collected studies of the 1930s and 1940s to develop at least as well intellectually and socially as children who have stayed at home. Recent studies on day care, moreover, including those of the author, have demonstrated that given adequate standards, infants cared for during the day in groups can thrive as well or better than infants cared for exclusively at home.

Despite continuing expressions of concern, the expanding social need in parallel with accumulating evidence suggest that group care is apparently here to stay. The long-run social need is just too large to stop it. The only question remaining is the form group care will take and the methods to be employed. The most obvious gap in the field of early care is the absence of a consistent philosophy and set of guiding principles which can encompass the social and educational needs of all children cared for in groups.

The Need for Comprehensive Early Child Care and Education

Current practice in the newly emerging field of day care borrows heavily from the philosophy of the open curriculum of free play characteristic of the traditional nursery school. Central to the guiding ideal is an image of the young child's need for warm and loving care. Closeness of relations, cuddling, and concentration on socioemotional development have been dominant themes in theory, if not always in practice, in the centers that are all too frequently poorly staffed with poorly trained personnel.

These orientations to early child care should not be downgraded. But loving care, informal social relations, and play alone do not make a complete curriculum to foster development. The laboratory nursery school is a creation of the university and research centers, generally attended only a few hours each day by selected groups of upper middle-class children from highly stimulating homes. The nine to ten hour days children from the broad population of both working-class and middle-class homes now spend in day care demand that careful attention be devoted to the comprehensiveness of programs.

One effort of this kind has been the "Head Start" programs for poor children, which have sometimes planned educational experiences for infants and pre-school children to compensate for the barren circumstances of a slum community. Whatever the merits of such programs, including whether they build sufficiently on the positive features of the child's culture, they are essentially research programs not widely available for the community at large. The more widely distributed Head Start type of programs for the poor have focused more on health and basic care than on cognitive development.

Methods derived from borrowed philosophies and specialized research programs must give way or be integrated into a generalized strategy arising from the character of group care itself. Group day care must be taken seriously and defined in its own terms if day care is not to descend to a drab system of institutionalized baby sitting. But even in the nursery school field, curriculum reform has been underway for some years. There is growing recognition that any institution where little children daily spend substantial periods must construct an ecologically complete social framework that tends to the complete developmental needs of the child—physically, socially, emotionally, and cognitively.

Recent research on deprivation, pointing to the combined importance of early stimulation and quality care, has aroused interest in devoting more systematic attention to the variety and quantity of dimensional, number, classification, and other concepts in the nursery school program. For one thing, even the favored laboratory schools find children benefit from an enriched curriculum, while many nursery schools are organized and increasingly serve working parent clientele in ways that are scarcely distinguishable from other forms of group day care. The total field of early group care is more and more one in which all the different forms of nursery schools and day care are merging into a common need for a total ecological program of child care and education. Whether children are cared for in institutions serving day care, nursery schools, cooperatives, or children with handicaps, emotional problems, or special disabilities, the children's needs for development are always comprehensive. In this book we shall use the terms *day care, group (day) care, (pre)-schools,* and *nursery schools,* more or less interchangeably to apply to any type of setting where young children are cared for and educated in groups.

Sources of the Approach

The approach to day care discussed in this book can be traced to a variety of sources. There are first the various cognitive, social, and behavioral theories of development and learning (notably those of Piaget), and psycholinguistic rule theory. I have formed these into a conception of human development as developmental learning, which combines both cognitive and socioemotional processes. The conception is one that sees mental processes and behavior operating as a unified whole in real life situations, uniting problem solving, learning, the emotions, and perceptual-motor action in all spheres of behavioral and linguistic activity, social and nonsocial alike. The approach thus also draws heavily on Lewinian traditions in social psychology, as well as psychodynamic theories of interpersonal and ego psychology, and sociological perspectives of social roles, structures and institutions. The model is in brief interdisciplinary in form.

A second set of sources is the large body of concepts and accumulating studies on the role of experience, especially early experience, in children's development. In the history of psychology the most prevalent beliefs on development have centered on the mind and body as preformed or at least predetermined by biology. Growth from birth to adulthood was seen essentially as changes in the size of basic structures present in miniature form at earliest conception (preformationism). The influence of Darwinian theory in evolution strongly supported the biological basis for development, but recognized that development consists of changes in form as well as changes in size.

The most systematic account of development as predetermined by biology in this way is found in the extensive writings of Gesell, one of the chief founders of the field of child development. His careful normative observations of children at successive ages have influenced generations of developmental psychologists, teachers, and other practitioners in the field of early education and child care up to the present time. In Gesell's framework, characteristics predominant at each age were described for several areas (language, motor, adaptive, and personal-social) in stereotypic patterns. The norms of children growing up in a single, middle class university community (Yale University) were confidently affirmed as universals of development for every child in every culture. This approach had some advantages in reassuring teachers and parents that children sometimes grow out of their current problems as they moved to the next age. But such a bias, viewing development as a series of biologically determined age stages that automatically succeed one another, left little room for individual and cultural differences and the prevention and resolution of children's problems through manipulating experience. The fact is that children did not always grow out of their problems with the arrival of the next age. Some even got worse, and children in some settings (those living in poverty or broken homes) seemed to have more chronic difficulties than others.

In recent times, several strands of research, theory, and growing public awareness of important social problems have combined to advance a more rounded theory of human development that brings into prominence the role of experience and early child care in fostering development. Probably the most significant influence has been public awareness, growing out of research and national and world political pressures, of the role of poverty and cultural differences in child development. Development in the urban ghetto and poverty-stricken rural areas has been discovered to follow a course of cumulative failure in school, very different from the idealized development of the middle-class world of the Yale University community. This awareness has been buttressed by studies collected over many years showing how widely abilities and school achievement vary (by both type and level) with conditions of family life, culture, and socioeconomic background.

Whether emphasis is placed on the child's life in poverty or on racial and ethnic discrimination and the failure of schools to adapt to and build on the intrinsic strengths of each child and his or her culture, both factors challenged squarely the old view of development as an automatic, biologically regulated process. Moreover, many research studies, by showing that development could be varied systematically through planned early education programs, further reinforced the new views. Children often regressed or reverted to their indigenous patterns once special programs were terminated and children entered school. Public schools and community programs apparently failed to match what systematic research programs could deliver.

Paralleling this development of public and professional consciousness of the influence of socioeconomic background on children's development has been the work on early deprivation in both children and animals. It had long been observed that infants reared in residential institutions (popularly known as "orphan asylums" and now generally abandoned) often did not do as well as children reared at home. More careful observations have confirmed that various developmental trends of apathy, hyperactivity, lack of social involvement and low order abilities are characteristic outcomes of early confinement to residential, mass care institutions. Partly spurred by these observations, researchers undertook to compare the development of dogs, monkeys, and other animals under various conditions of restricted early experience, such as isolation from other animals and reduced light, sound, and activity. Patterns of rigidity, turbulent relations, withdrawal, and a reduction of curiosity and of intelligent and adaptive behavior, similar to the patterns developing in institutionally reared infants, were typical.

Each of these separate lines of investigation appears to point to the same strong conclusions. Experience exercises powerful effects on children's development, and the effects of early experience may be particularly pervasive. The earlier, more pervasive, and more persisting the deprivation, the more difficult it is to reverse the damaging effects; conversely, within broad limits, the better the care and stimulation, the better the development. It has become obvious that, while our basic biology may define the forms and limits of human development in a general way (our genotype), experience is vital to realize our individual potential (phenotype).

From the research on deprivation of infants reared in institutions, however, there arose a separate, worrisome question. Perhaps it was not the poor quality of care alone that produced the damaging consequences, but the separation from the mother and the absence of the maternal bonds of loving care and attachment. Institutionalized infants were invariably children reared apart from their parents, who had died, or had abandoned or were otherwise incapable of rearing their children. A separate line of research has pointed up the apparent dependency of infants on maternal attachment and the stress that separation from parents entailed. In the light of the accelerating expansion of day care right down to infancy to accommodate the changing role of women, the question was not an idle one. Although *day* care does not involve full time or permanent separation of the child from the mother—a point that was often lost sight of in the heat of debate—it often does mean complete separation from home for most of the infant's waking hours, five days of every week. Could children adapt and develop away from home for such prolonged daily periods, as well as they do at home, even under the best forms of group care, let alone the typical, "average" quality likely to prevail in most day care centers?

The evidence is certainly not all in on this and many related questions. But there have been enough substantial investigations, including my own two major longitudinal studies* to make us believe that day care can be a healthy supplementary setting in which to rear children. Children in various regions, countries, and types of day care have been regularly found to thrive as well or better than children reared exclusively at home. Studies have included infants almost from birth, with care provided ranging in quality from moderate to high

* A developmental learning approach to infant care in a group setting. *Merrill-Palmer Quarterly*, 1972, *18*, 145–175.
   Day care and its effects on early development: A study of group and home care in multi-ethnic, working-class families. Toronto: Ontario Institute for Studies in Education, 1978.

level, children from many backgrounds of culture and class, and frequently children of single, working mothers. This is not to say that day care is necessarily an adequate environment for young children, as the survey of common forms of early group care in Chapter 3 makes clear. It also is in the nature of research studies, on which our knowledge of day care depends, that an important effect of an investigation is to improve the quality of care. Day care workers respond to the attention, as well as the knowledge that they are being judged, by devoting more effort to care. Investigations often bring extra resources in the form of materials, enriched care, and specially designed, stimulating educational programs.

Nevertheless, if ordinary day care does not always come up to standards, the point has been widely demonstrated that, at least under the right conditions, separation from parents and home each day need pose no threat to the child's development. Indeed, the problem of separation and maternal care is something of an invented problem, inasmuch as vast numbers of children, including infants, have been daily separated from mothers who work throughout the world for generations, as we have earlier pointed out. Children have been cared for historically in multiple care relations by other members of the extended family or neighbors, and more recently by baby sitters, while the mother works in the fields, community, or on the job. Although there are consequences, they do not appear to be either necessarily bad or necessarily good. How children develop, in other words, *depends more on the quality of care* than on the setting or the fact of a single caregiver versus many caregivers in day care and the home. Group day care, moreover, offers certain possibilities for enriching the variety of social, intellectual, and play experiences that are often difficult to match in all but the wealthiest homes. Yet the bond, and the quality of loving attention, between parent and child may even be enhanced through the day care experience, as some studies show.

What is most consistently evident from studies on the effects of early experience on children's development is that a multiplicity of factors jointly determine developmental progress. It is difficult to isolate any single factor or cluster of factors that make a difference; it is the total, cumulative effects of care and stimulation, the *ecology of relations* in the child's life situation of home and day care that determines the outcome.

The best research programs in specialized schools, group day care settings, and the home all incorporate a number of features that together foster development. And in programs designed for group settings, whether for schools or day care, the most successful involve close relations between the family and the institution. There may be varying emphases and different strategies, but there are generally a number of central features of care and education attended to in some constructive manner. Among them are involvement of the child in positive social experiences, both with adults and with peers; supportive emotional attitudes and flexibility in handling the child; stimulation of language, concepts, and other forms of cognitive learning; attention to perceptual motor processes, including (usually) mastery of whole body processes; availability and arrangement of the environment and materials conducive to play; and some concern for individualization by pacing and sequencing activity to each child's developmental level. The principles and methods presented in the text represent an attempt to synthesize these features in a systematic conception of care and learning.

I

HUMAN
DEVELOPMENT

1

The Nature of
Human Development

First steps

The Setting for Human Development

The Social and
Environmental
Basis of Knowledge

Children do not learn by chance; they develop according to the practices of the worlds in which they live. Children grow up in many worlds: the world of the family, the world of school and playmates, and the world of culture, community, and work. Each combines a physical setting, ways of doing things, and ideas, that combine to furnish distinctive experiences that shape children's lives.

The process of acquiring the knowledge and ways of their worlds is called socialization, the way in which children become competent social beings. The range of characteristics children can develop are set by biology, but the particular combination of characteristics the individual child actually learns is

3

determined by the worlds in which he or she grows up. Thus, although children have the potential to learn a great many things, they will learn only what the environment and culture provide.

Culture: The Historical and Collective Nature of Knowledge

Children acquire knowledge primarily through learning from others, because the world is too complex for them to master alone. The child cannot discover how the world works without the aid of knowledgeable persons—parents, relations, playmates, neighbors, storekeepers, and day care teachers. The knowledge that today enables us to construct complicated machinery and computers has taken thousands of years to develop. No individual could hope to learn a small fraction of the many intricate ideas we take so much for granted, even through a lifetime of experimentation, without building on the learning of past generations. The child will not develop language, counting, and mechanical skills through exploration alone, essential as direct experience may be. The guidance and example of those experienced in life and skilled in society's knowledge are essential.

Knowledge is thus above all a social thing, collectively acquired and collectively passed on. Every society and culture possesses a body of knowledge—practical knowledge for everyday living (coping and work skills), social knowledge about its institutions (such as its form of government), and basic knowledge about the nature of things (like gravity). This body of knowledge develops through historical accumulation and cultural diffusion. From earliest times, each generation has passed on what it knows to succeeding generations, and information spreads from one culture to another in varying degrees. In each case knowledge is added to and transformed by the uses to which each new generation and receiving culture put the knowledge transmitted. Thus the principles of steam engines, first applied to operating mine and mill machinery in England in the eighteenth century, were later applied to running trains and steamboats. And the use of steam engines gradually spread to all countries, but at different speeds and in different forms depending on their degree of industrialization and type of resources (using steam to mill lumber or to weave cotton, for example). No single individual, even an Einstein or a da Vinci, contributes relatively very much to any society's store of knowledge; it is the collective effort of each generation that significantly advances the level of knowledge available. It was not Einstein alone who developed the theory and methods for using atomic energy, but the combined efforts of a generation of scientists and engineers throughout Europe, America, and the industrialized world. Moreover, this work built on the physics and engineering of earlier generations and prepared the way for present attempts to build non-polluting nuclear energy plants (fusion).

Knowledge is not equally distributed, nor is all the knowledge of any generation passed on. Because different members and segments of society make different contributions and have different needs, the information passed on combines the trivial and the irrationally traditional with information that is significant, useful, and socially and aesthetically valuable to the life and problems of rising generations. People who work at different occupations learn different skills, for example, when technological change replaces one invention with another (as electric and diesel trains replaced steam trains) or when tastes in art, fashion, and even child rearing change.

Goals and Values: Culture and the Functional Basis of Knowledge

Knowledge is as much a tool as an abstraction. Much of what a child learns is society's concepts of goals to strive for and means to attain them. The range of occupations and skills are very different, for example, in agricultural and industrial societies, in fishing and farm communities, and for rich and poor within the same society. Correspondingly, children in different social settings will be socialized according to a variety of concepts and skills. There are basic concepts about the nature of things common to all cultures, such as that things have color, shape, size, and can be described in words. But there is variation in how many colors are recognized, how objects are labeled and grouped, and which language is learned, according to the ways in which cultures have put together their experience over many generations in adapting to the environment. Eskimos are highly skilled at detecting small changes in weather, ice, and snow, skills necessary for survival in the north. People of the New Guinea rain forests have developed similarly complex knowledge about the characteristics of plant and animal life in their areas. Children of the urban poor in a big metropolis become adept at learning the daily survival skills of life in the slums.

Socialization is thus a process through which children learn the ways people have developed historically for getting along in the world. Skills are not merely handed down and enforced by cultural tradition, but are also learned because they help one to cope in a given environment with a given group of people. This functional or practical basis for much of our knowledge extends to the social rules of manners and cooperation as much as to the obviously practical things of living like eating, sewing, hammering, or counting. Without some form of manners and methods of cooperation, family, friends, neighbors, and working groups would live in constant conflict, and could not divide and coordinate their daily tasks. No child or adult learns and lives alone. We all learn and do things in relation to the groups of people in the various milieus in which we live.

Inequality: Variations in Knowledge and Socialization

Not all that children learn in the culture and milieus in which they develop is equally beneficial or even socially functional, however. Families occupy different social positions and work roles. Inequality in income, jobs, and social status creates different degrees of advantage and disadvantage for parents in socializing their children to acquire the range of skills and socioeconomic positions the society offers. Differences between families are small in the once-prevalent folk communities that are being eliminated by the spread of urban civilization. Except for a few specialized roles such as those of tribal leaders and priests, families pretty much all followed the same community pattern of food gathering, hunting, fishing, or tilling the land, according to the way the tribe or village lived. However difficult life became during periods of drought, flood, or scarcity of game, children were all reared in a common way, close to the activities of the adults. The skills they learned were rather similar and adaptive to the way of life of the culture.

There has, however, usually been one sharp exception to this pattern of uniformity in folk cultures. Boys and girls have typically been reared in different ways. Girls have learned skills centering around their biological role of bearing children. This role extended beyond tending the children themselves to a variety of related activities of household maintenance, such as cooking, cleaning, making clothes, and varying degrees of agricultural activity. The rearing of boys, in contrast, has been directed toward more active tasks in the wider community, such as hunting, fishing, tending animals, making tools and weapons, providing houses and community buildings, defending the community, and generally supervising and engaging in planning, decision-making and leadership roles. While cultures have varied in the way they have actually divided the tasks, and some cultures have developed a considerably wider scope of responsibility and leadership for women, the historical trend of male predominance and prestige is widespread and persistent.

The development of complex social systems was made possible by the invention of complex tools. The invention of the wheel, the working of metals to forge tools and weapons, and the ability to fashion wood, stone, animal skins, and plant fibers in increasingly complicated ways for housing, clothes, food, and transportation, led gradually to an increasing division of labor. Different trades emerged in which people began to specialize in skills such as tanning, making weapons, stone working, carpentry, and many others. Differences in child rearing, heretofore evident mainly between the sexes, began to develop in many ways.

The growth of technology and specialization, even in the early periods of civilization, brought people together to work and live in common areas for ease in manufacture and trade, leading to the establishment of cities and the growth of the supporting service trades and government that city life required. These in turn led to the development of elite groups, who worked and associated together to further their own interests, and who socialized their children to follow their special pathways. The development of trade associations and leadership elites, and the growing disparity between working the land in the country and the specialized skills needed in the city extended social stratification throughout society. Differences between work roles of families and subgroups in the society not only brought differences between types of knowledge, skill, and the way children were reared, but also led to inequalities in opportunity to acquire the knowledge needed for more varied and skilled ways of living. The different ways in which children (especially boys) were reared to fit the roles of their parents became adaptive in highly particularized ways. (Few opportunities for specialized skill development appeared for girls until the beginning of the industrial revolution in the fifteenth century.) However, these differences were also partly maladaptive, especially for the less skilled, lower income groups, whose opportunities for educating their children to gain more complex skills and higher social positions became increasingly restricted.

Few societies in the modern world do not share these problems of differences between children in opportunities for socialization. Today in North America and elsewhere we speak of the skills of the educated middle class as those necessary for adapting in the complicated work and social roles demanded of a technologically dominated society. Yet we still have large populations internally in each industrialized country, and externally in the developing third world countries, whose skill patterns are well adapted to the concrete patterns of farming, hunting, fishing, and rural life, but poorly adapted to the abstract manipulations required in contemporary urban society. The problem is accelerating because technology is growing rapidly, with little social planning, and the skills once demanded mainly of the more privileged middle class are increasingly required of all members of society. There are fewer and fewer jobs for unskilled labor and more and more work roles demanding complicated mental manipulations with abstract symbols (language and mathematics). The problems of advantage-disadvantage and discrimination between the sexes in opportunities for socialization are thus fundamental aspects of the social context to consider in studying and equalizing human development.

The Mind and Personality

Some Definitions

The *mind* is a term we use to describe a capacity for thinking and understanding. *Cognition* or *cognitive processes* are terms that have recently come into widespread use, because they emphasize processes of understanding and knowing in an active way. *Competence* is now often used in place of the older terms, *intelligence* and *abilities,* because it suggests particular skills to perform tasks that can be learned, rather than capacities fixed at birth.

What the Mind Does

The mind is the basis of all human activity. It is a complex product of the influences of the physical and social environments experienced by a person. The activities of the mind cannot be observed, of course, except through our behavior (what we do and say), since they take place inside the head, and consist of nothing more than the activities of the brain. The brain is a complex organ. It is the agent through which information is sent to and received from the environment, by directing and coordinating the sensory (seeing, hearing, touching, etc.) and motor systems. The brain also sends and receives information to and from the other organ systems of the body. The term *mind* tends to suggest the cognitive (intellectual) functions of mental processes, while *personality* places more emphasis on the emotions. For our purposes, we are here using them synonymously to embrace all of the emotional, cognitive, and social aspects of mental functioning.

The mind is formed by the effects of environmental stimulation on the brain, working through the sensory and motor systems. These two systems, working closely together, are the means through which we get a running picture of the world and are able to navigate and act effectively. But the brain does not receive stimulation from the environment like a mirror. It *actively chooses* among all the sights, sounds, and touches presented to it, and puts them together to form its own organized picture and way of doing things. *How* it chooses and organizes is a constantly changing and developing process throughout life, depending on how the mind has already been formed from past experience and what choices are available to it in the present.

The mind is thus the central governing or regulating agency of all understanding and feeling, through its continuing interaction with both the outside world and our entire body system. It is the source of all of our planning and decision making, and the center of our feelings about everything.

Mental Processes: Concepts (Ideas) and Rules

The mind makes use of concepts for the purpose of understanding and adapting to the environment. The information the mind contains is not a fixed thing, but a constantly changing set of ideas, or concepts, about the world and our own actions. Concepts are based on *general* rules for understanding and doing things. Rules vary with the type of knowledge or skill being dealt with, but in general the regularity of things in the physical and social world makes mental rules the basis for the way the mind works. We can utilize these mental rules because the environment can often be understood on the basis of general regularities. We shape our pictures of the world in terms of the regularities we have previously experienced.

When we think of "a chair" or "dishwashing," for example, we are usually concerned less with the features of any particular chair or dishwashing process, than with the general features and uses of any chair or any dishwashing that we attend to. We make use of the *critical* features that distinguish chairs from tables and other objects, and we distinguish washing from drying dishes or other activities. We generally pay little attention to a lot of other particulars that are unimportant in using the chair (size, material) or in getting the dishwashing accomplished (color or shape of the soap). Thus, concepts are defined by rules that enable us to recognize and use the items concerned, such as that chairs have seats for sitting on and backs for leaning on, or that washing dishes involves material for cleaning and liquid (water for dissolving and washing away food and the cleansing agent). In short, our ideas and actions are governed by generalized pictures we form about things, which we gradually learn over the course of development.

But even when we talk about some unimportant (nonrule) feature of a *particular* chair or a *specific* time we washed the dishes, we discuss particulars in terms of rules about *general* qualities. We say, for example, this is a *big* chair or the dishwashing took a *long* time. In both instances, it is clear that these are generalities ("bigness" and "longness"), each recognized by its own special rules. Rules for how much space an object occupies, relative to other objects, define "bigness"; and rules for how much time has elapsed, relative to other activities, define "longness" (in the time sense).

Types of Concepts

There are three kinds of concepts that serve different purposes in our relations with the environment. Each type of idea is known through the rules that define the critical characteristics of the concepts. These three forms of mental processes consist of: (1) concepts and rules about things, or the *knowledge* we acquire about the world (real and imaginary) and how it works; (2) concepts and rules for *problem solving,* or rules for figuring out problems, reasoning, and carrying out actions to reach goals; and (3) language rules for *coding,* or rules for representing ideas in some shorthand or abstract form.

Knowledge Rules

Rules of knowledge make up the pictures we have of everything in the environment, objects, plants, animals, and people. There are also ideas about how things work and change, as well as imaginary ideas and the pictures we each have of ourself and our own goals and activities. Our knowledge constitutes a kind of map or plan of the world, serving as a framework enabling us to understand and carry out activities in the home, school, at work, and everywhere else in daily life.

The examples above about chairs and dishwashing illustrate two knowledge concepts and some rules that are used for working with them. One case was a common object, the other a common activity (a series of actions with objects). *Bigness* and *longness* illustrated knowledge concepts of another type, that of relations between objects (size differences) and between activities (how long processes take). There are many other types of knowledge, each with its rules by which we know and use it, ranging from the characteristics of things, like *color, shape,* and the *material* of which it is made, to complicated concepts like *factories* and *computers,* and imaginary ones like *fairies* and *stories.* Knowledge consists essentially of rules for guiding us in the general patterns of how the world is constructed and functions.

Problem Solving Rules

The rules for solving problems are the mental processes and strategies we employ when acting to gain and use knowledge, whether or not expressed in physical action. All behavior involves some sort of problem solving, or figuring out what means to use in order to reach goals. All human activity involves seeking goals, ranging from the trivial designs of doodling to major life goals of studying for degrees or choosing trades; in each activity we must figure out what means to employ. One can, for example, draw with a pencil or pen and get different results, or select different schools and combinations of courses, or choose from a number of different jobs in the same occupational field. Even in routine tasks of eating, preparing for bed, or bathing a baby, there are continuing problems of deciding what to do next and how best to do it. Most of the important goals we seek are part of a chain of generalized goals extending over time, in which achieving immediate goals are steps in achieving the larger, long-range goals. Thus, buying a new tool and learning a new skill are goals involving various means to reach these ends, which in turn are means to longer-range career goals like job advancement.

The rules for mental action (figuring out) and physical action (trying out different ways and carrying out the ones found to work best) are thus the set of *rules for working on means and ends.* Chief among these are *analytic* rules (which help in the search for particular methods and especially in recognizing relevant or important tool objects and features) and *synthetic* rules (which help to relate or pull things together, to use several skills or features at once or in sequence to reach a goal). In letter writing, for instance, we have to pick particular words (analyze) and string them together (synthesize) to convey what we wish to say. In helping a baby girl learn to eat, we need to guide her to recognize the handle of a spoon (analyze) and hold it (synthesize), keep the spoon right side up (synthesize), see her food (analyze) and use the ladle of the spoon (analyze) for scooping up her food (synthesize). There is such a similar structure of means and ends to every task, which often includes many intermediate goals, to analyze and integrate, using such additional rules as *abstracting, sequencing,* and *coordinating* over a period of time.

Coding Rules

Every thought and every action is coded in some form, either in language or in some other method of physical representation. We cannot have any idea of a thing unless it appears in some form or medium. There must be a *vehicle* in which the rules of knowledge about plants and houses and other things are carried, a process which involves *coding,* or representation of the knowledge in some systematic shorthand form.

The first and simplest method of coding our ideas is through physical action itself. This is the most direct and least abstract method, and thus appears first in the period of infancy. Actually, sensory and motor processes work together in action systems that become generalized to a variety of similar types of means-ends activities (what Piaget calls "schema"). Though it may not seem that way, when an infant reaches for a block and puts it in a cup, he has in mind a *general* action picture of reaching, grasping, placing, and inserting movements in space that enables him to repeat the action with almost any object and container of similar size, and to vary the angle and distance of his movements in many ways. Among these general rules of the basic sensorimotor code are those of the idea of objects as a goal, regardless of shape, size, position, etc.; the idea of physical means as tools to reach ends; the idea of substitutibility of means and of goals (that different means can be used to reach a given goal, or that the same means can be used to reach a similar but different goal), and so on. The basic sensorimotor code is thus a set of rules for mentally representing and acting on the environment in *direct action.*

Starting at birth, the infant experiments with all aspects of means and ends activities, using principally her hands and eyes. In the course of these experiences, and guided by parents and others, she gradually forms more and more complex general action pictures in a whole series of steps. Starting with looking and grasping, independent of one another, she advances through coordinating how she looks and grasps, to a stage during the second year when she can herself devise any number of combinations of methods and goals, even using hidden objects. At each step along the way she forms a generalized *action* picture of each new component (the new and different steps involved and how to organize them into new strategies), thus always coding her ideas about things in a sensorimotor code of rules.

As the infant develops further, she begins to make use of visual imagery and language codes. Much of our experience in modern life involves gaining information from pictures, books and magazines, television and the movies. *Coding for visual imagery* consists of rules for using a number of cues that indicate three dimensional space in objects drawn or photographed on a flat plane (such as shading, size differences and perspective), rules that babies learn from looking at pictures and comparing them with real objects.

Learning how to put knowledge rules in a *language code* (language learning) also begins early, but with development becomes increasingly more important than either visual or sensorimotor codes. Language codes are not directly tied to a situation like sensorimotor rules, nor do they "look like" the thing represented as do objects coded in pictures or diagrams. The highly abstract character of language codes makes language an extremely flexible and precise tool for communication and understanding. Using the rules of language we can move quickly and selectively to any situation and moment in time, real or imaginary, describing things in detail or in general terms according to need. We can choose exactly what knowledge we wish to deal with, such as the shape or other features of things (adjective rules like "round" and "large"), what is acting on what (subject and object rules, like "the child painted a picture"), or relations between things (prepositional rules, like "on, in, or under the box").

The strength of language is, however, also its limitation: its abstract flexibility makes it a poor vehicle for acquainting us with new things unless we can see them. For this reason, language communication often works best when accompanied by direct (sensorimotor) experience, or at least pictures of unfamiliar objects and events. Parallel sensorimotor experience is ordinarily essential for young children, since their competence in language is not fully developed, and their knowledge is so limited and concrete.

Coding Rule Subtypes. There are variations for each of the three primary forms of knowledge coding. There are specialized sensorimotor and game codes for athletics, constructed especially of whole body and leg movements, and aesthetic codes for dance, singing, and playing musical instruments. Visual imagery codes include drawing, sculpturing, and making diagrams, all of which may be fairly abstract. Language too has many complex, specialized, and aesthetic forms, such as those in mathematics, music, poetry, and novels. Many of the forms overlap, such as the involvement of both sensorimotor and language systems in singing and playing musical instruments.

Mental Organization

The Mind as a System

The three types of mental processes work together in an organized way. Knowledge does not appear separately from problem-solving or coding rules, and problem-solving and coding are also interrelated. Every mental act, and the physical action which frequently accompanies it, invariably occurs in such a way that all three cognitive processes serve key roles in an integrated system. Only a few rules of each type are typically involved in any single act, but some of each type are necessarily involved. Knowledge of a thing (an object or an event) *requires* the involvement of some rule about the way it is used (problem solving rule) and a form (coding rule) in which the idea is represented. When a child learns to ride a tricycle, for instance, she not only becomes familiar with key features and functions of tricycles and her body (knowledge rules), but she uses strategies for identifying and using key parts of the tricycle and her body in a coordinated manner (problem solving rules). She is also making use of

FIGURE 1-1
*Relations between
feelings and ideas.
The child's
confidence in his
own skills affects
his feelings about
the task.*

Lack of confidence in skills leads to
negative feelings toward skills.

High confidence in skills makes the child
see a problem as a chance to demonstrate
skills.

sensorimotor coding (direct action rules). If she were looking at pictures or telling about riding, she would be employing pictorial and language codes, respectively.

There is a structure and sequence to human activity that always follows some variation of a basic pattern. At the beginning of a cycle we are presented with a situation in the context of a social setting. Based on whatever knowledge we have of the situation, we select goals according to some combination of the situational elements and our own interests. We engage in problem solving strategies until we reach a satisfactory level of goal attainment, at which point the problem is solved, the cycle ends and we proceed to a new event sequence. Of course sequences of events typically form part of a continuing chain of events, though each has a defined beginning, middle and end, consisting of goal identification, means selection and use, and goal attainment or problem resolution. Shopping for groceries, making a cake, taking a walk, and writing a letter each follows a natural sequence of this kind, though each may also be part of a larger chain of events and long range goals, such as doing the daily chores that help to support a home and family. In every case we make use of the rules of knowledge applicable to the situation; we draw on the rules of problem solving to accomplish our task; and our thought and action are expressed in one and often more codes of rules.

The Relation between Feelings and Ideas

The ideas we have about things are closely linked to the feelings we have about them. Thus we have favorite books and foods, books and foods we actively dislike, and others we pay little attention to. We also encounter things, people, and events in our daily lives that we fear. Without some knowledge of an object, the feelings we have about it are largely a general aura of pleasantness or unpleasantness derived through vague associations with other objects or events perceived as pleasant or unpleasant. Unfamiliar experiences or objects

FIGURE 1-1
continued
*A longer-range
goal can affect the
child's feelings
about a task.*

Child's reluctance to go to bed creates negative feelings toward washing his face.

Child's excitement over preparing for a party eliminates negative feelings toward washing his face.

may in themselves also be interesting or frightening, or arouse a chain of pleasant or unpleasant associations.

The direction and intensity of feelings and attitudes we have toward things grow in proportion to the positive and negative satisfactions we have cumulatively experienced in the course of development. The experiences may be direct, such as enjoying well-prepared food or disliking it when it is overcooked. But a great deal of our feelings toward things are derived indirectly, through our ability to symbolize ideas about things in pictures, language, and other codes, and to connect one thing with another because of similarities. Thus we can become almost as anxious over a picture or a story of a car accident as we are at the danger of a real car accident. The similarities between the dangers or pleasures of moving trains and moving cars can in the same way arouse anxiety or anticipation over a train trip even though we have travelled in cars before but not in trains. Understanding in itself is usually a major source of positive satisfaction. Knowledge acquired and skills mastered are among the greatest sources of enjoyment. Conversely, ignorance (lack of knowledge) creates uncertainty over what to expect or how to do things, and a sense of failure when one is unaware of things one is expected to know.

It is not only the immediate value of information or success with skills that determines our feelings toward things, however. Most concepts and skills fit into a general scheme we have of things, the patterns and tasks of our occupations and interests. We may dislike or be unskilled in certain aspects of our office work (such as bookkeeping) or housework (such as washing dishes), but if there are not too many parts that we actively dislike or find difficult, and if our general satisfaction in getting the job done or earning a living is high, the unpleasant parts will be accepted as routine means to maintaining the desired overall end. In other words, we have particular feelings toward everything we know and do, but much of what we feel will depend heavily on how we value things as part of our general patterns of life.

FIGURE 1–2
Unity and continuity of mind. Early experience forms the mind and personality in certain ways that set the direction further development is likely to take. Early neglect and abuse create short-term behavioral problems and can lead to long-term behavioral and personality problems—in this case inability to concentrate and rebelliousness.

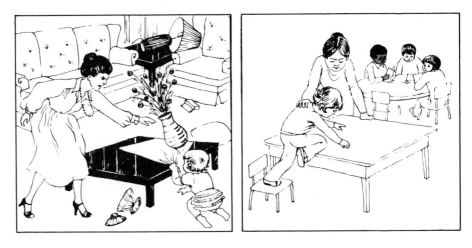

Perhaps most emotional conflict, and satisfaction, comes from learning to get along and finding a place for ourselves in the social world. Learning to cooperate and to maintain independence are both crucial to the adequacy of our personality development. If we have much knowledge and many skills, so that we can earn a living or maintain a home, but cannot understand or cope with the intimacy of love, friendship, or work relations with others, our functioning as persons will suffer. Knowledge and feeling thus work together in both the social and workaday worlds.

Unity and Continuity of Mind:
The Developmental Structure of Means and Ends

When we discuss human emotions, it is evident that each person is first of all a whole being, in whom all of the specific concepts and feelings that he or she has cumulatively acquired operate together as a system. The specific concepts of language, knowledge, and problem-solving have no value, except in relation to oneself (one's mind) as a single, unified person. We may well act differently in each situation, as a function of the different social roles and tasks we are expected to perform at work, in the home and at play. But we carry in our minds—always—a history of all the situations we have traveled through; they become registered, cumulatively, as we follow our course of living.

This continuity and unity of mind means that each new event, each new concept we encounter, is related to what has happened to us before *and* to our present situation; new concepts have no effect, no meaning, unless they are incorporated *in some active psychological way into our mind as it becomes organized from past experience.* Our minds are not empty bowls into which we pour ideas; to perceive a new tree or person for the first time requires us to compare and fit each into our scheme of what we know and how we feel about trees and people. New trees and strangers mean different things to forest rangers and desert nomads.

FIGURE 1-2,
continued
*Early and
continuing
exposure to an
activity arouses
short-term
pleasure, and leads
to long-term
interests that
children enjoy
alone as well as
with others.*

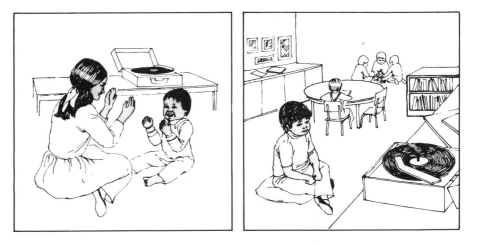

As we develop, our minds become increasingly complex; we learn more different concepts, and more complicated ones, the extent depending on the scope and depth of our experiences. But each new event also affects how we organize, and constantly reorganize, our understandings into categories. These, in turn, are continually interrelated to form general patterns of understandings, feelings, and goals for living. Every book we read or movie we see, for example, gives us information about how people do things, at play, in love, or at work, which we fit into what we know already about these categories. Some books, movies, or other events, like learning to read or meeting a specialist in one's field, provide information more directly related to one's development than others, but all are related to what we know and value in some way, however vaguely. On first seeing the word "lepidoptera" (butterflies and moths), for example, we may just say, "It must be a scientific term."

The structure of human functioning is a continuous process of change and development, in which we try to do things (seek goals) that we consider to be important. To do this, we use our reasoning skills to figure out effective means which we then apply to accomplish our chosen end. Depending on how much we value the chosen end, and on how well or how poorly we solve the problems of overcoming obstacles and selecting and exercising skills, we experience emotional pleasure or pain—usually in some mixture. Few actions are either completely successful or unsuccessful, few goals either totally desirable or undesirable. Diverting a child's attention does not necessarily stop unwanted behavior nor does anger always hurt a child's feelings. But in the course of completing any set (or chain) of means-ends activities, we acquire new knowledge and skills. When the concepts acquired are important, they may lead to new perspectives about the things and goals we value. The process is a cycle which repeats itself in ever-changing forms throughout life, sometimes leading to further development (increased sense of responsibility through job promotion), sometimes to a narrowing or regression of interests (sorrow and staying home from loss of a child), depending on circumstances and how well or ill prepared we are from our past history.

Child Development and Learning

Although no two people acquire quite the same set of understandings and feelings in the course of development, there is a general sequence of cognitive development and social activities which people in every culture and environment tend to follow. Generally speaking, as the child develops from infancy to adulthood he typically acquires more—and increasingly more complex and abstract—knowledge and skills (social, work, language, problem solving, and counting and measurement skills). These lead to extended planning of longer range goals (such as a career), adult work roles, and greater social responsibilities (such as raising and teaching children or leading people).

These universal patterns arise from a combination of things: the skill potentials characteristic of our species; the fact that such activities as walking, talking, work, and play are common to adaptation in every culture and environ-

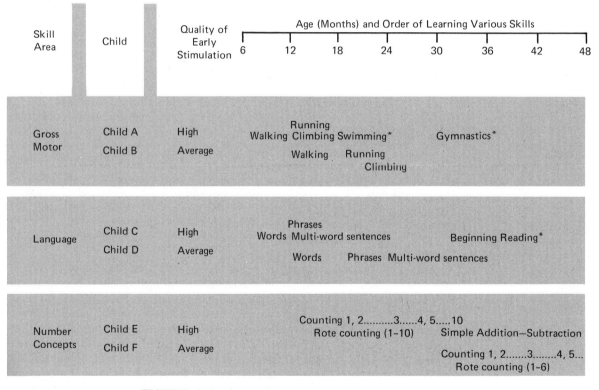

FIGURE 1-3
Effects of experience on development. Unusual early encouragement and stimulation advances the rate of development of the skills in which the child is stimulated, but does not change the order in which they are acquired. Thus, children A, B, and C advanced considerably in their respective gross motor, language, and number skills, while children B, D, and F progressed at culturally average rates through similar sequences. Children A and B also learned certain special skills very early (marked with an asterisk) that not all cultures necessarily teach at any age.

ment; and that the difficulty of ideas and tasks necessarily determines the order and time it takes us to learn them during development. The child must walk before he can run, talk before he can read, and count before he can calculate. But how well we learn the general patterns, as well as many other complex skills unique to our culture, depends on the quality of care and stimulation we experience cumulatively over the course of our childhood.

Definitions

But exactly how does development come about? The term development means the process of growing in some way, usually implying change in form as well as in size. It is easy to see how children grow physically taller and larger as they develop, but loss of baby fat, reduction in relative head size and maturing of muscles and sexual characteristics are also important changes occurring with development. Children acquire knowledge and understanding as they develop; they learn new ways of understanding when they learn to speak, read, write and work with numbers, as well as increasing their store of knowledge when they expand the size of their vocabularies and the number of facts they know.

Learning and development are closely related. Learning is more often applied to acquiring specific knowledge over relatively short time periods, however, while development implies major changes taking place slowly over a period of months or years. These often almost invisible changes come about through the many small things children learn that prepare them for major developmental changes. Thus babies listen to the sound of language and notice how their parents use words many times before they say their first words— with apparent suddenness. The child must learn about counting all kinds of things in many situations before he develops a consistent abstract idea of number. In the same way, he must learn to share with other children in many small tasks before he develops a responsible sense of cooperation.

As the foregoing suggests, development is a long-term learning process that requires a series of small steps to reach a new level or stage of development. In the course of the developmental cycle of childhood, a child goes through many such stages, each incorporating and building on the simpler stages of the past. There is much similarity to the general form and sequence of development every child goes through, but the type and complexity of rules each child acquires at any stage vary considerably according to the quality of his or her experience. For example, nearly all children learn to talk by late infancy, but few to speak well; most learn to run and jump before school, but few learn gymnastics; most learn how to group together things that are similar by early school age, but few to classify systematically; most to share with a friend during early childhood, but few to play cooperatively in a group without adult supervision; some learn about frogs and trees, others about stamps and furniture, and still others about city streets and dodging traffic.

Sources of Developmental Experience

Since each child has only one lifetime for development, the quality and variety of every child's experience is equally precious. There are several types of experience from which a child learns. These are:

1. from the environment itself—the setting, materials, and objects that continually surround the child, how they are arranged (in cities, suburbs, or

country; neatly or in chaos) and how they affect him or her (temperature, noise, and light changes);

2. from the child's own activity in reacting to and exploring the environment (self-regulated activity);

3. from contact with adults;

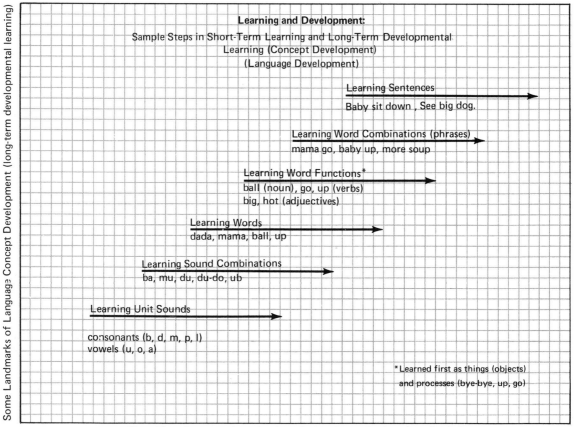

FIGURE 1-4

Learning and development: Sample steps in short term learning and long term developmental learning. Children develop in phases and jumps. Thus, when learning language, they learn a series of individual units (i.e., individual sound units) which lead them to develop a new concept (how to combine sounds in a series). This in turn leads to learning different sound combinations until they understand a further new concept—how sounds represent words. The order in which major concepts are acquired is more or less fixed, but the order for learning units in the phases at each concept level can vary considerably.

4. from peer relations (relations with other children);
5. from the impersonal media of written and pictorial material—books, magazines, film, and television—all of which have come to occupy a profound and pervasive influence on every detail of the modern child's development.

Each of these sources of experience serves a different, essential function in developing the child. Under ideal circumstances, various experiences occur regularly, in some balance, to promote the child's development. The environment is the material basis that underlies all knowledge and activity. The child will come to understand and act intelligently, however, only through acquiring from others the knowledge historically accumulated by his culture and society. By himself the child will not survive, let alone learn any of the many complicated things to know. Thus the child learns and develops in large part through three sources: through socialized adults—parents, day care workers, teachers,

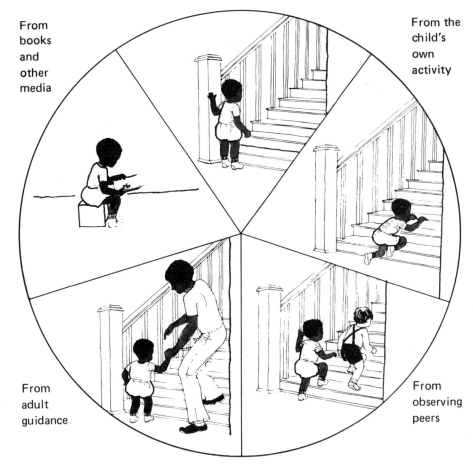

From the environment

From books and other media

From the child's own activity

From adult guidance

From observing peers

FIGURE 1-5
Where children learn: Sources of developmental experience.

neighbors, babysitters, storekeepers, etc.; through activities with peers in various stages of socialization; and through experiences with pictorial and verbal media, once she has learned these codes. Adults and peers both help the child to learn rules about things, but the adult is more of a teacher, providing accurate models and guidance, while the peer is more of a work and playmate with whom to test ideas in joint activity. The variety and complexity of ideas that can be presented through books, TV, and other media makes them increasingly important as development advances. Mass media are impersonal, lacking the guidance, flexibility, and sometimes support which only personalized instruction can provide. But since media materials can be carefully constructed and reach large audiences for little cost, they are an invaluable source of information.

However vital guidance and mass media are in imparting what society has learned, rules about the world learned without active, direct experience are sterile and impractical. It is knowledge in the abstract, absorbed—to the extent it can be—without the technique or interest needed to use it to do things. Direct experience means more than tuition accompanied by reference to examples, such as *showing* a child how to do a task along with describing it. It includes providing opportunities for the child to *experiment independently* through self-guided play (self-regulated activity) in an environment well stocked with learning materials. Mastery of concepts, which the child has only partially grasped, requires time to experiment alone with varied examples of previously taught concepts and their related concepts to deepen and broaden his understanding. If a child is shown something about how songs are made up of melodies and notes, for example, he will soon be observed listening to songs more closely, trying out different records, perhaps humming part of a tune. Play is especially valuable because it provides experience in self-directed inquiry to perfect the strategies of problem solving taught through guidance. Taught to look for round-edged pieces to match round-edged holes and angular-shaped pieces to match angular-edged holes in a given jigsaw puzzle, the child still needs plenty of practice with other puzzles before he can use the strategy easily.

Play in a setting with groups of children enhances the child's experimentation in two directions. First, it adds to the knowledge of concepts and examples realized through experimentation. The child gets the benefit of all the "experiments" of his playmates, which no single child would be likely to think of alone. Second, playing and working with peers adds human resources with whom to carry out more complicated cooperative activities, such as elaborate construction projects (building a ship or town) or sociodramatic play involving many social roles (doctor, nurse, patients; or supervisor, mechanics, customers, etc.).

Experimentation in groups provides direct experience, moreover, in the vital domain of social knowledge. Social rules learned through adults, while important, are generally theoretically oriented, appearing as verbal instructions of "dos" and "don'ts," rather than the give and take of actual relations. Relations with adults *do* provide knowledge about authority (leader-follower) relations of a kind that can only be had with adults, but peer experimentation in loosely supervised play provides a broad range of more practical, varied, and flexible leader-follower relations with peers who vary in age, assertiveness, and competence. Activity with peers, particularly in sociodramatic play, also provides experiments in equalitarian social roles that cannot easily be duplicated with adults, even with adults who engage in social play with children.

It is evident that all of these sources of experience contribute to different but equally significant aspects of learning. Each will naturally appear in some form and proportion throughout the development of every child. Few children in any contemporary culture or social class grow up without considerable exposure to adults, older children, opportunities for play, some environmental variation, and at least TV, movies, and comic books—even if the exposure is not always constructive. Variation, moreover, is the stuff of which interesting differences between personalities and cultures are made, differences between dancers and bookworms, between the fishermen and women of Japan and the mountain guides of Nepal. Yet in modern life serious neglect of any of these sources may lead to a corresponding underdevelopment in some way—to poor general cognitive and emotional development (neglect by adults), to social isolation or timidity (isolation from peer experiences), to passivity, overseriousness, or lack of curiosity and creativity (lack of opportunities for play), to poor general or current knowledge (lack of exposure to books or any media), or to narrowness of interests and rigidity (monotonous environment). Variation is both normal and desirable, but only in some fruitful balance beyond certain minimal levels of adequacy for each area of experience.

Types of Activity in Early Childhood

Four basic types of activity dominate in early childhood, each of them determined by a characteristic need of the period.

1. *Basic care routines.* Much of the infant's life is occupied with attention to hunger, sleep, and other basic needs in culturally prescribed routines of physical and socioemotional care. This type of care activity is required by the basic state of dependency and ignorance of the infant, coupled with each society's desire to socialize its children according to its traditions.

2. *Play.* When awake, on her own, with her needs satisfied, the infant's natural inclination is to explore and experiment with the world through sensorimotor, social, and symbolic play.

3. *Planned or sequenced learning.* Frequently teachers and parents take time to teach children little things about the world, sometimes in traditional forms of social play (peek-a-boo and nursery rhymes) and sometimes with the deliberate idea of teaching a concept. The amount of time parents spend in this important activity, which arises from the need to educate babies, varies greatly from home to home.

4. *Excursions and trips.* Families also differ in the amount of time and variety of experience they offer their children on excursions; but whether for errands, trips, vacations, or purposely educational purposes, time away from home answers the young child's need for broader experience to widen the base of her development.

All of these activities continue in changing proportion throughout early life, and in some form well into the period of formal schooling. In each of them, all sources of developmental experience and forms of learning (knowledge, problem solving and coding) are usually present in some combination, as we shall describe shortly in Chapter 2. But first we need to know what principles and methods to apply to the tasks of caregiving in various activities.

The Environment, the Child, and Principles of Early Care and Education

Where do principles for teaching and caring for children come from? Principles develop from the nature of the task they help to accomplish. Since the task of early care necessarily deals with the child in the environment, we must look to see how the nature of the environment and the child's own nature affect the task. The environment and the child independently do not determine the nature of caregiving principles. The principles we choose must of necessity be founded on the nature of *relations* between the two, the ways they interact to determine the child's welfare.

Caregiving does not concern the child's immediate welfare alone. Good care is educational, looking as much toward fostering development as it does toward serving immediate survival needs. The environment and child interact in a process of continual change, which, given appropriate educational principles, leads to the formation of the child's mind and personality. Successful child care takes account of the cumulative interaction between environment and child that fulfills present needs and shapes the child's mind according to his biological potential for coping with the environment. To the degree that principles fail to consider this basic, progressing relationship between the world and the child, they will fail to help the child develop to his full potential.

In Table 1–1 is presented in outline form a picture of the pattern of significant relations between the environment and the child, along with a list of child care and educational principles that follow from this pattern of relations. There are ten basic characteristics or conditions that appear to define the nature of the world. These are listed in the first column. Note that "the world" is not limited to the physical environment, but very much includes the *social* environment, which is the basic source for so much of the child's knowledge and development.

Each of these environmental conditions is then matched (in the second column) with corresponding characteristics of the child during early life that relate to how well the child can cope with that condition. The infant's potential for development during early childhood with respect to that condition is also included. In the final column are listed the child care principles needed to help the child develop the ability to cope with the respective environmental conditions. In each case the principles listed are based upon the *potential* the child has for learning and development during the first few years of life.

It is evident that the ten environmental conditions listed are not all that could be found and that each could be described somewhat differently. Other aspects, such as the separateness and relationships of things could be used. However, these are included under the categories of concreteness, regularity and abstraction. As it is, conditions like regularity, complexity, and abstraction

TABLE 1-1. Relations between the environment, the child, and principles of early care and education

Nature of the World (Environment)	*Characteristics of the Child During Early Development*	*Principles of Early Care and Education*
I. *Resources.* The environment contains food, material for clothes, housing, and other resources for people to live. It requires energy and skill to obtain environmental resources.	Physically and mentally undeveloped. Dependent on others to provide for basic needs (hunger, shelter, contact, etc.) Has potential for growth in strength and health and for learning many cognitive and perceptual-motor skills to increasingly provide for own needs during early development.	1. Providing care adequate to fulfill the child's basic, developing needs in a daily cycle of routines. 2. Guiding infants and young children in learning concepts and skills to cope with the environment autonomously (independently). 3. Providing opportunities for exercise to develop strength and health. 4. Providing experiences in self-directed perceptual-motor play to develop mastery and autonomy (independence) in a broad variety of fine and gross motor activities.
II. *Social Life.* People are social beings who live, work and play together to survive and satisfy human needs. Human development is a process of socialization, or acquiring the ways the cultures and society have developed to adapt to the environment.	Completely unsocialized as well as helpless, unskilled and undeveloped. Highly dependent on others for emotional care and socialization of development. Open to acquiring the rules, feelings and forms of social life without which child cannot survive, adapt, or develop into an adult member of society and culture.	1. Providing emotionally supportive care and guidance to develop positive self concepts and feelings towards others. 2. Fostering positive attitudes and ways of relating between children (peer relations), and between children and adults (authority relations), in play, care routines, and work tasks, maintaining a balance between each child's autonomy (independence) and cooperation with others. 3. Teaching children to work alone and in groups to develop responsibility, good work attitudes, and competence. 4. Encouraging achievement standards in activity and fair play in social relations through promoting care in work and play and consideration for others. 5. Fostering awareness and appreciation of differences in cultures, families, and individuals. Avoiding cultural, sexual, and individual stereotyping. 6. Developing aesthetic interests, values, and skills (see also Condition VIII, Abstraction).
III. *Concreteness.* The world is basically physical, defined by color, form, texture, movement, and other concrete characteristics. Even live things have a material basis with concrete features.	Knowledge of the world is gained primarily through direct, perceptual-motor experience with the surface characteristics of the environment (especially early in development before an organized body of knowledge, abstract codes, and coping strategies have been acquired).	1. Providing extensive sensory and motor experience with materials to develop direct knowledge of the nature of things. 2. Providing guidance and experience in actively exploring and manipulating materials to develop sensorimotor coding skills and problem solving strategies to enable the child to cope directly with the environment.

TABLE 1–1—(Continued)

Nature of the World (Environment)	Characteristics of the Child During Early Development	Principles of Early Care and Education
IV. *Regularity*. Order and relative stability underlie all things; objects are relatively permanent. Regularities in the environment appear in the: 1. *Similarities* between objects, features, and relations of color, size, substance, use, etc. 2. *Organization* (structure) of things, the form of relations between things, ranging in complexity from simple objects to abstract systems (see Conditions VI and VIII, below). 3. *Spatial Arrangements* of objects, features, and other characteristics (e.g., closeness, isolation, continuity, and clustering). Environmental regularity (consistency and repetition in the environment) at many levels of abstraction establishes the possibility and utility of human *memory*.	Initially lacks objective knowledge of (understanding of general rules about) environmental regularity but can begin to learn simple regularities from earliest infancy. As the child knows little and has little experience with regularity—how things repeat themselves—the child's *memory* is limited in time and scope. Knowledge of environmental regularities (rules of knowledge) will develop in proportion to opportunities to observe and use them through guidance and experimentation.	1. Providing cognitively oriented care and instruction; explaining things because there are regularities that can be understood. 2. Teaching general rules (concepts) about regularities instead of collections of unrelated facts. 3. Drawing attention to similarities between environmental characteristics through matching objects and processes which have similar features, functions, or other characteristics. (Used in connection with principle of discriminating differences listed below under Variety, Condition IX). 4. Arranging features illustrating a concept to be learned so that they stand out clearly for the child. 5. Teaching knowledge systematically to aid the child to build up gradually an organized and comprehensive picture of the world (the structure of knowledge). (See also Condition VI, Complexity, and Condition VIII, Abstraction.) 6. Providing activities to develop memory for regularities of objects and events (hiding, discussion, etc.).
V. *Change* (Processes): Things are constantly in the process of changing, developing, or declining at different rates, in different forms (mechanical, chemical, biological, social). Changes are *caused* by certain things (means) acting to produce *effects* (ends) in sequences over *time*.	The infant's awareness of change, time, and causality develops through responding to stimulation and through adapting needs to activity cycles that follow sequences in time. Open to understanding many aspects of causality, function, order, and other concepts of change, in conjunction with learning to adapt to the environment in increasingly complex ways.	1. Teaching rules for ways change occurs through helping the child to cope with and master the environment in daily care routines and learning activities. 2. Teaching causality, predictability, relations between means and ends, form and function, sequence, and other concepts of change as the child develops. 3. Showing how change involves the appearance of new arrangements and forms through experimentation and creative play. 4. Teaching creative skills through providing opportunities for experimentation, and guidance in creative play with different types of materials. 5. Developing an increasingly objective (logical) sense of time through (1) maintaining routine and activity cycles and (2) gradually introducing the preschool child to the measurement of chronological and calendar time. 6. Keeping in mind that both short-term and long-term changes are characteristic of children's development.

TABLE 1-1—(Continued)

Nature of the World (Environment)	*Characteristics of the Child During Early Development*	*Principles of Early Care and Education*
VI. *Complexity.* World is intricate and complicated in space and time (see Condition IV, Regularity).	Child's reaction to world is simple and undeveloped. Has no knowledge and skills; initially capable of little more than adaptive reflexes to need provision (such as nursing) and stimulus changes (such as startle reactions); has perceptual preference for stimulus variations and complexity (such as looking more at moving objects or patterned surfaces than at stationary objects or plain surfaces). Has potential for gradually acquiring complex concepts and skills if sufficiently simplified and ordered.	1. Guiding children's learning systematically to build up an organized general body of knowledge adequate for coping with the complexity of the environment (see principle 5, under Condition IV, Regularity). 2. Using techniques to simplify and order concepts to ease learning and foster cumulative mastery of a complex body of knowledge.
VII. *Problems.* Conflict and problems are inherent in the differences, change, and complexity in the environment. Human activity consists of solving problems to adapt to the environment and conduct cultural life.	Lacks objective awareness of nature of conflicts and problems. Child's awareness is subjective, centered on problems of satisfying personal needs. Problem solving skills are initially limited to simple, relatively automatic reflexes. Difficulty in distinguishing between the subjective and objective (between his own imagination and reality) makes play the main way the young child experiments with the environment to work out problems in early development. Open to gradual development of competence in problem solving according to the quality of guidance and opportunities to experiment, dramatize, and play with developmentally appropriate conflicts and problems.	1. Using a problem-solving approach to child care and education through presenting care tasks, experience, conflicts, and concept learning as problems to be solved through experimentation, understanding, and effort. 2. Providing extensive self-directed experience in problem solving through free play. 3. Using problem-oriented social and object play techniques in conducting concept learning activities. 4. Teaching the child means-ends and other strategies (rules) for solving problems systematically.

TABLE 1-1—(Continued)

Nature of the World (Environment)	Characteristics of the Child During Early Development	Principles of Early Care and Education
VIII. *Abstraction.* Many environmental regularities (1) are obscured by surface disorder and irrelevant perceptual characteristics and (2) transcend local space and time. The human brain is capable of coding information to select, organize, and represent knowledge about the world in abstract form, either real or imaginary, in terms of what is represented. There are a variety of abstract codes, of which the main ones are pictorial, verbal, mathematical, or various aesthetic codes (music, painting, dance).	Oriented toward the immediate and concrete. Relies directly on perceptual-motor systems. Is undeveloped but has potential for rapidly acquiring abstract regularities and language codes.	1. Teaching the abstraction of regularities through guiding the child to select the essential aspects of regularities and ignore the irrelevant detail and local conditions. (See also Conditions IV and VI, Regularity and Complexity.) 2. Teaching symbolic codes (picture, language, mathematic, aesthetic, etc.) as tools for abstracting regularities, mentally manipulating concepts, and enjoying and representing experience in aesthetic form.
IX. *Variety.* There are many different things and types of things to know.	Limited in variety of knowledge and skills. Capable of mastering foundation concepts and skills in a representative sample of all major areas of knowledge.	1. Providing experience in discrimination and understanding differences in environmental characteristics through presenting objects and processes with contrasting features. (Used closely with principle of teaching similarities listed above under Regularity, Condition IV.) 2. Developing awareness of the extent of variety in the world through exposing the child to many different concepts and areas of knowledge. 3. Using a wide variety of examples for each new concept to enrich the child's grasp of ideas. 4. Selecting generally important topics and skills in various areas of knowledge in order to develop a representative variety of knowledge.
X. *Quantity.* There are endless things to know.	Limited in amount of knowledge. Can learn some concepts and skills about everything, and learns much specialized information and develops a greater degree of competence in a few areas.	1. *Quantity:* Presenting lots of information for the child to learn because there is so much to learn. 2. *Intensity:* Engaging the child regularly each day in guided learning without sacrificing play and recreation. 3. *Selectivity:* Choosing what is important since we can't learn everything. 4. *Specialization:* Encouraging each child to develop specialized types of competence according to his emerging interests and skills.

necessarily overlap, though they are all included separately to emphasize their separate contributions to understanding how the world appears to work.

In the same way, the matching list of characteristics of young children and the list of child care principles could be stated in different ways and there is again a certain amount of duplication. Just as the various environmental characteristics are all interrelated, so too are the characteristics of the child, who after all is a unified whole creature. The child's dependency is listed at least twice, for example, opposite the environmental condition of resources and again for that of social life. Aspects of principles of cognitive stimulation are listed in connection with regularity, complexity, abstraction, and other conditions. These repetitions are useful to emphasize somewhat different aspects of the child during early development. For example, dependency is listed as a characteristic the first time with respect to the infant's inability to obtain resources from the environment alone. The second time concerns the fact that the child is dependent *on people,* thus stressing the fact of the infant's relationship to social life. The duplication of child care principles serves similar purposes.

An extensive discussion of the pattern of environmental child relations and educational principles outlined in Table 1–1 is contained in Appendix A, following the same organization as the table. The sections on child care principles include considerable description of methods for applying the various teaching principles.

Bibliography for Part I

Ausubel, D. P., & Sullivan, E. V. *Theory and problems of child development* (2nd ed.). New York: Grune & Stratton, 1970.

Baldwin, A. L. *Theories of child development.* New York: John Wiley & Sons, 1967.

Bernard, H. W. *Human development in western culture* (4th ed.). Boston: Allyn and Bacon, 1975.

Bloom, B. S. Stability and change in human characteristics. New York: John Wiley & Sons, 1964.

Bossard, J. H. S., & Boll, E. S. *The sociology of child development* (3rd ed.). New York: Harper, 1960.

Bower, T. G. R. *A primer of infant development.* San Francisco: W. H. Freeman, 1977.

Brackbill, Y. (Ed.). *Infancy and early childhood: A handbook and guide to human development.* New York: Free Press, 1967.

Bronfenbrenner, U. *Two worlds of childhood: U.S and U.S.S.R.* New York: Russell Sage Foundation, 1970.

Bruner, J. S., & Anglin, J. M. (Ed.). *Beyond the information given: Studies in the psychology of learning.* New York: Norton, 1973.

Caldwell, B. M. The usefulness of the critical period hypothesis in the study of filiative behavior. *Merrill-Palmer Quarterly*, 1963, *8*, 229–242.

Clarke, A. M., & Clarke, A. D. B. *Early experience: Myth and evidence.* New York: Free Press, 1976.

Cole, M., & Bruner, J. S. Preliminaries to a theory of cultural differences. In I. J. Gordon, *Early childhood education, Yearbook of the National Society for the Study of Education*, Part 2, 1972, *71*, 161–179.

Cole, M., Gay, J., Glick, J. A., and Sharp, D. W. *The cultural context of learning and thinking.* New York: Basic Books, 1971.

Dewey, J. *The child and the curriculum* and *The school and society.* Chicago: University of Chicago Press, 1971.

Flavell, J. H. Concept development. In P. H. Mussen (Ed.), *Carmichael's manual of child psychology* (3rd ed.), (Vol. 1). New York: John Wiley & Sons, 1970, 983–1059.

Flavell, J. H. *The developmental psychology of Jean Piaget.* New York: Van Nostrand, 1963.

Fowler, W. Cognitive baselines in early childhood: Developmental learning and differentiation of competence rule systems. In J. Hellmuth (Ed.), *Cognitive studies*, (Vol. 2) *Deficits in cognition.* New York: Brunner & Mazel, 1971, 231–279.

Fowler, W. Cognitive learning in infancy and early childhood. *Psychological Bulletin*, 1963, *59*, 116–152.

Fower, W. The development of competence and deficit and some Canadian perspectives. In T. J. Ryan (Ed.), *Poverty and the child.* Toronto: McGraw-Hill Ryerson, 1972, 90–114.

Fowler, W. Sequence and styles in cognitive development. In I. C. Uzgiris & F. Weizmann (Eds.), *The structuring of experience.* New York: Plenum, 1977, 265–295.

Gagné, R. M. Contributions of learning to human development. *Psychological Review*, 1968, *75*, 177–191.

Gagné, R. M. *The conditions of learning* (2nd ed.). New York: Holt, Rinehart, and Winston, 1970.

Glick, J. Cognitive development in cross-cultural perspective. In F. D. Horowitz (Ed.), *Review of child development research* (Vol. 4). Chicago: University of Chicago Press, 1975, 595–654.

Hartup, W. W. *The young child: Reviews of research* (Vol. 2). Washington, D.C.: National Association for the Education of Young Children, 1972.

Hartup, W. W., & Smothergill, N. L. (Eds.). *The young child: Reviews of research* (Vol. 1). Washington, D.C.: National Association for the Education of Young Children, 1967.

Hess, R. D. Social class and ethnic influences on socialization. In P. H. Mussen (Ed.), *Carmichael's manual of child psychology* (3rd ed.), (Vol. II). New York: John Wiley & Sons, 1970, 457–557.

Hunt, J. McV. *Intelligence and experience.* New York: Ronald, 1961.

Infancy and Early Experience. In P. Mussen (Ed.), *Carmichael's manual of child psychology* (3rd ed.), (Vol. 1, Part II). New York: John Wiley & Sons, 1970.

Isaacs, S. *Intellectual growth in young children.* London: Routledge, 1945.

Leiderman, P. H., Tulkin, S. R., & Rosenfeld, A. (Eds.).

Culture and infancy. New York: Academic Press, 1977.

Lesser, G. S., Fifer, G., & Clark, D. H. Mental abilities of children from different social-class and cultural groups. *Monographs of the Society for Research in Child Development*, 1965, 30 (Whole No. 102).

Lévi-Strauss, C. *The savage mind.* Chicago: University of Chicago Press, 1966.

Luria, A. R. *The role of speech in the regulation of normal and abnormal behavior.* New York: Liveright, 1961.

Luria, A. R. *Cognitive development: Its cultural and social foundations.* Cambridge, Mass.: Harvard University Press, 1976.

McCandless, B. R., & Trotter, R. J. *Children: Behavior and Development* (3rd ed.). Holt, Rinehart, and Winston, 1977.

McGurk, H. *Ecological factors in human development.* Amsterdam: North-Holland, 1977.

Mead, M., & Wolfenstein, M. *Childhood in contemporary cultures.* Chicago: University of Chicago Press, 1955.

Middleton, J. (Ed.). *From child to adult: Studies in the anthropology of education.* Garden City, New York: The Natural History Press, 1970.

Miller, G. A., Galanter, E., & Pribram, K. H. *Plans and the structure of behaviour.* New York: Holt, Rinehart, and Winston, 1960.

Montagu, A. *Culture and human development: In-sights into growing human.* Englewood Cliffs, N.J.: Prentice-Hall, 1974.

Mussen, P. (Ed.). *Carmichael's manual of child psychology* (3rd ed.), (Vols. 1 and 2). New York: John Wiley & Sons, 1970.

Neisser, U. *Cognition and reality.* San Francisco: W. H. Freeman, 1976.

Piaget, J. *The origins of intelligence in children.* New York: International Universities Press, 1952.

Sameroff, A. J. Early influences on development: Fact or fancy? In S. Chess & A. Thomas (Eds.), *Annual progress in child psychiatry and child development.* New York: Brunner/Mazel, 1976, 3–33.

Schultz, C. B., & Aurbach, H. A. The usefulness of cumulative deprivation as an explanation of educational deficiencies. In S. Chess & A. Thomas (Eds.), *Annual progress in child psychiatry and child development.* New York: Brunner/Mazel, 1972, 258–271.

Stott, L. H. *The psychology of human development.* New York: Holt, Rinehart, and Winston, 1974.

Uzgiris, I. C., & Weizmann, F. (Eds.). *The structuring of experience.* New York: Plenum, 1977.

White, B. L. *Experience and environment: Major influences on the development of the young child* (Vols. 1 and 2). Englewood Cliffs, N.J.: Prentice-Hall, 1973 and 1978.

Zaporozhets, A. V., & Elkonin, D. B. (Eds.). *The psychology of preschool children.* Cambridge, Mass.: MIT Press, 1971.

II

DAY CARE:
THE ACTIVITIES
OF CARE AND
SOCIALIZATION

The Tasks of Caregiving: A Model for Interaction

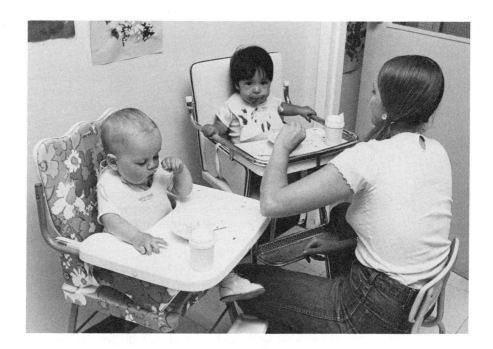

*Developing
autonomy*

How do we apply principles of caregiving in practice? There are many problems to be considered, depending on the setting and type of activity. Two of the most important are how we relate to the child (processes of interaction) and how we can adapt our interactions to the developing child (processes of development). Interaction and development apply to all human activity, of course, but take special forms when applied to the care of young children. The first problem calls for methods that promote relations *between* the child and a caregiver, *not* simply actions *by* a caregiver. In order for the child to develop at all, both caregiver *and* child must be active agents in accomplishing tasks. The second problem suggests that as the child learns more and different forms of activity, the caregiver must adapt the way he relates and teaches to the levels and styles of the child at each phase of development.

33

Interaction and development occur between adults and children, between children (peer relations), and between the child and his or her physical environment. In caregiving, the key relation is between a child (or group of children) and a caregiver, both of whom are engaged in the task of meeting the child's needs. In this chapter, we shall outline the major types of caregiving activities characteristic of early care and socialization. We shall also present a general model for interaction in caregiving, discussing the chief characteristics in terms of an example from the routines of basic care. Although the model is applicable to any caregiving situation and phase of development, the general form of the interaction process will center on a specific routine and age period. How the process works in other activities and phases of development will be dealt with in later chapters and the appendices.

Types of Caregiving

There are many aspects to caregiving, if only because there are so many characteristics of the environment for the child to learn about, and so many processes involved in the child's development. Caregiving activities fall into four main types as outlined in Table 2–1, which taken together can fulfill the multiple goals of care related to children's needs in early development. Each type of caregiving is coupled with a characteristic form of activity in the caring relationship with the child. The third column summarizes the main developmental goals of socialization in each of the processes; the column on the far right lists a few of the important tasks characteristic of each type of caregiving activity.

Planning around these four activities is a practical way of organizing early child care as a workable system. When carried out as I shall describe, both the quantity and quality of intellectual stimulation, social learning, and other requirements for healthy development are amply met. Many preschools, day care centers, and parents follow these procedures in one way or another, since children's care almost naturally seems to follow certain forms. Basic needs for food, elimination, warmth, etc.; children's dependency; and cultural demands combine to make the routine of personal care a highly specialized and essential activity of early care. Infants would neither survive nor learn how to care for themselves adequately and in socially acceptable ways if these routines were not followed with care. The child's needs to explore and experiment with objects and other children calls for a different form of adult activity to help the child get the most out of her play. Planned learning experiences (guided learning) are needed to insure that a variety of fundamental concepts about the world (size, that things can be classified, time) are covered systematically, which calls for a still different form of caregiver activity, special preparation, and selected blocks of time for organized learning. Excursions with the child to other learning environments demand particular adult skills for guiding movement and focusing and responding to children's interest in shifting panoramas.

While most people raising children practice these four activities in some form, few caregivers or programs give them the attention and thoroughness they deserve. Basic care is too often a hurried chore; some children get few or no ordered concept-learning experiences; play is frequently discouraged, hectic, or unimaginative because materials are missing or inappropriate and super-

TABLE 2-1. The activities and goals of caregiving

Type of Caregiving	Form of Caregiving and Teaching	Socialization Goals	Representative Tasks

Basic Care Tasks and Routines	Providing care and guidance for basic physical needs and social tasks (Chapters 2 and 5)	Competence in personal-social care: Self regulation of physical needs according to personal styles, group definitions and prevalent familial-cultural practices
		Competence, responsibility, standards, and cooperation in performing socially defined work tasks
			Personal Care Routines:
			  Eating-drinking
			  Elimination
			  Sleep-wake cycle
			  Dressing-undressing
			  Washing-bathing
			  Physical movement
			Work Routines:
			  Meal-snack preparation and clean up
			  Playroom-program preparation and clean up
			  Bath-change room preparation and clean up
			  Running errands

Play	Non-obtrusive guidance and mediation of play activity and sociodramatic play (Chapters 6 to 9)	Development of sensorimotor skills, strength, and diversified interests in both fine and gross motor activities
		Competence in inquiry, experimentation, problem solving, and creative-construction activities; skill, imagination, and both specialized and diversified, self propelled interests
		Language and communication skills
		Interpersonal competence in socioemotional relations with peers; autonomy, cooperation, and regulated emotional expressivity in both peer and leader-follower relations and in varied social roles and areas
		Aesthetic forms: competence and interests in musical, literary, and art forms
			Sensorimotor activities:
			  Fine motor: problem solving, concept and creative-construction toys and materials
			  Gross motor: gymnastic (climbing, tumbling and problem solving (blocks, mazes)—outdoor and indoor
			Sociodramatic activities:
			  Microsphere: blocks and miniature replicas of people, animals, vehicles, tools, etc.
			  Macrosphere: blocks, tools, clothes, and other props of typical social and work scenes and activities; simple games
			Language communication and play:
			  sounds, words, sentences, meaning-themes, poetic forms alone and accompanying much of sensorimotor and sociodramatic play
			Informal play with specialized aesthetic materials:
			  Art-crafts, musical records, instruments, songs, dance, picture-stories, and poems

Guided Learning	Systematic sequential teaching of competencies in any area (Chapters 10 to 14)	Systematic development of competencies and motivations for a representative variety of areas of knowledge of the physical and social world, problem solving, and language (including sensorimotor and creative skills, inquiry and experimental orientations, and development in aesthetic forms)
		Systematic encouragement of selected specialized competencies and self-propelled interests, according to emerging personal dispositions
			Sensorimotor programs:
			  Fine motor: object and spatial relations, conservation, dimensional concepts (color, size, shape, etc.), sequence, causality, process, time, classification, etc.; skill and coordination
			  Gross motor: gymnastics, swimming, wheel vehicles
			Language programs:
			  Oral-aural, picture viewing-drawing, early reading
			  Math-measurement concepts (number, length, area, arithmetic operations, numerals)
			Information-knowledge programs:
			  Social: family, group, community, culture, economics, etc.
			  Biological: plants and animals
			  Geographic-geological: terrain, rivers, mountains, etc.
			  Human-made: furniture, building, transportation, factories, etc.

TABLE 2-1—(Continued)

Type of Caregiving	Form of Caregiving and Teaching	Socialization Goals	Representative Tasks

			Aesthetic programs:
			  Art-Craft: drawing, painting, sculpture
			  Music: listening, appreciation, singing, dance, beginning instruments; reading music
			  Literary: oral and written stories, rhymes, poetry

Excursion-travel	Guiding children in tours of community institutions and activities (Chapter 7) Guiding children on trips and vacations	Expanding direct knowledge of local community—its economic and other institutions such as stores, factories, offices, streets, building and road construction, transport junctions, etc. Expanding direct knowledge of geography—woods, lakes, rivers, mountains, etc. Expanding direct knowledge of other communities and regions—other cities, towns, countrysides, cultures, etc. Expanding knowledge of and competence in using local public transit systems—buses, subway, street cars—and walking through city streets, traffic, etc. Expanding competence in running errands and simple shopping for groceries, hardware, etc. Introducing knowledge of and competence in using regional and wide range transportation systems—buses, trains, planes, etc. Expanding direct knowledge in special topics through community resources—such as zoo, acquarium, science center, local farms and flora in parks or countryside	Errands and shopping expeditions to stores of all kinds—walking and using all forms of public transit Visiting community institutions—stores, factories, gas stations, street and building construction sites Utilizing community resources—zoos, science centers, parties, beaches, countryside, ethnically different urban communities Travel to a variety of geographically different natural areas—lakes, rivers, woods, ocean, mountains Travel to other cities, towns, and countries

vision is unstimulating or restrictive; and excursions fail to broaden children's interests because children are dragged from place to place with little adult communication, or never go anywhere at all outside the home or day care center.

Cultural Differences   Cultures vary widely, of course, in the procedures they employ for rearing children. Many of these practices make sense for the way of life in the culture, at least in traditional, settled communities. Simplicity of dress, advancement in motor development, and delay in language and toilet training are common practices in the cattle raising and agricultural communities in the warm African climate. Direct physical experience in concrete activity with plenty of space leads children naturally to adapt to the unchanging practices of adults in rural folk communities. Similar practices are characteristic around the world and back into history, wherever living patterns remain close to the land, involving only simple tools and changing little from generation to generation. Abstract verbal concepts and generalized units of measurement are not missed in discussing the recurrent problems of village life or in carrying out the limited measures of pasture and food distribution that children can easily and gradually learn by observing and imitating adults. Our ancestors in Britain, for example, used stones for measuring weight; rods for fields; inches, feet, and yards for shorter lengths (as we still do, though metric measurement is increasingly universal); and hands for the height of horses. The more generalized, abstract use of numbers only gradually developed with the growth of urban life, trade across wide areas, and industrialism. Wherever social life and the skills demanded became more complicated, formal schools began to be established, most widely in Europe and North America during the nineteenth century.

Our problem today is that what is concrete and practical for a traditional culture in its own environment may not work well in another. Isolated, small communities are dying out, and rural populations make up a rapidly diminishing percentage of the population in every country. More and more families are moving to cities and their increasingly extended suburbs, often within their own traditionally rural countries such as Mexico, India, or Brazil, but also frequently emigrating to highly industrialized countries like Germany, Canada, and the United States. The black migration from the rural South to the urban areas of the United States, and the immigration of Puerto Ricans and Mexicans over the past decades is part of this worldwide process. The general results of this migration is extensive concentration of populations in urban areas, including large numbers of recent immigrants from a variety of different cultures and regions within a country, who yet have much in common. They all bring with them skills and related child-rearing methods that were functional for the practices of their traditional, small communities, but not for the complexities of modern urban life. Our problem in providing day care, then, is to design our caregiving methods to fit the needs of children from different cultures. The goal is to teach children the abstract skills of an urban technology and those values of the mainstream culture that are worthwhile, while preserving language, specialized skills, and practices of their own cultures.

Designing programs in relation to culture has another dimension. The traditional way in which boys and girls are reared in most cultures, in developed and less developed economic systems alike, is for boys to be the active doers and girls to be the homemakers. These different roles, which may have been useful as a means of dividing the labor in the past, are increasingly less useful today and in fact exclude women from the working world. Preparation for the adult world begins in the daily play—and types of toys—accessible to young children. Both boys and girls need exposure to the full range of activities and materials available in day care or schools in order to equip them equally with the skills they may need later. Thus the questions of culture and sex role socialization must be progressively resolved in the practices of early child care, since early experience establishes the framework for later development.

Basic Care

Graduated guidance according to
planned routines

Informal care and everyday examples

Play

FIGURE 2-1
*Types of adult
guidance in
different types of
caregiving activity:
Comparison
between group
care practices in
an industrial
society and
extended family
life in a traditional
folk community.*

Orchestrating play and occasional
guidance on specific problems

Background watching while working

Caregiving Activities

Basic Care
Routines

Basic child care consists of procedures to fulfill the child's basic personal
needs. These are the primary, biologically regulated needs on whose fulfillment
the infant is dependent for survival and comfort. Milk and other food, water,
clothes according to climate, sleep styles, movement for safety and health,
cleanliness, and training bowel and bladder activity are central preoccupations
of early care in every culture. While families and cultures vary in the timing

Guided Learning

Guidance in planned learning sequences   Guidance in necessary work tasks

Excursions

FIGURE 2-1
continued

Guidance in educational outings   Guidance on practical lore in natural setting

and the degrees and form of attention devoted to satisfying the child's needs, they are always tended to in some way.

In any culture we find two different goals involved in basic care: to satisfy the child's primary needs, and to teach the child to care for himself in the way the culture prescribes. Every child must eat, but *what* he eats—potatoes, spaghetti, or beans; the tools he is taught to use—spoons, forks and knives, chopsticks, or fingers; and the manner of eating—whether to chew with the mouth

FIGURE 2-2
*Basic orientations
to caregiving:
Interaction and
development.
Involving the child
in performing the
task gradually
develops the
child's autonomy.*

6 months   18 months

open or closed—are matters of cultural practice, not survival or health. Socialization is nonetheless equally important in learning to adapt to the environment as fulfilling the child's hunger for food. For this reason care that merely accomplishes the task, such as feeding the child, without involving the child at his skill level in learning the prescribed cultural manners, language, and skills, fails in the task of socialization. Of course this form of attentive care is highly dependent on the number of caregivers available (see Chapter 3).

The basic care activities shown in Table 2-1 are organized in terms of the primary personal and social need processes characteristic of early development in every culture, however different the forms of care in each culture. Typically in the United States, daily attention to these processes in some form continues well into the preschool period, when the child can move about freely on her own, express her wants, eat without help, dress herself, and go to the

FIGURE 2-2
continued
*When the
caregiver fails to
involve the child,
continuing
dependency and
growing conflict
result.*

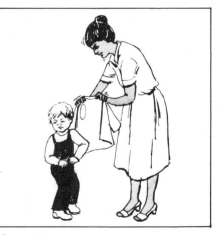

6 months   18 months

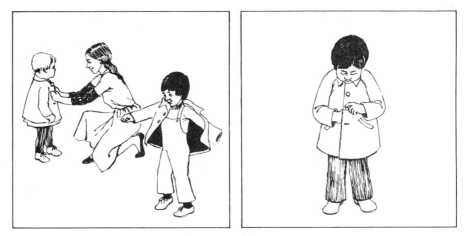

FIGURE 2-2
continued
*Involving the child
promotes
increasing
autonomy.*

30 + months   36 + months

bathroom without being reminded. Afternoon naps, night attention to bath-room routines, or help in cutting meat, tying shoelaces and performing similar specialized, difficult tasks may, however, continue into the early school years.

While there is a wide range of procedures for accomplishing each task from which caregivers may choose, according to need, culture, and preference of both child and caregiver, it is indispensable to establish a routine schedule. Because many procedures must be repeated several times a day, organizing basic care tasks into routines is a convenience in both day care and family life. Without a system of routines, it is easy to become disorganized and even forget important procedures. However, it is important not to allow routines to become too ritualized, or they will stifle affection or dull stimulation.

Work routines are grouped with basic care tasks because they are closely

FIGURE 2-2
continued
*Failure to involve
the child promotes
dependency and
conflict.*

30 + months   36 + months

associated in everyday life. Food must be prepared before we can eat it, and cleaning up and washing dishes are basic to health. In the same way, arranging and tidying up play areas is essential to the intelligent use of materials. Unless materials are regularly arranged and rotated, children will not see their possibilities (see Chapters 8 and 9), while involvement in preparation and tidying teaches the child something about cognitive organization and classification, as well as work habits. The obvious context to learn constructive work modes and attitudes is through activities that are visibly useful and closely related to the play or social task concerned.

Basic care activities resemble guided learning activities in that both demand some planning and organization in ordering learning experiences. Guided learning tasks are less ritualized and repetitive, however. They are usually presented in projects and graded in difficulty with a kind of detail that leads to learning a series of specific concepts (e.g., length, width, height). Caring for children's needs early in life, moreover, is a more constant process, taking precedent over all activity in the day care center and home, until the child learns to assume more responsibility for his or her own care. Children's basic personal needs must be tended to day after day, but if the tasks are also at least partly graduated in difficulty, the child can be encouraged to participate, and the tasks will provide much cognitive learning. Further discussion on techniques and problems of caregiving routines will continue later in this chapter and in Chapter 5.

Play

The second major form of caregiving activity, play supervision, is required by the way little children think, through experimentation in sensorimotor and sociodramatic play. Because of limited knowledge and capacity to see details in relation to the whole, the young girl or boy is often more interested in how things work, the relations between means and ends, than in actually producing some result. The child also often fails to distinguish between the effects of her own actions and externally produced events (the difference between pushing something and something rolling downhill). To the child many things just happen—the movement of toys and objects around the house, the appearance of meals and clothes—with little discrimination as to exactly how they occur and whether and when she can make them occur.

It is through experimentation in play, both with objects and with other children that the child comes to grips with concepts on her own terms. Although the young child plays directly with objects, as she begins to think more with symbols (guided by language) she begins to pretend. She uses objects and toy figures to imagine how things work and how people do things, mastering and generalizing concepts through play with many examples. It is less that the child discovers new conceptions of things during play than that she works out the subleties of things, verifying that the ideas she has heard can really work in practice, and in many different ways.

The role of the teacher in play is to promote good relations between children and imaginative use of materials. The caregiver must know how to start and keep children's experimentation going with a minimum of intrusion. This process calls for ways of organizing the child's interactions with toys and peers, in ways that are often more complex and subtle than the simple interactions typical of basic care routines, or the structured interactions needed for planned concept-learning programs. The goals of care in play center on clusters of children learning to play together in constructive and elaborate ways, which often takes weeks of patient development. Play will be discussed further in Chapters 6 through 9.

Guided Learning

Planned learning projects are as important as basic care and play in the day care program. Through repeated attention to a related body of ideas (about time, or about the characteristics and habits of fish), organized learning projects insure that the child acquires comprehensive information about the world and effective problem solving strategies. Although information about a topic needs to be complete and organized, the manner of teaching can vary in many ways, depending on the philosophy and skills of the teacher. The approach can vary from one scheduled in time, place, and order of presenting concepts, to teaching only when the child shows interest or when a convenient occasion arises. The extremes of interest-based teaching and spontaneous teaching, however, make it difficult to develop learning programs that are balanced in coverage, depth, and logical order. Without some structure, sessions become erratic and infrequent, allowing inadequate time and placing no demands on the child to persist. Temporary enthusiasms of a shallow sort, for example, in obvious size differences between common objects (such as the difference between a tiny chair and a very large chair) come and go at the expense of the deeper engagements required to attend to comparisons of length, width, height and area. While flexible methods are preferable, they need not interfere with regularity in scheduling. Scheduled learning allows the teacher to systematically monitor each child's progress and cover key areas of knowledge. These and other problems of guided learning techniques will be taken up in Chapters 10 through 14.

Excursions

Stimulating and caring for children on excursions also presents particular requirements. Trying to teach and interrelate in the context of a shifting panorama of sights, and varying travel demands, makes flexibility one of the main requirements for handling children. Most excursions are brief errands around the community, when the child is taken along by a parent for convenience in child care. Others are pleasant family outings on picnics to the zoo or to the country. Longer vacations include camping trips or other extended trips by car, plane, or train.

The excursions of day care and nursery school groups are likely to vary from strolls around the neighborhood and picnics in the park to organized visits to stores, construction sites, bus stations, the waterfront, or the zoo. But all travel with children, whether local or distant, no matter who guides it, provides opportunities for extending a child's first hand view of the environment.

Communication with children on outings is usually irregular. Even brief errands present too many different scenes to hold the attention of little ones continuously. The demands on adults to navigate and attend to the business of the trip, moreover, necessarily leave the child to his own resources part of the time. There are nevertheless many techniques to help the child to learn about the activity of adults in real life situations during trips around a community. Drawing attention to the bus driver and passengers, the passing buildings, trucks, and street construction, will do much to add zest to a trip. Methods of care and stimulation on trips, and how to coordinate experiences with guided learning themes, will be discussed in Chapters 7 and 9.

Model for Care and Stimulation: The Dimensions of Interaction in a Basic Care Routine

Ideally, most caregiving tasks incorporate a number of vital psychological processes, regardless of the type of activity. Every caregiving task holds a potential for rich emotional experience and a great deal of concept learning. The extent to which this is possible has been illustrated in Table 2-2, using the common routine of dressing a one to two year old infant. At the top of the table is a list of recommended procedures for this sample task, which bring into play the psychological processes that follow. Moving in order from the top downward, we see that good caregiving involves five basic processes—knowledge of the physical world, social concepts, feelings or emotions, perceptual-motor problem-solving skills, and language rules.

In practice, not all elements of every process can be included in every routine, or in all play and guided learning activities. Interaction with adults is less frequent in play and more specialized in guided learning. Yet the items in each process are more than a theoretical list to be used only under ideal circumstances. If items listed are built into the caregiver's way of doing tasks, caregiving routinely becomes a meaningful experience that also gets the task done. The items under language, for instance, are simply an outline of the major rules for good language communication and aesthetic experiences (such as rhymes and songs). In the same way the items concerned with emotion comprise a generally positive and warm mode of relating to children, though the items concerning values and standards will vary with the circumstances and activity. How well and to what extent these and the other three processes are brought in will depend on the care exercised by adults to weave them into the caregiving procedures. Many aspects of these processes, such as learning to cooperate with a caregiver or another child in dressing, are always included in an approach to caregiving that is interactive and careful in attention to detail.

The complexity of the concepts the caregiver demonstrates and the extent of the child's participation in tasks will increase with development. Yet rules and processes from every category should be incorporated regularly in basic care routines, guided learning, excursions, and in briefer contact between adult and child in play. How the dimensions of quality care and stimulation can be implemented in various areas will be discussed below. Techniques for monitoring the quality of care in routines are outlined in Chapter 5.

Emotional Climate   Every caregiving task should be approached in a warm and friendly manner to help the child feel positive about himself, the caregiver and the task. The in-

TABLE 2-2. Some major cognitive rules and socioemotional processes represented in developmental caregiving activities: sample task for infants

Caregiving Activities for Morning Dressing for a One to Two Year Old	**Items of Clothing:** 1. Diapers and protective pants 2. Undershirt 3. Shirt or blouse 4. Pants or skirt 5. Socks 6. Shoes

Recommended Procedures

1. Place child on change table and guide and assist him or her to sit and lie down.
2. Change diapers: remove pins and soiled diaper (and protective pants), clean child and rediaper (protective pants replaced as part of dressing routine)—involve child in lifting buttocks, and locating fresh diapers (and possibly pins if care is exercised).
3. Help child stand with support.
4. Guide and assist child in selecting and putting on clothes, each item in turn; guide child to orient items to his or her body and appendages; guide child to locate holes in sleeves, pant legs (or skirt); guide and assist limbs through sleeves, garment on head around trunk, etc.; guide and assist child to locate and pull zipper (or buttons; button holes and buttoning-unbuttoning allow involvement but require total adult action until later in development).
5. Cuddle, pat, hug, kiss, etc., child now and then.
6. Use language freely to label objects, details and movements, timing descriptions with actions of self and child.
7. Smile and sometimes laugh (e.g., in play).
8. Embellish tasks with interesting peek-a-boo games, smiling, nursery rhymes, language, phrasing and imagery, musical and similar play activities.
9. Occasionally, introduce and label a picture or toy to hold attention and for learning, where task requires waiting and/or is too difficult for child to participate.
10. Carry out all phases of task smoothly and quickly—*but without hurrying the child.*

Knowledge of Physical World Child Can Learn During Effective Caregiving Routines	*Identity and characteristics of objects*—part-whole relations, features, texture, color, form, etc. *Spatial relations*—positional relations, container-contained. *Means and Ends*—causality, movement, processes and functions (of things). *Social order*—beginning concepts (e.g., routine place and order of dressing); activity time (beginning, middle, end). *Elements of classification*—clothes versus other things; types of clothing, etc. *Aesthetic concepts*—of color, design, and general taste in clothes.

TABLE 2-2—(Continued)

Social Rules and Relations Child Can Learn from Effective Caregiving	*Self concepts*—definitions of self as responsible, competent, and personable, built up according to effectiveness of caregivers in involving child and imparting rules and skills while performing tasks. *Cooperative and following relations*—child being involved and guided, following gestural and verbal directions, and contributing to task in cooperation with caregivers. *Autonomy*—developed through involvement, participation and encouragement of initiative by caregivers—guiding and expecting gradually increasing self-regulation of tasks by child. *Social communication*—developed through gestural and verbal interaction in task cooperation, play, and conversation. *Peer relations*—sharing and cooperation with equals, developed when caregivers work with children in pairs and small groups.
Emotional Processes Involved in Effective Caregiving	*Love and affection*—developed in the child by good physical and psychological care and attention. *Trust and respect*—developed in the child when adults provide reliability and sensitivity to child's needs with which care, help, and guidance provided; continuity of attachment relation(s). *Positive feelings and motivations*—such as satisfaction, achievement, perseverance, efficacy, elation, sensory pleasure and playfulness; according to attitudes, styles, and ease with which tasks carried out by caregiver and involvement of child. *Delay of gratification*—learning to wait, take things in series, etc. *Valuing*—objects, activities, social (self, relations with other people), and cognitive aspects according to attitudes of caregivers and positive quality of experiences. *Valuing work and standards*—valuing effort, completing tasks, and valuing quality of performance and outcome.
Problem-solving Skills and Rules Child Learns from Effective Caregiving	*Perceptual-motor skills*—central to all tasks especially in early development; coordination, timing, sequencing and speed of movement are basic to all caregiving procedures. *Analyzing and synthesizing*—the significant parts and functions of object structures (i.e. clothes), actions, and language in the course of dressing; organization of means and ends relations. *Cognitive inquiry*—every caregiving task is a problem to be figured out; should be a joint inquiry of child and caregiver of what to do next, how to do it, and what things (tools) are needed to do it. *Play*—integral to all tasks for young children; should provide opportunities to playfully experiment in the natural form of activity, trying things out socially and physically.

TABLE 2-2—(Continued)

Language Representation Rules Involved in Effective Caregiving Routines	*Phonology*—sound patterns of speech of adult as example and self experimenting in circular feedback systems. *Syntax and semantics*—names of objects (nouns, pronouns), actions (verbs), features (adjectives), etc.; sentence structure rules and relation of language rules to the world. *Social communication*—language understanding (receptive language) and speech, conversation. *Aesthetic concepts of language*—through rhymes, poems, songs, imagery, metaphor.

fant's emotional capacities to love, display affection, and trust others are rooted in the quality of affection and respect he encounters in his first adult-child interactions, particularly those concerned with his basic needs.

How well or poorly a child learns the daily routines of personal care—washing, dressing, eating habits, and the like—depends on the attitudes adults show toward these events. If an adult is impatient, sloppy, or holds such care tasks to be unimportant, the child's own developing standards of care will be negatively influenced. Such an adult, constantly impatient of "getting the task done," without regard to quality or attitude toward the child, is a model for low standards, instant gratification, and mean attitudes.

It is important to praise the child's efforts to participate, being careful not to overstress standards of performance, which may arouse feelings of resentment towards work and a sense of failure and incompetence in the child. Fostering a growing sense of self-worth in the child through making participation itself a positive experience is as important as accomplishing the task. Notice the child's small efforts to cooperate, such as extending an arm to a sleeve—even if it's the wrong arm or the arm is extended at an awkward angle. If adults do not exercise patience in involving the child, it is difficult for children to develop a tolerance for small delays and a commitment to daily small efforts to achieve the goals of a task. Ordinary tasks can become enjoyable learning rituals punctuated with only minor irritations, rather than chores to be anticipated with dread.

Develop a relaxed style with children by speaking freely and welcoming a bit of play. Express tenderness physically through an occasional kiss or by cuddling. Try to become sensitive to the moods and differences of a wide range of individual personalities and to adapt the demands of the task to each child's styles and cultural background.

Obviously, caregivers too have their individual styles and mood shifts, which sometimes result in negative feelings toward the child, her behavior or aspects of the task (e.g., disgust over a soiled diaper, concern for cleanliness, annoyance over spilled food, anger at the child's resistance). Conflict can be minimized by adopting a flexible approach. Within reason, time your requests so that they occur during shifts in the child's attention, such as asking a child to find her sweater at the point she stops looking at a mobile. Vary the routine to make it interesting. Sing a song one day, say a rhyme another, and change the order of dressing (alternating between socks, or between shoes, or between shirt and skirt). The order of certain steps, like undershirt before overshirt and

Language: Talking to the child about the task helps him learn how words represent things and processes.

Knowledge and problem solving: Guiding the child in solving problems helps him to acquire knowledge.

Emotional processes: Warmth and approval develop responsibility and self-worth.

Social rules: Encourage the child to initiate (develop autonomy) and cooperate with adults.

FIGURE 2-3
Fostering cognitive rules and socioemotional processes in a typical basic care routine.

socks before shoes, which cannot of course be changed, help teach the idea and purpose of order, thus contributing to cognitive development (see below under knowledge). Avoid direct confrontations; rather, dissolve the child's resistance by diverting her attention. Hand her an interesting toy or name the act being performed (e.g., hooking the zipper). Even better is to transform the resistance by involving her in the task ("Where's the sock?" "Let's find the front of the pants").

The Development of Social Concepts

Everything a child experiences is bound up in his emerging sense of self, which is at the core of his well being. His self concept comes in a large part from how others behave and feel toward him in everyday activities. The basic routines of early care are packed with so many essential concepts that it is difficult to inflate the importance of these daily experiences in shaping a child's beginning conceptions of himself, his sense of competence, and his ability to interact with others.

Regulating a child's social behavior during caregiving tasks is as vital to development as providing emotional warmth. Emotional expression smoothes and sustains the child's acceptance of task demands. Social control organizes the interactions between adult and child into a mutually satisfying and productive form.

Social interaction in caregiving tasks is concerned with the amount of *autonomy* (self regulation) the child is permitted, and the degree of *cooperation* between caregiver and child. Provide as much opportunity for self care in every routine as the child's understanding and personal history permit. In this way, infants will continuously expand their range of competencies for personal care.

Cooperation, which is the basis for successful accomplishment of a caregiving task, is essentially coordination of effort between caregiver and child. Cooperation requires engagement rather than use of physical force or fear (intimidation), which will develop passive and frightened children, or excessive indulgence, which will neither accomplish many tasks nor socialize children in self care.

Effective caregiving thus depends on maintaining a balance between self-regulation by the child and control by the caregiver. This balance is decided mainly by the adult whose greater knowledge necessarily makes him the leader. Naturally, the younger the infant, the greater the scope of adult control. During infancy the degree of autonomy of which the child is capable is confined to carrying out one small part of a task, like picking up a hat or lifting a foot, a detail in a particular routine. Decisions on when to get dressed, the order of dressing, and so on, fall to the caregiver. Only as learning progresses can the child be engaged in such larger questions of strategy and choice as which clothes to wear, when, and in which order.

Social concepts cannot be learned through relations between adult and child alone, however skilled the caregiver. Certain rules of cooperation can only be learned through relations between equals. How to stand up for one's own interest while considering the needs and rights of others is forged in give and take with those who are roughly equal in age, competence, and status. The superior competence and status of adults in the adult-child relation is no basis for learning to cope reciprocally with equals.

As social abilities develop during late infancy and the preschool period, small groups of three or four children can be involved in dressing together. Children can be guided to collaborate in locating lockers, finding items of clothing, choosing the order, and suggesting what comes next. Little should be expected, of course, until well into the preschool period (ages three to four) in terms of children helping one another in such complicated tasks as putting on an entire jacket or snowsuit, or tying a shoelace. But efforts to help and suggest

Be relaxed . . .   . . . but not sloppy

Keep the task in mind . . .   . . . but don't overlook the child

FIGURE 2-4
*Some do's and
don'ts for
caregiving
routines.*

techniques to one another should be encouraged in these daily routines. Genuine willingness and knowledge of *how to cooperate* can only develop when built into the activities of daily living.

Many of the social concepts specific to relations with peers, such as sharing toys and play space or assuming different social roles in dramatic play, develop best in free play activity. Adults need only monitor the play, for example, to maintain cooperation between passive and domineering children. More complicated rules for cooperating, involving a plan of work, a division of work roles, and leader-follower relations are also sometimes easier to develop during the less pressured periods of free play (see Chapter 9).

Cooperative activity during basic care routines is also an important basis for learning the chores of family living. It is particularly important to involve

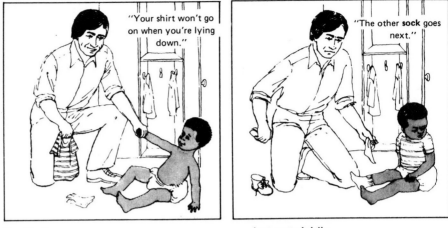

Set limits . . .   . . . but not rigidly

FIGURE 2–4
continued
*Some do's and
don'ts for
caregiving
routines.*

Bring in some play . . .   . . . but don't lose sight of the task.

boys in learning how to work cooperatively in such chores. If they are not to fall into the traditional ways of many cultures of leaving all household tasks to the women, boys as much as girls will need experience in this form of cooperation. Obviously, such basic routines as setting and clearing the table, and tidying up the bathroom and playroom are particularly key areas in which to work toward cooperation as a matter of routine.

The role of the adult in care routines (and guided learning sessions) is necessarily more active than in the looser relations of play. The caregiver must organize the tasks and children's roles in an explicit way. Tasks that are performed many times as routines teach children how to cooperate in more detail and more automatically. Through play, children experiment on their own with the concepts of cooperative relations presented to them in guided learning and care routines. Methods for handling children cooperatively in small groups will be discussed at length in Chapters 9 and 13.

Stimulation of Knowledge

Not only do routines encompass many different types of activity, from dressing to running errands, but they enable children to gradually become skilled at increasingly complex tasks. They learn, for example, concepts of order through putting on and taking off clothes; matching and spatial concepts through fitting clothes to the body; ordering, classifying, and memory skills through setting tables and putting away toys correctly; and the many different functions of all kinds of everyday objects.

Children acquire a great deal of knowledge when the routines of caregiving are sufficiently cognitively oriented. What is cognitively oriented caregiving? It is an approach that draws the child's attention to the means, ends, and concepts involved in accomplishing tasks, and makes clear the nature and purpose of the activity. The regularity and frequency of these experiences helps to insure that exposure leads to mastery. Moreover, promoting the child's understanding of tasks is important in eliciting willingness to cooperate.

The child's understanding may be developed through task activity in at least four ways:

1. observing the caregiver's normal performance of actions;
2. having his or her attention drawn to a task object or demonstration of an action;
3. experimenting with the various movements in a task; and
4. being aided and guided in efforts to carry out a task.

Under ideal conditions, all processes shown in Table 2–2 should be systematically used in all but the briefest caregiving routines. Regularly involve the child as much as possible, given the demands of the work load and the need to complete the task. Draw attention to the significant parts, functions, and relations in each task (sole of shoe, sole protects foot, sole is attached to shoe, and sole sets on floor). As the child develops, the child will normally be able to absorb more complex and abstract concepts. For example, progress from drawing attention to the whole shirt alone, to its sleeve, to distinguishing between the top and bottom of a sleeve. When the child begins to identify individual features and functions, begin to compare sizes and classify types of clothing. An entire gamut of concepts about the physical world, like those listed in Table 2–2, can gradually be taught in this manner.

Depending on the nature of the task, it is additionally stimulating to introduce miscellaneous objects and pictures for learning and play. During diaper changing routines, before the child can do much to help, a few well placed pictures on the ceiling, and mobiles (which should be changed occasionally) along with a box of hardware gadgetry, small toys, and household items for the caregiver to label and for the infant to handle make useful supplementary learning materials. Similar materials can be helpful at other times when the child must wait, such as meal times. Care must be exercised, however, to avoid disrupting the main goals of completing the routine and teaching the child responsibility for his own care in the various routines.

The Use of Language

Language is an indispensable, always available tool of caregiving, requiring no other resources than the human voice, and restricted only where quiet is desirable (such as sleeping areas) or by the language skills of the caregiver. The free use of language during caregiving activities is a major factor in developing the child's competence, not only in language, but in cognitive processes in general. Speech is *the* means we employ for communicating with others and for organizing thought to represent the world and our activities in abstract form. The social and technological organization of civilization could hardly have reached even Stone Age levels without language to aid in conceptualizing and coordinating our activities. The following are a few highlights of techniques for fostering language development.

Selectivity and Simplification

Language necessarily lags behind knowledge in infancy; it comes into use only gradually over a period of years. Yet language is complex and difficult to simplify without speaking in an artificial manner such as saying, "eat carrots", or "put shirt". To teach anything worthwhile we have to say something like, "eat the (or your) carrots" or "put your shirt on", thereby often introducing more abstract qualifiers and relational terms like articles (the), prepositions (on), and adjectives (your).

There are several ways around this apparent dilemma. One way is to isolate single nouns and verbs as labels for specific objects and actions, saying the word distinctly *as one points to the object* ("spoon") *or performs a particular action* ("zip"). In this manner numerous concrete nouns can be repeatedly used with relative ease, although verbs pose more difficulty. They generally describe movements whose beginnings and ends are not always clear (such as eat, go, take), and more than one verb is commonly employed to describe the same or similar movements (for example "go to" and "walk to"). Nevertheless, repeated use of the more concrete describers of action (verbs), such as "walk," "zip," "button," "sit," "lie," "touch," "kiss," will advance the child's comprehension and add to his store of verbs. Consistency in labelling is important in the early stages. Try to stick to the same terms much of the time (choose either "give me" or "hand me") and minimize pronouns and other more ambiguous terms until speech is well started. (It helps day care workers to discuss and agree on some of the common terms and minimize complicated verbs until the child's speech is really taking hold, some time during the second year.)

A second approach to simplifying language is to *stress the most relevant term in a sentence,* again being sure to time the stress with attention to the object or event it designates. One can say, for example, "Put your *foot* in the *hole*," while pointing first to the child's foot, then the pantleg hole, or, "Put your foot *in* the hole." It is advantageous to employ this method frequently, since complete sentences provide an important model for learning *all* the rules of language, including sound patterns of stress and intonation and the rules of grammar and meaning. There is a substantial period of time (between 6 and 18 months) when the infant is mainly learning to *understand* language (receptive language). He must understand many rules about syntax (sentence rules) and meaning before he can begin to use them in the more complex and creative task of constructing his own sentences.

Variations in the Use of Language

There are several variations in the way language can be used with children to combine enjoyment with learning. One way is as a tool to describe and explain what is going on in a task. This is the relatively direct method we have been discussing so far.

Language can also be used dramatically in surprise and suspense activities such as "peek-a-boo" and "hunt-and-find" play. Because the infant's understanding of objects is still expanding and her search skills are limited, objects that are still visible or only half hidden will often arouse as much or more excitement than completely hidden objects. In any case, vary the hiding place and adapt the difficulty to the child's abilities. To heighten the drama, ask questions with enthusiasm and an element of mystery. Express surprise as well as enthusiasm when you or the child "find" the missing object. For example, if you say, "Where's the diaper?" (or "meat on the plate," or "sweater") or, "Can you find the diaper?", involve the child in the search. Pause briefly for her to look. Exclaim, "There's the diaper!" if the child locates it, using a tone as if a mystery had been solved. Ordinarily, allow only as long for the child to search as she shows an active interest before "finding" it yourself, saying, "Here's the diaper!" with the same surprise at the instant of bringing it into view. Occasionally, when time is available, it is fun to prolong the suspense, continuing to search and make puzzled statements ("Where's the diaper? . . . I can't find the diaper . . . Where *is* the diaper?") even when the infant does not actively search but may continue to watch with interest. The dramatic use of language in this manner is highly effective, both for teaching and for holding the infant's attention in routines.

As the child moves into later infancy more complicated relations between objects, events, and social roles can be dramatized, and the role of the child in hiding and searching expanded. Play on language meanings and grammatical rules for preschoolers during meals can be fun, if it does not get out of hand. Pretend games during dressing can make these routines enjoyable and creative experiences.

Literacy and poetic play with language is particularly valuable and easily woven into many of the routines of caregiving. The opportunity that routines provide for repetition make them ideal situations for poetry, even leading to memorization without apparent effort. Nursery rhymes and simple poems, particularly if memorized by the caregiver and accompanied by movements to represent the ideas in action, can serve many purposes. Their rhyming, lilting, verse qualities give the child a feel for the sound patterns of language as nothing else can. Since rules about sound are the first language rules learned, infants are easily captivated by verse. Poetry not only develops the child's auditory discrimination skills for language, it also lays the basis for an aesthetic appreciation of language. Moreover, ideas and grammatical forms exist as much in poetry as in prose. The imagery and metaphor in poetry stimulate early imagination. Not the least of the functions of poetry is its value in relieving the sometimes burdensome tedium of routines for both caregiver and child.

Singing little songs, particularly repetitive ones, is still another method for teaching language, while at the same time contributing to an early appreciation of music. Melody has special qualities for soothing or arousing children at times of fright, stress, or boredom.

Language and Culture

Children in day care and preschools are usually exposed to a variety of language styles, because caregivers come from so many different backgrounds. Even when not following a bilingual program, community life today is so cosmopolitan that urban centers in almost every country include caregivers from different language, dialect, and regional groups. All may speak the mainstream language well, but use different accents, expressions, and even grammatical rules. How do these differences affect children who are learning to talk?

Probably only in small ways in the long run, as long as the children enjoy plenty of skilled language stimulation. The language children learn when exposed to a mixture of styles for any length of time may be something of a blend of the different patterns, but the complexity of their speech may even be enhanced. Exposure to differences enables children to make comparisons which sharpen and extend their knowledge of language rules. Their vocabulary becomes richer (they will use both "there" and "yonder"; "get and fetch") and their use of grammatical forms becomes more varied ("aren't" and "ain't"; "am coming and be coming"). Usually children eventually develop two distinct systems: their own dialect or the language at home, and the "standard" language used in day care.

The age of the child, the duration of exposure to differences, and the extent of the differences (among caregivers in preschool or day care, and in the home) will all affect development, but again usually in small ways. Children who spend their infancy in day care, during the period when language is first learned, are likely to be more influenced than children who enter preschools after age two or three, when language as it is spoken in the home is normally quite well established. Yet even with infants, the ties of attachment and the consistency of forms make the home the dominant influence in the development of language, despite the long hours children may spend in full time day care. However, lack of attention to language stimulation at home, or family conflict, can undermine this influence.

There are a number of ways to strengthen the child's own cultural style and language. Helping parents to take pride in their own styles is perhaps the most important way. Reassure them that children can easily learn more than one way of saying things, that children will gradually learn to be comfortable in using both their own dialects (or language) and the standard language. Providing caregivers who speak the children's home dialect or language is helpful, and becomes feasible when a number of children come from homes with the same dialect. Where the center is composed of children split into two or even three groups of children from different language backgrounds (Spanish, an Afro-American dialect, and standard English, for example) it may be valuable to regularly conduct a portion of the daily activities with the children grouped with caregivers who share the child's background. This method will serve to provide children with more systematic and frequent learning experiences in their own language or dialect than may be possible at home. Because of the

Traditional Experience

FIGURE 2-5
*Broaden the
experience of girls
and boys. Provide
girls and boys with
both traditional
and contemporary
types of experience
to ensure rounded
development.*

wider experience with adults (especially professionals) and other children outside the home, the language is acquired more solidly, in a generalized form.
This experience can help a child to feel comfortable and natural in her own
language outside the home, as she develops her home language and culture as
an important and socially valuable part of her self concept. Relations between
home and day care are also strengthened, making it easier for caregivers to
avoid or work out other problems of learning or adjustment that may arise.

Of course, it is often difficult to match caregivers or teachers and children
by dialect and language, if only because of the multiple responsibilities and
irregular schedules of caregivers. But in cities where centers can draw children
from a number of different language backgrounds, selecting caregivers from a
good mix of backgrounds will ensure that as many children as possible are
exposed regularly to their own language and cultural style in a community
setting. Just as important, a language and cultural mix in caregivers will make
caregivers more sensitive to differences and will help both caregivers and children feel that their own styles are valued by the community.

Consistency in language stimulation is nevertheless helpful to children in
learning a language, whether it is their native language, a second language, or
the standard language of a community. It is well to assign children to caregivers for experience in a language they are to learn, preferably for some part
of each day. Regular daily sessions are needed to provide enough contact for
the child to become skilled in a language. Pronounce words distinctly and
clearly and make an effort to use complete sentence forms, at least some of the
time, but avoid becoming stilted. Once you have formed a practice of speaking
clearly, it will become natural for you.

Sex Differences

One of the common problems in using language with children is the different
way adults tend to talk to girls and boys. They tend to talk a lot with infant
girls, making frequent eye contact and holding them close. With infant boys, on

Contemporary Experience

FIGURE 2–5
continued
*Broaden the
experience of girls
and boys. Provide
girls and boys with
both traditional
and comtemporary
types of experience
to ensure rounded
development.*

the other hand, adults often talk less, letting them crawl, encouraging them to play more, and cuddling them less. Caregivers also talk about different things with boys and girls. They talk with girls about the way they look, dress, and please adults. Speech with boys is more often used to teach them the names of things, how they work, and what their functions are. Boys may learn less language, but what they learn is a better tool for solving problems in the physical world. Girls not only learn more language, they also learn more about language as a means of personal expression and social communication, although in a somewhat dependent way, often trying to please others at the expense of asserting themselves and mastering skills for coping with the physical environment.

Clearly, these traditional ways of teaching language to boys and girls leave each sex disadvantaged in important ways. Boys need plenty of experience in talking about how to please and get along with others, in being cuddled and talked to quietly and personally, if they are to become sensitive to their own and others' feelings. Girls need corresponding experience in learning to label tools and other objects, guidance in how to use them, and encouragement to play with mechanical things on their own.

Problems in Language Stimulation

One of the chief pitfalls of adult-child verbal communication is the tendency of adults to rely on language at the expense of physical directions. Unless employed selectively, and well coordinated with actions, descriptions can confuse rather than clarify. Excessive speech, however clear, will irritate or stifle a child. And talk "to" or "with" the child, rather than "at" her in a manner that fails to respond to her reactions.

Some caregivers may have an opposite problem. For reasons of culture, personal style, or limited experience, they tend to be quiet even with adult friends. There are probably limits to how much adult personalities can be changed, but special training, through demonstrations, supervised practice, and role-playing sessions, can help day care workers and preschool teachers (and parents) learn to talk to children more freely and enjoyably during common routines as a matter of course.

Inexperienced day care workers, otherwise not normally silent, sometimes find it difficult to appreciate the value of talking to babies. They may rely almost exclusively on gestures, because infants, not having speech, appear to understand so little. Even for teachers with good scholastic backgrounds in child development, there is no substitute for seeing for oneself how talking with babies stimulates curiosity and causes language skills to flourish. Once a skeptical caregiver works with a few infants during their first 12 to 18 months, and sees for himself how speech advances as a result of his early efforts, he usually becomes an enthusiastic user of language with the youngest infants.

Using language and other forms of play too freely during caregiving routines, however, can prolong the routine and prevent the child from learning the task itself, causing frustration and power struggles between adult and child. Keep the basic goals of each caregiving routine always clearly in mind, maintaining a main line of progress toward completing each task. Remember, getting the task done not only tends to the child's needs with dispatch, but it also is part of teaching the child that caring for her needs *can* be accomplished without strain.

Teaching Problem-Solving Skills

The routines of care are well fitted for teaching the infant strategies for solving problems, because, like knowledge, solving problems is built into the actions of caregiving. Care routines are all physical activities at the infant's sensorimotor level of development. Working with means and ends to get things done teaches the child many of the basic rules of problem solving, of how to figure out key parts of a task and put them together in certain ways.

Every caregiving task provides natural opportunities to engage the child in figuring out how to accomplish the task. Dressing entails finding the correct items of clothing, identifying the critical parts (front and back) and using them in the proper order and relating them to one another and the body. Eating requires finding the right tools (spoon, fork, knife, glass) and identifying and using their key parts in certain ways with different foods according to custom.

Although the child experiences many such practices almost automatically in routines, taking the time to guide the child greatly advances the child's development of independence in problem solving and as well as in self-care. Show all the various steps in each task, at different times in order not to prolong the routine at any one time. Demonstrate slowly and carefully in a way that captivates the child's attention, providing encouragement and giving the child time to imitate. Guide the child in trying out the difficult stages, being sure to encourage him or her to work out steps that can be handled and experimented with independently. Bring in alternative ways of doing things where appropriate, in order to broaden the child's skill and mental flexibility. Pause long enough to give the child a chance to try and to think, in order to encourage independence and the ability to reflect and figure out.

Ask questions to get the child thinking, preferably in a way that asks the child to *do* something, rather than answer in words. The learner needs to practice a task in order to master it, not give formal explanations, which in any case are usually beyond the ability of infants and many preschoolers. While explaining what you (and the child) are doing while you are doing it teaches a lot, an infant girl herself cannot be expected to make such descriptions. Language is too new to her, and she will understand what you are saying much more rapidly than she will be able to express herself. Ask the child what comes next, or better, ask such questions as, "Can you find your shoe?" "Where's the hole for your foot?" "Where does your foot go?" and "Which way (direction) do you hold your shoe to put your foot in? Show me."

Effort is a key to solving problems. Encouraging the child to work on her own at tasks within her competence takes time, but the time expended will reap long term advantages. The child will become able to care for herself earlier and more easily and confidently at every subsequent phase of development, and will have learned to persevere at solving problems. Usually it is wise to compromise between the practical demands of meeting schedules and the limits of adult patience, on the one hand, and the need for the child to gain experience in self care and problem solving, on the other. There is also a danger, if too many demands for participation are placed on the young child at one time, that the child will tire and become frustrated. It is the continuing, well-guided daily experiences over the course of development that produce competence in problem solving.

3 The Social Environment

*The home and
day care*

How well principles of child care are realized in practice depends greatly on the characteristics of the physical and social environments. Because they exert a pervasive influence on children's care, we shall discuss the qualities of the social environment in this chapter before describing those of the physical environment in the next. Not only the quality of care but the choice of principles caregivers apply are directly affected by the social structure of the setting. The values and goals of the day care or school leadership, the social and psychological supports available, the forms of decision-making, the qualifications of the staff as a whole, and especially the adequacy of the teacher-child ratios are critically important to the type of child care provided.*

The Home and Day Care

What most distinguishes day care and nursery schools from any of the traditional forms of childrearing is the professionalization of practice. Group care programs are characteristically organized and operated by specially trained personnel, according to planned methods spelled out in the clearly defined duties and limited personal commitment of a job. Activities in the home are built around life in a family, where children are reared by adults who have personal involvement in and permanent commitment to parental roles, following methods intuitively derived through cultural practice and personality style. Thus the home care curriculum is essentially personalized and variable from home to home, while the group care curriculum is routinized in a number of basic minimal practices, and is relatively uniform from center to center.

The continuing growth of urbanization, travel, and communication is, however, bringing about a convergence in practices between the home and group care. This convergence is accelerated by the expansion of parent education services through popular media (TV, newspapers, magazines) and social agencies (welfare agencies, well-baby clinics, visiting nurses), the increase in the number of women working and the growth of day care itself. The rise of women's consciousness through the women's liberation movement is also a generally significant force spreading knowledge of rational, humanistic principles of child care. I shall have more to say about home care and its relations to group care later on.

The Effect of the Social Environment on Child Care

Despite a considerable uniformity in philosophy which prevails in the various forms of early group care, in practice there are many variations in the social environment that influence the quality of care and education provided. Among a number of key social features are the qualifications of the staff, the ratio of teachers to children, the form of administration, the size of the institution, the quality of inservice training, and the relations with the parent. Some of these, such as teacher competence and staff-child ratios, affect the children's education directly; others, like the administrative structure and inservice training, influence the quality of a program indirectly because they affect the morale and competence of the staff. The administrative social structure of the adult envi-

---

* Many of the dimensions we shall discuss can be defined in reasonably exact form, as has been done in the "Environmental Profile" which appears in William Fowler, *Curriculum and Assessment Guides for Infant and Child Care* (Boston: Allyn and Bacon, 1980).

ronment is also a model for social living for the children*. In the discussion to follow we shall review the characteristics and problems of these features.

Staff Qualifications   Competence is the heart of qualifications for caregiving personnel. A competent staff member will have knowledge and skills in child care and development, interest and effort in caring for children, and background competencies of culture and everyday coping skills. Culture includes an interest in music, literature, art, other peoples, and general knowledge needed to stimulate the aesthetic, social, and intellectual development of children. Everyday coping skills are made up of the ability to get along in relations with other teachers, assistants, supervisors and parents, and the ability to solve practical problems in the varied job, community, and home tasks of daily life. Permeating every

* Detailed descriptions and rating scales for evaluating most of these conditions are presented in Form 2 of the 'Environmental Profile' in the companion volume to this text, *Curriculum and Assessment Guides for Infant and Child Care.*

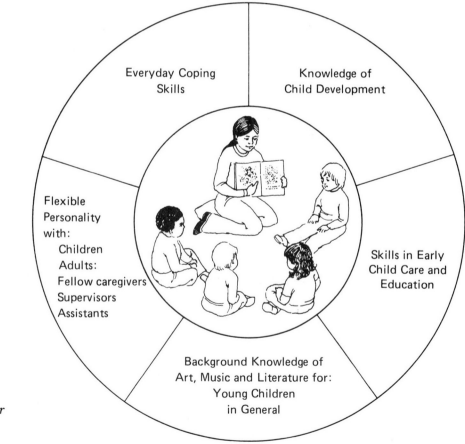

FIGURE 3–1
Qualifications for caregivers and teachers

facet of caregiver competence is a variety of personality characteristics, such as flexibility, warmth, and imagination, that determine how adaptively the adult interacts with and stimulates children.

Competence may be acquired either through training and experience in formal teacher educational systems or through personal experience, but is usually the result of some combination of the two. Although public standards stress professional background, day care or nursery school directors are likely to assign a great deal of weight to background competencies and personality characteristics when they hire a day care worker or teacher. The only thing wrong with this practice is that such qualifications are rarely defined openly and systematically and few teacher education or day care training programs furnish training in these vital aspects.

However attained, teacher qualifications should be based on objective definitions of competence, *measured in performance terms,* rather than merely by the paper qualifications of degrees and years of experience. As noted, teacher education programs often fail to attend adequately to the development of background competencies. How the day care teacher in training actually relates to children, handles a group, stimulates concept learning, reads poetry, rotates toys, solves practical scheduling problems, communicates with different parents, or does her share of the tidying tasks is best taught through courses closely related to intensive guidance in practice teaching. And they are best measured, not through written exams, but through observations of performance in live caregiving and teaching activities, by the use of rating scales, check lists and similar devices.

Cultural enrichment is of course a much broader thing, often acquired through growing up in a family and milieu in which literature, music, and general knowledge are valued and regularly explored. But a strong liberal arts background of courses in literature, art, music, and social studies, and even a course or two in a teacher education program can contribute importantly to interests in this direction. Culturally-oriented teacher education courses probably develop greater understanding when some of the cultural material selected, the literature or music, is discussed and tried out with children.

Day care, particularly day care for infants, is a recent and rapidly expanding enterprise. It will be some time before day care teachers with such comprehensive qualifications, which only a few laboratory nursery schools already provide, can be available in large enough numbers through improvement in teacher education programs. One strategy for improving staff qualifications is to train unusually well qualified day care directors who are capable of developing in their staffs a program with goals based on a comprehensive set of competencies. A concentration of resources in programs to educate highly skilled directors would multiply the benefits of improved staff to day care groups through improving the ability of directors to develop continuous inservice teacher training programs and to provide curriculum leadership. These directors should be more than administrators or senior staff. They should be selected on the basis of performance qualifications to provide personal and educational leadership.

**Adult-Child
Caregiving Ratios**

Dedication and competence in caregivers cannot adequately compensate for numbers. The quality of care and intellectual stimulation children receive in preschools and day care is very much dependent on the number of caregivers present to tend to the children. The tasks of care can only be fulfilled to the extent teachers and caregivers are available to carry them out. But it is of course the number of caregivers *in relation to* the number of children that counts, the teacher-child ratio, not simply the number of caregivers. Thus 10 caregivers would be a lot for a center with an enrollment of only 20 children (a ratio of 1 to 2) but very poor for a center with 100 children (a ratio of 1 to 10).

The caregiver-child ratios outlined in Table 3–1 are levels necessary to provide the *best quality care* in fulfilling children's needs associated with the activities summarized for the different age groups. These are *ideal* ratios, even beyond the U. S. Federal and many state standards, and only specialized research and training centers would be likely to attain them. Since the aim of child care is to promote development in the best manner possible, and not merely to provide minimum attention to meeting the immediate needs of children, ratios should come as close to the ideal as practicable.* While recognizing the practical limitations on most day care centers, we shall discuss the problems of how ratios affect quality in terms of those ideal levels. They represent goals to aim for.

Because the activity cycles of little children are typically irregular and of short duration, not only should ratios be adequate but caregivers need to be regularly close at hand. During the first year infants are so immobile and dependent on adults that the repeated cycle of eating, movement, sleep, elimination and clothes changing, and the problems of providing access to toys and other forms of stimulation make infant care especially demanding. Many caregiving tasks either demand the full attention of a caregiver (e.g. changing diapers, dressing) or, in those like feeding in which more than one infant *can* be managed, it is often managed only through prolonging or rushing the feeding, and cutting the quality of care.

Toward the end of the first year and the beginning of the second (exact timing depends on a child's progress), the infant takes a number of important steps toward greater mental, social, and physical autonomy. Crawling and walking begin, immediately expanding the variety of interesting activities the infant can reach; need cycles become relatively stabilized and of longer duration; awareness of other children increases; language comprehension sharpens, speech begins and the child's play becomes more complex and self-sustaining. While more planning may be necessary, demands on direct adult caregiving become less constant and detailed.

Toward the end of the second year further developmental advances occur: mobility is mastered and speech begins in earnest. It becomes easier to explain things to the child and for the child to explain her wants. The child plays for much longer periods, and engages in social play with others. Intervals between the demands for eating, napping, and changing become longer and soon the major developmental landmark of independence in toilet routines is established.

* A rating system for assessing the adequacy of ratios is included in Form 3 of the "Environmental Profile" in *Curriculum and Assessment Guides for Infant and Child Care.*

TABLE 3-1. Developmental age groups and teacher child ratios: characteristics of different infant age groups that affect care-giving ratios (Reprinted from W. Fowler, "How Adult/Child Ratios Influence Infant Development," *Interchange,* Vol. 6, No. 1/1975, p. 18)

Characteristic	Younger Infants (birth to 12 months)—Recommended Ratios[a] 1:2	Toddlers (13 to 24 months)—Recommended Ratios[a] 1:3	Beginning Preschoolers (25 to 36 months)—Recommended Ratios[a] 1:4–5
Physical mobility	Minimal: none to crawling	Moderate: Walking to beginning running	Mastery: Walking, running, stairs, climbing, jumping, beginning wheel toys
Degree of infant participation in physical care	Minimal: Development of interest in comfort and cooperation in component actions of care routines	Regular participation in routines: relative autonomy in components of routines—with help and supervision, e.g., eating, dressing, toileting	Relative autonomy in certain routines, e.g., eating, toileting, stair climbing, getting into cot; routine participation and partial autonomy in all others, e.g., dressing
Scheduling	Highly individualized and flexible; high ratio of sleep, eating, and other routines to waking and play	Moderate stabilization in routines; long periods of play and wakefulness	Good adaptation to flexible routines of a group; typically one nap per day
Language	Beginning comprehension; babbling but no speech	Single words and rudimentary sentences; extended comprehension	Complex syntax and more elaborate comprehension
Sensory motor play	Highly circumscribed and focused in direction, distance, number of objects, and relations; interested mainly in objects as ends in themselves rather than as tools for a purpose (except hands as instruments)	Extension of focus beyond immediate environment; interested in means and ends, how they work, and in objects as instruments for other purposes, e.g., simple tools, puzzles, form boards, pull-push toys	Interested in multiple patterns and object relations; perseveres over simple obstacles in a chain of means-end activities
Social and emotional relationships —with adults	Attachments to preferred adults (parents and favored care-givers); responsive and dependent interaction with single adults	Relative autonomy in a familiar and friendly environment; adapts well to care and (individualized) guided learning in groups of two to four children (but limited peer interaction)	Multiple adaptation; some cooperative interaction; considerable competence in social rituals, adaptive to care and guided learning in groups of three to five children
—with peers	Responds briefly to and explores (looks at and touches) single infants within proximity	Some initiating of contact but interaction limited in quality and duration	Initiates and interacts socially with others functionally with some persistence; begins to interact cooperatively in play in small groups.

a Ratios indicated refer to on-floor ratios of adults to children, i.e., the number of adults in the room or immediately on hand when needed.

From this point on, more and more of the child's care can quite adequately and even beneficially be provided in small groups of three to five children. The child is becoming sufficiently self-reliant and advanced in understanding and social skills to get enough individual attention and instruction in the remaining parts of tasks she still can't accomplish on her own. (See Chapter 13 for techniques of small group management.) Some tasks like putting on pants, jackets, and snowsuits will continue to require special help for some time. Most activities need to be carried out either individually or in small groups throughout the preschool years, to avoid the developmental problems more likely to arise in large groups from the decrease in personal monitoring by the teacher.

There is scarcely any aspect of the social environment more important yet more expensive to maintain than a high ratio of caregivers to children. There is a constant financial temptation for day care administrators to cut corners here above all other places—to enroll an extra child or two; to cut staff by just one; or to get by without substitute teachers. Yet anything less than a full staff quota, or more than a full infant quota, inevitably increases the staff work burden and tensions, diluting the quality of care. An occasional slight drop in ratios for a day or two is unlikely to matter much over the long run, of course, but financial pressures make it easy to slip from the occasional to the frequent.

The problem is complicated by the difference in length between the infant's and the caregiver's day. Teachers typically work about an eight hour day, while many infants must be transported by their parents before and after their own eight hour working day, making the infant's day at least nine hours long. Variations in parent starting and stopping schedules extend the day care schedule to 10 or 11 hours. Such a length of day necessitates staggering staff schedules. A full staff complement is present only during the middle five hour period of the day, usually between 10:00 and 3:00. Fortunately, variations in parent work schedules tend to reduce attendance during the earlier and later periods of the day, but not as much as the shorter staff work day cuts down the number of caregivers available during these periods. Actual, *on the floor*, ratios are further undermined by staff housekeeping tasks (e.g., record keeping, folding diapers, tidying), and staff needs for coffee breaks and lunch—to say nothing of time for discussion and program preparation. Those housekeeping duties that can often conveniently be done in a corner of a playroom will at least keep another caregiver present (on the floor) to tend the children from time to time, even if her attention is partly distracted. Scheduling problems also seriously interfere with maintaining continuity of care, and make it difficult for teachers to coordinate their efforts and plan the center's program. It is readily apparent that realistic staffing must allow for these scheduling and housekeeping problems, to insure that planned ratios provide adequate *on floor* ratios during the entire day. There are several types of day care systems that can fulfill ratio requirements at a reasonable cost, which will be reviewed later in the chapter.

Administration

Probably next in importance to staff qualifications and ratios is a democratic approach to administration. Who makes decisions about policy and principles, the administrators alone or some combination of staff and leadership? There are many advantages and few disadvantages to involving the caregiving staff in policy planning and administration, though the type of involvement should probably vary with staff competence, the stage of program development, and other circumstances. Teachers will poorly understand or support principles of child care that they have had little share in formulating. Experienced teachers will resent highly controlled leadership and less skilled staff will fail to develop under rules they must follow slavishly. When caregivers must carry out methods and schedules just as the supervisors decide, teaching and care become boring rituals without life or thought. Human relations and learning are dynamic, evolving processes in which only general principles can be formulated in advance. Principles need to be applied adaptively in many different ways to meet changing circumstances and to fit the individual styles of children and teachers.

Teacher participation in making program decisions promotes group discussion which stimulates the development of ideas less likely to come to any individual singly. Joint curriculum planning will make better use of any specialized skills members of the staff might have in music, carpentry, literature, drawing, and even administration and parent liaison. Not the least advantage of staff involvement is the increased harmony that can come from cooperatively dividing the necessary housekeeping and administrative chores almost no one likes but someone has to do.

Staff planning, openness of psychological atmosphere, and even flexible scheduling are all likely accompaniments of a group process approach to running a center, and a good measure of its quality. By its nature, group decision making leads to the identification of problems, a search for solutions, and cooperative planning to implement solutions, all of which foster friendliness, better care and coordination of effort to avoid program conflicts and chaos.

Working together, teachers are likely to set flexible schedules because they are the ones who experience first hand the problems that arise from rigid scheduling. Tight schedules make it difficult to coordinate events, discourage persistence in children's play and learning, and create tension in teachers and children alike. Cooperative planning also makes all aware of the different needs and competencies of individual teachers in setting and timing duties of all kinds.

Group decision making also leads to problems, however, which can usually be resolved if anticipated and worked through. For example, teachers with limited verbal skills may still be afraid to raise questions and will remain silent or voice agreement just to get along with an articulate authority who may hold the key to job security. Sharp divisions of opinion among staff may lead to rivalry and factionalism which tax a director's mediating skills. Continuous inservice teacher development programs, frequent changes in staff responsibility and above all willingness of supervisors to work things through are the best safeguards against such distortions of group decision making.

Working out ideas and plans through group discussion takes more time than issuing instructions from above. It often takes a series of discussions to reach agreement on some method or child problem, even when staff must work within the framework of a defined philosophy of child care. The time is well spent, however, because problems and solutions emerge that would be overlooked by a leader working alone. Group processes also lead to depth of understanding and genuineness of agreement that foster involved teaching instead of a mechanical application of poorly understood directives.

Democratic policy making need not—indeed should not—eliminate active leadership or even the use of a particular theory of education. Group process without leadership tends to work chaotically and lead to uncoordinated teaching practices, the dominance of strong personalities and factions, conflicts, program oversights, and even neglect of the children. Guidance, support, and coordination by supervisors are indispensable if teachers are to work together smoothly and pleasantly to produce a good program. As a minimum, democratic planning requires shared decision making on different ways of carrying out the principles and goals of a program. When there is a definite philosophical framework and set of program goals determined by a director or leadership board, they should be clearly spelled out in advance. These then serve as guidelines and principles for the day to day practices worked out between the caregiving staff and the supervisors. There should be no "hidden agenda" of implicitly taboo topics and principles. No day care worker wishes to discover through a cold comment from a supervisor that center philosophy discourages efforts to toilet train infants before 18 months, when he is leading a 13 month old to the toilet. Rules and the rationale for them should be known and discussed by all.

The Effects of Size on Social Atmosphere

Bigness alone need not depersonalize relations in day care, though it often does. Personalized care, informality, and staff equality are difficult to maintain in centers housing many children. The problem lies in sheer numbers, and the hierarchy of relations that tends to come about in large organizations. A center of about 30 to 50 children and 10 to 15 teachers organized into three groups is ideal for communication. This size is large enough to afford a diversity of resources yet small enough for cooperative planning and informal relations to flourish. A center of this size takes on the intimacy of an extended family or small community, in which staff, parents, and children (except younger infants) come to know one another fairly well.

There are nevertheless advantages to centers accommodating as many as one hundred children and problems in running centers of less than thirty children, nor need size inevitably preclude intimacy and community. The chief advantage of size is the lower per child operating costs of large building facilities and land; bulk purchasing of food, housekeeping equipment, toys, and equipment; and pooling resources (in effect combining those of several small centers). The savings realized permit more frequent replacement and the purchase of a wider variety and higher quality of educational materials that can be shared by all groups. Large centers may even afford a highly qualified director, a number of master teachers, a curriculum resource person, a diet specialist, and a part-time psychologist. Size also enables centers to create a number of floating teacher positions to meet fluctuations in children's needs and program demands, and provide greater continuity of relations for children than substitute teachers can provide.

There are several ways of preserving a sense of community. While bigness does require planning and organization, it does not require day to day control by the director of resources and children's welfare. In one model, a center of 200 children could be separated for operating purposes into 5 or 6 semidetached work groups of 35 to 40 children. Each group would be run as a separate group with a distinct identity, its own rooms, facilities, and toys, and local policies and practices worked out in local discussion groups. Overall guidelines of educational principles, administrative coordination, and resource allocation could be prepared by a central body composed of the center director and teacher representatives of the various groups. An abundance of such resources as a library, gymnasium, circulating toys, specialized science, art, and playground facilities, and specialized teachers, offer children a greater pool of talent, playmate choices, and program diversity than is available in a small center. The only problem is to ensure that the multiplication of opportunities does not fragment relations and learning.

Inservice Teacher Education

Inservice education for staff is as much a creative approach to operating a day care program or nursery school as it is a means of maintaining teacher competencies.* Teacher evaluation is integral to this process. Teachers are often evaluated when they are hired, but unfortunately, few initial judgments are made on the basis of *performance,* the expression of skills in *practice.* Well-intentioned references, resumes, and detailed interviews do not convey complete information even to insightful interviewers, and caregivers adapt differently to the circumstances of each center. Since all teachers have strengths and weaknesses, regular performance assessments in a program of continuing inservice education benefits everyone in some way, adding to the general quality of care. The best assessments are the day to day *working observations* teachers make of one another and themselves in the course of caregiving. Constructive guidance often comes out more readily if there is a daily 15–20 minute period for discussion between a working staff of caregivers and their supervisors, when they can be free from the immediate responsibility of care tasks. Their shared familiarity with the children, the closeness of a continuing working relationship as a team, and the freshness of the day's problems make it natural to discuss alternatives ("This child needs more direct handling," "That child needs simpler examples of how boats move") and difficulties ("How do you handle Nellie's biting?"). Both poorly qualified and highly qualified teachers have much to gain through such inservice education experiences, the former in general development, the latter in refreshing old skills and acquiring new ones.

The best inservice program approaches teaching as constant experimentation with the many aspects of learning and human relations, which change continuously and can never all be known or controlled. Fundamental to this approach is a background of team work and joint questioning on the part of the staff and administration, to continually build the day care program. There must be a balance between maintaining stability and consistency of care to foster security for the children, and trying out new things to keep the program alive and stimulating. Child care is a dynamic process of constant development, not a prescribed program of fixed procedures.

Effective inservice education programs will include:

1. Above all, frequent and open communication between teachers at all levels and areas of a center. Openly talking things out develops teacher awareness of differences in approaches, and perspective on children's development in different areas, age levels, and phases of the program. Harmony of relations and philosophy cannot be maintained without intensive communication.

2. Constant analysis of problems and formulation of approaches to child care, with respect to both cognitive learning and interpersonal rela-

* See Form 2, "Environmental Profile", *Curriculum and Assessment Guides for Infant and Child Care.*

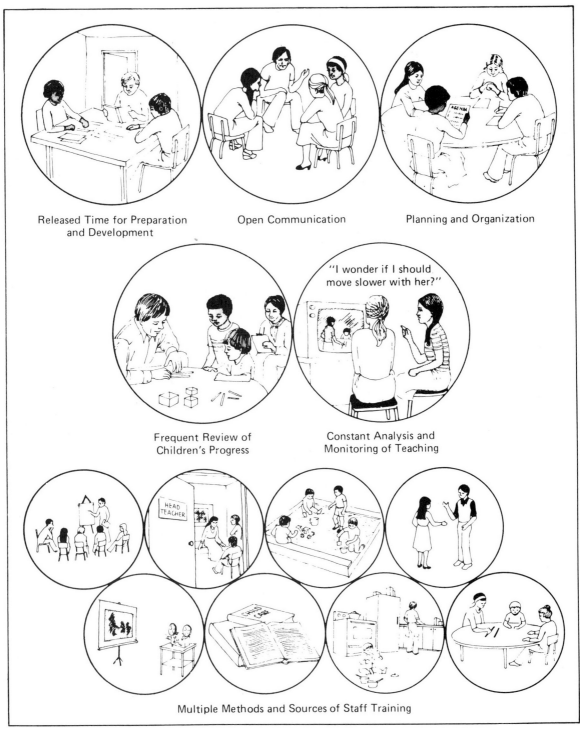

Released Time for Preparation
and Development

Open Communication

Planning and Organization

Frequent Review of
Children's Progress

Constant Analysis and
Monitoring of Teaching

"I wonder if I should
move slower with her?"

Multiple Methods and Sources of Staff Training

FIGURE 3-2
Techniques of in-service education for caregivers and teachers.

tions. Friendly analysis of one another's strengths and weakness in the context of constructive *working observations* is intrinsic to healthy working relations in handling children.

3. Regular access to many sources of ideas, including the director, other teachers, parents, books, films, visiting experts, or visits of staff to other centers or conferences. Frequent exposure to outside sources will prevent a staff from becoming too ingrown, as well as enable a center to learn of new developments in child care.

4. Careful planning and organization of inservice training and discussion sessions to make sure that a comprehensive program is maintained, that no important methods or ideas are overlooked. However stimulating spontaneous communication may be, without the support of planning it can easily lead to one-sided development in a program, and the unwitting neglect of essential aspects of learning or the individual needs of children, teachers, and parents.

5. Routine released time for staff to prepare programs and materials, observe children and monitor their development, and develop their professional skills. Such periods of thirty to sixty minutes are needed several times per week in addition to personal break periods. The quality of programs and child care will improve in direct relation to the regularity of such practices.

6. New concepts and techniques of teaching are acquired through a variety of methods, all of which need to be systematically employed to build a strong inservice program. The first method is staff discussion, both for playroom staff teams and for larger groups involved in general teaching problems. A second is through demonstrations of methods, problems, and the use of materials, either live with children or in some combination of videotaped and live presentations. Direct observation makes clear the actual operations of teaching practice in a way that the abstract discussion with language alone can never do. Discussion, on the other hand, is useful for formulating and evaluating general principles and considering alternatives, and is often most helpful following (and/or preceding) a demonstration, or based on detailed case study facts about a child or problem situation. A fourth method is experience itself, not merely in the day-to-day practice of caring for children, but performing under direct supervision, especially when videotaped (see Chapter 14). Teachers are often timid about being observed directly, but usually can adapt to videotaping themselves. The tape is then available for repeated review and objective evaluation by the teacher herself and by others. She is able to gain an outside view of herself not easy to obtain in any other way.

7. Continued monitoring and evaluation of staff and director, as described later in chapters on strategies of care and stimulation.

8. Keeping in mind that the goal of inservice training is the welfare and education of individual children, inservice training might include at least weekly reviews of the children's progress by the teachers who are responsible for each of them. Discussion can be directed toward how each child is progressing and what new problems have arisen. Each caregiver's problems, and different methods to try, can thus be worked out directly in relation to

the children's needs, while the problems are fresh. General principles and techniques make more sense for teachers when they are examined in terms of how they work with particular problems and children. The principle of flexibility, for example, becomes more meaningful to a caregiver when he sees it means occasionally letting a child run down the hall when she's anxious to get outdoors, or to overlook one child's exaggerated self-assertive style, while working on the aggression of another who already copes successfully. Since this is so vital to the intelligent and smooth operation of a program, time should be allowed for teachers to prepare and discuss when calculating caregiver-child ratios.

Parent Involvement and Community Relations

Involvement with parents and relations with the general community are two aspects of a general outlook, in which the day care staff and administration see themselves as part of the life of a community, rather than simply as an agency of experts on child care. Making ties to the local community helps to build closer personal relations in our sprawling cities and suburbs so dominated by commercial relations and technology. For a variety of reasons, the development of extensive relations with both parents and various segments of the local community, such as storekeepers, park personnel, and neighbors, will do much to enrich the cultural life and the feeling of belonging in a day care center.*

There is also a deep obligation to further relations between day care and home because the parent has the major responsibility for the daily care of the child and has continuing responsibility for socialization throughout childhood and youth. It is important to coordinate the modes of child rearing used in the two settings to minimize conflicts for the child, as we shall discuss in Chapter 5 on strategies of child care. Most parent groups represent a pool of talent (e.g., carpentry to repair and make toys, guitar or piano playing) and a diversity of cultures for the day care staff to draw on in order to enrich the program and teach the children the broad array of values characteristic of the world at large.

Although in parent-operated centers and parent-teacher cooperatives, parents vote on policy questions, the important thing in all day care and school settings is some degree of parent participation in curriculum planning and in handling problems of child care and education. The general curriculum plan and educational principles may be established by the professional staff or board, but there is much to gain when parents work with staff on the actual application, including both discussing methods and assisting in the playroom as they have time. Parent participation is a potent tool for adding to the pool of teaching skills, educating parents, and dealing with the differences between school and home. Unfortunately, the time and involvement of many parents is inevitably limited, particularly for single parents or working mothers, but parent participation can be meaningful and regular if parents are asked to help out with committee work, and expectations of some sort of participation are made clear at the time of the child's enrollment. Day care should not become merely a convenient parking place for thoughtless parents who do not take their child-rearing responsibilities seriously. Indeed, involving parents is likely to increase

* See Form 2 of the "Environmental Profile" in *Curriculum and Assessment Guides for Infant and Child Care* for methods of assessing program quality on these points.

parental satisfaction through furthering understanding and helping to find solutions to conflicts with children.

Building relationships with different groups in the local community contributes to many social aspects of day care besides a sense of community. Visits to stores, libraries, the post office, fire houses, plumbers, and other commercial and community services provide children with wider social knowledge, including exposure to a diversity of cultures. Frequent educational excursions identify the day care center in the neighborhood, and help develop mutually beneficial efforts to improve the quality of community life. Scheduled contributions of staff and parent time, effort, and even money to community social, cultural, and improvement organizations will help. A day care center may find itself isolated in a gradually deteriorating or hostile neighborhood, in part through the center's own failure to contribute to the development of stronger community relations and services. A center which has cemented itself in the community may find temporary support in times of financial crisis, in the form of donated goods, money, or prizes for fund-raising activities.

Serious consideration should be given to the possibility of extending the services of a day care center to fill other community needs. At a minimum, day care centers usually have a number of rooms, some of them large enough to serve as activity and meeting rooms for community groups, and most of which remain vacant night after night. Renting rooms to community groups is also an additional source of income.

In a broader sense, day care centers are more community oriented when designed as one component of a community activity, social, and cultural center. Many urban and rural areas lack physical facilities and social activities to enliven the sociocultural life of the community. Single parents and small nuclear families are typically isolated from the larger (extended) family and friends. They are often lonely and bored, in part because of the absence of a friendly, informal gathering place, offering low cost social and recreational activities. A multipurpose community center which offers day care, art, craft, carpentry, photography, music, dance, literature, cooking, and other activities serves many social, cultural, and educational needs of the community. It is also a useful setting for an information clearinghouse for community social services like parent education, vocational retraining, family financial and personal counselling, family planning, welfare, and job placement. And it is a useful basis for developing community awareness and action groups for solving local community problems. Families who initially come to a center for one reason, such as day care, social activity, or a pottery class, may discover other interests, such as parent education and poetry. Community centers are not panaceas for involving everyone or solving all social problems, and they do usually require governmental or agency support. They are, however, one useful means of providing community alternatives to the isolation of the family in the home, or the street idling and car riding of youth.

Types of Group Day Care: Characteristics and Problems

There are at least five basic types of day care centers, determined by type of sponsorship and administrative organization, each of which has its characteris-

TABLE 3–2. Characteristics of day care/schools for young children, (ages 0–4 years)

Sponsorship: Administrative Structure	Special Features	Problems

I. Government	1. Low or income-scaled fees; government subsidized.
	2. Standards: generally adequate programs, staff (professional), and caregiving ratios.
	3. Hierarchical administration: government system control.
	4. Facilities and equipment: generally adequate and sometimes outstanding in upper middle-class areas.
		1. Scaling fees may limit participation of middle-class and two-parent (intact) families.
		2. Subsidy rarely sufficient to support high quality programs, ratios, etc.
		3. Standards:
		   a. Programs: seldom high quality, especially in education
		   b. Staff: adequate but director usually selected on the basis of seniority rather than ability to provide educational leadership.
		   c. Staff-child ratios seldom attain optimum levels.
		4. Little parental involvement in policy or programs.
		5. Bureaucratic: impersonal control by large systems; insufficient local center and teacher autonomy; when group processes employed in staff meetings, they are usually authority-centered.
		6. Often requires extra parental commuting time.
		7. No provision for care if child is ill: often means extra babysitting costs for working parents, or threat of job loss.
		8. May be socially and/or ethnically segregated, depending on community.

A. Social service (welfare): Municipal day care	Modification of government model: Child-care oriented (physical care and socioemotional development).	Modification of government model: Little educational programming
B. Educational (public schools): Junior kindergarten	Modification of government model: 1. Combines education (cognition and learning) with child care and development. 2. No family fees. 3. Enrollment and social relations related to the local community.	Modification of government model: Staff-child ratios typically inadequate

TABLE 3-2—(Continued)

Sponsorship: Administrative Structure	Special Features	Problems
C. Educational-social service (public schools—welfare): High school day care	Modification of government model: 1. Combines education (cognition and learning) with child care and development. 2. Combines parent education (theory and practicum) for high school students with day care staffing, leading to: a. Improved staff-child ratios at low cost. b. Professional staff stimulation. c. Improved, experimentally oriented program. d. Possibly improved parental communication. e. In specialized centers for school-age parents, enables them to complete high school.	Modification of government model: Program instability and practical discontinuity of adult-child relations through unevenness of student competency and number and rotation of student assistants.
II. Cooperatives	1. Low fees: parent shares in teaching; may also be subsidized. 2. Standards: generally adequate program and staff (professional-parents); good to excellent staff-child ratios because of parent participation. 3. Cooperative model: a. Sets example for children in socialization. b. Relates the personal ways of the home to the professional ("rational") ways of day care. c. Provides parental inservice education in child care. d. Tendency toward group processes in decision making. 4. Facilities and equipment: variable.	1. Fees seldom adequate to provide high quality. 2. Standards: large daily fluctuations in quality of program, staff competence, and staff-child ratios because of number of different parents teaching each day, who vary widely in competence and who must often shift schedules to cope with children's illness. 3. Time for caregiving may be a burden on some parents. 4. Administration and group process orientation extensive and time consuming. 5. May be factional groups polarized on issues such as discipline, professionalism, degree of cooperation, life style, etc. 6. Extra commuting time for working parents. 7. Few nonmiddle-class groups served, separates mothers at home from working mother population. 8. Generally no provision for care of child during illness, but nonworking parent status makes this less of a problem. 9. May be socially and/or ethnically segregated, depending on community.

TABLE 3-2—(Continued)

Sponsorship: Administrative Structure	Special Features	Problems
A. Parent-professional cooperatives.	Follows basic cooperative model.	Follows basic cooperative model.
B. Parent cooperative (including university student-faculty and community cooperatives)	Modification of cooperative model: 1. Low fees: parents (and volunteers) are teachers. 2. Standards: program and staff competence variable; may reflect casual and cooperative communal life styles; often quite personalized, extended family atmosphere.	Modification of cooperative model: Standards: absence of professional leadership and tendency to adopt alternative life styles results in: 1. Intuitive versus rational basis for methods of child care, sometimes with basic ignorance of child development, educational content, and occasionally nutrition; child assumed capable of reasoning and social responsibility level of adults. 2. Respect for individual sometimes extreme; hampers group processes in planning and decision making. 3. Larger variability in goals of care competencies, methods, and schedules, depending on availability of parent skills. 4. Permissiveness sometimes to point of extreme disorder and disorganization. 5. Contrasts in expressions of good feelings and hostility.
III. Agency-professional, nonprofit	1. Fees: Highly variable, depending on subsidy and policy. 2. Financial basis often sufficient to permit high quality. 3. Standards: generally high quality, often individually tailored and developmentally and educationally oriented program; competent staff and leadership; good to excellent staff-child ratios. 4. Parent involvement usually high; special reports on child to parent typical. 5. Hierarchical administration: board-directorial control. 6. Facilities and equipment: adequate but variable.	1. Fee levels may be exclusionary, limiting social class membership; elitist, upper middle class status oriented, along with a special scholarship group. 2. Teacher autonomy and participation in policy making and program design may be restricted by administration, though control tends to be personalized in director and local board; staff meetings may be authority centered. 3. Parent participation may be shunted to social supportive (coffee and cake) and fund-raising roles. 4. Extra commuting time for working parents. 5. No provision for care if child is ill; often means extra babysitting costs for working parent or threat of job loss. 6. May be socially and/or ethnically segregated, depending on community.

TABLE 3–2—(Continued)

Sponsorship: Administrative Structure	Special Features	Problems

A. University laboratory-demonstration nursery schools and day care (latter usually with community college)	Modification of agency-professional model:
	1. Professional teacher training and research programs which are involved with school often serve to:
	  a. Raise caliber of staff competence academically to teach students.
	  b. Improve staff-child ratios through the pool of students in training.
	  c. Develop innovative, experimentally oriented curriculum through student teacher and research projects.
	2. Facilities and equipment generally exceptional.
		Modification of agency-professional model:
		1. Elite; attendance is drawn heavily from academically oriented university community.
		2. Head teachers likely to enjoy "master" status and considerable autonomy, commensurate with instructor–practicum supervisory roles; policy thus made by a collection of independent individuals rather than through collaborative group planning.

B. Private school day care Liberal-intellectual oriented	Modification of agency-professional model: Sometimes has a teacher training program involved.	Modification of agency-professional model: Sometimes less teacher autonomy, greater directorial-board control.
Social status-tradition oriented	Modification of agency-professional model: Stress on social definitions and greater variability in standards and facilities.	Modification of agency-professional model: Standards: program may be more socially biased and less adequate educationally: program, staff competence, and ratios vary more in quality, depending on financial resources and ratio of cultural/intellectual to social status values of school.
C. Social service agency (private welfare organizations and religious or church groups)	Modification of agency-professional model: 1. Greater stress on low-cost service to include more poverty and/or special handicapped (learning disabilities, physically handicapped) groups. 2. Greater variability in standards varying from delivery of minimum adequate care to as many special need groups as possible, to delivery of highest quality individual care to a small number of high-need children.	Modification of agency-professional model: 1. Fee policies (scaling) favor poor rather than middle class, though not the poorest noncoping families; centers for the handicapped may be more middle-class biased. 2. Teacher participation and group planning may be more extensive and democratic because of social service ethic; specialized competencies in centers for the handicapped may result in greater teacher autonomy and consequent erosion of group planning. 3. Parent involvement likely to be greater because of social service ethic, and specialized child and family needs, but attitudes toward parents may also be patronizing because of "charity" framework and familial vulnerability.

TABLE 3–2—(Continued)

Sponsorship: Administrative Structure	Special Features	Problems
IV. Commercially operated (profit)	1. Fees: standard, unscaled 2. Standards: variable 3. Business management administration. 4. Facilities and equipment: variable. 5. Mixed social class composition, though generally for working mothers.	1. Fee levels may be high because of tremendous unfilled demand by working mothers, and profit basis in an intrinsically high cost field (especially in personnel costs). 2. Standards often less than adequate and even poor because of cost-profit basis that undercuts adequate staff ratios and competencies needed to individualize care and develop a planned educational program. Salaries are often lower than the average of this uniformly poorly paid profession and the business orientation fails to attract competent staff who will often work for less in a more idealistic framework (e.g., in a cooperative). 3. Staff seldom has much voice in policy and program, which are determined by manager or owner-director and based upon cost considerations. 4. Parent involvement in decision making generally minimal, although there may be some social activities and reporting on child's development. 5. Generally extra commuting time for working parents. 6. No provision for care of child during illness; means extra babysitting costs or threat to job security for working parents. 7. May be socially and/or ethnically segregated, depending on policy and community.
A. Owner-operated (private profit in the community)	Modification of commercial model: Facilities generally in partially remodeled old homes.	Modification of commercial model: 1. Fees may run lower at the sacrifice of quality. 2. Standards are generally lower due to high unit costs of small operation and lack of capital to construct new or remodel old facilities; insufficient funds and competence to select a good director, competent staff, or good toys and equipment. Facilities may be grossly overcrowded, underequipped, understaffed, and staffed with poorly trained, even abusive personnel.

TABLE 3-2—(Continued)

Sponsorship: Administrative Structure	Special Features	Problems
B. Corporate: multiple-center chain operations	Modification of commercial model: Large capitalization and lower unit costs may result in: 1. Standards: competence of director and some staff may be high. 2. Facilities and equipment generally good to excellent.	Modification of commercial model: Problems of standards may center in numbers of staff more than in staff competence, facilities, and materials. There may be an educationally oriented program, parent reporting, etc., but with less than adequate staff-child ratios, program tends to be organized in oversized group activities and individualization suffers. Problems of depersonalized communication associated with large scale corporations.

C. Industry operated: factory or office setting	Modification of commercial model: May be subsidized by industry as a fringe benefit to attract and stabilize employment:
	 1. Fees may be reduced.
	 2. Standards may be improved: higher salaries to attract a competent director and staff, good care ratios, and a quality program (though not necessarily educationally oriented).
	 3. Facilities and equipment may be excellent.
	 4. Eliminates extra commuting for parent, who is also close at hand in case of children's need.
		Modification of commercial model:
		 1. No commuting problems for parents.
		 2. Modifications mentioned under special features. Problems of staff and parent involvement generally remain.
		 3. Working parent enrollment of child at place of work increases leverage of company over employee behavior.
		 4. May not serve management purposes:
		   a. Does not stabilize employment, since children rapidly outgrow the need for day care unless a long age span is accomodated, or
		   b. Works well only for large plants or those with a high proportion of young workers with small children.
		 5. Limited, single industry population, though may embrace several occupations and social strata.

D. Apartment management operated: residential setting (high rise or housing complex)	Modification of commercial model:
	 1. Some inclination to improve quality as a fringe benefit for tenants (similar to industry goals).
	 2. Eliminates extra commuting time for working parents:
	   a. Parent is not immediately available.
	   b. Child can be easily returned to home apartment for working parent.
	 3. Potentially neighborhood oriented.
		Modification of commercial model:
		 1. Similar problems to industry model, including problems of enrollment stability and problems of tenant-management relations.
		 2. Limited social class composition of housing category; housing group may not reflect wider neighborhood of community.

tic features and problems, as outlined in Table 3–2. The terms group care or group day care in this context refer to any method of care that brings children together in groups at a common place of activity during the day, full or part time. Both schools and family day care are included under this definition, although the latter stands apart from all other forms because of the small size of the group of about five children who are cared for in someone's home, usually outside a professional framework.

The order in which the types of care and preschools are outlined is not intended to reflect either the order of importance or the relative frequency of types in use, although the first two categories (government and cooperatives) appear to represent major growing trends. The field of early day care and education is expanding and changing rapidly, but in any case types frequently overlap. For example, the provincial government in Ontario, Canada, in effect sponsors many private agency centers, both profit and non-profit, by subsidizing 80 percent of the costs of care. Cooperatives will sometimes accept a few children whose parents will be unable to participate at all, and residential apartment day care centers may be run on a cooperative basis.

Each of the types of care outlined offers solutions to various problems, but none of the systems comes to grips with all problems, even in centers high in quality for the type. Solutions to one problem often create problems of another kind. A classic illustration is the different advantages and disadvantages we have discussed of small and larger day care centers and schools. Even union-operated centers, in which union membership serves as a basis for parent participation in policy making, nevertheless bind parents to a particular job setting, a problem for which no union grievance procedure has much relevance.

There are two systems of group care, however, which despite their particular problems, deserve special attention, because each promises an answer to the biggest plague in day care delivery, the dilemma of quality versus cost. The problem centers on adult-child caregiving ratios. Teacher salaries typically account for as much as 60 to 80 percent of the costs of running a center. To illustrate the dilemma, we have only to consider the effect on costs of a small shift in ratios. In a center of 45 children, 15 in each of three age groups from a few months to age three, an average ratio of one teacher for every five children (1:5) would amount to an annual cost of $72,000, assuming an average salary of $8,000 for 9 teachers, hardly a large figure in this time of inflation. This figure compares with a range of likely costs for rent, maintenance, materials, and food services from perhaps $25,000 to $35,000 (including two to three supporting staff salaries of $6,000 to $8,000, for janitors and cooks), or at the most about a third of total operating costs. But if we attempted to bring this ratio in line with the average ratio of 1:3 recommended in Table 3–1, the number of teachers would jump to 15, an increase in salaries of $48,000 to a total of $120,000 or at least three quarters (77 percent) of total operating costs. The individual figures may fluctuate, but the relations remain comparatively constant. While the figures do not take into consideration initial capital costs for down payment, remodeling, and primary equipment and materials, these are largely one-time costs that do not match the repeated, year-after-year costs of salaries. Nothing is so costly yet so important in the maintenance of infant care as staff-child ratios. The critical aspect of ratios is that even highly skilled and dedicated caregivers cannot perform competently if they have too much to do.

FIGURE 3–3
The social and educational benefits of parent-teacher cooperatives and high school day care and preschools.

The two types of day care that come closest to combining quality with low cost are high school day care (item IC, Table 3–2) and cooperative day care or schools (item II, Table 3–2). Each of these serves essentially different parent populations, but together they are capable of satisfying much if not all of the high quality, low cost day care required in any community. High school day care could easily fill the demands of the entire population of parents working on fixed, full time schedules. Cooperatives could meet the needs of all parents willing and able to share time teaching in day care because they do not work, work only part time or enjoy flexible work schedules (e.g., students and college faculty). Non-working parents who, for various reasons, such as illness or number of children, are unable to work in cooperatives could have their children admitted to the high school day care services. Neither system, however much expanded, is likely, however, to stop the growth of other care and school systems (laboratory, nursery schools, junior kindergartens, union, industry and apartment operated) designed to meet other community needs or special interest groups.

The particular virtue of high school day care is that it provides badly needed parent education and child care practice for high school students, while providing a supplementary means of staffing day care centers with student assistants at little cost. Every high school boy and girl deserves the opportunity to take at least one course in child development that combines academic work with several months of inservice training in care methods with infants. High school day care centers are most conveniently located in nearby elementary schools because of their younger age atmosphere, and because many schools now have vacant classrooms resulting from the current decline in birthrates. A core staff of professional teachers is required to insure continuity of care, and to provide training and supervision of students on tasks easily within the learning competence of the average high school student. This approach to staffing day care is already well established in many high schools. Most programs are designed to combine parent education with training in infant care for school age parents, but a few provide similar training with both infants and preschoolers for ordinary high school students.

Cooperatives, which have a long history in several forms, follow the same basic structure as high school day care, except that parents rather than students serve as teachers or assistant teachers. Given the differences in age and status, parents in cooperatives generally have far more responsibility for running a program than students do in high school day care. Parents are also frequently associated with a particular cooperative during one or more years of their child's infancy, while students at best remain one or two semesters. Moreover, cooperating parents usually work with a professional staff to manage a center, even if it is also government subsidized. Student-assisted high school day care is ordinarily operated by the school system, perhaps in collaboration with the municipal social service department, giving the professional staff the essential management responsibility.

Neither of these approaches to group day care solves all problems and each type is prone to problems of its own, as Table 3–2 makes clear. The chief problem in both cases is the tendency toward inconsistency in program quality as a consequence of the numbers of assistants, the rotation of schedules, and the unevenness of response to training of both parents and students. However, much of this problem can be tempered and even turned to an advantage, given the diversity of talents available, if the professional staff is skilled enough to make full use of these resources. The key is to select directors and staff for both cooperatives and municipally operated high school day care centers on the basis of motivation and ability to give educational leadership, and not just on the traditional grounds of seniority. Despite their problems, both cooperatives and high school day care enjoy a great potential, each in its own form, providing good quality care at a price even many low-income parents can afford, and without burdening taxpayers with excessive subsidies.

There are other problems inherent in the different types of day care outlined in Table 3–2, such as the problem of added commuting time for the working parent, who must drop off and pick up his or her child en route to and from the job. This problem can be solved by selecting a center located close to the home, or at the job site, but both of these solutions raise other problems, such as, what happens when the parent moves or changes jobs?

Another, little-noted problem is what happens when the child in day care becomes ill? Almost no type of day care or school system will or probably even should care for sick children. Many day care agencies will keep an ill child until the end of the work day, knowing the threat to a parent of job loss from leaving work. It is also common for day care centers to admit children with mild colds and diarrhea, recognizing the burden to parents without relatives at home of extra expense for babysitters. But no really sick child should be exposed to the stress of temperature changes and movement to and from the center, and healthy children should not be exposed to any illness that could spread to other children in more serious form. Clearly, public support for a system of low cost home visiting caregivers, or provision for isolating several moderately sick children in day care on a routine basis, is badly needed. Since well-run residential care centers for children routinely cope with this problem, why can't day care? Working parents, particularly single parents, need to be able to provide for their children's care during illness, with the assurance they will be well cared for, without feeling guilty of neglecting them, and without the worry of added expenses. Since there is probably no good substitute for parental attention to the seriously ill child, paid sick leave is needed for working parents to tend their children during important illnesses.

Each form of group care is subject to special problems and any form can be abused or operated inefficiently. The social environment is rarely perfect. The most common problems are inadequate staff-child ratios, and inadequacies in teacher motivation and competence (in both of which inadequate center leadership plays an important role). Quality day care rests especially on the quality of the social environment, which is never secure; it must always be worked for.

4 The Physical Environment

Facilities scaled to size

The Influence of Physical Structures on Mental Structures

Each environment has distinctive characteristics that influence what and how the child learns. In a playroom, for example, the way in which furniture, partitions and toys are distributed; the kind of toys available; the properties of objects—their color, shape and size—and how they are arranged; are all physical conditions that define the sorts of learning possible (see Chapter 7). We must not assume, however, that the way an environment is organized provides a mold which is literally "stamped" into the mind of the child. The flexibility and inventiveness of young children in play reveals the powerful role played by fantasy and the organizing capabilities of the mind in making different uses of an environment. Moreover, the aims of child care in general, and the arrangement of environments and learning materials in particular, are to teach mental principles for problem solving and adapting, not the slavish use of materials. There is plenty of room for individual differences in well-designed playrooms.

Each setting has its own dimensions and boundaries which determine the direction and range of learning available. The basis for this frequently overlooked aspect of life is to be found in three conditions of the physical and human world, two of them very general and one specific to the nature of development in the early years. These three conditions are:

1. All behavior is affected by the characteristics of the environment where it takes place.
2. The infant is particularly dependent on the physical environment.
3. The ways in which each environment is arranged can greatly help or hinder young children's learning.

Activity always happens *somewhere*, in a *specific environment;* we cannot do anything or even exist without being in some particular place. Moreover, it will not be just any place, but one of a certain size, shape, color and texture. At a day care center, a baby is in a crib, in a particular area of a playroom, on someone's lap or shoulder, or in some other place; but always a place with special characteristics that determine what he can see, hear, touch, taste, do, and play with—as well as what can be done with him.

As adults we have become so accustomed to the objects and environments generally available in our homes and cultures that we deal with many places and things in routine ways rather automatically. We hardly observe the common, everyday things, seeing and reacting only to a limited number according to their use and the task we have at hand—the clothes we wear, the pencil and paper we use to write, and the food we eat. Even our interest in familiar objects varies according to our cultural values and our personal histories. We have grown to like certain clothes, food, and ways of arranging our household— plenty of jazz records in one house, classical music in another, and none in a third. The ordinary stimulus characteristics of familiar objects like the hum of the refrigerator, the length of a spoon, or the pattern on a rug, and their arrangement—whether cluttered or orderly, full of sharp edges and hard surfaces or rounded edges and soft textures—affect our actions much less than they affect a child's. We tend to forget how different environments offer different

FIGURE 4-1
The preschooler is influenced by her surroundings far more than the adult is.

possibilities and demands—how continuous TV noise and confusion interfere with the child's attention to explanations and demonstrations of how to do a task, or how a large overstuffed chair makes a better hiding place than a straight chair. We think and act as if our actions occur free from particular physical situations; we must not assume that the same is true for infants.

Our second point is that for the infant the nature and organization of *his immediate object world is fundamental,* both because it is all relatively unfamiliar and because the infant does not yet operate on an abstract level. His is a world of physical movement and direct feeling of things. It can only have meaning for him through his senses; he learns to use his hands and feet as instruments for acting in the physical world—grasping, picking up objects, moving them, using them as tools to do other things, and for moving himself from place to place. During infancy language is primarily used only in direct relation to an immediate situation. The infant's goals and actions, his reactions to objects, are simple, short and shifting; the infant is always preoccupied with things and simple physical actions.

The nature of this first learning period gives great importance to the infant's physical environment. A home or institution limited in the number and variety of toys and objects available is a barren environment psychologically, because it narrows the range of experiences the baby can have. Impoverished homes and the big, empty rooms of the old-fashioned infant institutions (orphan asylums) are difficult settings in which to lay a good foundation for the human mind. Even with the best caregiver intentions, barren environments

FIGURE 4–1 continued
The preschooler is influenced by her surroundings far more than the
adult is.

tend to leave perceptions and understanding shallow and dwarfed, dampening
knowledge of how to do things, or even the desire to try to develop that knowledge.

Third, it is not enough to think only of the quantity and variety of objects
and living arrangements available for infants and young children in their everyday worlds. An abundance of objects can still mean chaos. Objects vary in
color, size, and other features, so that similarities between objects (shape or
size, for instance) are *easier for children to learn when arranged or clustered*
together in certain ways.

The parts of similar objects also serve similar functions—the legs of chairs
and tables, the viscosity (flow) of liquids, the enclosing quality of containers,
the flexibility of cloth. Only through experience with objects arranged according to their similar and different features and functions does the child develop
general concepts about the world. Merely perceiving the size or color of individual objects which may stand out to the sight or touch leaves the child in a
psychological world bereft of sense and purpose. The importance of the way
the child's environment is ordered can be seen most acutely by viewing extremes. Children growing up in very disorganized homes, regardless of social
class, are slow to learn to order their thoughts and classify objects according to
their similar features and functions. There are also differences in what must be
ordered. Thus children from Arctic regions learn all about many different types
of ice and snow and many more words exist in their language to represent
these many types than are found in English or other European languages. Chil-

Clutter and Confusion   Areas of Concentration

FIGURE 4–2
Children's activity is influenced by the arrangement as much as by the quantity of things in the environment.

dren in a jungle environment learn to classify and label many more types of leaves, butterflies, and other local natural objects than either we or Arctic children do. Inner city children learn an extensive street and urban lore that baffles suburban middle-class children, white or black.

The child's encounters with the environment can thus be either more or less meaningful depending on the *selection* and *arrangement* of materials, and the relation among patterns present in a whole series of well arranged experiences. The grouping of materials should not be arbitrary or inflexible, but should be designed to bring out the structures and processes intrinsic to the natural world. In group care, on the one hand, we need to avoid piling or scattering toys without any plan; on the other hand, if all objects of the same size are invariably placed together, there will be less opportunity for a child to see and learn about size differences without constant teacher intervention.

The Surrounding Community

The location of a day care or nursery school facility is likely to be more a matter of opportunity than choice. The availability of property, financial considerations, and requirements of city codes within the community usually determine the selection of building sites. All communities need group care and educational facilities for all ages and types of families, from the many cultural neighborhoods of the inner city to the middle-class suburbs and farm, mining, and industrial communities. Obviously, the nature of the environment where a center is located will be heavily determined by the character of these very different communities.

Whatever the setting, local conditions can be exploited in full to enlarge even the infant's horizons. It is important to distinguish between the immediate circumstances of the street where the center is located and the resources of the extended community. Thus in the inner city of any metropolitan region and in many mining and manufacturing communities some streets are further from the beaten track of traffic, construction, factory fumes, and noise, than others. A tree-lined street and stretches of lawn furnish aesthetic features in addition to health advantages of oxygen, shade, and quiet. In our concern for providing the basics of day care, we too seldom attend to the quality of the surroundings that contribute to children's health and aesthetic development.

Features that are absent in the immediate locale of the day care setting may be available in some combination in the vicinity. Streets that have no yards and trees may be located near a park. While the block itself should be tranquil, proximity to factories, warehouses, stores, and garages provide useful sources of experience for children as young as two years, as do train and bus depots, or air, sea, and lake ports.

The residential, social class, and ethnic homogeneity of many neighborhoods, in the suburbs and inner city alike, require compensatory experiences in exposure to a diversity of age and social groupings if we are not to perpetuate ignorance, fear, and bigotry. The material limitations, social chaos, clash of

FIGURE 4–3
Adequate settings and landscaping for nursery schools and day care centers can be found in many neighborhoods.

cultures, and physical harshness of lower-income working-class communities is matched by the narrow, sterile role playing, empty refinement, and TV stereotypes in the perceptual world of the suburbanized middle class. Rich cross-cultural experiences need to be built into all day care programs, exposing children to many types of people and ways of life.

Building Designs: General Consideration

Few day care administrations are likely to be in a position to design their own plant according to ideal principles. Most must use existing facilities, usually selected because of restrictions on cost. It is useful nevertheless to outline principles which can be used for designing new centers and modifying existing structures.

The first consideration is the general setting. It is desirable to select an area large enough to support a generous structure surrounded by spacious grounds. The building needs to be completely detached and sufficiently removed from neighboring buildings to maximize light, flow of air, and sound control. An irregularly shaped structure sprawling over one (ground) level has numerous functional and aesthetic advantages by creating varied play and work spaces. Time and energy are also saved when activities are all on one level and rooms are placed in a design that makes communication between them easy, using, for example, 'U', 'T', or radial plans, possibly with an inner courtyard.

Such a spacious plan may be impossible in inner city areas, but the principles involved can be kept in mind even where the social setting dictates fundamentally different physical arrangements. Often the facilities for the young child must fit into some large complex, yet this need not mean any serious sacrifice of design principles. Almost any building complex or high rise can guarantee at least two sides free and be far enough from adjacent buildings to furnish plenty of light, cross ventilation, and viewing space for its young children's unit. Vertical construction provides no special obstacle to placing the set of facilities needed for an infant or preschool unit all on one floor, leaving staff offices, dining, and supporting activities on other floors. Nor is it any real problem to provide ground, lawn, and outdoor water play areas on penthouse roofs or other similar raised areas in high rise apartments, office buildings, or community center complexes.

Among the few constraints on design are the size of trees and the ready availability of wooded and wild areas. Experience with these and other special environments, like factories, zoos, and stores, will usually have to be incorporated into the children's program through regular excursions.

Perhaps the most serious problem in attaching infant and early child care centers to larger establishments is to insure that the sensitive needs of young children do not become submerged in the depersonalization that often develops in large elementary schools. There are, however, many advantages to be derived from combining educational units across age spans from infancy on (see Chapter 3). The chief benefit is the reduced cost that comes from pooling building overhead and supporting services. Again, trouble can arise from the problem of coordinating infant schedules, demanding greater flexibility and irregularity, with the tighter schedules of older children for use of playrooms, observation and testing rooms, gyms, dining facilities, playgrounds, etc. Scheduling problems multiply with the number of individuals and age groups.

Educationally, there are many advantages in planning and coordinating programs for children across a broad age span of development. It is possible to design programs that prepare the young child for the kind of learning situations encountered in older age groups, and conversely, plan approaches for later periods with concrete knowledge of the kind of earlier experiences each child has encountered. Despite these advantages, at present there is little individualized program coordination between age groups, often within a single center, and almost none between early and later childhood periods to permit educational planning that takes account of the cumulative nature of development.

Functional Designs and Human Environments

Advances in architectural concepts and engineering offer limitless possibilities for the design of children's environments. Unfortunately, cost considerations, and the worship of efficiency and fashion, have frequently interfered with the creation of satisfactory designs for the developmental needs of children. Sheer cost often necessitates the decision to make do with whatever building can be found and remodeled to meet minimum health, fire, and other safety standards. But cost alone has not been as determining as the limits of imagination. Administrators, child care staff, and contractors are not familiar with design principles, and few centers can afford architects. Those that can are often frustrated by designers who mount great plans without consulting the users, despite the designer's lack of knowledge of the needs of child care systems. An emphasis on fashion and functionalism frequently overshadows understanding of the personal world of the child. Nevertheless, it is not difficult to reconcile cost and need, and still make use of many rich design concepts.

One such method is modular construction, which provides flexible and varied design at low cost. Prefabricated activity rooms, offices, baths, etc., can be assembled and decorated on site, in different combinations in great diversity. The cost of modular construction decreases according to the number of units manufactured once the basic design is set. To be most economical, it requires either that a large organization plans day care units for many communities, or that a community plans a variety of residential, school, and working units. An educational park, serving the educational and recreational needs of many children of all ages in a large community may also be large enough to justify the initial overhead expense of modular construction.

Even without the cost savings and social communication facilitated by large scale, community-based designs, an approach that integrates good design with children's needs is still possible. The principles of good design are variety, flexibility, and an attempt to consider both the aesthetic characteristics of design and their relation to the purposes of the users. Good design is therefore above all functional, but not in the narrow, instrumental sense of serving a single purpose for the least cost. In the name of efficiency, a multitude of centers all over the world have been constructed on the model of one or two oversized playrooms of steel, concrete, and glass. Easy to clean and maintain, flexible to furnish and arrange, the result is often a cold, barren, and noisy activity environment which tends to destroy culture and individuality.

There are many dimensions of the child's world to be considered when relating the structural principles of design to the child's modes of functioning. The first concerns the problem of constructing a building that makes survival possible for the center as a whole. Durability of structure, low cost of initial investment, and ease of maintenance are important priorities in this category. Closely related is convenience, how well the layout and facilities of playrooms, supporting rooms, and playgrounds support the caregiving staff in their day to day work. A third concern is features that often directly affect the physical and psychological welfare of the children. Here we include such matters as the effect of different materials, lighting, and room shapes on the psychological atmosphere and quality of play. None of these categories should enjoy significantly greater priority in designing a center than any other; they are all vital to its successful operation. But somehow cost and durability are usually granted first priority, for reasons we have outlined, despite the fact that the second and third categories involve matters that are at least as closely related to the purposes for which a center is established.

Administrators and builders who make most of the decisions on investment and operational costs have such well-established design and construction patterns that little further comment is needed. Here and there schools and centers have sprouted up, however, which have combined a variety of common materials to create imaginative designs. Color, texture, and form are used to create an environment that is rich and friendly for children, convenient for staff, and reasonable in basic and maintenance costs.

Designs to Serve Communication and Privacy

Indoor Arrangements

A central concern of child care personnel is the control and flow of social traffic and communication. Both children and adults can function more effectively if the physical structure lends itself equally to separation and communication between activities. Periods of privacy and insulation from distracting stimuli are essential, but communication between and rearrangement of separated groups should be rapid when needed.

There are several ways of realizing these twin goals, some of which may be employed in combination to also satisfy such additional educational requirements as adequate natural light and ventilation, noise and visual control, and adequate space. Perhaps the most flexible and least costly solution is the use of movable partitions within a single oversized playroom designed to accommodate a large group of children who regularly share activities in common. There are also advantages to a suite of different sized rooms in a close-knit complex, arranged in circular, rectangular, or irregular patterns to facilitate both communication and separation as shown in Figure 4–4.

Each of these designs provides a number of rooms of different size to allow for complete visual and auditory separation of various activities. In each case a central corridor permits access to each room without intruding into the activities of another room en route; this corridor could also be used for a gross motor play area, which is little disturbed by traffic.

Each design has certain advantages and disadvantages. The circular and rectangular designs are similar in their degree of separation and ease of communication, but circular structures may be a little more costly, and more awkward for arranging furniture and utilizing space. The possible slight gain in ease of communication is also offset by the fact that natural light comes entirely from one side—though fortunately the wide arc side—in every room. The four corner rooms of the rectangular structure have light coming from two sides.

The chief advantages of the irregularly designed structure are the amount

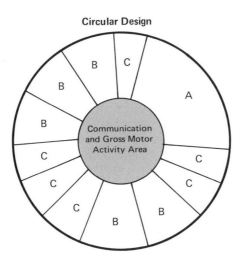

Room Functions

A — *Large* (extended playrooms: gross motor play, parent meetings, sleep, and other supporting activities as designed and needed).

B — *Medium* (music, dance, sociodramatic play, adult lounge, eating, kitchen, and other supporting functions as designed and needed).

C — *Small* (individual and small group activities; testing and observation; and office, library, toilet and change rooms, kitchen, storage, and other supporting functions as designed and needed).

Note:

Various walls may be movable to increase flexibility in room size

FIGURE 4-4
Designs to facilitate group separation and communication.

of light afforded nearly every room and the amount of separation between activity rooms. The chief disadvantage is the increased cost of heating, important to consider as a continuing cost in a period of rising energy costs. The additional heating cost may be partially offset from the diminished need for artificial lighting.

The protruding structures permit all except one small room to be free from having a common wall with more than one adjacent room, and the common corridor. In both the circular and rectangular designs, each room shares walls with two other activity rooms and the central corridor. The irregular arrangement should cut noise interference problems to a minimum, since noise tends to travel through all except the most expensive forms of wall construction—making permanent walls more efficient than movable partitions. The additional travel time between some of the playrooms is probably inconsequential, given the fact that there is no passage through other activity rooms—except the gross motor play area. In this latter design, incidentally, the gross motor area benefits from a small amount of natural light, although in any case skylights may also be installed to provide a more extensive source of natural light for this internal area in all designs.

All three of the foregoing designs are readily adaptable to the accommodation of additional children's groups, simply by repeating the same pattern on two or more floors. Stairs, or even escalators and elevators for multistory buildings, can all be placed in the central communication area. For the most part, moreover, groups can be arranged to minimize the need for communication between floor levels. Even where family-type (vertical age) social groupings are preferred, the basic floor plan can be made large enough to encompass as many as fifty to one hundred children, which would thus embrace two or three age levels even in a large day care center.

This reintroduces the question of building vertically rather than spreading out horizontally. Heating costs are less with a plant distributed over several stories, and maximum separation between suites is obtained. But construction costs also tend to rise, because of the additional reinforcement and fireproofing required by government safety regulations for buildings of two or more stories.

Single floor designs present problems of space availability, particularly in urban-suburban areas where population density is often high. But, as we have pointed out, previously, it is difficult to operate institutions for group care and schooling of young children beyond a certain size without depersonalizing relations, despite the cost and resource advantages. Intimacy with peers and adults is particularly important for the emotional well-being of children during early development. Between 30 and 50 children can be educated and cared for reasonably economically and well on a human scale. As enrollment starts to climb above 50, the personal dimension and informality of a small community, where nearly everyone knows everyone else, is more and more difficult to develop and maintain. The caring in smaller settings may sometimes take negative forms, but problems are more visible and both children and teachers are less likely to become lost or alienated.

Indoor-Outdoor Arrangements and Communication

One of the biggest problems of multistory structures is providing close communication between indoor and outdoor areas of activity. It is important for children to spend a substantial amount of time outdoors, not only for the exercise, body movement, and communication learning involved, but also because of the need for frequent movement between indoor and outdoor activity with changes in weather. It is easier to coordinate supervision and communication between indoor and outdoor play with single floor designs. Staff resources can be more effectively utilized and programs made more flexible, in the same way a common corridor will improve communication between activities indoors. In both cases teachers do not have to herd children great distances, up and down stairs, or move children as frequently, since children can easily move back and forth singly or in small clusters as they desire or as the program requires. In many cases, teachers can often supervise adjacent indoor-outdoor play areas, at least for short periods, further easing demands on staff time and conflicts over transitions between activities.

An illustration of a design maximizing communications between indoor and outdoor areas of activity is shown in Figures 4–5 A, B and C, each of which is a variation on Figure 4–4. Once again, the circular and rectangular shapes are more compact and probably less costly. All three designs include additional open structures without sides to multiply the number of occasions when children can play outdoors. The rectangular area contains a single, protected play space designed to be shared by two playroom groups. Open structures are especially suitable for mild climates, but most climates permit many days each year of outdoor play in sheltered areas. These shelters have the effect of multiplying indoor play areas considerably at low cost, because they permit more concentrated forms of cognitive and perceptual motor play that depend on relatively small and fragile materials (e.g., puzzles and miniature figures) to occur outdoors.

Large expanses of glass may be installed in all outdoor walls to provide a generous amount of light and bring the outdoor and indoor environments closer together. Double- or even triple-glazed glass and special blinds to be closed during off hours will greatly reduce heating costs, while the added natural light cuts the costs of artificial lighting. Outside doors on rooms next to outdoor areas will further the closeness between playroom and playground.

Control of Communication and Noise Interference

Noise from playground activity may intrude on children's concentration in many of the rooms in Figure 4–5A (circular design) and could interrupt adult seminar, office, and testing activities. The layouts in Figures 4–5B and 4–5C give better control of this problem, because most of the specialized activity rooms (B and C sizes) are located in parts of the building removed from the main playground areas. Activity in the landscaped garden areas of Figure 4–5C is likely to be quieter. In all three designs, children in the major playrooms can be restricted from the playground during certain periods of indoor free play, since the large rooms are designed to accommodate all children in a play group. At other times, when free flow between in and outdoors is desired, playrooms are even large enough to enable much of the continuing indoor activity to take place at some distance from the louder outdoor activity. This is especially true of the design in Figure 4–5C, where only the narrower end of each playroom is located next to the playground and outdoor protected areas.

The playing children will be spread over a greater surface area, reducing the overall volume of noise.

There are other methods of controlling noise and visual distraction. A hedge barrier or row of small trees around the vulnerable rooms in the circular design can lessen both noise and visual interference. Windows may be inserted at levels above the eye height of children, or blinds and curtains can be in-

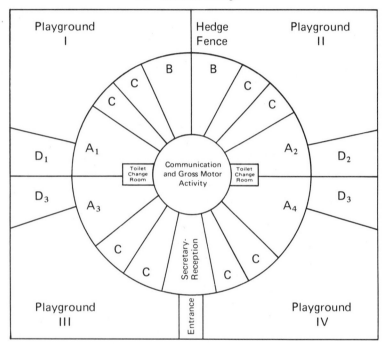

Legend:

A_1, A_2, A_3, A_4 :   Main playrooms for each of 4 groups.

D_1, D_2, D_3, D_4 :   Protected outdoor area for gross motor play in rainy or hot weather; all types of play as desired.

B — *Medium* (music, dance, sociodramatic play, adult lounge, eating, kitchen, and other supporting functions as designed and needed).

C — *Small* (individual and small group activities; testing and observation; office, library, toilet and change rooms, kitchen, storage, and other supporting functions as designed and needed).

Note:

Various walls may be movable to increase flexibility in room size.

FIGURE 4–5
*Designs to
facilitate group
separation and
communication.*

B.   Rectangular Design

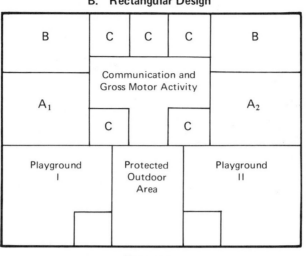

Entrance

Note: Various walls may be movable to increase flexibility in room size.

Legend:

A_1, A_2:   Main playrooms.

B — *Medium* (music, dance sociodramatic play, adult lounge, eating kitchen and other supporting functions as designed and needed).

C — *Small* (individual and small group activities; testing and observation; office, library, toilets and change rooms, kitchen, storage, and other supporting functions as designed and needed).

C.   Irregular Design

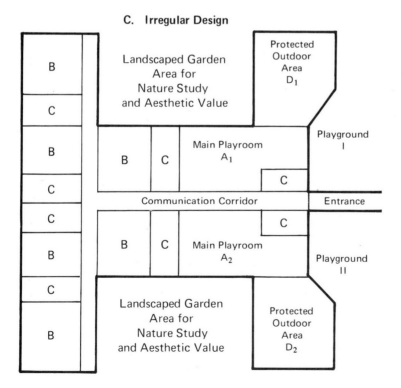

Legend:

B — *Medium* (music, dance, sociodramatic play, adult lounge, eating, kitchen, and other supporting functions as designed and needed).

C — *Small* (individual and small group activities, testing and observation, office, library, toilets and change rooms, kitchens, storage and other supporting functions as designed and needed).

Note:

Various walls may be movable to increase flexibility in room size.

stalled to cut distraction at times when more concentration is needed. The building may also be constructed with the main floor a few feet above ground level, reducing noise slightly and eliminating visual distraction, but still permitting easy communication through shallow ramps or stairs.

Social Density: Safe Play Requirements

Recommended standards for the amount of play space needed for young children in group care range from a minimum of 30 square feet to a preferred (if ideal) level of 50-plus square feet of functional play space, perhaps less for children under two. Functional play space means all areas in a child's "home base" playroom, including space occupied by the children's furniture, mobile toys and book shelves, but excluding built-in storage cabinets, teacher's desks and other furniture, and large items like pianos, aquaria, and indoor sand tables, which utilize a great deal of space. The lower figure of 30 square feet is in fact very minimal since the intensity of psychological activity and conflict increases as the physical space available decreases. The more children crowded into the same area, the closer together they must play, which diminishes the floor space they can use for extending buildings and roads, running wheel toys, spreading out paper for painting and drawing, and similar space-demanding activities. Inevitably, the amount of conflict grows, as children move frequently, bump into one another, hamper one another's play, and damage one another's products and creations. The space problem is magnified for younger children because the increased teacher-child ratio demanded for the age group means more adults to consume physical and social space. Failure to maintain adequate child-space and child-teacher ratios results in neglect of care and stimulation, intensified conflict, and increasing rigidity of social organization and program structure, with less free play, movement, exploration, and program flexibility.

Ratios defined for playrooms apply equally to any other space in the center where children are cared for or participate in activities; the critical aspect is the number of children (and adults) who regularly or frequently occupy a given enclosure in any time period. Even in sleeping rooms, children will disturb one another more and be more difficult to quiet as the social space per child decreases.

Given these basic considerations, it is not always easy to decide on the total floor area required for a child care center. There is a simple number versus size formula, based on multiplying the number of children enrolled by the optimum (50 square feet) or the minimum (30 square feet) play space per child available. But, while such a formula tells something about the space required for constructive social relations to occur in a playroom, it leaves many questions to be answered. For example, some of the furniture and equipment, such as desks, piano, or sink, which take up play space may also add a few interesting "bridges" to crawl or run toys under, or places to hide behind.

Moreover, the number of children scheduled to use a set of rooms during any one period does not take into account the efficiency of space use throughout the day. There is usually much latitude in program planning with regard to alternative use of facilities, that is, to use the same rooms for several purposes. To illustrate, a low-cost center may be forced to operate in two modest playrooms, each about 15 by 25 feet, making a total area of 750 square feet, plus one office 10 by 15 feet or 150 feet in area. A similar small, but better supported, center may enjoy the use of three offices, each approximately 150 square feet in area, in addition to two basic playrooms equivalent in area to those of the first center. The difference in functional space available for the two centers can be enormous.

Take the case of a center with children over two who seldom require more than one nap per day. For the first center, all supporting work must be compressed into the single office, unless some of the items, such as a limited adult library, reserve toys, equipment, and art materials are moved into one or both of the playrooms; and the amount of space available for play will be correspondingly reduced. Probably at least 75 square feet of each of the two playrooms will be needed for storage of materials and equipment that will not fit into the single office. The balance of 600 square feet will accommodate from 12 to 17 children, depending on the play space standards adopted.

In the second center, not only can supporting activities and equipment be distributed over three offices, but even such items as certain children's book shelves or play tables and chairs can be placed in one or more of the offices, to be brought out when needed or used in the offices for special activities. This means that one can calculate quotas on almost the full playroom space, say 730 square feet (an upright piano and sand table together occupy about 20 square feet), making space available for 15 to 21 children. This arrangement would increase the enrollment quota by 2 to 4 children without undue crowding or deprivation of staff use, even if preferred standards are followed. Equally important, there is more space for equipment and for staff communication, discussion, planning, and relaxation. The availability of additional small rooms also permits longer periods of concentration in varied learning activities.

Neither of these examples is ideal: no provision is made for separate staff lounges, and playrooms must serve many functions despite the fact that a few of the play and learning activities can be held in the small rooms in the larger center. Well-equipped centers with generous space are necessarily considerably larger and furnished with an even greater variety of rooms and equipment, such as special rooms for dining and sleeping, small rooms for learning projects or water play (equipped with child-size sinks and water resistant floors), child-size kitchens, carpentry rooms with work benches, rooms with props for social role play, and ecology rooms for nature observation. Infant centers include special feeding, diaper changing, and sick rooms to permit separate and specialized handling of two or three babies at a time, and larger sleeping rooms to fit the irregular napping patterns of infants. Laboratory schools and child research centers are usually equipped with special purpose rooms for observation, testing, calculation, research staff offices, and seminars. Clearly, total size requirements are—within limits—highly elastic according to purpose and financing.

Movable Partitions and Multiple Room Use

The multiple use of room space is greatly facilitated by modern architectural and engineering techniques, particularly by movable partitions that permit rooms to be readily divided into segments. In more expensive systems several ceiling tracks placed at varying angles to one another permit a large room to be subdivided into rooms varying in size, number, and arrangement.

The advantages of such a system are numerous. A single large room can be varied in size according to the number of children enrolled or in attendance at the center. The method permits flexibility through simultaneous scheduling of activities according to the number of children and amount of space required. There are, however, problems of sound control and distribution of natural light with movable partitions. Most of these can be minor in well designed systems, supported by carpeting and drapes to muffle sound and large windows or skylights to extend light.

Supporting Facilities

There are other physical features important to staff and children that building designs can incorporate without difficulty if they are properly planned for. No day care center can run well without some space for supporting facilities, such as storage, kitchen, staff eating, rest and washroom facilities, office facilities, library, and discussion areas. Adequate storage space for reserve supplies and equipment, separate storage for each playroom group, and a spacious and convenient storage area for janitorial and kitchen supplies are all very useful.

Kitchen and Serving Facilities.   The adequacy of facilities for preparing and serving food to both children and staff contributes much to morale and the smooth operation of a center. The traditional nursery school for middle-class children is often confined to a half day program in which lunch may or may not be served. In such settings a modest pantry equipped with a counter, a few cabinets, and a refrigerator are sufficient for the storage and preparation of morning or afternoon snacks of juice or milk, fresh or dried fruit, cheese, crackers, etc. A hot plate for preparing coffee for adults or to involve children in limited cooking may round out the arrangement.

Day care centers and a few larger scale nursery schools operate on a fundamentally different basis. They are particularly tailored to meet the needs of the working parent who must leave the child from early morning until late afternoon, as long as ten to eleven hours. Under these conditions, complete kitchen and serving facilities for both children and adults is necessary. Large stoves, refrigerators, work counters, storage areas, and dishwashers are appropriate, particularly in large centers (over 50 children and 10 caregivers). A full time cook-housekeeper and an assistant or two are needed to plan and prepare the schedule of special breakfasts, snacks, and meals required.

Another arrangement sometimes recommended is the separation of the children's food preparation area from that of the adults. This is often an expensive and unnecessary duplication of facilities, since there is no reason why all cannot enjoy the same meals. There are some advantages to a separate diet kitchen for feeding children under two, as they need softer, blander diets, and the preparation of formulas may interfere with group meal preparation. This, and the necessarily higher standard of hygiene required during infancy, makes a diet kitchen a reasonable consideration if the cost can be met. However, a separate, well-defined area in a large kitchen, with a small extra stove, work space, storage shelves, sink, and one corner of a large refrigerator may be satisfactory; mutual access to the separate storage, food, and cooking resources will encourage economy and a cooperative atmosphere.

If the expense can be managed, a small room next to the main kitchen may be outfitted with limited cooking facilities for children. When properly introduced, cooking is an interesting activity for both sexes because of its pleasurable outcomes and its social learning value. A stove, sink, and a counter area, all scaled down to the height of preschoolers, together with storage areas and possibly a small refrigerator, will complete the setting. Only centers of high enrollment can probably afford such facilities.

The kitchen and eating areas are placed close together to reduce the amount of labor and time required to serve, and a serving window with a counter that extends on the same level into both the kitchen and eating areas is a great convenience.

Sleeping Areas.   Throughout the preschool period, most children need to nap or rest in the early afternoon. During the first year of age or so it is wise to follow an entirely flexible pattern of nap and play according to individual need. Many babies learn to adapt to the limited facilities of local cooperatives by falling off for catnaps on their own in the midst of other children at play, which is easily managed if caregivers take a child to a quiet, partitioned-off corner of the room when they note signs of fatigue, and sit for a moment until the child falls asleep. This combines a degree of privacy with convenience for staff watchfulness in case of need, at low cost. Some older children, who have difficulty learning to nap in another room, will drop off to sleep near the scene of activities. There is often insufficient insulation from noise, however, for many children to settle down. The problem of noise control, coupled with the problem of heightened responsiveness to distant visual stimulation, usually becomes greater as the child gets older.

On the whole, there are numerous advantages to separate sleep rooms at every age. If there is more than one playroom, one of them can double as a sleeping room since, except for babies, sleeping areas are basically only needed for a period in the early afternoon. Cots are easily dismantled and cribs can be crowded into one section of the room, leaving space available for play. The value of having at least two playrooms for each play group should not be underestimated, however, because it may be better for children who have outgrown or are poorly adapted to napping to play or read quietly in another room. There is no value in forcing children to repeatedly lie awake in frustration.

Placing the sleeping rooms close to the suite of rooms where the children play will minimize transition problems and help to budget caregiver resources. If each sleeping room shares a wall with one of the playrooms and a window (with a curtain the teacher can pull aside) gives visual access to the children sleeping, one teacher can assist in attending to both sets of children. A curtained alcove or door communicating between the two rooms at one end gives superior noise control. Movable walls are certainly in order here, particularly if furnished with a curtain-covered doorway and window to allow the teacher to check on sleeping children without opening the partition.

Sleeping areas need to be well ventilated and cool but without direct drafts, and darkened to induce sleep. It is often preferable, particularly in cold weather, to air a sleeping area just before rather than during nap periods. Cribs

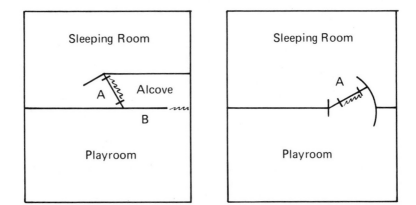

FIGURE 4-6
*Sleeping room
arrangements.*

A — Door with curtain covered window
B — Open doorway with curtain

and cots range in size from about 18 to 24 inches, suitable for the tiniest babies, to 20 to 24 inches for larger and older children, and length can vary from 30 inches to 60 inches. Cribs should be of sturdy construction, with sides that can be raised high enough to prevent active infants from climbing and falling during an unwatched moment. High springs and mattresses will ease the strain on the caregivers' backs from constant lifting of heavy infants.

It is useful to leave enough space between cribs and cots for privacy, and for caregivers to tend children freely and comfortably. Two sample arrangements are illustrated in Figure 4–7.

In the diagram on the right, two age groups of infants, each with different sized cribs, are placed to provide maximum separation, consistent with good use of room space. In the left hand diagram, a few more infants of the same two age groups and crib sizes are fitted into the same amount of space, still allowing room for movement between every pair of cribs. While the second plan is satisfactory, the increased crowding brings greater difficulties in settling children. The center partition in both plans provides some additional visual but not auditory separation between the main body of both groups. It is low enough to permit caregivers to view activity on the other side, however.

The transition from crib to cot comes when the child can climb in and out of his cot with ease and safety. The relative independence of older children minimizes the need for adult passageway between cots. Children with less settled sleeping habits can be separated or placed in a separate section of the room. Thus the arrangement of cots is less of a problem.

Staff Facilities

A separate staff lounge and eating area with kitchen and washroom facilities will do much for morale and is psychologically important to enable caregivers to withdraw from the wearing demands of children from time to time. However much teachers may enjoy children, the endless care and stimulation children require builds up a strain that needs to be completely removed at definite peri-

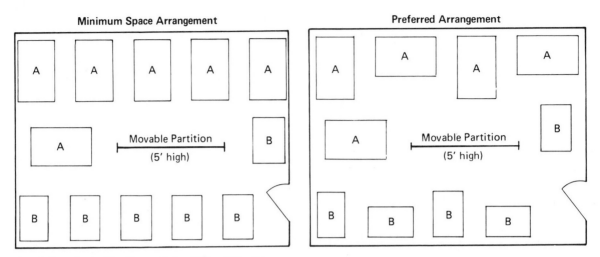

A   Older infants (7 - 18 months) — 30″ x 48″ cribs
B   Younger (preclimbing) infants (1 - 7 months) 24″ x 36″ cribs
    Scale: 1/6″ = 1′

FIGURE 4–7
Sample sleeping room arrangements.

ods. Otherwise day care workers (and parents) fall into a self-protective style of pacifying and mediating without fostering curiosity, problem solving, and complex social relations. Every center needs at least one staff room, large enough to avoid crowding (at least 35 square feet per person). Space must be sufficient to meet the periods of highest demand, such as lunch periods and nap times, when nearly all of the staff gather and occasional visitors may be present. If parents regularly participate, as in a cooperative, space should be expanded accordingly. Ideally, in centers staffed with more than a half dozen caregivers and office personnel there are two separate rooms, one for general conversation and dining and a smaller room for retreat, private discussion, and professional reading.

In small centers that cannot set aside special rooms for staff, a number of the ordinary social needs of caregivers can be met by alternating the uses of auxiliary rooms or even of playrooms. Here again, the availability of movable partitions is helpful. But such arrangements seldom substitute satisfactorily for the continuing availability of a separate room where privacy is assured, since rooms used for projects, conferences, and other purposes are often found to be occupied at the moment of staff need.

Office Space

Office facilities in a day care center are likely to vary from almost none (in a low-budget cooperative) to a whole suite of offices (in a laboratory nursery school). Even in well-equipped centers, however, it is rare for caregivers to have their own desks; a single desk in some corner of a playroom, if the room is large, is a typical arrangement.

However, a desk is not the only means of providing personal work and storage space, and a private office is not only expensive, but tends to isolate staff from one another; each becomes more concerned with his or her own contributions and development at the expense of coordinating activities, program, and interpersonal relations.

What is needed is an arrangement encouraging communication and cooperation, mutual stimulation, and the pooling of ideas, and still permitting separation of activities and individual concentration when needed. A work room of moderate size (12′ × 15′) equipped with a center work table, storage cabinets and a desk or two can accommodate three to six adults in just such an arrangement. One or two portable study carrels may enhance work privacy.

Similar arrangements are desirable for secretarial and administrative personnel, although they may find separate offices advantageous because of the amount of office work, telephoning, and private conversations. On the other hand, multipurpose office-reception-conference rooms, which are even combined with office use for teaching staff, are convenient and inexpensive arrangements for all except very large centers, which must regularly support numerous staff for teacher training, research, and development activities.

Office machines are useful but expensive, and require maintenance. Electric typewriters, duplicating machines, photo copiers, and calculators will not only expedite office work, but are useful for developing and circulating program materials, and maintaining more systematic and comprehensive records.

Equipment may lead to formality, however. Although simple written guides are often invaluable, concepts are usually not absorbed clearly unless they are worked out in discussion; a program must be at hand in the mind of the teacher, however impressive it may appear on paper. Since written communication is more impersonal, too much of it may lead to the development of greater hierarchical control by supervisors unless regularly accompanied by intensive group discussion. Inexpensive portable typewriters, miniature electronic calculators, and ditto machines that can turn out handwritten outlines, diagrams, and pictures, can efficiently maintain informality while minimizing the work load.

Library

An adult library of some kind is a must for every child care center. Selected textbook sources on child development, early education, and child care, and a body of curriculum materials, should be easily accessible. A basic stock consists of at least 30 to 50 books discussing a range of age levels, including periods of development before and after those of the children actually attending the center to help teachers maintain a long-range developmental perspective. A good library also covers many topics, such as intellectual, social, emotional, and physical development, health, norms of development, and practical descriptive guides and case studies oriented to children's problems. Subscriptions to journals on child development, day care, and early education are especially useful, as many of them cover a range of current topics and give practical suggestions on caregiving and early education. The complexity of the materials is determined by the education of the staff, but a few technical and clinical references for supervisory personnel and consultants are always useful. Advice from a local community college or similar resource will provide the guidelines for a good basic selection.

However fine the library, it will be of little value unless it is easily accessible and regularly used. The materials need to be placed in a convenient and pleasant room, and each staff member needs a definite period of at least 15–30 minutes each day set aside for library use. Where no extra room is available, a small room already in use can be reserved for exclusive use during certain hours. Given the premium on their time in most centers, unless staff have some time when they can feel free to read, only the most dedicated and educated will take the trouble to do so. Occasional staff discussions, visiting speakers, and regular participation by parents will also stimulate staff to read more regularly. Parents often have special interests, insights, and competencies not available among the staff.

Observation, Testing, and Conference Rooms

Even the smallest center benefits from places where adults can meet for quiet discussion and children can be separated for periods of special observation, testing, or learning activity, individually or in small groups.

The number and variety of special purpose rooms will, of course, depend on the size and quality of the center, but in all except the largest centers, an efficient use of space demands that various small and medium, special-purpose rooms serve many needs on a rotating basis. Small centers will probably encounter more scheduling problems and noise conflicts, but, however limited, some provision for a range of such individual activities is essential. The quality of a program is heavily dependent on the *particularized* communication, assessment, and teaching that are difficult to fulfill without divided space. The biggest problem for small centers is often the lack of division in one or two oversized playrooms, a problem that can be handled by movable partitions, including homemade plywood partitions or even sheets of canvas or blankets suspended on ropes across the corner of a room. Well-designed centers are ordinarily furnished with several specialized rooms, each containing different sorts of equipment, depending on demand and resources available.

Workshop and Repair Rooms

Every center needs some arrangement for the maintenance and repair of toys and materials. Many items are expensive to replace, many breakages require only minor repair, and imperfect toys are a chronic source of irritation to children and teachers alike.

A small work room which could also serve as a children's carpentry and construction area would suit the purpose; additional adult tools and supplies that are too fragile or dangerous for children can be routinely kept in reserve for adult use.

If there is enough skill and enthusiasm to draw on, parents and staff can be encouraged to design and construct simple toys and equipment at low cost.

Occasional evening toy construction and repair sessions will accomplish this purpose, especially when combined with social activities. Walking boards, climbing apparatus, arches, bridges, gates, various wooden wagons, trucks to ride, play houses, doll houses, and playground equipment such as "ocean liners" and "rocket ships" are all valuable additions to school equipment. Besides providing equipment for the school, activity of this kind provides a model of creative construction work for children. It is sometimes feasible for moderate and large sized centers to combine janitorial maintenance with an equipment construction and repair role. Older, semi-retired people will often find this an interesting combination, if cleaning duties are not too demanding. Parents in cooperatives, and sometimes even working parents, may like to repair or construct an occasional toy.

Materials and Decoration

We come now to the single most consistently ignored aspect of the design of children's centers, the perceptual features of color, form, and texture that contribute to a positive emotional ambience and the cognitive and aesthetic development of children. They are the surface details of things that help determine whether surroundings are pleasant or unpleasant, stimulating or boring to work and learn in. While social relations, adult guidance, and play materials are the major sources of variety in children's experience, the colors and shapes in their daily environment in day care and at home play an important role. The background of structural and decorative design in the children's playrooms is a

Barren and Cold   Warm and Appealing

FIGURE 4-8
The effect of decoration and materials on room atmosphere.

supporting framework for cognitive stimulation and development of taste. Playroom decoration has a special value for educating parents whose poverty or background has prevented development of interest in design.

There are a number of specific features that make up a perceptually constructive environment. Large portions of the walls and floors of playrooms should be surfaced with soft materials of irregular texture, and ceilings should be covered with acoustical tile or plaster to absorb the sounds and echoes of children's play. Hard, smooth surfaces bounce sound around, multiplying its intensity and frequency to drown conversation, spoil musical activities, and generally wear on the nerves of staff and children alike. The problem is particularly acute in children's centers because children's voices are high-pitched, their emotional expression is freer (they cry and shout), and because many playthings are constructed of hard, smooth materials (hardwood blocks, metal toys) that make sharp, penetrating sounds when knocked together.

Wall to wall carpeting, so advantageous for sound absorption, is best limited to those areas where wheel toys will not be used, since it impedes their movement. Area rugs can be moved, to leave a square area of hard floor surface suitable for block-building and the operation of miniature vehicles. They are easily removed for cleaning and slightly damaged or irregular sized remnants can be obtained at reduced cost.

Pieces of carpeting can also serve as wall hangings; they absorb sound efficiently and make a good surface for attaching children's art and decorations. Burlap or any soft curtain material is appealing because of the variety of rough textures and many interesting colors. Slabs of cork, crude or refined, absorb sound well and provide a rich, natural appeal and an excellent surface for fastening pictures. Crude cork is darker, but refined cork echoes sound more.

Perceptual diversity in visual materials is important for enriching aesthetic and cognitive development; a bland, uniform background is unstimulating both emotionally and perceptually. However, variety alone is not synonymous with interesting design, which can be extremely simple and selective. Interest can be achieved by varying the decoration scheme periodically and by retaining an overall plan of good, simple design for every activity room, while varying details regularly. The cork board display areas can be used to add perceptual variety in two ways: to display children's creative products, and to hang materials like bits of cotton, wool, silk, metal, stones, wood, to expose children to the nature of materials and how they vary in texture, form, and color. Materials that are placed close to children's eye height can be handled (and perhaps taken down for learning occasions) easily, and can be rotated to vary the experience.

Harmonious design and perceptual enrichment are realized through such characteristics as simplicity; symmetry of form and color; balance of overall compositional effects; continuity of line and rhythm; and balanced proportions among shapes and colors. In general, lighter colors make cheerful settings for children's activity but natural and earthy colors (rich browns, rusts, and deep mustards) are warm and expressive. Some areas of activity could be made softer by the use of subdued shades and rounded forms, while others might offer very active stimulation through strident, clashing colors (orange and bright pink) with angular or even jagged lines and shapes. Perceptual contrasts (such as checkerboards, bullseyes and irregular patterns), and mobiles and other types of moving materials are also stimulating, particularly for small infants confined to a given area. They should be changed periodically, and occasionally removed entirely to offer a more placid background.

It is useful to consult guides on design and decoration, leaving many of the decisions to those among staff and parents who are interested. Any day care center is likely to have several adults involved who value or have talents in design to serve as enthusiastic and inexpensive resource persons. On the other hand, teachers naturally want some voice in the decor of the rooms in which they must work every day. Beginning in infancy, children can become more and more involved with questions of decoration and design, mainly through the display of art works they produce. It is important to help both children and teachers to become conscious of the value of different dimensions of design through guidance and focused, but non-competitive, comments. For this reason, some understanding of design is needed in the training of day care workers.

Natural Environments

Direct contact with the earth, plants, and animals develops children's understanding of the natural world. The energy, ecology, and pollution crises of our time show the significance of making such experience integral to development. There are three basic methods of obtaining such experiences. First, through nature excursions; second, through the methods we have discussed for designing indoor environments in close relationship to outdoor environments; and third, by designing miniature natural ecologies according to the climate and space available, both indoors and outdoors. Landscaped gardens of plants and flowers, vegetable gardens, and natural and simulated "live" environments of woods, meadows, deserts, ponds, and seas, provide a wealth of experience in the ways of plants and animals hard to duplicate in any other way (see Chapter 8). About the only essential features necessary for indoor simulation of various water and land environments are one or more air tight, enclosed spaces or rooms, together with temperature, light, air flow, and moisture control apparatus, and at least one viewing window. If aquarium size (about one by one by two feet to two by two by three feet in volume) dimensions are employed, two or three such spaces can be readily serviced by one set of control apparatus at a reasonable cost. These specialized environments should be positioned so that the child can easily view them, and manipulate material as appropriate.

The effort and expense of recreating real-life ecologies in some form are well worth the cost. The awareness of life processes that these simulated environments develop rivals the value of experience in the original settings. Convenience, accessibility and control of time, place, and vantage point for observation make up for much of what is lost in scope and variety in the real environments.

Strategies of Child Care

*Encouraging
responsibility*

A Clinical-Developmental Approach to Care

Ideally, methods of care take account of two basic aspects of children's development. First, good caregiving is adaptive to the child as a unified whole. The care given to a little girl affects not only her skill for the task at hand, but her entire mind and personality. Learning to complete a puzzle, for example, can affect development of spatial concepts, motor skills and how success or failure

109

FIGURE 5-1
The whole child and his history: The clinical developmental approach to development. Each child has a history, which has developed an overall style and prevalent reactions. Each child needs to be handled differently to best further development. Early history.

Child A   Child B

Child A   Child B

FIGURE 5-1
continued.
Overall style.

affects her view of herself. Second, good caregiving considers the long-term history of the child's personality and mental development. Success in teaching the child at any moment depends on her age and how her personality has been shaped by past experience. Thus, past exposure to cooperative versus competitive relations would affect how the child is taught to share.

These two cardinal points of human development mean that child care needs to be both clinically oriented (concerned with the dynamics of the whole child in her current life situation) and developmentally oriented (concerned with the dynamics of relations between past, present, and future likelihood of development). It is convenient to discuss care processes that concern personality and social development separately from those that concern other areas of knowledge. Socioemotional development is perhaps more intimately embedded in the processes of everyday living than what we ordinarily think of as

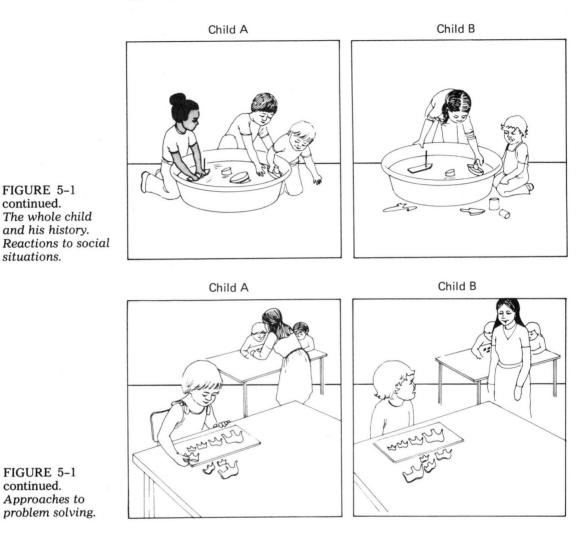

FIGURE 5-1 continued. *The whole child and his history. Reactions to social situations.*

FIGURE 5-1 continued. *Approaches to problem solving.*

"learning," or acquiring, knowledge and skills. Methods and strategies for guiding environmental learning about shapes, size, number, language, etc., which lend themselves more to planned learning programs, will be discussed later in the book. In the present chapter we shall consider the developmental-clinical approach to care in terms of social rules and emotional development.

Setting Limits: Techniques of Control

The curious and active nature of young children determines the caregiving techniques for regulating their behavior. The fewer the rules to enforce, the less the conflict and confrontation in child care. Freedom for the child to explore is essential for encouraging curiosity and creativity. Development of these pro-

cesses will be hampered in proportion to the number of tempting but dangerous or valuable objects within reach, whose exploration must be inhibited by a
constant harassment of "No's." The necessary rules chiefly concern safety
(light sockets, household poisons, falling, sharp instruments, appliances, cars,
etc.); the comfort of others (biting, hitting, and noise in crowded living conditions); and damage to valued possessions (tearing books, damaging furniture,
breaking vases, etc.).

The chief method of limiting the number of rules is through *child proofing.*
Young children are easier to care for in an environment free of dangerous and
fragile objects and under conditions where their play will not disturb others. A
good stock of toys and learning materials, and other children to play with,
make it easy to stimulate and channel children's energies into constructive
activities with a minimum of adult guidance. Day care centers (and nursery
schools) are normally easily arranged to meet these requirements; homes
can—within certain serious limits—be similarly arranged.

Problems of child proofing are greatest in the home, which parents should
be encouraged to check for potentially valuable or harmful objects to place
beyond the child's reach. Crowded and rundown tenements among the poor,
high rise apartments of the middle classes, are confining, ill-equipped, and vulnerable to noisy play. The problem of managing child care and household duties in an environment not designed or equipped for constructive play makes at
least part time day care attractive, even to many nonworking mothers. As the
child moves into the preschool era the range of activities in the home and
neighborhood expands. Yet, without increasing the risk to the child, access to
potential "conflict areas", such as city traffic or play in a suburban yard close
to a power lawnmower, can proceed no faster than the child's awareness,
skills, and sense of responsibility permit. Details of how to organize the environment and supervise children in play are described in later chapters.

A second major technique of control is selecting and *sticking to a few rules
that should and can be enforced.* There are inevitably objects the child must
learn to handle in certain ways. For example, the child must learn to look at
books without tearing or marking pages, to treat other children with care and
consideration, and not to throw things that become missiles. Restricting infants
to cloth or cardboard books will limit their picture-story experiences; aggression hurts others; and missiles may injure or break. If a good stock of objects
for free exploration is essential to development, so is the opportunity to learn
rules about handling certain things with care. Learning such rules teaches the
child to value our cultural tools according to their use and their aesthetic and
moral value. Many rules like limits to exploring a room can be regulated with
considerable flexibility, as long as obvious hazards (knives) and cherished
things (vases) are removed, but there are always limits of some kind.

Lags in the child's understanding of the importance of a rule create conflict. It takes time to grasp the difference in toughness between paper and
cardboard pages, or the different dangers of dropping glass and plastic glasses,
and that the different materials require that different amounts of care be taken.
Consistency helps. Until the child understands such differences, enforcing rules
for handling *all* books and *all* glass-like containers carefully from the beginning will hasten the child's understanding and acceptance and reduce conflict.
Conflicts arise mainly from rules that are unclear or inconsistently enforced.

Limiting the number of such rules, therefore, minimizes interference with exploration, while avoiding confusion or burdening children and caregivers with too many special rules to insure a reasonable chance of success.

A third technique for regulating children's behavior is by *diverting* wayward exploration into other channels. It is often easier to avoid confrontations with rules difficult to enforce consistently by diverting the child to areas or materials free from conflict. While it may be valuable for a child to learn that there are rules beyond her understanding that must be accepted, it is well to limit their number. There are plenty of essential rules to teach the lesson well, without inhibiting the child's developing curiosity by frequently resorting to a string of arbitrary "No's."

When an exploring child is on the verge of causing damage or danger, it is useful to present another task likely to capture his immediate interest. In place of simply saying "No," when a child begins to throw blocks or mark across another child's drawing, start building with the child or offer another crayon and a new piece of drawing paper. Often he will readily turn away from the previous activity to the alternative offered. Quite often some little comment is in order, such as "You might hurt someone," or "That hurts Billie's drawing," but the chief emphasis is on arousing interest in another activity.

What one offers is naturally dependent upon age and interest. The simplest diversion is usually an age-appropriate toy of known appeal, such as an interesting puzzle, a wind-up toy, or a favorite stuffed animal. Real items from the adult world, such as pots and pans, a bunch of keys, or a rugged alarm clock (supervised), offer a high probability of success. When conflicts arise it is sometimes possible to encourage cooperative relations in play by suggesting that the children involved work together, for example, suggesting, "How about you and Billie drawing together, one on each side of this large piece of paper?" being sure to hand them materials and start them off.

When a child is slow to shift attention because he is too angry or excited, the discouraged behavior is too inviting, or such behaviors have been too inconsistently discouraged in the past, a combination of techniques is often necessary. Pausing to play with the child for a minute or two adds the incentive of adult attention. Involving the child in some ongoing adult activity, such as folding a diaper, sweeping the floor, or getting out blankets for naptime may appeal to an interest in the world of adults. When the behavior persists, diversion is best combined with physical removal to another activity in a different place. Allowing the behavior to persist only heightens the conflict for the child, while it can also threaten the safety, or is not fair to the interests of other children.

Caregivers should not hesitate to gently but firmly remove children when behavior poses serious difficulties, diversions fail to work, or harassed caregivers are unable to hit upon imaginative devices. This fourth method of regulating behavior is often more appropriate for young children than verbal guidance alone, because language is still a recently acquired tool for them. They live much of the time in the physical world of action. It is usually advisable, however, to accompany the removal with a brief explanation of the reasons for the move. It is important to work toward helping a child understand the reasons for controlling behavior, even when the child's present resources fall short.

Actually, much of the time a combination of methods is likely to be the best approach for resourceful day care workers and mothers. Removal of a child in a friendly way is usually more easily accepted when accompanied by a diversion and a simple comment, thus employing a combination of physical means and social incentives to attract the child toward a new activity.

Times of emotional stress and strong aggression are definite occasions for removing children from the scene of their play. When caregivers remove a child they usually assume, often implicitly, that the child understands but has been incompletely socialized in the social rule in question, that is, a little girl may know the rule but cannot control her feelings. Most caregivers also believe that negative methods are ultimately indispensable for teaching rules, or that regardless of whether the child knows and accepts a rule, certain rules *must* be enforced for the social good of all. Biting hurts and tearing books interferes with the pleasure and learning of others. Some minimum of social order is necessary to conduct life in day care and family settings, although the range of tolerance for disorder varies among individuals and cultures.

Whatever the reasons, the important thing is the attitude with which a technique is applied. Negative attitudes expressed through punishment are generally less effective than positive emotional approaches, and may in the long run have negative consequences for socialization. The child who is punished somehow feels wronged; the focus shifts from the rule in question to her relations with authority, toward whom she becomes more or less angry and rebellious, often covertly. Spanking a child for hitting is doing the same thing to the child as she has done to another child. Even scolding hurts a child's feelings (her self esteem), making her feel sorry for herself and resentful to the teacher (or parent), instead of developing her awareness of how she has damaged something of value or hurt someone else's feelings. The child may learn to stop her aggressive ways in that instance, from fear of further scoldings, but inside her resentment comes out in other, more covert and indirect forms of aggression. She may destroy a child's drawing when no one is looking, shirk her share of work tasks, or get others to throw food at the table, thus getting back at teachers. Punishment thus sows the seeds for the development of rebellious attitudes and emotional, unreasoning ways of dealing with rules.

A few bad incidents probably make little difference over the long run. A pattern of negative experiences, however, can accumulate to shape a hostile personality alien to itself and society. It is just the child who persistently misbehaves, of course, due to a history of previous spankings, scoldings, family conflicts, or inconsistent handling, who provokes caregivers to exasperation and chronic punishment. The child becomes the scapegoat of a play group, earning constant punishment but usually also stirring up rebellion in other children, which further adds to destructive activity and disruption of the interests of the group.

The only real alternative is a complete change of approach through involving the child in caring, and developing constructive ways and self control. A child who displays a pattern of aggressive behavior, whether in play or toward teacher or peers, usually responds best to special attention combined with a firm hand—applied in a positive, or at least neutral, non-angry, manner. When carefully planned, regular attention is paid to a little boy who is involved in some interesting story, or other play and learning activity, he is able to build up a positive idea of himself as worthy of special care by an adult. At the same time, it is important to apply clear and definite limits to the child's antisocial behavior, but with positive attitudes that will not undermine his newly developing self image. Wholesome self control can only come where the child sees himself as a worthwhile member of the human community, in which the demands for good behavior are not only rewarded by love and interesting play with adults, but in which all activities, including demands for good behavior, are conducted with mutual respect. Through these combined means and attitudes the child comes to accept the values of cooperative behavior, and to exercise self control which in turn brings more satisfying constructive play and relations with other children to further cement the process.

Removing a child from the play group is only effective when applied consistently in a balanced manner. When used in this way, with a matter-of-fact, non-hostile attitude, separating a child from a conflict situation also serves to calm all parties concerned, including the misbehaving child. As long as the child is merely asked to play or reflect a few minutes alone and is not exiled in hostile isolation, the technique both aids the misbehaving child's development and maintains the constructiveness of the play group. Short, clear explanations, even friendly and sympathetic to the child's struggle, are desirable. Again, the aim is to teach rules and the effects of "bad" behavior, not to humiliate a child. Long verbal statements are often punitive or at least mind-dulling, producing essentially negative effects. Remember, rules are not learned overnight. The best care is preventive, through maintaining conditions that develop constructive play and social activity rather than conflict.

Adapting Caregiving to the Child's Current Problems

In order to meet a child's changing needs, caregivers must adapt to personality changes caused by ups and downs in the child's life circumstances. Family crises at home, such as a parent's loss of job, death or serious illness, financial worries, a move to a new apartment, sibling rivalries, emotional conflict between parents, and other similar events, whether temporary or chronic, all serve to undermine the social harmony of the family and the relations between parent and child. Similar effects can result from role shifts and job turnover among caregivers at the child's school or day care center. In either case, the child's security tends to be undermined from breaks in the continuity of relations and activities.

Little children seldom have either the understanding or the coping skills to deal with such problems. If the sources of conflict are both severe and chronic, difficult-to-manage emotional reactions are likely to appear. Children become chronically tense and hyperactive, seldom able to settle into any activity for a substantial period of time. They may be edgy, irritable, and prone to cry easily. They may become withdrawn, mistrustful or rigid, never going along with peer group or caregiver task demands without extreme patience and sensitivity on the part of the caregiver. They may vacillate between extremely dependent and extremely independent behavior, or form clinging attachments to one caregiver while remaining shy and hostile toward others.

Mild signs of insecurity, such as periodic thumb-sucking or bouts of irrita-

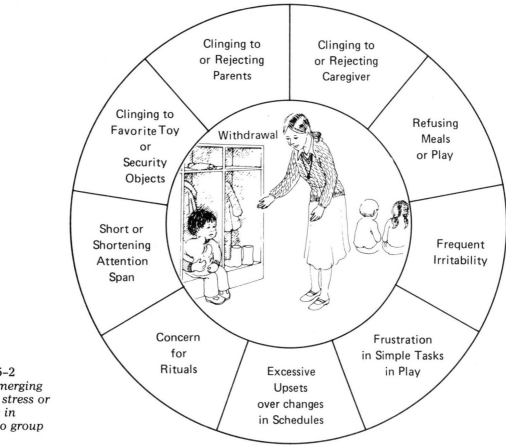

FIGURE 5–2
Signs of emerging emotional stress or difficulties in adapting to group care.

bility, are likely to appear occasionally in most children as problems arise in various settings. Such temporary patterns are normal to development, although some children experience more and some less than their share of these problems. Often a great deal of patience and attention, combined with emotional support (such as extra hugging) and a certain amount of indulgence in idiosyncracies (adhering to ritual ways of putting away socks, or the order of eating food at meals), are needed to complete tasks the child would normally undertake with little strain. This can be trying when there are other children and household or day care duties to attend to. It is often not possible during care routines to give the kind of prolonged attention a child seems to hunger for. Most programs, however, can afford to set aside a special time daily for a fond caregiver to devote undivided attention to a distressed child, which will often ease his anxieties or grief. Usually a quiet activity with a story or a puzzle is helpful, but some children from strict or highly active homes find more relief in individual attention during vigorous activity in the playground.

Sometimes the methods used to solve problems result in new problems worse than the original conflicts. For example, while added attention and flexibility may partially relieve a child's current insecurity, if continued too long they may lead to an unduly inflated ego or excessive dependency on adults. Again, balance is important. Extra care and tenderness will help, but only when some minimum demands for cooperation and self care are maintained, lest

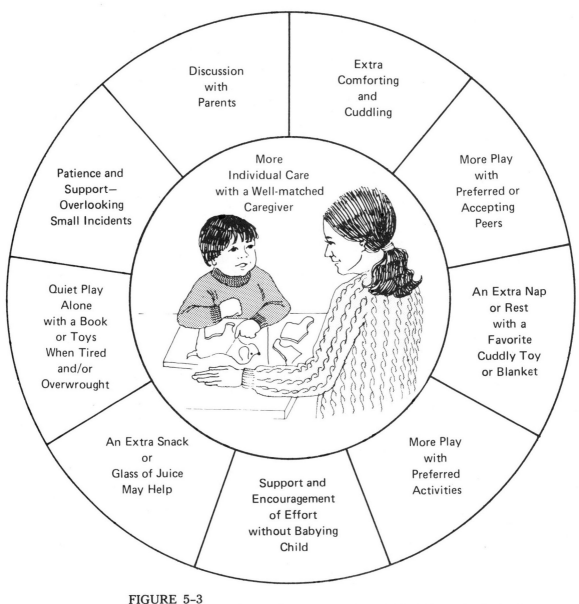

FIGURE 5-3
Some child care aids to relieving emotional difficulties and adaptation problems.

unrealistic expectations and poor coping systems develop in the long run. If, despite judicious handling, major problems persist, it is probably wise to seek professional guidance, usually in cooperation with the parents.

Situational conflicts (disputes with other children, for example), fatigue, and illness all have effects similar to those arising from major upsets in a child's life, although they are usually less pervasive. Small upsets will usually pass quickly if the child is handled with sympathetic understanding, is encouraged to play quietly alone for a short period, enjoys a good nap, or recovers from illness, as the case may be. Many children who feel irritable toward meal times will recover their normal disposition in the course of a good meal. This is partly due to restoration of blood sugar levels, but is also more characteristic of children who have come to strongly associate eating with security and a state of well being. Different events upset children, and children vary in the type and intensity of their reactions. One child may feel slighted over a child grabbing his toy, while another simply turns to something else or grabs it back with only momentary irritation.

Each situation has a personal meaning for each child, a way the event is seen in his own picture of the world. To a little girl whose parents do everything for her, adults may seem large and powerful. Day care workers must anticipate "babyish" reactions to their efforts to involve such a child in her own self care. A child whose parents encourage self reliance will probably like to do things for herself and may resent even essential help. Styles also usually generalize to other areas. Faced with a puzzle, the "babyish" child will be likely to give up quickly, while the self-reliant child will persevere. Caregiving is above all based on knowing the children and building a repertoire of caregiving skills to match particular personalities and particular situations.

Individualizing the Continuity of Developmental Care

The home offers continuity but few choices, while the multiple roles and varying schedules in day care offer many choices but less continuity. Fortunately, the stability of styles in the home tends to build the infant's personality to fit the personalities of the family in some workable way of life. The reserved mother develops a restrained child, or perhaps a highly uninhibited child because she encourages the openness she wishes she had in her own personality. Within limits, whatever the sources of conflict at home, the types of relations are known and predictable.

The number of different people in the day care setting, and the variety of personalities in the familial and cultural mix of modern living, inevitably widen the range of adaptation problems. One solution to this diversity of relations in day care is to assign children to individual teachers according to how well the styles of adults and children match, thus enhancing continuity of care.

There are at least two methods of matching, both of which are feasible in adequately staffed centers and schools, and can also be applied in some form in slightly understaffed centers. The first method is to assign clusters of children to each teacher for limited care and monitoring, but not continuous care. The second is to assign needful children to particular teachers for the bulk of their care during periods of emotional crises. These methods yield the greatest advantage when used together as complements to each other.

Matching may be as simple as merely observing which children and staff "take" to each other or as complex as making formal ratings with personality scales, similar to the diagnostic ratings described in Chapter 14, which discusses strategies for guiding developmental learning. One system, equally applicable to children and adults, is presented in Table 5–1.

It will be observed that this scheme of analysis encompasses four categories of personality functioning: cognitive styles, motivation, object relations, and social relations, each of which includes a number of characteristics. Cognitive styles refer to the different ways children figure things out (problem solve) in play and social activity. On the form, problem-oriented children, for example, notice when there *is* a problem and try to figure out what's wrong. At the other extreme, non-problem-oriented children remain confused or just turn away. Motivation refers to how interested children are in an activity, how well they concentrate or persevere in overcoming obstacles, for example. Object relations include ways the child uses and plays with toys and other objects in the physical environment, while social relations are the types of relations children experience with people, either adults or other children (peers).

Characteristics may be scored in two ways, either along the indicated 7 point scale or, to make it easier to use in the practical context of day care, in terms of plus or minus. A high number on the 7 point scale (6 or 7), or the plus area on the form, represents a high value on the characteristic concerned; showing much initiative would gain a high score on the dimension of autonomy. Low numbers (1 or 2), or the minus area, represent low values, such as being passive and dependent with respect to autonomy. On most characteristics, the average child would be expected to score in the middle range, compared to his peers, (from 3 to 5 on the 7 point scale, or the zero area on the plus-minus form). If lines are drawn between the plotted scores, the result gives a profile picture of the strengths and weaknesses in the child's way of coping with people and things.

A parallel form for rating adult skills in guiding children on the same characteristics is shown in Table 5–2. Ratings made on day care staff and children during the same period (during the same week) provide a useful tool for assigning children to teachers on the basis of how well a certain teacher's styles match a given child's needs. Each child can be placed under the wing of some staff member who is strongest on the traits in which the child most needs to develop. It will be noted in Table 5–2 that ratings on a teacher are defined in terms of how well a teacher *fosters* a characteristic in children, rather than simply whether he possesses the trait in question. In this fashion, one can determine the best fit between teacher and children. A child weak in analytic functioning (under cognitive styles on the form), but fairly socially adaptive and autonomous might, for example, benefit from close experience with a cognitively (intellectually) stimulating teacher who enjoys drawing attention to the significant details of how things work.

Below the profile section, on both the child (Table 5–1) and the teacher (Table 5–2) rating sheets, are spaces for brief written comments for each of the major areas (cognitive styles, motivation, etc.) and a section to summarize

TABLE 5-1

Diagnostic-Development Monitoring Assessment Form for Children (1975)

William Fowler and Nasim Khan

Developmental record of _____, _____, _____ for the period _____ to _____ _____
Child's Name   Group   Age   Date   Date   Name of Adult(s)

Setting (home, day care, indoor, outdoor, free play, guided play, physical care, etc.)

Cognitive Styles	Motivation	Object Relations	Social Relations — With Adults	Social Relations — With Peers	Representation	Loco-motor Skills	Physical State

Representation — Verbal

Top labels (high end):

Cognitive Styles: Analytic, Integrative, Reflective, Flexible, Problem oriented, Complex
Motivation: Inquisitive, Concentrative, Attentive, Persevering
Object Relations: Adaptative, Constructive, Productive, Creative
Social Relations With Adults: Cooperative, Adaptive, Autonomous, Empathetic
Social Relations With Peers: Cooperative, Adaptive, Autonomous, Empathetic
Representation: Comprehension, Production, Pictorial, Number
Loco-motor Skills: Fine motor, Gross motor
Physical State: Energy level, Health

High-end descriptions:

- Focuses on significant details
- Puts things together
- Thinks before acting
- Adaptive
- Perceptive of problems
- Likes complex things
- Explores the unfamiliar
- Highly absorbed
- Follows an activity
- Overcomes obstacles
- Likes things
- Uses material positively
- Accomplishes things
- Original combinations
- Interacts constructively
- Friendly and trustful
- Shows initiative
- Sensitive to others' needs
- Interacts constructively
- Friendly and trustful
- Shows initiative
- Sensitive to others' needs
- Excellent understanding of language
- Excellent speech/babbling
- Excellent use of pictures
- Excellent understanding of numbers
- Excellent use of fine muscles
- Excellent use of large muscles
- Functions at a high level of energy
- Maintains excellent health

Scale (left and right margins):

```
      7                                7
  + 6                                6 +
    5                                5
  0 4                                4 0
    3                                3
  - 2                                2 -
    1                                1
```

Low-end descriptions:

- Overlooks significant details
- Disorganized
- Impulsive
- Rigid
- Poor awareness of problems
- Likes simple things only
- No interest in the unfamiliar
- Loses interest easily
- Scattered attention
- Gives up easily
- Little interest in things
- Destructive
- Finishes no product
- Unimaginative combinations
- Very little constructive interaction
- Withdrawn
- Aggressive
- Passive dependent
- Attention demanding
- No awareness of others' needs
- Very little constructive interaction
- Withdrawn
- Aggressive
- Passive dependent
- Attention demanding
- No awareness of others' needs
- Little understanding of language
- Little speech/babbling
- Little use of pictures
- Little understanding of numbers
- Poor use of fine muscles
- Poor use of large muscles
- Functions at a low level of energy
- Maintains poor health

	Cognitive Styles	Motivation	Object Relations	Social Relations — With Adults	Social Relations — With Peers	Representation	Motor Skills	Physical State
Comments on child's patterns in different areas								
Summary of adult's strengths and problems								
Suggested methods for improving child's development and learning								

Reprinted by permission

TABLE 5-1 continued

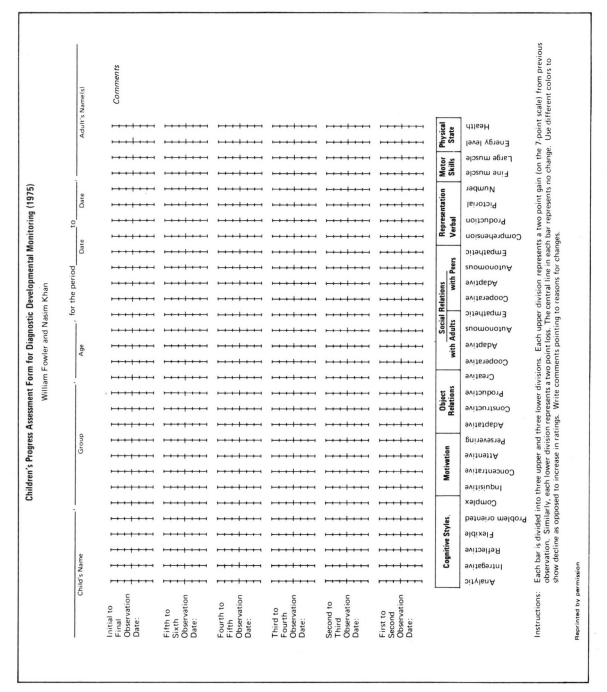

TABLE 5-2

Diagnostic-Developmental Monitoring Assessment Form for Caregivers (1975)

William Fowler and Nasim Khan

Profile of _____ , _____ for the period _____ to _____ | _____

Caregiver's Name   Group   Date   Date   Child(ren)'s Name(s)

Setting (home, day care, indoor, outdoor, free play, guided play, physical care, etc.)   Age(s)

	Cognitive Styles	Motivation	Object Relations	Social Relations				Representation	Loco-motor Skills	Physical State
				With Adults		With Peers				
								Verbal		
	Analytic / Integrative / Reflective / Flexible / Problem oriented / Complex	Inquisitive / Concentrative / Attentive / Persevering	Adaptive / Constructive / Productive / Creative	Cooperative	Adaptive / Autonomous / Empathetic	Cooperative	Adaptive / Autonomous / Empathetic	Comprehension / Production / Pictorial / Number	Fine motor / Gross motor	Energy level / Health

Encourages Child to:

Focus on significant details / Put things together / Think before acting / Adapt / Perceive problems / Like complex things — Explore the unfamiliar / Be highly absorbed / Follow an activity / Overcome obstacles — Like things / Use material positively / Accomplish many things / Original combinations — Interact constructively / Be friendly and trustful / Develop initiative / Be sensitive to others' needs — Interact constructively / Be friendly and trustful / Develop initiative / Be sensitive to others' needs — Excellent understanding of language / Excellent speech/babbling / Excellent use of pictures / Excellent understanding of numbers — Excellent use of fine muscles / Excellent use of large muscles — Function at a high level of energy / Maintain excellent health

7										7
+ 6										6 +
5										5
4										4
3										3
− 2										2 −
1										1

Leads Child to:

Overlook significant details / Be disorganized / Impulsiveness / Rigidity / Poor awareness of problems / Like simple things only — Lack of interest in the unfamiliar / Lose interest easily / Scattered attention / Giving up easily — Little interest in things / Destructiveness / Finishing no product / Unimaginative combinations — Very little constructive interaction / Withdrawing / Aggression / Passive dependence / Attention demanding / No awareness of others' needs — Very little constructive interaction / Withdrawing / Aggression / Passive dependence / Attention demanding / No awareness of others' needs — Little understanding of language / Little speech/babbling / Little use of pictures / Little understanding of numbers — Poor use of fine muscles / Poor use of large muscles — Function at a low level of energy / Maintain poor health

	Cognitive Styles	Motivation	Object Relations	Social Relations		Representation	Motor Skills	Physical State
				With Adults	With Peers			
Comments on patterns in different areas								
Summary of strengths and problems								
Suggested methods for improving caregiving skills								

Reprinted by permission

TABLE 5-2 continued

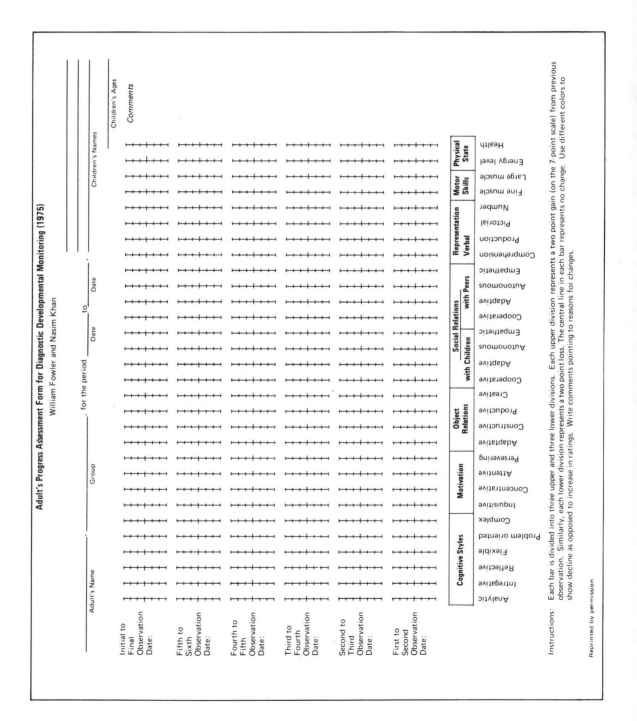

Adult's Progress Assessment Form for Diagnostic Developmental Monitoring (1975)

William Fowler and Nasim Khan

Instructions: Each bar is divided into three upper and three lower divisions. Each upper division represents a two point gain (on the 7-point scale) from previous observation. Similarly, each lower division represents a two point loss. The central line in each bar represents no change. Use different colors to show decline as opposed to increase in ratings. Write comments pointing to reasons for changes.

Reprinted by permission

overall trends. At the bottom of the child rating sheet is space for writing recommendations on helping the child solve any problems identified through the ratings and comments. The corresponding space for comments at the bottom of the teacher's sheet would contain suggestions on changes in style recommended for improving his handling of his assigned children. As will be seen shortly in the section on monitoring, teachers usually respond best to suggestions for changing their approach when they are involved in rating themselves or when making joint ratings with another caregiver.

Regardless of what techniques of assessment are used, it is well to expect that not all caregiver-child matches will work out in practice. Assessments are, after all, abstractions which do not take into account all aspects of personality, nor how people really get along and change from day to day. Since no two personality patterns are ever exactly alike, even in identical twins, there are usually a number of possible teacher-child matches. Each of these may take into consideration different sets of traits, often on a complementary basis, matching opposites, for instance, as when an especially friendly teacher is matched with a mistrustful child, or a reflective teacher is assigned to an overly impulsive infant. Fortunately, the availability of choices (several caregivers and many children) meets the practical demands of multiple scheduling which make some matches more convenient to arrange than others.

There are two situations when individualized attachments with teachers are especially valuable. The first concerns the emergence of family crises for children who have otherwise been getting along reasonably well in day care. When crises arise, the small social adjustments and learning problems children typically face become inflated and generalize to many aspects of their day-to-day activities. The limited ratio of caregivers to children in the average day care center necessitates careful use of staff resources to minimize the confusion and emotional drain such crises create.

The second special situation concerns the occasional child who has difficulty in adapting at all to day care. Most children feel some insecurity on the first separation from the familiar environment and close attachments of parents and the family. Unfortunately, few working mothers can arrange a gradual separation, remaining with the child as a security base and staying for a few minutes or even hours each day until the child is well adapted to the people and the setting (see Chapter 9 for methods of graduating admissions). Fortunately, as long as the day care or school staff makes special efforts to make the child feel at home during the first week or so, most children will adapt very quickly. They readily exchange daily separation from parents for interesting playmates and activities as long as there are also other caring adults around.

There are always a few children, however, whose developmental problems or sheltered history prolong the adaptation process. With these children, a deeper attachment with a well-matched caregiver will usually accelerate the process of adaptation, though the process may last a month or more. Separation problems are often greatest during the second six months of infancy, a period when the child is both forming a strong attachment to his primary caregiver (traditionally the mother) and becoming more aware of differences between friends and strangers. His growing understanding of the identity of people and things makes him more aware of differences, but his still-short memory and still-forming ideas make him uncertain of just whom he can count on, and when. Will his favorite caregiver really return, and who is this new person? Is it really someone new, or has the caregiver he knows in some way changed?

It is perhaps easier for infants to adapt if they are first enrolled before or after this sometimes critical period. However, children from overprotected homes or from homes with very close family ties may experience various degrees of adjustment problems throughout childhood, unless they gain healthy experience in group care and other community relations. The only residual problem after a week or so of gradual adaptation to a group setting may be signs of stranger anxiety upon the approach of an unfamiliar person (a visitor, another parent, or a new worker in day care). Hesitation, staring, withdrawal and a tendency to cry and turn to a familiar caregiver are indications of this reaction. The reaction can soon be dispelled for most children if they are held and comforted by a trusted caregiver and allowed to gradually get acquainted with the stranger. Adapting to group care is not necessarily prolonged even during the developmental stranger-anxiety phase, unless it occurs in combination with a history of having been overprotected.

Adaptation to group settings, even for overprotected children, is usually easier to work on during early development than at school age. Children become more fixed in their habits and uncertainties with age, and adults come to expect more of them, making less allowance for timidity. Elementary schools have large classes that limit the amount of attention available from teachers. The social isolation of living in urban apartments, being an only child, or even in living in suburban communities where there are few young children makes early exposure to good social experiences outside the home advisable. Flexibility, personal attention, and gradual involvement of the child in activities with other children soon leads even most overprotected children to adapt comfortably to the broader social life and activities of group care.

It is well not to wait for crises or adaptation problems before instituting some system for individualizing care. Once emotional problems get started, children develop defensive methods of coping that are difficult to reverse. Problems of interruptions in care can be resolved through arranging for caregivers to tend to one another's children during periods of staff absence. Assigning two caregivers to each small group of children, one with the main responsibility and the other as a backup or relief caregiver, can also soften the move of a child to a new main caregiver as a result of staff turnover. Continuity of relations between caregiver and a set of children gives both children and caregiver a sense of belonging in a family-like group, deepening their understanding and feelings for one another. Individualizing care also tends to increase the commitment of caregivers, because of the increased opportunity provided to plan for each child's overall development and to follow a child's progress. The caregiver has the opportunity to see the results of her efforts emerge in the developing child, and to see how different areas of development fit together to make the changing whole.

Culture Clustering

Just as staffing a school with teachers from cultures represented among the children creates respect for cultural differences, so clustering teachers and children from the same background will further support the child's cultural and language identity. Since it is equally important to make use of every teacher's special caregiving styles and interests that cut across ethnic backgrounds, some method is needed of matching teachers and children for individualized care by *both* background *and* personal characteristics. One way this can be accomplished is to assign children to different caregivers for different purposes. First, for individualizing care, a few children could be assigned to each caregiver on the basis of how caregivers and children matched in personal styles. These caregivers would be responsible for seeing to the overall adjustment of their children.

Teachers and children could then be clustered again, this time on the basis of ethnic background, such as placing Latinos, Chinese, blacks, Anglo-Saxon and other similar children, each with a teacher from a similar background. (The problem of unequal representation of teachers and children from the same background would often necessitate compromises, as when there are no teachers available for two or three children from Chinese or Italian-speaking homes.) Teachers in these roles would be responsible for organizing for their cluster of children special culturally related theme activities, such as special food at occasional meals, appropriate trips, stories, music, and discussions (see Chapter 7). Such activities need not—and indeed should not—be at the sacrifice of scheduling cross-cultural experiences for all children to better broaden cultural awareness. But such arrangements would help to cement the cultural identities of the children and reinforce their native language skills, especially when the main school language is not their own. It would also serve to bridge relations between the child's way of life at home and in day care. In these roles, teachers could also become sensitive to children's problems that arose from cultural conflicts, such as eating problems over differences in the foods at home and in day care. A Latino or Italian teacher would notice a boy's need for more hugging in day care, knowing that he receives more hugging in his home compared to the greater physical reserve applied to boys in Anglo-Saxon homes.

While there is much that could also be said for grouping boys and girls in separate activity groups to work on the special problem each sex faces from cultural pressures, until more males become teachers and day caregivers in early educational programs, such arrangements are usually not available. Moreover, sex clustering may also lead to further sex role stereotyping instead of, for example, helping boys to become more emotionally expressive and share with girls instead of excluding them, and girls to engage more in problem solving with construction toys than in doll play alone.

Monitoring Personality Development

In order to provide the care each child needs, it is useful to monitor development by keeping a continuing record of the different ways each child is developing. Without monitoring, care at best becomes a good but general approach, ill-adapted to individual differences and changing needs. Monitoring furnishes the knowledge that enables caregivers to provide the individualized care each child needs.

The process of monitoring is an extension of the initial personality evaluations made on entry to day care, but with differences in emphasis. Initial assessments are concerned with gathering knowledge on each child's behavior patterns in order to plan how best to handle him or her. This purpose is implicit in matching children with teachers. The emphasis in monitoring, on the other hand, is on how a caregiving plan is working out, based on awareness of the child's history. The best of plans require frequent modification in practice; first, because it is impossible to foresee every aspect of how a child will behave and, second, because children and even caregivers change in the course of time.

There are many different approaches to monitoring. It may be informal, or systematic (like the entry assessments), and may vary in frequency, in the variety of material covered, in the setting where it occurs, and in who does it. In general, the less the continuity of individual care, the more important it is to keep written records. When the care for a child constantly shifts among a number of caregivers, it is difficult to keep track of the child's progress in various areas without written records. Under these circumstances, periodic, comprehensive assessments are also valuable to further objective discussion in staff meetings. They provide an overall picture of the child against which staff notes drawn from scattered incidents can be evaluated. Written records are especially useful for making comparisons, both between the child's rate of development in different areas, and between the child's present and past status on any characteristic. It is wise to minimize making comparisons between children, however, because such comparisons shift attention from analyzing and trying to better the course of each child's development to fostering unhealthy competition and passing harsh judgments on children. Sorting children into the "easy", "average" and "problem" children solves no caregiving problems. It leads to useless stereotyping that is particularly destructive for minority group children, who already face chronic social discrimination, and for children from upset homes who already find it difficult to cope.

When each staff member is responsible for the same small group of three or four children much of the time, the teacher naturally gets to know each child well. Provided the caregiver is reasonably competent in child development and care techniques, he or she can easily become very familiar with children's distinctive characteristics and keep fairly good mental records of how they are developing. Under these circumstances, systematic monitoring, while still very useful, is less essential.

In the absence of individualized teacher responsibility, continuity of attachments and care are greatly diluted, as are clear pictures of how the children are developing. Where each is responsible for all, who is to keep—who *can* keep—detailed mental records on an entire playroom of 10 or more children? In multiple caregiving, both the well and the poorly developing children will stand out for different reasons, while the larger group in between is frequently lost sight of. Even on the extremes, important details will be lost. With no objective method of checking, busy day care workers will tend to stereotype, to see no flaws in favorites and few good points in "problem" children. Favorable caregiver ratios will minimize but are unlikely to eliminate such trends, because the problem really centers on the impossibility of keeping in one's head the emerging histories of so many children.

Children's development can be monitored systematically in many ways. Two useful aspects of development to monitor are (1) the personality patterns of individual children, and (2) the pattern of relations among children and staff in different activities. The former is essential to pinpoint how each child is progressing. The second sheds light on conditions in the day care center that are influencing development.

Individual development can easily be monitored on the Progress Assessment Forms of the same rating scales employed for the entry assessments of children (Table 5–1 and Table 5–2) previously mentioned in the discussion of matching children with caregivers. The profile system enables a caregiver to tell at a glance how each child and teacher is performing on all characteristics, make quick comparisons with previous patterns, and ascertain how well the initial matches between each teacher and her set of charges are working in practice. It is seldom necessary to shift any child to a new teacher except for reasons of staff turnover, but any characteristics on which a teacher and child are both low indicate areas where the teacher may need to change the method of handling that child. For example, a passive-dependent child (low on the scale in autonomy) with whom a caregiver is over-controlling (low in fostering autonomy), needs to be encouraged to experiment more on his or her own.

Parenthetically, personality processes do not usually change to the same degree as progress in cognitive development. Abilities show a continuing advancement in complexity with development, while personality and social characteristics tend to rise and fall more according to the home situation and other circumstances. Personality characteristics like adaptiveness, concentration, and flexibility can be seen in the youngest babies.

Children's personal styles must be compared with their own age groups, because the child's social abilities (which also become more complex with development) influence the way these processes are expressed. Both babies and preschoolers cooperate in some form of sharing. This is seen in an infant's degree of willingness to explore a toy alongside another infant without grabbing it away from the other child, while in the preschooler, cooperation can be measured by willingness to coordinate actions with another child to solve a puzzle or paint a scene. Though four-year-olds concentrate on more complex tasks, like riding a bicycle or building a road, while a ten-month-old merely watches a mobile or explores a wheel toy, either can display varying degrees of concentration, from as little as a second or two to as long as 30 minutes or more. Familiarity with the behavioral complexity of the age group is thus an essential basis for judging the quality of a child's personality traits.

The style of an individual teacher is not the only factor influencing a child's development. Relations with the home, which we shall discuss in the next section, obviously have a profound effect. So does the child's status among the other children and with the other day care staff, who must interact with each child frequently even where individual teacher responsibility is the rule. Quite often ratings will show a child low in characteristics even when the teacher is rated as quite skilled in fostering the same characteristics. For example, the primary day caregiver for a passive-dependent little girl may regularly provide the form of interaction and opportunities for experimentation needed to foster autonomy, but the child's first efforts to assert herself with other children may be too timid to gain acceptance in a lively group, thus perpetuating her dependency.

This information might not come to light unless the second method of monitoring is employed, one which gets at relations between peers. One common technique for monitoring relations in a group is sociometric rating. The technique, which is discussed further in Chapter 14, consists of making ratings on each child's relations with each of the other children in the group. Sociometric ratings can also be used for monitoring staff relations or relations between staff and children, but in this case should be used only with staff consent and involvement to protect privacy and interests. Children's interests are best handled by extensive staff-parent discussion and evaluation of consequences.

Ratings may be made on a variety of characteristics, ranging from simple preference (like-dislike) to judgments on popularity or leadership skills. Older preschoolers at least can be rated in terms of how they are viewed by others, indicating each child's relative popularity by placing ratings in rank order. By putting together the information from the list of ratings for the entire group, one can then diagram each child's popularity position in the total group. Ratings can focus on specific characteristics, such as popularity, skill, or interest in different activities.

Preschoolers will usually be able to make the necessary choice if asked to compare a picture of each child with one of every other child ("Whom do you like to play with more, this one or that one?") and similarly, asking which of a pair a third child would like to play with better. In Figure 5–4, for example, the pattern of peer choices among a group of four year olds reveals a kind of pecking order in which child A is at the center of many choosing children, two of whom are themselves chosen by two or three others, but most of whom apparently just follow along. This sociometric diagram provides a useful picture of the children's play group patterns for staff to consider in encouraging the formation of new relations among the children, as described in Chapter 9 on running a free play program. In the example shown in Figure 5–4, the staff would probably wish to work out a plan for providing leadership experience for a number of children (D through J) who appear to follow most of the time, and especially to search for a play partner who would match the (probably) timid style of the social isolate (K) who never even dares to choose anyone at all. Monitoring the children's relations with each other and the styles of caregivers and their assigned children brings together information from two complementary sources to fashion a more coordinated approach to caregiving.

Any staff member is capable of performing some monitoring techniques and they can be applied as often as is useful and feasible, to follow a teacher's development, profile the quality of any child's care among staff, or provide other similar information on the actual quality of care. Simple checkoff lists are easy for caregiver and parents with little training. A checkoff list for monitoring the quality of care provided in basic care routines with infants is shown in Table 5–3. (Similar checkoff guides for monitoring the performance of teachers in free play activities and guided learning activities are illustrated in chapters 9 and 14.) Such a list is valuable because it combines quickness of scoring with completeness of assessment. While not probing each teacher's characteristics in the detail possible with the method shown in Table 5–2, this basic care check

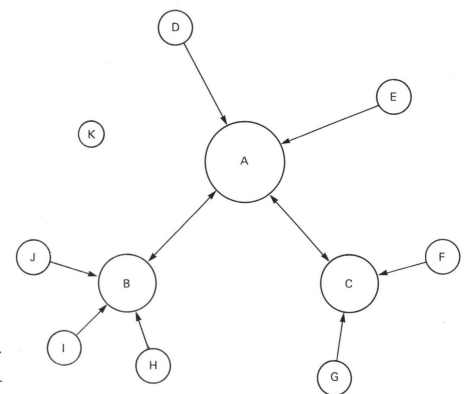

FIGURE 5–4
*Sociometric
illustration of peer
relations among a
group of four-year-
olds.*

list does furnish clear information on two or three important behaviors contributing to three basic aspects of development. The framework is interactive, and
even a dimension of problem solving is implied in the task involvement of the
child and the introduction of materials for play and learning. Useful information is furnished at little cost and much benefit to the quality of care.

The basic limitation of monitoring techniques is more often time than competence, since given time, a day care director can usually furnish the guidance
needed for staff to master even the more elaborate assessment techniques.
Practice will do the rest. A few trials with any of the different techniques will
readily demonstrate their value in providing more exact information to improve the handling of children and to further teacher development. It cannot be
emphasized too much, however, that unless the center leadership believes that
monitoring is sufficiently important to include routinely as part of each caregiver's assigned duties and schedules, the monitoring will not work. Teachers
are not likely to take seriously and use constructively what may appear to them
simply an added burden, unless supervisors show their utility, provide guidance, and help the teachers work them into their schedules smoothly. Even so,
the adequacy of adult-child caregiving ratios is obviously crucial to affording
the time to monitor effectively.

Day care staff are likely to find monitoring useful for evaluating their own
characteristics as well—but only if they are involved in the process. In fact,

TABLE 5-3. Monitoring basic care routines[a]

Categories and Behaviors	Yes	No
Language Stimulation		
1. Teacher talked to child 3–5 times		
2. Teacher labelled 3–5 objects, events and relationships		
Cognitive Stimulation		
3. Teacher encouraged child to help with 2–4 different parts of the task—child was involved		
4. Teacher introduced 1–3 miscellaneous play materials and tasks for child to learn about		
Socioemotional Development		
5. Teacher cuddled, hugged, petted or smiled at the child (at least once)		
6. Teacher attended to child without scolding, threatening or punishing		
7. Teacher gave reasons or suggested alternatives when using "No"		
Totals		
Means		

a To be used for assessing a teacher's performance during a single session in any given care routine (snack period, dressing, diaper changing, bathroom routines, etc.)

they will naturally tend to resist using any scales (including sociometric ratings) even for evaluating children's development if supervisors employ them for evaluating teacher competence without involving the teachers in making them. The threat to job security, promotion, and personal integrity is too great. One way to use the information constructively is for inservice training. If at least some of the ratings are made jointly by a supervisor and caregiver, the ratings can be compared and discussed with the goal of helping the caregiver to improve his techniques of child care. Joint monitoring is more stimulating and adds objectivity difficult to achieve through self ratings alone. Videotaping the teacher-child caregiving sessions provides a permanent, objective record for a teacher and supervisor to use in common (see Chapter 14 on strategies for stimulating development). Because both supervisor and teacher can now see the events in the same objective way and play over the various incidents as often as they like, rating videotapes is most helpful in reaching agreement on the teachers' strengths and weaknesses.

The main purpose of monitoring teachers, however, is to determine the appropriateness of their styles for handling various children. Hopefully it is the teacher who wants the insight needed to alter or improve his or her styles. Involving teachers in videotaping and rating together in pairs contributes to both the objectivity and the excitement of the process. Each has the advantage of seeing and comparing his own and the other teacher's performances from an

Reduction of child's conflict by coordination of methods between home and group care

Improved relations between teachers and parents

Better adaptation of children to group care

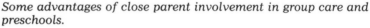

FIGURE 5-5
Some advantages of close parent involvement in group care and preschools.

objective angle, which can bring out many more ideas than would occur to anyone working alone.

Working in pairs has the added advantage, as pointed out earlier, of providing alternates for teachers in the case of absence. Assuming little staff turnover, stable assignments will further continuity in monitoring children and teachers, allowing staff to follow development over substantial time periods and to see the effects of various techniques they try out. Over the course of a series of sessions, caregivers will develop sharper insights into handling different children and closer working relations that will strengthen their cooperation in caring for one another's children.

The frequency of monitoring depends on its purpose. Learning records can profitably be maintained daily to match the small changes in children's knowledge and skill likely to accumulate from day to day (Chapter 14). Children's personality processes and teacher learning styles, on the other hand, usually change more slowly over a period of weeks. Monitoring these processes loses its impact when applied more than once every week or two, except for purposes of teacher training.

Relations Between Day Care and Home

There are several barriers to communication between home and day care that may seriously affect the development of the child. One barrier is the difference in the form of their social organizations, discussed in Chapter 3 on the social environment. Child rearing in the home is relatively intuitive, personal, and permanent, and is based on the traditions of culture, while day care is more professional, temporary, and uses child rearing methods that are relatively

Improved behavior and relations at home

More skills and materials for preschool or day care center

Better knowledge of the children and more program ideas

FIGURE 5–5 continued.

planned and rational. Such differences may create a wide psychological gulf in interests and understanding between day care workers and parents.

Related to this first problem are differences in size and power between the day care center and the family. Even a small center consists of a number of staff responsible for numerous children, while in a family only a pair of parents is typically responsible at most for several children. These differences of scale, combined with the formal basis for a day care center's organization, enables its leadership to negotiate from strength in its dealings with each of the many unrelated families.

A third barrier is the diversity of child rearing philosophies and methods among the families whose children are enrolled in a center, compared to the relatively unified approach a day care staff must necessarily adopt to maintain a minimum of working harmony. The cosmopolitan character of culture in urban life greatly magnifies such differences. Even when all members of a day care group live in a community, sharing a common culture, differences between families may be substantial.

A fourth barrier appears simply in the time limitations and the physical separation between homes and day care. It is difficult to expand day-to-day contact beyond brief exchanges when the parties are a commuting parent who often lives at some distance and must get to her job or home, and a busy day care worker who must simultaneously handle several children and talk with several parents at arrival and departure times. Lengthy conferences, parent evenings, and the like, while extremely important, can neither be arranged very often for working people (parents or staff) nor match the ease with which daily contact can settle problems when they are fresh.

These barriers between home and day care, the two dominant settings in the life of the child, create two fundamentally separate and often contradictory forms of experience.

For a number of reasons it is important to reconcile background differences in the interests of furthering wholesome, integrated forms of adaptation in the child. When differences are neither great nor intense, the child is likely to cope effectively, adapting flexibly to the different demands of home and school. When differences between milieux are marked, problems are likely to develop. A child who is expected to keep perfectly clean and neat at home, but is allowed considerable latitude at day care or grandmother's, may easily develop two distinct patterns of cleanliness and orderliness in the separate settings. Such a dichotomized form of development may lead to poor adaptation to the more moderate demands characteristic of later school and other community settings. Or, in the case where the parents place intense and rigid emotional stresses on obedience and order, these standards may generalize to make the child feel conflict over independence and casualness in any setting.

Even apparently minor differences between approaches can occasionally be confusing to a child. For instance, parents may have ideas of bundling children up to go outdoors in a manner that interferes with the free movement early childhood programs deem essential for physical development. Regular communication between parents and day care staff can prevent minor problems from growing into serious conflicts and can further personal acquaintance and trust. Despite limitations, casual, daily contact helps to keep everyone in touch with current developments in both settings and contributes to the formation of shared outlooks.

There is also an advantage to planning extended conferences with parents periodically, to permit a more detailed and systematic review of each child's development. It is easy to overlook significant details in the friendly disorder of casual communication. The important problems and negative trends are just the ones which find the greatest difficulty in surfacing. A carefully planned conference can provide greater assurance about areas of progress and agreement between day care and home, but also can bring into focus the child's problems and the differences in expectation between parent and day care staff.

No communication system is likely to resolve all differences in approach to the child's development. Culture and value differences cut deep, parents and day caregivers have different types of responsibility, and discussions can never faithfully recreate the experiences each has encountered. (Parent involvement in day care policy to insure parent interests are represented is discussed in Chapter 3.) Fortunately, as we have suggested, complete agreement is never entirely necessary, since even infants can adapt constructively to more than one way of doing things. Communication and agreement need only be sufficient to coordinate approaches and insure emotional harmony, a process which is critical during the highly formative periods of early development. It is up to the day care staff to reduce most conflicts for the child, not by erasing all differences, but encouraging respect for personal and cultural differences, except where family styles appear to harm the child (physical or psychological abuse) or otherwise interfere with development (too much exposure to TV violence or insufficient sleep). Differences can even be a source of stimulation to the development of an inquiring mind, and are a basis for the survival of cultural pluralism in the world. After all, unless each family can feel there is room in its children's lives for its own language or dialect, food, taste for music, and other traditional ways, we shall all become alike as robots.

Bibliography for Part II

Achenbach, T. Behavior disorders in preschool children. In H. L. Hom, Jr. & P. A. Robinson (Eds.), *Psychological processes in early education.* New York: Academic Press, 1977, 261–293.

Aronoff, F. W. *Music and young children.* New York: Holt, Rinehart, and Winston, 1969.

Baumrind, D. Will a day care center be a child development center? *Young children,* 1973, *28,* 154–169.

Baumrind, D., & Black, A. E. Socialization practices associated with dimensions of competence in preschool boys and girls. *Child development,* 1967, *38,* 291–327.

Becker, W. C. Consequence of different kinds of parental discipline. In M. L. Hoffman & W. Hoffman (Eds.), *Review of child development research* (Vol. 1). New York: Russell Sage Foundation, 1964, 169–208.

Birch, H. G. Functional effects of fetal malnutrition. In S. Chess & A. Thomas (Eds.), *Annual progress in child psychiatry and child development.* New York: Brunner/Mazel, 1972, 96–113.

Boguslawski, D. B. *Guide for establishing and operating day care centers for young children.* New York: Child Welfare League of America, 1966.

Breckenridge, M. W., & Murphy, M. N. *Growth and development of the young child* (7th ed.). Philadelphia: W. B. Saunders, 1962.

Bronfenbrenner, U. Developmental research, public policy and the ecology of childhood. *Child development,* 1974, *45,* 1–5.

Bryan, J. H. Children's cooperation and helping behaviors. In E. M. Hetherington (Ed.), *Review of child development research* (Vol. 5). Chicago: University of Chicago Press, 1975, 127–181.

Caldwell, B. M. The effects of infant care. In M. L. Hoffman & L. W. Hoffman (Eds.), *Review of research in child development* (Vol. 1). New York: Russell Sage Foundation, 1964, 9–88.

Caldwell, B. M. What is the optimal learning environment for the young child? *American Journal of Orthopsychiatry,* 1967, *37,* 50–67.

Caldwell, B. M. Can young children have a quality life in day care? *Young children,* 1973, *28,* 197–208.

Caldwell, B. M. Aggression and hostility in young children. *Young children,* 1977, *32,* 4–13.

Caldwell, B., Wright, C. M., Honig, A. S., & Tannenbaum, J. Infant day care and attachment. *American Journal of Orthopsychiatry,* 1970, *40,* 397–412.

Campbell, J. D. Peer relations in childhood. In M. L. Hoffman & L. W. Hoffman (Eds.), *Review of child development research* (Vol. 1). New York: Russell Sage Foundation, 1964, 289–322.

Chandler, C. A., Lourie, R. S., Peters, A. D., & Dittman, L. L. (Eds.). *Early child care: The new perspectives.* New York: Atherton, 1968.

Chauncey, H. *Soviet preschool education,* Vol. 1, *Program of instruction.* New York: Holt, Rinehart, and Winston, 1969.

Chilman, C. S. Programs for disadvantaged parents. In F. D. Horowitz & H. N. Ricciuti (Eds.), *Review of child development research* (Vol. 3). Chicago: University of Chicago Press, 1973, 403–465.

Chukovsky, K. *From two to five.* Berkeley, Calif.: University of California Press, 1968.

Crase, R., & Crase, D. Helping children understand death. *Young children,* 1976, *31,* 21–25.

deMause, L. (Ed.). *The history of childhood.* New York: Harper & Row, 1974.

Dennis, W. *Children of the Creche.* New York: Appleton-Century-Croft, 1973.

Erikson, E. H. *Children and society.* New York: Norton, 1963.

Fein, G. G., & Clarke-Stewart, A. *Day care in context.* New York: John Wiley & Sons, 1973.

Flint. B. *The child and the institution: A study of deprivation and recovery.* Toronto: University of Toronto Press, 1966.

Fowler, W. Design and values in the nursery school. *Inland Architect,* 1965, 9, 12–15.

Fowler, W. The patterning of developmental learning processes in the nursery school. In A. J. Biemiller (Ed.), *Problems in the teaching of young children.* Monograph Series No. 9, Ontario Institute for Studies in Education, Toronto: 1970, 27–46.

Fowler, W. A developmental learning approach to infant care in a group setting. *Merrill-Palmer Quarterly, 18,* 1972, 145–175.

Fowler, W. Infant education. In N. Byrne & J. Quarter (Eds.), *Must Schools Fail?* Toronto: McClelland & Stewart, 1972, 104–125.

Fowler, W. How adult/child ratios influence infant development. *Interchange,* 1975, *6,* 17–31.

Fowler, W. *Day care and its effects on early development: A study of group and home care in multiethnic working class families.* Toronto: Ontario Institute for Studies in Education, 1978.

Fowler, W. *Guides to early care and teaching:* Supplement to *Day care and its effects on early development.* Toronto: Ontario Institute for Studies in Education, 1978.

Fowler, W., & Burnett, A. Models for learning in an integrated preschool. *Elementary School Journal,* 1967, *67,* 428–441.

Fowler, W., & Swenson, A. The influence of early language stimulation on development: Four studies. *Genetic Psychology Monographs,* in press.

Furstenberg, F. F., Jr. *Unplanned parenthood: The social consequences of teenage childbearing.* New York: Free Press, 1976.

Gilbert, R. (Ed.). *The Weavers' song book.* New York: Harper & Row, 1960.

Ginsberg, H. *The myth of the deprived child.* Englewood Cliffs, N.J.: Prentice-Hall, 1972.

Giovannoni, J. M., & Billingsley, A. Child neglect among the poor: A study of parental adequacy in families of three ethnic groups. In S. Chess & A. Thomas (Eds.), *Annual progress in child psychiatry and child development.* New York: Brunner/Mazel, 1971, 323–334.

Gonzalez-Mena, J. English as a second language for preschool children. *Young children,* 1976, *31,* 14–19.

Gordon, I. J. *Baby learning through baby play: A parent's guide for the first two years.* New York: St. Martin's Press, 1970.

Gordon, I. J. (Ed.). *Early childhood education.* Yearbook of the National Society for the Study of Education, 1972, *71,* Part 2.

Gordon, I. J. Parenting, teaching and child development. *Young children,* 1976, *31,* 173–189.

Greenberg, M. The male early childhood teacher: An appraisal. *Young children,* 1977, *32,* 34–38.

Grotberg, E. (Ed.). *Day care: Resources for decisions.* Office of Economic Opportunity, Office of Planning, Research and Evaluation, Pre/R. (undated).

Kritchevsky, S., & Prescott, E., with Walling, L. *Planning environments for young children: Physical space.* Washington, D.C.: National Association for the Education of Young Children, 1969.

Hanes, M. L., Gordon, I. J., Breivogel, W. F. (Eds.). *Update: The first ten years of life.* Proceedings of the conference celebrating the tenth anniversary of the Institute for Development of Human Resources, College of Education, University of Florida. Gainesville, Florida: Division of Continuing Education, University of Florida, 1976.

Hapkiewitz, W. G., & Roden, A. H. The effect of aggressive cartoons on children's interpersonal play. *Child development,* 1971, *42,* 1583–1585.

Hardgrove, C. B., & Dawson, R. B. *Parents and children in the hospital: The family's role in pediatrics.* Boston: Little, Brown, 1972.

Helfer, R. W., & Kempe, C. H. (Eds.). *The battered child* (2nd ed.). Chicago: University of Chicago Press, 1974.

Hess, R. D., & Bear, R. M. *Early education.* Chicago: Aldine, 1968.

Hess, R. D., & Shipman, V. C. Early experience and the socialization of cognitive modes in children. *Child development,* 1965, *36,* 869–886.

Hoffman, L. W. Effects of maternal employment on the child. *Developmental psychology,* 1974, *10,* 204–228.

Holzman, M. The verbal environment provided by mothers for their very young children. *Merrill-Palmer Quarterly,* 1974, *20,* 31–42.

Hom, H. L., Jr., & Robinson, P. A. (Eds.). *Psychological processes in early education.* New York: Academic Press, 1977.

Honig, A. S., Caldwell, B. M., & Tannenbaum, J. Patterns of information processing used by and with young children in a nursery setting. *Child development,* 1970, *41,* 1045–1065.

Honig, A. S., & Lally, J. R. *Infant caregiving: A design for training.* New York: Media Projects, 1972.

Horowitz, F. D., & Paden, L. Y. The effectiveness of environmental intervention programs. In B. M. Caldwell & H. N. Ricciuti (Eds.), *Review of child development research* (Vol. 3). Chicago: University of Chicago Press, 1973, 331–402.

Houston, S. H. A reexamination of some assumptions about the language of the disadvantaged. *Child development,* 1970, *41,* 947–963.

Hunt, J. McV. The psychological basis for using preschool enrichment as an antidote for cultural deprivation. *Merrill-Palmer Quarterly,* 1964, *10,* 209–248.

Hunt, J. McV. *The challenge of incompetence and poverty: Papers on the role of early education.* Urbana, Illinois: University of Illinois Press, 1969.

Kenniston, K., & The Carnegie Council on Children. *All our children: The American family under pressure.* New York: Harcourt Brace Jovanovich, 1977.

Kessen, W. (Ed.). *Childhood in China.* New Haven, Conn.: Yale University Press, 1975.

Kessen, W. *The child.* New York: John Wiley & Sons, 1965.

Kohen-Raz, R. Mental and motor development of kibbutz, institutionalized, and home-reared infants in Israel. *Child development,* 1968, *39,* 489–504.

Labov, W. *Language in the inner city: Studies in the black English vernacular.* Philadelphia: University of Pennsylvania Press, 1972.

Landeck, B. *Songs to grow on.* New York: William Sloane Associates, 1950.

Landeck, B. *More songs to grow on.* New York: William Sloane Associates, 1954.

Lavatelli, C. S. (Ed.). *Language training in early childhood education.* Urbana, Illinois: University of Illinois Press, 1971.

Lee, P. C., & Gropper, N. B. Sex-role culture and educational practice. *Harvard Educational Review,* 1974, *44,* 369–410.

Levitan, S. A., & Alderman, K. C. *Child care and ABC's too.* Baltimore: Johns Hopkins University Press, 1975.

Lewis, M. State as an infant-environment interaction: An analysis of mother-infant interaction as a function of sex. *Merrill-Palmer Quarterly,* 1972, *18,* 95–121.

Lichtenberg, P., & Norton, G. *Cognitive and mental development in the first five years of life: A review of recent research.* Washington, D.C.: U.S. National Institute of Mental Health, DHEW Publication No. (HSM) 72-9102, 1972.

Macrae, J. W., & Herbert-Jackson, E. Brief reports: Are behavioral effects of infant day care program specific? *Developmental psychology,* 1976, *12,* 269–270.

McLaughlin, C. J., with Frisby, D. R., McLaughlin, R. A., & Williams, M. W. *The black parents' handbook: A guide to healthy pregnancy, birth, and child care.* New York: Harcourt Brace Jovanovich, 1976.

McLaughlin, R., & Schliestett, P. *The joy of music: Early childhood.* Evanston, Ill.: Summy-Birchard, 1967.

Meers, D. R., & Marans, A. E. Group care of infants in other countries. In C. A. Chandler, R. S. Lourie, A. D. Peters, & L. L. Dittman (Eds.), *Early child care: The new perspectives.* New York: Atherton, 1968, 237–282.

Messer, S. B., & Lewis M. Social class and sex differences in the attachment and play behavior of the year-old infant. *Merrill-Palmer Quarterly,* 1972, *18,* 295–306.

Miller, M. (Ed.). *The neglected years: Early childhood.* United Nations Children's Fund, 1973.

Moerk, E. Principles of interaction in language learning. *Merrill-Palmer Quarterly,* 1972, *18,* 230–257.

Moore, S. C. The effects of television on the prosocial behavior of young children. *Young children,* 1977, *32,* 60–65.

Murphy, L. B., & Moriarty, A. E. *Vulnerability, coping and growth.* New Haven, Conn.: Yale University Press, 1976.

Paraskevopoules, J., & Hunt, J. McV. Object construction and imitation under differing conditions of rearing. *Journal of Genetic Psychology,* 1971, *119,* 301–321.

Parker, R. K., & Knitzen, J. *Day care and preschool services: Trends and issues.* Atlanta: Avatar Press, 1972.

Prescott, E. In collaboration with E. Jones, S. Kritchevsky, C. Milich, & E. Haselhoef, *Assessment of child-rearing environments: An ecological approach.* Part I: *Who thrives in group day care?* Part II: *An environmental inventory.* Pasadena, California: Pacific Oaks College, 1975.

Prescott, E., Milich, C., & Jones, E. *Day care* Vol. 1: *The "politics" of day care.* Washington, D.C.: National Association for the Education of Young Children, 1972.

Prescott, E., Jones, E., & Kritchevsky, S. *Day care* Vol. 2: *Day care as a child-rearing environment.* Washington, D.C.: National Association for the Education of Young Children, 1972.

Provence, S., & Lipton, R. C. *Infants in institutions.* New York: International Universities Press, 1962.

Provence, S., Naylor, A., & Patterson, J. *The challenge of daycare.* New Haven, Conn.: Yale University Press, 1977.

Rafael, B., & Marinoff, S. L. Using videotape for teacher training. *Young children,* 1973, *28,* 217–219.

Raymond, T. A. *A history of the education of young children.* London: Longmans, Green, 1937.

Ricciuti, H. N. Social and emotional behavior in infancy. In S. Chess & A. Thomas (Eds.), *Annual progress in child psychiatry and child development.* New York: Brunner/Mazel, 1969, 51–71.

Robinson, H. B., & Robinson, N. M. *International Monograph Series on Early Child Care* (Volumes 1–12). *Early child care in Hungary, Sweden, The United States of America, Switzerland, Britain, France, Cuba, Poland, Yugoslavia, India, Israel, The Union of Soviet Socialist Republics.* London: Gordon and Breach, 1972.

Roby, P. *Child care—who cares?* New York: Basic Books, 1973.

Rogers, D. *Issues in child psychology.* Monterey, Calif.: Brooks/Cole, 1977.

Roher, C. K. Racial and ethnic identification and preference in young children. *Young children,* 1977, *32,* 24–33.

Ruderman, F. A. *Child care and working mothers: A study of arrangements made for daytime care of children.* New York: Child Welfare League of America, 1968.

Ryan, T. J. (Ed.). *Poverty and the child.* Toronto: McGraw-Hill, Ryerson, 1972.

Schaefer, E. S. Parents as educators: Evidence from cross-sectional, longitudinal, and intervention research. In W. W. Hartup (Ed.), *The young child* (Vol. 2). Washington, D.C.: National Association for the Education of Young Children, 1972, 184–201.

Schaffer, H. R. (Ed.). *The origins of human social relations.* London: Academic Press, 1971.

Schaffer, H. R. (Ed.). *Studies in mother-infant interaction.* London: Academic Press, 1977.

Seeger, R. C. *American folk songs for children.* New York: Doubleday, 1948.

Shure, M. B., & Spivack, G. *Problem-solving techniques in childrearing.* San Francisco: Jossey-Bass, 1978.

Sigel, I. E. Developmental theory and preschool education: issues, problems and implications. In I. J. Gordon (Ed.), *Yearbook of the National Society for the Study in Education,* 1972, *71,* Part 2, 13–31.

Sigel, I. E., & Perry, C. Psycholinguistic diversity among "culturally deprived" children. In S. Chess & A. Thomas (Eds.), *Annual progress in child psychiatry and child development.* New York: Brunner/Mazel, 1969, 196–201.

Skeels, H. M. Adult status of children with contrasting early life experiences. *Monographs of the Society for Research in Child Development,* 1966, *31* (Whole No. 105).

Soloman, R., & Décarie, T. G. Fear of strangers: A developmental milestone or an overstudied phenomenon? *Canadian Journal of Behavioral Science,* 1976, *8,* 351–362.

Spiro, M. E. *Children of the kibbutz.* New York: Schocken Books, 1965.

Spock, B. *Baby and child care* (Rev.). New York: Simon and Schuster, 1968.

Spodek, B., & Walberg, H. J. (Eds.). *Early childhood education: Issues and insights.* Berkeley, Calif.: McCutchan, 1977.

Stein, A. H., & Friebrich, L. K. Impact of television on children and youth. In E. M. Hetherington (Ed.), *Review of child development research* (Vol. 5). Chicago: University of Chicago Press, 1975.

Stewart, I. S., Denson, R. A., & Stone, N. K. Competency and early childhood teacher education: Beginning at the beginning. *Young children,* 1976, *31,* 188–194.

Stone, L. J., Smith, H. T., & Murphy, L. B. (Eds.). *The competent infant: Research and commentary.* New York: Basic Books, 1973.

Swift, J. W. Effects of early group experience. The nursery school and day nursery. In M. L. Hoffman & L. W. Hoffman (Eds.), *Review of child development research.* New York: Russell Sage Foundation, 1964.

Taylor, K. W. *Parents and children learn together: Parent cooperative nursery schools* (Rev.). New York: Teachers College Press, 1967.

Tizard, B., Cooperman, O., Joseph, A., & Tizzard, J. Environmental effects on language development: A study of young children in long-stay residential nurseries. *Child development,* 1972, *43,* 337–358.

Tronick, E., & Greenfield, P. M. *Infant curriculum: The Bromley-Heath guide to the care of infants in groups.* New York: Media Projects, 1973.

Ward, W. D. Process of sex-role development. *Developmental psychology,* 1969, *1,* 163–168.

White, B. L. *The first three years of life.* Englewood Cliffs, N.J.: Prentice-Hall, 1975.

Williams, J. E., & Morland, J. K. *Race, color and the young child.* Chapel Hill: University of North Carolina Press, 1976.

Williams, T. M. *Infant care: Abstracts of the literature and supplement.* Washington, D.C.: Consortium on Early Childbearing and Childrearing, Child Welfare League of America, 1972, 1974.

Williams, T. M. Infant development and supplemental care: A comparative review of basic and applied research. *Human development,* 1977, *20,* 1–30.

Willis, A., & Ricciuti, H. *A good beginning for babies: Guidelines for group care.* Ithaca, New York: Cornell Research Program in Early Development and Education, Department of Human Development and Family Studies, Cornell University, 1974.

Wolfenstein, M. Trends in infant care. In Y. Brackbill and G. G. Thompson (Eds.), *Behavior in infancy and early childhood: A book of readings.* New York: Free Press, 1967, 473–483.

Wolins, M. Group care: Friend or foe? In S. Chess & A. Thomas (Eds.), *Annual progress in child psychiatry and child development.* New York: Brunner/Mazel, 1970, 218–245.

Yarrow, L. J. Conceptualizing the early environment. In C. A. Chandler, R. S. Lourie, A. D. Peters, & L. L. Dittman (Eds.), *Early child care: The new perspectives.* New York: Atherton, 1968, 15–26.

III

PLAY:
THE ACTIVITY
OF EARLY
CHILDHOOD

6 Play and Development

Cooperation

Play has been defined as the essence of childhood. Its informality and comparative disregard of purpose and reality lend it a quality that makes it readily distinguishable from work and structured goal-seeking. In play, the ratio between the influence of imagination and the physical dimensions of the environment is almost the reverse of that found in the ordinary means-ends activities of everyday adult life. Is this reversal a characteristic difference between children and adults, or is it a result of the role in which we place children?

Children spend much of their time with things called toys that have little use beyond the play itself. Adults pass the bulk of their time performing actions with things that function primarily as means to ends; they use tools to make things, vehicles to transport people or things, and books and television to communicate ideas. Yet play may occupy a vital position in the life of every person at all stages of the life cycle, merely varying in form according to the culture, situation, and type and stage of development.

In this chapter I shall explore some of the dimensions of play, and its meaning for both children and adults. I shall try to define its similarities to and differences from work and task activities; I shall also furnish a classification of

141

common forms of young children's play and the major lines of development of its structure. Methods of stimulation and the role of teachers will be largely left to discussion in other chapters.

Definitions and Boundaries of Play

Play at every age has multiple functions. Not every person enjoys all of them, nor does every type of play permit all of them to be expressed. But, whatever its varieties, play is principally defined by its *detachment from purpose external to itself.* Whatever end or personal needs it satisfies must be sought in the character of the processes themselves. Although play may in fact contribute to the individual's development or goal seeking, the relations between play and goal-seeking activities are more indirect than direct. When children play with toys or adults play games they are often performing tasks in which they employ means to work toward ends. The adult shakes dice to move pieces on a playing board (Parcheesi, Monopoly) in order to reach an ultimate goal that may additionally implicate a network of means-ends processes. The young child's activities in play are far simpler in rule structure but such means-ends actions as placing a doll in a bed for sleep, or banging a block to hear the sound, may be identified. None of these activities, however, is directed toward accomplishing serious purposes. The activity is essentially complete in itself as far as goals are concerned. External goals *can* be imposed on play or game activity, but that is not its main function when play is engaged in *for its own enjoyment.*

It is difficult to capture the exact psychological sources which impel us to play. The definition we have advanced is more a statement of what play is *not* than what it is, a problem common to theorists who attempt to define play. It is, in fact, easier to observe many psychological needs that play (and games) appears to serve than to identify a single, underlying motive which draws us into play. The lack of consequence for the real or serious goals attached to one's social role enables play to be satisfying in itself and to feed a variety of needs and motives. Why? It is not the absence of control alone that creates the satisfaction, although periods of freedom from strong demands for achievement is a condition necessary for play activity to thrive. Play is a psychological process in which imagination and fantasy, more than the nature of the external environment, determine the character and course of action. Yet the child in play does not lack orientation toward the things and stimulation in a situation; he elaborately and extensively explores toys or any objects at hand, such as pots, pans and kitchen utensils; he fingers, pokes and pulls; he assembles, sorts and builds; he imitates common uses of objects and creates uses of his own. What, then, makes play different from ordinary tasks and work?

Once more we must fall back on the primary distinction that tasks and work are invariably related to some socially defined goal that is valued beyond the activity itself. The mother uses pans to cook food to eat; the child either pretends to cook or uses pans for purposes of his own design in the interest of the *(creative) processes themselves.*

The boundaries between play and work, between play and rational problem-solving, are not always as wide as they seem. In many of their daily tasks,

Social Play   Social Tasks (Work)

FIGURE 6-1
*Children at work and play. Differences between work and play depend
mainly on the context and the social necessity of the goals.*

adults encounter problems requiring unfamiliar solutions, which demand new
analyses and manipulations. Particularly where tasks enter uncharted territory—a new math problem; composing sentences, even in one's native language; visiting an unfamiliar part of a city—we must bring to bear different
mental reorganizations that cannot be mapped completely in advance. These
activities do not only involve logically direct, step-by-step analysis of each
dimension of the new task or aspect of an old task; they also require us to build
on our own experience, to use our minds intuitively to search for new ways of
putting things together, forming mental images in a sort of trial and error mental logic to find the best fit. These processes involve the same sort of imaginal,
integrative processes that characterize the play of the child. Playing with a
problem is often the shortest route to solution. It is in the process of making a
new synthesis that intuitive interplay among the acquired understandings of
the mind takes place.

Seen in this perspective, play is not a segregated branch of mental activity
unrelated to work, problem-solving, and other apparently more structured
forms of activity. It is rather a type of loose, free-flowing mental activity, in
which the expression of inner mental structures over predefined tasks is salient, and which may or may not be related to accomplishment. The predominance of imaginal, constructing processes is proportional to the degree of openness in a situation, and to the mental flexibility of the individual.

The structure of play and imagination tends to be governed by the forms of material available in an environment, but latitudes of expression are wide, according to the social definition of a situation and the quality of the player's past experience. Narrowness and ritual in task demands and routines in work minimize the operations of play and imagination, while complexity, novelty, and indefiniteness of cues and guidance increase them. Removal of task or achievement demands increases the expression of imagination in play.

The Functions of Play

The most obvious function of play is the production of learning, ranging all the way from the new-born's first visual exploration of shapes to the intricate rules of strategy and tactics in complex games. Thus the learning to which children are exposed through play covers all of the dimensional, process and informational rules by which objects can be structured, varied, and related to one another. The child can learn, for example, whether a toy is long or short, how it moves, and what sort of social object (toy stove) or natural object (stone) it is. The expression "the learning that *can* occur" is used here to emphasize that play in and of itself is no guarantee that any learning *will* occur. Much of the learning in play, particularly during early development, results from children's experimenting with examples of concepts, such as "long" or "short," or "fathers" and "storekeepers," that children are first exposed to through guidance, observation, and cultural media (books, TV). Without such experiences, not much learning can be expected to occur during play. The learning in play, in other words, is principally that of enriching concepts through experimenting directly with many examples, rather than learning brand new concepts. Social deprivation thus means above all deprivation of stimulation from adults and older children and opportunities to observe a variety of human activities.

Play is filled with many other qualities that enrich the child's development. It is a process that combines many of the sets and sequences of mental operations that make up problem solving and reasoning. The exploration of a situation or a problem, an inquiry orientation, scanning and analysis, identification, and synthesis of means-ends parts and relations, are all built into many of the activities of playing with toy people, vehicles and blocks, form boards, and activities with playmates in sociodramatic play. The quality of problem-solving will depend on circumstances and how the child has been stimulated during past and current development.

There are few functions that play does not serve; and it fulfills them so flexibly and organically that it is universally powerful as an agent of human development. Play is the vehicle through which children explore new areas and widen their understanding; it is an important means of refining competence and understanding of the social roles and developmental tasks of everyday cultural life such as manners for eating, reciprocity in authority and peer relations, and structures of the family and community; it is a means of resolving emotional conflicts attached to social experiences and activities. The exploratory-manipulatory aspects of play provide sensory pleasure as well as sensori-motor feedback and learning; play is an arouser of curiosity, and a generator of creativity.

Comparisons between the Play of Adults and Children

The value of play for children can be better understood through assessing the change in its general character over the course of development from childhood to adulthood. The most significant change in play activity is the evolution from outer to inner expression and the shift from physical to symbolic manipulation. The complexity and logical ordering of the forms of playful processes are also considerably increased as the child develops. The development of the abstract tool of language enables older children and adults to go beyond the concreteness of specific situations to reflect about problems and try out alternatives in their minds without always being tied down to immediate action. This shift from sensorimotor or direct action systems of mental processing to abstract language systems produces most of the characteristics of adult play: the inner control, the intricacy of logical ordering, the abstract mapping, and the long-range linking and coordination of means and ends.

The *absence of a genuine work ethic in early life* is closely related to the limits upon abstract and complex representation inherent in the young child's direct action systems of functioning. Work is built on instrumental striving for non-situational goals, *distant* in time (painting a picture for a display next week) and abstract in concept (saving up money to buy a bike). The child cannot plan and organize his activity to work for long-range goals until he develops the abstract mental systems needed to do so. The child must play because he cannot work. How do the adult's ability and necessity to work affect his play?

Historically, the pressure of economic necessity has always meant unimaginative labor from dawn to dusk, with few periods of leisure and play, for the vast majority of adults. In contemporary society, however, the rise of industrialism and its attendant expanding productivity have led to greater diversification and complexity of work roles and the extension of leisure time. Greater leisure and role complexity are both conditions that produce diversity in the forms of mental activity likely to encompass the intuitive mental manipulations we have defined as play.

What specific forms of activity does play encompass in adult life? Hobbies, games, sports, and the many varieties of art expression all incorporate styles of play in differing degrees and circumstances. The rituals of courtship and love play, strolling and window shopping, urbane conversation, language repartee and teasing also embrace elements of fantasy, expressivity, exploration, and experimentation that feature so much in play, and serve many functions similar to those experienced by the child. The adult learns about social relations informally, and often better through play than through work roles. The adult also resolves tension and conflict, rehearses for work roles, experiments and creates, as the child does, though through different forms and levels of complexity. Product orientation and concern with serious achievement goals are also commonly secondary to the course of these activities.

Just as the child's block construction activity and sociodramatic play are expressed within definite material forms (see Chapter 7) and follow certain rules, so many of these adult play-like activities are contained within the limits of abstract codes (language, music), design rules, material forms, game rules, or physical limits. It is not the absence of complexity or high abstraction that determines whether or not play processes are involved; it is the presence in the activity of experimentation, spontaneity, and the expression of fantasy, which are important to creativity. Art creation, and literary and musical composition, almost of necessity incorporate such processes, though they vary widely in width of expression and originality. Acting, performing music and viewing paintings also demand wide latitudes of interpretative play to become emotionally meaningful. Scientific activity as well by its very nature is built on experimentation with processes of means and ends, trying out different models and methods, such as preparing vaccines at different strengths, quite often in playful activities (but often on paper), similar to the way children try out toys. Though these fanciful manipulations may be part of systematic planning with definite ends in mind (such as curing people), the concern with processes and the use of the imagination are quite the same. Actually, children in play also often care about an end product (completing a puzzle, building a tall building), though the end is usually secondary to the processes, especially in sociodramatic play, as in "fixing" a pipe with a wrench to "be" a plumber.

In a different way, conversation, hiking, and window shopping can involve considerable spontaneity and randomness of expression. Dialogues with the computer and model building are additional forms of expression in contemporary life that permit variations in creative interplay. Sports and games can become so ritualized that the process qualities of play are stifled, or they can remain informal and imaginative in their variations. Many physical power sports like track and swimming focus more often on speed than the creative aspects of form stressed by activities like diving and gymnastics; but even activities with a high premium on speed require exploration and experimentation with skill, like the puzzle play of a three-year-old.

Thus adult play differs from child's play in some ways more in its forms of physical expression and levels of abstraction than in its degree of spontaneity or concern with purpose and goals. Play can hardly be excluded from any major phase or form of contemporary culture. If the work of the preschool child is indisputably play, little directed to larger plan or purpose, then the forms of leisure of the adult depend heavily on the expressive and fantasy games of play, however concrete or abstract. But the role of play does not stop here. The work of the adult, in an increasingly differentiated society, consists more and more of complex, creative activities, which cannot be effectively performed without regular infusions of imaginative play with ideas. In a society where soon almost everyone will pursue some form of post-secondary education, few completely ritualized jobs will remain. We must therefore insure that the early foundation of children's experience is enriched with many creative play activities.

Types and Complexity of Children's Play

The young child experiments with processes in play in a variety of types or forms, varying from the simplest act of touching or looking, to complex social interactions and intricate problem-solving processes. Play also varies according to the nature of the materials and situation, and the social, aesthetic, and functional purposes to which the materials are put; the latter depend on the experience the child has accumulated. A set of geometric shapes (e.g., triangles, squares, and diamonds) may be used as money in playing store (social play), to construct mosaic designs (aesthetic purposes) or to fit in a form board (functional purposes).

Most types of play have their roots in earliest infancy and can be observed at any age, given appropriate materials and circumstances. Even language play can be found in the infant as he experiments with his own simple sound productions. Social play also begins early, starting with the vocalization and smiling play of parent-child interactions. The complexity with which any given type of play is organized is determined as much by the general developmental level of a child's understanding (indicated for example by his general skill in using language and other symbols) as by his specific learning experiences with that particular type of play.

We cannot easily predict the types and complexity of play for any child or group, even if we are familiar with the interests and cognitive level of the child, the situation, and the type activities that the materials at hand will allow. There are endless combinations of rules for a child to choose from: for example, form board inserts can be used as walls and their parts as building blocks; stacking rings can be rolled like wheels, graduated by size horizontally in a row on a table instead of stacked in a vertical column on a ring, or even placed in two horizontal rows. We can be more certain about the *most* complex cognitive rules the child will employ if we are familiar with his competence levels. But the type and level of play he actually uses may vary considerably as his interests and those of his playmates dictate, in some situations hardly approaching his actual capabilities.

Unlike the well-laid out course that many adult tasks, older children's school work, and babies' developmental routines take, play typically follows no completely planned route. Unpredictability is basic to the spontaneous basis of play, though periods of planning can regularly be observed in the problem-solving and construction play of many children. Even infants will often place a series of trinkets in a jar one after another with studied deliberateness, insuring no item is neglected, then tip them out and carefully repeat the process.

The relative freedom of play from social necessity (from having to do it) allows the child to pursue any path that appeals to him or her along the way to produce endlessly unexpected outcomes. Work tasks must find a solution, defined within certain preconceived limits (the blocks must *all* be put away on the shelf), and this need for solution tends to determine many of the pathways allowable, and thus the form the activities will follow. In cleaning up after play *all* toys must be put away and they must be placed on *certain* shelves in some *order,* not just any old way or in a creative design.

The Structural Development of Play

Differences between work tasks and play are real, though relative. Play may not follow as steady a course as work but, like planned goal striving, it is similarly organized around the exercise and mastery of cognitive rules for doing things. Play processes, like all other activities, are concerned with the development of competence systems; cognitive rule processes are as integral to the many types of play as they are to formal tasks. Play is not a mere expression of feeling and fantasy, though both are integral to it; there is an order and organization to play, in which even the simplest touching and searching activities are patterned by rules of how things are structured and the relation, however primitive, of means to ends. For example, when exploring objects about which she is curious, a baby girl's movements are initially awkward and scattered, but she can be observed to move from place to place, and try to cover territory, two of the most basic rules of exploration. As she learns, over many months, she can be observed to move in a more orderly, less random manner, and more selectively among significant features (eyes, nose, mouth of a new doll), two additional rules that refine her search skills. Even exploratory play is serious and inescapably harnessed to ordering rules, despite the absence of planning to accomplish tasks. In more complex stages of development, block building, painting, sociodramatic role play, and all other types of play obviously conform to even more complex rule patterns.

Thus play is bound by the limits of materials and the structure of activities, and can no more transcend the iron framework of reality and activity organization than any other activity. It follows the same general route of concept development as the mental structures defined in earlier chapters. Though play is concerned with experimentation and fancy, its organization increases in complexity through the development of competence in the three basic types of processes with which all mental activities are structured, that is (1) knowledge, (2) problem-solving, and (3) language processes (see Chapter 1). The behavior of children in play throughout development can be analyzed in terms of a structure in which the interaction of these three sources of competence can be identified. They do not, however, always appear in equal measure.

The general character of structural development of mental processes is one of increasing complexity, its progression determined by the successive learning of rules about concepts. As more rules are acquired the child is able to act in play more intricately, more abstractly, and in a more generalized, yet increasingly selective, manner. In the section that follows, a few major rule transitions and systems of rules that determine the character and development of several types of play structures in early childhood are outlined. The emphasis is on types of play in terms of cognitive development, more than on the forms of play determined by the structure of materials. The latter will be discussed in detail in Chapter 7. These types of play development do not follow any marked progression in complexity levels, since all are found in some form at every age, although some (like exploratory and instrumental play) attain a relatively complete form earlier than others (construction and symbolic play). The former (especially instrumental activity) usually become greatly elaborated, however, and serve major functions in all activity throughout development. The latter (especially symbolic play) reach a complete structure somewhat later and are effectively infinite in variety and complexity.

Type I: Exploratory-Manipulatory Play.
(Object and Pattern Play)

In this simplest level of play activity, the behavior of infants in the first few months pivots around exploration of *single objects and closely spaced patterns in their immediate perceptual field*. Play at this level is based on the sensorimotor enjoyment of exploring shapes, colors, texture, and changes in environmen-

FIGURE 6–2
*Types of play in infancy and early childhood. Type I: Exploratory-
manipulatory play.*

tal characteristics. Our inherent responsiveness to environmental stimulation
is one of the fundamental sources of motivation—another is our physiological
need for food, water, warmth, etc.—leading us to understand and actively
regulate our actions to get along in the world. The basis for human curiosity is
stimulus responsiveness, a natural tendency to respond to movement, form,
color, light, weight, and other environmental stimulation. As the infant responds, various stimuli become increasingly familiar, leading to growing understanding of the rules by which things are patterned, and efforts to seek new
and more complex stimuli of sights and sounds. This basic responsiveness to
stimulation and mastery of increasing complexity is of course highly dependent on the sequence of events the child experiences. Development is not automatic, but will vary with the effectiveness with which the child's world is organized and interpreted by caregivers. The variety and complexity of toys and
other objects to explore, and of adult attention and relations with peers, must
constantly expand to maintain the child's curiosity and development.

At first, babies respond by little more than looking, listening, and touching,
shifting attention between two or three prominent parts of an object (the two
bright ends of a rattle, or the mother's moving eyes and mouth). The patterns
most frequently seen (mother's face) and the objects and events that most
regularly occur together (bottle and mother) lead to his making mental connections about regularities as first rules about how the world is patterned. Repeated encounters with objects touched stimulates touching, and visual contact stimulates looking, first separately, then *gradually together*, through the

repetition of chance coordinations of seeing objects that are touched and vice versa: the child has learned his first big rule for controlling his own explorations, that of coordinating his sensorimotor systems in exploratory play.

The *range of complexity* attained in the early forms of exploratory object and pattern play is confined largely to single units and relations in a kind of zig-zag chaining process. The infant moves from point to point, drawn more by the sharpness of definition of shapes, colors, sounds, and movements, than by any systematic plan of search. The child may be attracted first by the bright color, then the whole form of a rattle, then the handle if it sticks out, and finally the sound if it is shaken, turning to some other attraction, such as a face, voice, or mobile, when the shaking ceases. Familiarity and organized meaning begin to take shape in the child's mind, however, centering in those areas most prominent in his or her experience, such as the face and voice patterns of mother and other familiar caregivers; the baby's own hand and eye movements; the patterning of objects and events in feeding, and the characteristics of common objects. The child also attends to the rhythmic and intonational patterns of voices just as he explores any other stimulus (environmental) regularities. If language stimulation is ample and well-presented, the first year infant learns to enjoy the play with his own vocal patterns in babbling activities.

Exploratory play continues as one basic form of play and problem-solving throughout development, though operating on a constantly expanding foundation of mental structures of rules about the environment, problem solving, and language. It becomes, in fact, the basis for all play and coping activities where task uncertainty or openness of definition exists. A new rattle for the baby or a new puzzle for the preschooler is first an occasion for exploration to analyze and put together what the chief features are. Exploratory play is also the preliminary orientation and search activity preparatory to approaching and defining tasks even for adults, and is integral to analyzing new problems as they appear at any point in an activity cycle.

Type II:
Instrumental Play.
(Means-Ends Activity
Play)

Once a little girl masters the rules for coordinating her sensorimotor systems to *do* things with objects (to reach out and touch what strikes her eye), she is well on the road to competence in working with means and ends in instrumental play. This new step goes beyond simply learning how to touch and look at the same objects, which is the major rule we noted that the infant must learn in order to engage in exploratory play. She now begins to touch and look with a *purpose.* Through many encounters in exploring things, she forms a general rule about her own body (first the hands) as a means (tool, instrument) with which to purposefully accomplish things. This is the first big step in a sequence of the development of instrumental activity. The next move is recognition of how objects (besides her hands) can be used in a task as tools to produce effects on other objects (for instance, marking paper with a crayon or painting with a brush, first dipped in paint). Then follows a series of increasingly complex stages, through which she gradually learns to coordinate the actions of chains of objects to bring about complicated events.

Instrumental activity is the model for means-ends goal striving and problem solving for almost all activity throughout life, whether in play or in striving for achievement. When the first sequential connection between means and

FIGURE 6–3
*Types of play in infancy and early childhood. Type II: Instrumental
(means-ends) play.*

ends is recognized by the infant, she has discovered the basis for all *intention-ality.* She can form *cognitive maps* of routes to follow and means to employ to attain goals. She begins to understand that everything that happens has a relation to, is caused by, something else. There is no end to the complexity of processes that can be defined within this fundamental form. She starts with just two units (her hand and a stuffed doll) and a single general relationship between them (reaching-retrieving). But these multiply into long event chains, intricate sets of variable components (including language and social events), which can reach astonishingly complex forms of means-ends (problem solving) play even in young children, as, for example, when several four-year-olds manipulate toy figures and construction vehicles in sociodramatic play.

Typical forms of instrumental play activity in early childhood consist of sensorimotor *puzzle activities* and *manipulative play* with two or more objects that go beyond the exploratory handling of Type I. While instrumental activity is also integral to construction and sociodramatic play, it is more obviously displayed in the child's play with puzzles and in object-object manipulations. Placing a series of rings, graded in size, on a peg attached to a base entails means (placing rings) to ends (on a peg) relations. Inserting blocks of varied shapes (square, round, triangular) in form board holes and fitting jigsaw puzzles are similar examples.

The final step at the perceptual-motor level is awareness of *causality* as a general phenomenon. As the child learns to use her hands, then to use other objects as instruments, she learns to distinguish the movements *she* initiates from movements the tool object makes itself, finally noticing that certain things move on their own without effort on her part (for instance, that a ball or toy car can roll down a slanted table). This new knowledge enables her to expand her means-ends play into more subtle and indirect environmental manipulations, such as employing objects to produce effects through environmental forces (letting balls roll, letting herself fall downhill, dropping blocks into a pail, balancing) as opposed to using direct push-pull actions to do things.

As it develops, language also features in means-ends play. It becomes an instrument for engaging attention, attempting to influence or enlist the aid of others, permitting complex forms of corrective action (putting away toys) and sociodramatic play. Language is also a device for mentally rehearsing, defining, and steering the child's own actions, and is thus a tool for clarifying and furthering the progress of her play. As she shapes a figure in plasticene, the child may be heard to say, "This is an arm," then "she needs another arm." Saying it not only helps to tell her what is needed and what to do, but it helps fix the concepts and the rules for what to do in her mind. Later in development, language can become the sole medium for problem-solving (and other) play, all processes taking place through the manipulation of ideas. Children learn to calculate using words alone, for example, shifting from the need to manipulate objects as they add or subtract; but even before then, preschoolers carry on extended conversations about imagined family or job problems in their play. As children reach school age, however, they figure out problems more and more in their heads, without saying anything aloud.

Young children enjoy experimenting in instrumental play, sometimes repeating with endless interest the various placing or targeting tasks they originate (or observe and imitate). They like to practice fitting objects or dropping them into a box; placing a toy on, beside or under another; using a toy rake to capture a block at a distance, and aiming the wheels of their tricycles to run over a pebble. All of these activities follow the basic form of relating one (or more) object(s) to another in a variety of means-ends operations.

Type III: Construction-Creative Play

When a young baby discovers that one object can be related to another, he is planting the seeds of what later becomes the basis for all creative activity. From his infant experience, beginning with the first excited anticipation of the nipple at the approach of signalling cues (the sound of the refrigerator door, bottles rattling, sight of the bottle, or positioning at the mother's breast) the child gradually learns and enjoys seeing how things can be put together. In instrumental activity, objects are employed as tools, pathways, or mechanisms of some kind to do something with another object. In construction play activity, objects are also related to one another, but the interrelations do not follow such a direct course to a predesignated specific goal. Unless, for example, a child attempts to copy literally some other child's building block structure, what he builds himself will assume a form usually not well defined in advance; moreover, he can, as his fancy changes, change the mental plan of his structure at any point in the course of building.

This, then, is the key dimension that distinguishes the *model of construction and creative play* from instrumental play. There is no fixed set of combinations or single organization defining construction activity. *There are only rules for organization* and organizing, determined by the characteristics of the me-

FIGURE 6-4
Types of play in infancy and early childhood. Type III: Construction-creative play.

dia (Chapter 7) that we shall illustrate shortly in our discussion of how play is influenced by the design of materials. These rules do not, however, interfere with the main dimension of creative play, the openness to alternative structure.

Ordinary means-ends activity (instrumental play) also usually presents the possibility of alternatives—at least different means to the same end. Choices are trivial in simple sensorimotor puzzles and other predefined tasks, however (the child can only choose such things as the angle from which a block is inserted in a form board or whether a square or triangular block is inserted first), and generally defined relative to some fixed purpose even in complex tasks. An intricate maze may be designed with several successful routes and a jigsaw puzzle can be put together in different sequences, but neither offers more than fixed alternatives, in each case leading to one goal.

More open instrumental tasks, like reaching a toy on a high shelf, may challenge a problem solver to create new means, for example stacking boxes to stand on or fastening two Tinker Toy lengths together to lengthen his reach. But reaching a toy or even repairing a piece of complex machinery remain predetermined goals requiring less imaginative integrations than construction play. Riddles and verbal puzzles (how can a farmer transport a fox, a goose, and a sack of grain across a river in just two trips in a rowboat that can carry not more than two of the three items at once) are similarly limited to a fixed solution. Even reading tends to be more instrumental than creative, although all reading, especially literature and poetry, demands creative interpretation. Musical performance, dance, and acting, also provide opportunities for creative interpretation, but musical and literary composition (along with dance choreography, architecture, painting and any activity where new forms and combinations are constructed) are probably, for adults, more nearly comparable to children's creative and sociodramatic play.

Not being harnessed to a predetermined goal, creative activity follows a more structural, interactive route along several dimensions as compared to the linear course of instrumental activity. Since the final outcome is some sort of new form or structure (clay figure, picture of a tree, or block house), the path to this outcome can easily be worked on from several directions at different times. The constraints of gravity preclude building with blocks from the top down, of course, but they do not prevent working on any of the different sides at different times.

Inherent in creative, combinatory play of this kind is a concern with principles of structure and systems, the rules for how organizations are formed and hold together. Blocks must be centered to balance, it takes two blocks to support a third to make a bridge, and unit blocks fit smoothly together, while interlocking materials hook together in some way. Process and technique themselves become important, even when at later periods of development (starting with preschoolers) a goal is planned in advance (to build a castle with blocks or shape an alligator from clay) that dictates more of the content and form. Even designated creative goals originate in fantasy instead of in a fixed instrumental, single goal task, and are necessarily complex structures (instead of single ends) that can vary indefinitely in form (castles can be cubical and austere or multi-towered and embellished). Even in the most "free" forms, creative activities involve relating means to ends, but even the most restricted construction play is different in kind from instrumental play tasks. The task structure is never linear and the final outcome is not a single end but a new form, a creation following certain principles of structure.

The *range of skill complexity* for creating new forms, aesthetic, functional, or scientific, extends from the infant's first efforts to place any two objects side by side to the most intricate musical compositions and revolutionary scientific theories. All partake of the same cognitive effort toward imaginative integration, bound only by rules of structuring, and of which materials can form what structures, whether concrete materials like clay, or abstract symbols like musical notes.

The range for young children occurs mainly within the bounds of constructing with physical materials, as with all other types of play. The constructions and creations of early development, even in the later preschool period, seldom follow well laid out mental plans, though elements of planning can be observed—for example, gathering certain blocks to be used after a first is positioned. But the building takes on much of its structure only as the child goes along, adding blocks as they seem to fit, following whatever rules for structuring he has learned in a kind of cognitive, chain-associational process. He is, in other words, stimulated as he goes along as much by what structures the materials evoke in his mind as by his internal ideas. The young child has not yet internalized well-integrated, abstract rule systems about things and techniques. As he progresses through the early years he gradually adds to the number of units he can place together to make a structure and multiplies the number of relations and rules he can employ. He must learn to juxtapose objects horizontally and vertically (in linear, area, then cubical (volume) terms) to learn rules for positioning, balance, fitting, bridging, and ultimately for positioning and relating substructures to total structures (an arm on the top and side of a clay figure). As with instrumental play, the competence he acquires will depend on two things; the effectiveness of his general learning experience (from both adult guidance and his own activity) and his specific experience in different forms of creative and building play.

Type IV: Symbolic and Sociodramatic Play

Although symbolic activity is the basis for the most advanced and complex structures of both language and sociodramatic play, its foundations are in the primitive vocalizations and babbling play of early babyhood. This early activity is enjoyed for its own sake; the sounds produced do not appear to have meaning. Another foundation of symbolic play is the perceptual-motor action schemas babies develop. These schemas of reaching, grasping, or moving enable them to coordinate and sequence visual and auditory activities and are the beginning codes for mentally representing and symbolizing events. The formation of mental pictures of things (cognitive maps) is still another step toward complete abstraction (symbolizing). This can be demonstrated as early as six to 12 months, by an infant girl's first brief search for an object that has just been removed from her sight.

The first of these processes does not appear to involve much representation, since mental activity is tied so closely to the immediate situation. The anticipation and coordination of action sequences does, nevertheless, seem to

FIGURE 6–5
Types of play in infancy and early childhood. Type IV: Sociodramatic (symbolic) play.

encompass mental constructs at some level, as evidenced by the skill the infant acquires to redirect her attention to unexpected problems appearing in a supposedly familiar routine. She can at some point, for example, readily turn her bottle around when it is handed to her upside down, long before she gets any assistance from verbal language. Movements of this kind, however, suggest that mental pictures are also beginning to play a role in her thinking. She is apparently able to picture to herself that there is a "right" end that does not look like the end presented, in order to make such a shift.

It is doubtful that even mental pictures can provide the same possibilities as verbal symbols for recreating the world in fantasy, however. Once language coding starts—calling things, and soon whole events ("go bye-bye", "daddy come") by arbitrary but socially agreed upon patterns of sound—an endless world of truly mental play becomes possible. Picturing activity no doubt precedes language symbolization and continues to contribute to the child's mental creativity long after verbal language has developed into the major tool for mentally reconstructing and playing with the world. But it is hard to tell just how powerful visual imagery can be in representing the world. We can only observe that in her early actions, when both mental pictures and sensorimotor codes are evident, but before language, the infant does not use general rules about size, classification, or other abstract dimensions.

Once language starts, language and images often work together, particularly in childhood, just as symbolization in early childhood generally takes place in the context of physical activity. The child is not moved to mental play with ideas unrelated to stimuli at this stage. But when she acquires the capacity to symbolize things in play, she continues to bring into situations mental pictures of experiences drawn from prior events, as well as using words to describe and symbolize. The little girl driving a truck (e.g., a tricycle), the boy in grown-up clothes, the children, as they speak to one another and perform tasks in their make-believe roles, are concerned with how they look. This concern is evident in their attempts to imitate facial expressions, gestures, and postures typical of the roles they are enacting. Language and imagery complement one another to enrich the play.

The power of verbal symbols to extend the scope of play and problem-solving activity is incalculable. As we have discussed elsewhere, it is the capacity to *code* systematically according to a shorthand logic of its own that gives language its power to portray simply so many key points of a problem in general terms. Mental pictures of things are, as the words imply, tied to pictures of particular situations. The first use of language to symbolize things is therefore a major advance in the child's development. She is no longer tied to the world as it is; she can build her own physical and social world of make-believe, though starting from and making constant use of the real world.

Through language the child discovers that *any* object can become a symbol for something else. Once the child learns this power of arbitrary symbols, the only limit is her imaginative capacity. Unlike pictures, which look like the things they represent, through language she can call a block a boat, or a stick a sword, and transport herself into a different world. But the process does not stop here. She learns that she can *pretend,* making believe she has a long beard like a pirate or has a computer near her desk. She may also learn to pretend by observing her peers, but the development of make-believe is probably largely aided by the "carrying" value of language. Words and phrases serves as vehicles to carry the ideas of things through the course of play. With the aid of language, she can navigate with remarkably few props (becoming fewer still with development, until wholly internalized fantasizing—day-dreaming— emerges). She can transport herself anywhere in the world—real or imagined—that she is capable of conceptualizing. She can be a pilot, a computer programmer, a doctor, a poet, a mechanic, an aunt or grandfather; she can try out as many different occupational and other social roles as she is familiar with. The emergence of language as a basis for cognitive activity is thus the key to the development of play with the rules of social life (sociodramatic play).

Type V: Language Play

Children enjoy play with language just as they enjoy experimentation with the rules they are learning in any other concept area. Much of their play with language is directly related to their experimentation with social rules in sociodramatic play. In social play, they try out the expressions and use the questions, instructions and conversational dialogues they overhear in family and community life.

At certain periods, children can be observed to spend time trying out the forms of language themselves, the rules for how sounds are made, the rules of grammar, and the rules of how words represent meaning. Each of the three types of language play tends to become more prominent at different periods,

FIGURE 6–6
Types of play in infancy and early childhood. Type V: Language play.

those associated with the major language structures the child is preoccupied with learning. Thus babies play with vowel and consonant sounds in babbling, often starting during the first year; next they experiment with grammatical rules of word order, parts of speech (such as nouns and pronouns) and verb tense; and finally children play more with word and sentence meanings (such as what "now" means and how far "away" is). The distinctions are not always clear, however; and sound, grammatical, and meaning play are often intertwined once children have begun to learn words. For the first several years they are engaged in learning rule after rule about which word or expression means what, how to rhyme, and how to form plurals and verb tenses, regular and irregular in form.

Once past the babbling and single word stages, rhyming games, alliteration (six sloppy snakes), puns (the bear was bare) and similar forms of word play are activities which children enjoy with adults and playmates. Nursery rhymes and similar forms of poetry stressing patterns of sound are sources to draw on freely, but almost any poetry combines attention to sound, meaning, and grammar. Play with grammatical rules, the using of "hitted" when they are just discovering that "hit" is the correct form; and play with meaning, like calling a giraffe a hippopotamus, when they have just learned to recognize a giraffe, are both also enchanting to children.

Some children engage in play with language rules far more than others, usually a result of a combination of the richness and earliness of exposure to language and books, current parental and teacher interest, and the opportunity for solitary play. Of all the types of play, play with language is the least dependent on environmental props and most dependent on the continuing quality of conversational and literary stimulation by adults.

Play also develops in other related types of language forms, ranging from music, art, and dance activities to play with numbers and measuring things. All of these spring to life in any home or day care setting of reasonable quality, often separately in different corners of a playroom, and sometimes woven into sociodramatic play. But, like language play, none of them become major interests or major skills in early childhood except in homes, preschools, or day care centers that value them highly.

7 Toys and Materials: The Physical Basis for Concepts

A variety of examples

Children's play is influenced as much by the form of materials as by the child's purposes in play. The cognitive classification of play reviewed in the last chapter in fact derives to an important degree from interactions between the nature of materials and the structure of our mental processes as developed through experience. In this chapter we shall discuss dimensions of children's play determined by the physical nature of materials. Since many materials illustrate more than one concept, we shall consider freely how the structures of various materials influence learning rules for concepts in actual play situations.

159

Excursions - direct observation of vegetable farm and canning factory

Sociodramatic play of canning factory

Growing their own vegetables

FIGURE 7-1
Sample coordinated theme activity program: Growing and canning vegetables.

Sociodramatic versus Nonsocial Forms of Play

Play at almost any age occurs in relation to the approval and patterns of others (peers or adults). The uses of toys are planted in the social meanings defined by the culture in which we are socialized. The rug or rattle the baby first explores, and the blocks and paint the nursery school child uses to create new things, are all made by people. Even the plants and trees in a school yard are usually planted according to landscape designs. Only the wilderness is apart from human social life.

Certain activities, nevertheless, are *primarily* socially oriented in theme. Others, such as exploring household objects, working puzzles, modeling clay, while *utilizing* social objects and often relating to social themes, concentrate the child's play upon the nature of the materials and the structure of physical tasks and concepts. As development proceeds, all sorts of tasks are frequently interwoven in sociodramatic play.

The first signs of social interactive play are the smiling, vocalizing, and finger play babies engage in through the stimulus of others in the family. These become more complex as children develop; for example, they become fascinated with the mother's vanishing and reappearing face in "peek-a-boo" games. Soon they come to imitate some of these actions themselves, but with little more than one- or two-step, instrumental actions (pat-a-cake, fingers over eyes for peek-a-boo, feeding a doll) until the dawning of symbolic activity. This process fosters sociodramatic activity in a wide diversity of imaginative play.

Once the process is launched, there is a slow extension over the toddler period in the number of elements and events that can be included. The child begins to initiate dramatic play alone, then to initiate and respond in imaginary situations with peers. Eventually, older preschoolers are able to sustain, ver-

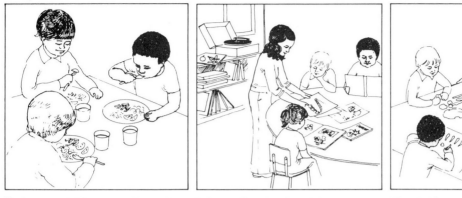

Eating vegetables grown from the garden

Information books, pictures, records, and stories on growing and canning.

Vegetable growing and canning themes in art work

FIGURE 7-1 continued.

bally define, and comment on an ongoing sociodrama with several children. A little girl might, for instance, play out the role of TV repair person for 20 minutes or more, saying what she and her assistant should do, commenting on what the problem is ("This wire is broken," or "It needs a new tube") and discussing with the owner such things as payment, removal, and when it will be ready.

The development of diversity and complexity in dramatic play depends on many things, including the range of social and occupational role materials available (the kitchen utensils and appliances, the tools and work clothes of various trades) and the child's opportunities to observe and participate in social life in the home and community. Does she ever visit the office or factory where her parents work, or at least get taken to stores, gas stations, offices, truck depots, and sports events to see all the types of work and other activities adults do? How much value do the adults she knows give to emotional expression and social relations? Boys in the patriarchal (father dominated) traditions of Western (and many other) societies are generally channeled into the mechanics of the physical world. These trends are reflected in their play preferences for instrumental and construction activities, to the relative exclusion of certain free form activities like painting and clay (which are sometimes mistakenly viewed as the only forms of creative and expressive activity) and sociodramatic play. The opposite trend persists for girls.

The home is often limited in its capacity to set up a systematic program of visits to community work and play activities and different ethnic neighborhoods, or even to guide children in play with an array of suitable props. Day care and nursery school institutions, on the other hand, can easily schedule regular community visits, providing the details of how people actually work, live, and amuse themselves in different cultural settings, which the child might otherwise know only from the distorted stereotyping of mass media (especially television). In contrast to the multiple role demands upon parents (work, cooking, house cleaning, chauffering, child care, relations with spouse, etc.) the overall role of group care institutions is education and care. They usually have far more play space and learning materials, and the presence of one of the most potent aids to dramatic play, many children.

The *material basis for dramatic play* originates in three sources: the pool of ideas children bring from their homes and neighbourhoods; observations during community excursions; and the guidance and play props and facilities available in the center itself. Standard nursery school practice has long overstressed the definition of social play as woman's traditional domestic role (household) activities, encouraged only a limited range of professional and skilled occupational activities (postmen, doctors, firemen), and ones that are often highly aggressive in theme (soldiers, cowboys and Indians, police). Thus, social play has tended to be sexually segregated, social class biased, and ethnocentric, as well as too often limited by the lack of imaginative guidance and stimulating play facilities.

Program components for rich imaginative play need to embrace experiences with a variety of ethnically and culturally different groups—even where, as in suburbs segregated by discriminatory living practices or in isolated rural regions, fewer direct contacts with varied social groups can be arranged than in urban, cosmopolitan areas. Picture books, stories and discussions are important substitute experiences when different ethnic communities are not accessible. Early and comprehensive socialization of children in cultural pluralism (familiarity with and respect for different peoples) is essential to break the historical bases of racism, sexism, and ethnocentrism that permeate much of the world. This practice can help each child to become more familiar with his or her own cultural practices and be proud of them while also developing in each child a positive attitude towards other cultural groups.

A planned *program cycle* of activities in group care will greatly expand the development of children's sociodramatic play. Settings that follow these methods will produce very different children from schools that follow culturally stereotypic programs with limited excursions and plan little or no diversity in guidance, materials and facilities. A program cycle may be composed of several types of activities that follow a planned *theme* selected for a time span of two or three weeks or more. In the following illustration of sea life and transportation, stimulation and play activities may proceed more or less concurrently as shown in Table 7–1.

Table 7–1 is elaborated to indicate the range of possibilities for two- to five-year-olds. The program can be adapted for children under two by shortening visits and simplifying the activities, visits, and types of comment and materials.

Several principles for reinforcing interest and enlarging understanding are employed, through providing coordinated experiences in several media and types of learning. Observations of the same scenes (in excursions) and the same picture stories are repeated several times to allow exploration of concepts in depth. The frequency of exposure to the same general theme, made possible by varying the activity over a several-week span, enhances the concentration of experience and the potential for concept mastery. Guidance is crucial for selecting and explaining key features in both the natural environ-

TABLE 7-1. Coordinated program for sea life and transportation theme

Excursions	Dramatic Play	Pictures and Stories	Creative-Construction Play
1. *Place:* Waterfront-harbor area, on ships, in boats, boating-yacht clubs, museums, fishing areas.	1. *Setting:* Rearrange a special play area in school with a fresh set of props (e.g., blocks stacked to represent mast, hold, and bridge of ship, etc.; drawing or picture of ship posted on wall background; a barometer, ship's clock, compass, helm; things (e.g., Tinker Toy rods, papier-maché) to represent masts, loading booms; sailor hats, work dungarees).	1. *Materials:* Preselect books and sets of pictures that illustrate clearly ships, sailors, boats, and sea activities. Dramatic stories of boats and ships, as well as simple descriptions of sea life and harbor activities. *Review* same stories and sets of pictures several times.	1. *Materials:* The usual drawing and painting materials, clay, building blocks (table, small unit and large hollow blocks); collage material that includes sea and ship items.
2. *Frequency:* One to two excursions per week. Where possible, repeat visits to settings to reinforce experiences.	2. *Frequency:* Plan time for activity every nonexcursion day, beginning with the day following first trip.	2. *Frequency:* One session almost every day during theme period; occasional sessions later on to encourage further interest in dramatic and creative play.	2. *Frequency:* Available each day if possible.
3. *Guidance:* 1 adult (teachers, aids, parents) for 2–5 children). *Answering questions. Comments* timed to fit close observation of specific activities (e.g., anchoring, docking, unloading, sailing, driving fork lift truck, etc.). Single out *people working* in different roles and tasks. Discussions on return from each trip.	3. *Guidance:* At beginning and at low or conflict points of play, suggest themes and label a few props. Demonstrate and/or participate at some points. Assign and shift children in roles occasionally, e.g., crane boom operator, helmsman, fork lift operator, oarsman, ship's cook; be sure to assign *both* girls and boys to *all* roles. Especially after initial assignments, encourage children to set up own physical arrangements. Encourage four or five children to play together in a small group.	3. *Guidance:* Point to and talk about pictures, involving children through asking them to find and describe items and activities depicted. Read and discuss stories.	3. *Guidance:* Usual supervision. For some activities, place children in small groups (4–6 children) in same area or around a table; suggest a theme and subthemes for entire group to work on, such as, "We're going to draw (make in clay, build, etc.) what we saw (the ships, fishing, harbor, etc.) yesterday."

ments and in pictures. It is also often essential for initiating and sustaining play activities until, after several such program cycles, many of the children will have attained relatively self-propelled and imaginative levels of functioning. Good arrangement and rotation of simple play materials designed to suit the theme of the cycle is an equally stimulating component of the program.

Macrosphere—Microsphere

Play varies according to the scale of the materials used in the activities. At one extreme, the microsphere, all materials are in miniature, of a size easy for small hands to handle. In this scale the child looms as a giant in a world of small buildings, roads, walks, etc., populated with small figures of people, animals, trees, vehicles, and other social objects proportioned to a size easily arranged and controlled. At the other extreme, the child works with materials more nearly proportional to the *macrosphere* of a child-size world. In this realm, the child is not restricted to constructing and manoeuvering objects (on this scale, the large building (hollow) blocks and social objects like kitchen utensils and steering wheels). Children can also personally act and interrelate with their peers in the macrosphere.

This large difference in scale produces fundamentally different forms of play. In the microsphere only the miniature figures and other objects are employed dramatically, while, in macrospheric play, the children themselves act out the various parts of the play, the movements, conversations, and facial expressions of family members, dancers, scientists or repair people, according

Giants in the Microsphere   The Reality of the Macrosphere

FIGURE 7–2
Differences in scale in children's construction and sociodramatic play.

to the character of the scene. On the other hand, the toy replicas and construction materials (e.g., small unit blocks) in the microsphere are generally more varied and refined, permitting more elaborate building and play activities than in the macrosphere. For children, the world of the macrosphere can perhaps more readily simulate reality as they imagine it, since they can physically perform gestures and interact with others to experience social phenomena at first hand. The demands and expressions of co-operation or anger by others toward each child's own efforts and feelings lend a quality to the experience that probably deepens a child's understanding of the rules for coping in real life situations.

Intimate involvement and development of sociodramatic play is by no means absent in the microsphere. There is opportunity to interact—though less physically—and as many parts and scenes for the miniature replicas of people to play as there are in large-scale sociodrama. In fact, the difficulty of simulating situations with materials in the large scale often means that play in the microsphere encompasses a greater range of community settings. It is expensive to make replicas of ships, airplanes, and animals on a child-size macrospheric scale, while small figures and construction materials are found in the market in abundance and variety. Because miniature creatures and scenes appear more removed from life, the child usually feels freer to express socially tabooed feelings and actions in his play. Fantasy is offered a greater scope, since all the participants recognize that "hitting" or "wounding" a doll really does no injury to anyone.

Each sphere has its advantages. What the microspheric play may gain in depth of expression and scope for the imagination is unmatched by the social reality of dramatic play in the macrosphere. The diversity and ease of manipulation of materials for physical construction tends to lead to a greater proportion of time in physically creative processes in the microsphere, while building processes usually move quickly to sociodramatic performances in the macrospheric world.

Sometimes the two worlds blend into one another, combining operations from each category. Constructing small buildings, roads and other landmarks of a community setting in the microsphere, accompanied by placement and manipulation of miniature figures and vehicles, may at some point incorporate a social dimension that involves the children physically as actors. Someone may start taking tickets for a toy train, which then prompts another child to act as gatekeeper for children to pass through some barrier he establishes. Manipulating toy animals may involve making first animal noises and then animal movements. The play may move in and out of focus at the two levels or even proceed in parallel for a period.

Skilled teaching can stimulate these variations in sociodramatic play without inhibiting the reality of the children's imagination. There are techniques for suggesting ideas and channeling play in a balanced way that will not cause it to die from too much intrusion nor let it descend into chaos from too little. The direction of play in each sphere can be regulated by the choice of materials, the setting, and the types of children who are introduced into the play situation, as discussed in Chapter 9 on guiding free play activities. Microspheric play on a table, on a small rug, or in a confined corner of the room is likely to retain its miniature focus more than play in the center of an extensive floor area. There are, moreover, at least two sizes of blocks, vehicles, and replicas of animals and people in miniature. One, on the scale of the standard ($2^{11}/_{16}$ by $2^{11}/_{16}$ by $1^{5}/_{16}$ inches) small unit block system is, together with accompanying replicas, designed for floor play. The other, of even smaller blocks and replicas, is more suitable for confined table play areas. Sets of multi-shaped blocks that come in boxes and various small Leggo and other interlocking construction materials fit a table setting well.

Within these categories there can be further variations. Some toy vehicles adapt equally well for either unit blocks or table blocks, but the smaller "Match Box" vehicles fit better in a table play environment. Very large (sometimes 18″ or more in length) dump trucks and fire engines often only work well near a sand box or in a gross motor activity setting. They are really too large for unit block microspheric floor play, tending to divert the creative development of the play, yet are also frequently too small for the physical scale of the macrosphere.

In both spheres, a broad selection of materials placed on shelves in sets will do a great deal to stimulate interesting and imaginative cognitive learning variations in construction and sociodramatic play. The accompanying Table 7–2 illustrates a few common materials by categories suitable for use in the two scales of play. They need not be presented in single categories. Play will follow a course according to the type and arrangement of the items selected.

The Material Basis of Fine Sensorimotor Object (Nonsocial) Play

Irrespective of whether objects employed in play are natural or social in origin, or whether the play involves social behavior, much of any play consists of manipulations of materials. The general structure of these manipulations has been outlined in the previous chapter. Within this framework we can further identify many different principles ordering children's perceptual-motor play, some of which form distinct systems of cognitive functioning and all of which concern specific cognitive rules about the structure of things. Some toys, for instance, teach rules about spatial fitting (such as form boards and jigsaw puzzles); but one set (form boards) usually deals specifically with rules about geometric forms, while the other (jigsaw puzzles) encompasses a broad range of rules for fitting things according to free-form curves and the shapes of objects.

In this section we shall present a rough classification of the *design characteristics* of sensorimotor play materials according to the concepts they serve to develop. We shall be concerned more with the *perceptual-cognitive rules inherent in the forms of materials and tasks* (concepts of the physical world required in using the material or performing the task) than with their value for sociodramatic play and learning. It is useful to stress that direct experience with these materials will not automatically lead to development of skills and concepts. The guidance of experienced people through demonstrations and explanations is needed. Concept learning is greatly advanced by combining guidance with plentiful self-guided experimentation through play.

TABLE 7-2. Common types of sociodramatic[a] and supportive play materials

I. Construction Materials	Microsphere[b]	Macrosphere
Modular	Cubes (plain and colored) Unit blocks Variable shape and color blocks (including stone blocks) Tinker toys, building bricks, and similar materials easily constructed to resemble many different structures stimulating sociodramatic play.	Large, hollow unit blocks (hard wood and cardboard) Unit construction boards Saw horses and portable walls Cardboard cartons for building (empty, sealed, 12-bottle cases of comparable sizes) Miscellaneous modular and free-form construction materials (blocks, interlocking building materials, clay, paints, etc.).
Free form	Play dough (to stimulate cooking activities) (Clay, crayons, paints, sand, etc., are better used in a separate context, although they stimulate imaginary constructions and social situations).	
II. Representational Materials		
Objects	*Miniature Replicas* Animate figures (Animals, plants, dolls, humans, puppets—including multi-cultural and imaginary figures) Household items (furniture, appliances, utensils, etc.) Food Clothes (ordinary and occupational) Transportation (vehicles, boats, planes) Community objects (stores, docks, gas pumps, street signs, etc.) Occupational tools and equipment (construction, postman, doctor, plumber, etc.)—real and simulated Farm materials (tools, agricultural equipment, buildings, animals) Play money (paper and coins—perhaps including real pennies) Other common objects (watches, pencils, erasers, etc.). *Small Pictures* (or drawings) of individual objects, especially of difficult to obtain replicas.	*Child-size Replicas or Nonhazardous Real Objects* Includes most categories of microsphere, excluding human and animal replicas because social interaction between children is paramount Items from many categories will need to be constructed by teachers and children because of cost and other limitations of commercial materials, coupled with the need for variation and the educational value of construction experience Items can be constructed of cardboard cartons, cloth, signs, boards, etc.—painted to indicate salient features (e.g., face of gas pump gauge). *Large Pictures and Drawings.*

TABLE 7-2—(Continued)

I. Construction Materials	Microsphere[b]	Macrosphere
Scenes		*Child-size Replicas or Real Objects*
	Miniature Replicas	Includes most categories in microsphere. Many scenes may have less detail than microspheric representations in keeping with flexibility and homemade quality of construction
	Doll houses, tents, replicas of different sorts of housing	
	Community buildings and settings (stores, gas stations, railroad stations and track systems, airports, construction sites, factories, dock areas, apartments, skyscrapers, etc.)	
	Communities (suburbs, ghettos, business sections, cities, small towns)	Natural environments used more for science observation than for sociodramatic play
	Natural environments (ponds, woods, etc.): mockup or miniature table scenes (aquaria and terraria)	
	Small Pictures (or drawings) of similar scenes.	*Large Pictures and Drawings.*
III. Supportive Play Materials	Selected Manipulative and Prop Materials	Selected Manipulative and Prop Materials
(To add perceptual diversity; to stimulate imagination in simulation for social play; to expand spatial problem solving)	(Real objects—small scale) Boxes and containers of all shapes and colors—scaled to size of microsphere Hardware and electrical gadgetry Pieces of cloth and paper (all colors and shapes) Miscellaneous objects (marbles, pieces of wood, pebbles, twigs, beads, spools, string, empty paper rollers, etc.).	(Real objects ranging in size from miniature to full size, depending on play utility. Similar sets to microsphere.

a Infants (younger than two) will in general exhibit less elaboration, persistence, and role interaction in dramatic play; materials and expectations should therefore be simpler, fewer and smaller (e.g., large hollow blocks and standard floor play unit blocks are generally too heavy and unwieldy for children under 18 months; it is helpful for representational materials to be designed more realistically (functional features should be clear), though without too many details (because infants lack experience), and more sturdily.

b Microsphere embraces two types of areas, the focused table and small rug area play and the relatively more extended floor play areas; materials should be scaled slightly smaller for the former than for the latter.

All materials may be typed according to rules intrinsic to (built into) their design. A toy or set of materials may be patterned to include more than one concept, as nesting cups illustrate rules of circularity, containment, fit, and serial order, among other things. Materials may also be used in ways that are extrinsic to (outside) their designed functions in loose sorting, piling, or mixing activities, and of course may be used symbolically to serve sociodramatic play, as for instance when a child uses a nesting cup for a coffee cup or a form board shape as a biscuit. It is useful for teachers to focus frequently on rules intrinsic to the form of the material, but it is better not to restrict children to using particular materials only according to their designed concept functions, as in the original Montessori approach. Children will tend to use materials as they were designed to be used because rules are built into materials. It is this characteristic of toy design that makes it easier to teach children concepts about how the physical world is structured. Using the same materials flexibly in other ways some of the time fosters the development of imagination.

Our system of rule classification will be analyzed in two ways. I shall review a number of *major dimensions* of play materials that broadly influence the form of children's play, such as specific purpose versus open structure, design versus content, and complexity of structure. At the same time, I shall discuss concepts inherent in designs of representative toys, such as how the concept of containment appears in using nesting cups, and modularity and verticality appear in using building blocks. The combined scheme is outlined in a chart in Appendix C (a Toy Curriculum), which shows a list of major concepts intrinsic to various types of toy designs.

Some Cognitive Rules Intrinsic to Toy Design: Major Dimensions

Specific Purpose versus Open-ended Materials

A large number of play materials, both professionally and commercially conceived, channel activity into specific tasks by their design. In contrast, there is another major group that encourages a broad range of activities, definite in form but open as to outcome.

The first category comprises means-ends linked devices, such as peg and form boards, number pegs, and jigsaw puzzles, that are constructed to produce the type of instrumental activity described in Chapter 6 on play. Although they sometimes permit alternative pathways, every pathway in the same toy leads to a common solution, a single, preconceived form. The second category, on the other hand, comprises sets of materials that can realize an indefinite number of outcomes. "Finished" structures are determined by the imagination of the builder interacting with rule constraints of the material, which are broad *principles of organization,* rather than rules defining courses to follow to complete a particular structure. This open structure material leads to the construction-creative activity also described in Chapter 6 on play, and includes modular block or other multiple unit construction materials, such as unit blocks, hollow blocks, bricks, stone blocks, geometric shapes, and collage; moldable materials, such as clay, play dough, and wet sand; and surface diffusable materials, such as those used for painting and drawing.

The learning potentials of the two categories cannot really be compared, since they are, for the most part, totally different. The first category brings into focus no more than a few highly specific rules about environmental structures and what can be done with them, such as fitting round—not square—things into round holes. Means and ends are very simple, precise and closely related. The second category may, at first glance, also appear to be based on no more than a few simple rules (marking paper or paint with crayon or brush, or fitting and piling blocks), but in fact the particular way of shaping or assembling

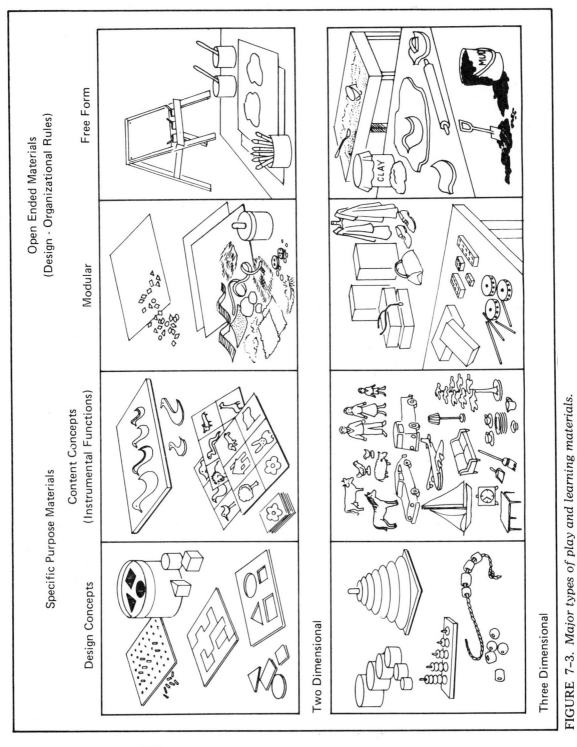

FIGURE 7-3. *Major types of play and learning materials.*

materials is secondary to other more general rules for creating structures. Blocks and other modular materials can be linked in different ways (inserted or placed flat against one another) to construct varied structures built according to many general rules (verticality, enclosure, bridging). Similarly, the specific rules of molding, shaping, and painting are simple, but again they are secondary to the many rules possible for structuring forms within the framework of the elementary rules of the medium.

Both categories of rules are important to knowledge and cognitive processing. The child who fails to learn a rich repertoire of specific rules about how the world connects together in very particular forms (who does not understand roundness or insertion) is as handicapped as the child who cannot integrate particulars to create new structures and forms. Broad syntheses and creations can be only as complex, as scientifically meaningful, or as aesthetically appealing as the specific rules with which we are capable of dealing will allow. We cannot combine or create with forms if we are ignorant of their particular spatial rules. A little girl cannot, for instance, build *any* structures with tinker toys—let alone imaginative ones—until she has mastered specific rules and skills about roundness and insertion. These concepts are probably easier to learn with simple form boards, where the rules about how round things fit in round slots are first isolated in closed tasks without distracting clutter, and with an easier fit and simpler design than tinker toy rods and knob holes. In the same way, engineers must learn the rules by which concrete and steel can be used to construct buildings, musicians the rules for manipulating musical notes and phrases to compose symphonies, and painters the rules for applying paint to paint pictures.

Modular (Multiple Unit) versus Free-Form Pliable (Moldable) Materials

Toys and materials in the open-ended category are of two kinds: modular and free form.

Modular materials have two basic characteristics in common: they are composed of discrete, rigid forms (modules) designed in multiples of fixed units of measurement; and they can be formed into complex structures which are rigid but vary in structure according to definite rules. Units may not all be alike, but units of different size are generally exact multiples of some basic and discrete unit of measurement. For example, tinker toy rods come in multiples of a basic one inch length, and unit blocks are multiple lengths of a basic unit of approximately $1\frac{1}{4}$ by $2\frac{1}{2}$ by $2\frac{1}{2}$ inches, namely, in lengths of about $2\frac{1}{2}$ inches, 5 inches, 10 inches, and so on.

Free-form materials, including surface diffusable (two dimensional) types, consist of materials that can be shaped, with no standard, prearranged unit of measurement. Because clay takes the shape it is given in molding, its unit of measurement is completely variable from one situation to the next, according to the wishes of the molder. The principles free-form construction follows to realize a structure are those of changing shape to achieve a form and coherence of material. Since there is no fixed standard of measurement, the problem of maintaining size consistency in shaping a form is technically more difficult than with rigid construction, modular materials.

Differences between materials are not just limitations, but types of freedom they offer to create some things but not others. Each material is a *medium* that has its own rules that determine what can and cannot be done. Basically, modular construction and free-form materials demonstrate two primary ways in which matter is organized and measured. The former is based on discrete (separate) units of noncontinuous matter like blocks or tinker toy rods, with measurement prearranged in an imposed standard unit (such as inches or centimeters). Unlike continuous (free form) material, measurement is integral to the nature of noncontinuous material and the purposes of the creator. Modular materials may be likened to oranges, marbles, and stones; free-form materials to earth and water.

The processes of creation follow different courses in the separate materials. Modular principles are essentially additive, adding fixed pieces (units) to build up a structure. The final size of the structure (as well as its shape) is not attained until the structure is completed. Free-form creation, on the other hand, often ends up with an object about the same size as the mass of material with which one started. For example, bits of clay may be added on, once the original blob of clay is roughly shaped, but the technique consists more of shaping an amorphous mass than adding pieces—which in any case must then also be shaped.

Free-form creation is probably better defined as a combined shaping and additive process, while modular creations can only be formed by adding on processes, since the unit materials themselves cannot be altered in shape. Adding on and building up processes play a more prominent part with free form materials other than clay; for example, wet sand. Children commonly make additions to their initial sand building and tunnel system, partly because there is usually a large inexpensive supply right at hand. The inferior sticking properties of sand also lead the activity into building more extensively than into the refined shaping of forms that clay permits.

Surface diffusable materials, like those used in painting and drawing (essentially two-dimensional media), are even more characterized by building up processes than wet sand, though the shaping process remains free form. A picture is formed by painting a stroke at a time, variable in width, length, consistency, color, though ultimately limited in final size by the area of the paper available. The total composition of the finished painting, moreover, typically bears some relation to the surface area and shape of the paper.

Since modular construction makes use of fixed, standardized and easily separable components, one of its learning values centers on rules about relations among and between parts and wholes, which are well defined in modular building. One can readily put together, take apart, and even copy or reassemble any toy brick or block building, and substitute and restore parts of the same or different dimensions with little difficulty. The fixed part (unit) rules for modular construction are difficult to duplicate in free form materials, which are more concerned with how things flow (rather than fit) together to make the whole. In the finished free-form clay figure or painting, for example, the whole is often more organically integrated and many parts run together to lose some visible identity (though somewhat less in crayon and pencil line drawings).

The remainder of the major cognitive rule dimensions of materials we shall discuss cut across the foregoing distinctions between and within specific purpose and open-ended materials and tasks. Each of them interrelates for the most part, moreover, with all of the others, but will be discussed separately for purposes of clarification. There are other distinctions which can be identified, such as the size, weight, color, and structural unity of materials; many of these will be mentioned in the context of what are felt to be the more overriding dimensions.

Complexity of Structure

The complexity of children's play is bound to be affected by the complexity of the materials to which they have access, although the uses to which materials are put will obviously develop with experience and general cognitive development.

Toys vary in complexity in several major ways, among them (1) irregularity of shape and color; (2) number of parts; (3) size of parts; (4) the intricacy of interrelations among parts, including the types of connecting mechanisms (hooks or snaps) and the degree of hierarchical ordering (pieces in the center of a jigsaw puzzle cannot be placed before certain edge pieces); and (5) toughness of the parts and interconnecting mechanisms (for example, snaps or zippers may stick). In general, the greater the irregularity, the greater the number of distinguishable parts, the more interrelations among parts, and the greater the intricacy of interconnections, the more complex the material. Toys with either tiny or enormous parts present special problems of fine or gross perceptual-motor control and visual perspective. Solidly attached or complex parts may demand special strength (tough snaps) or the use of tools (hammer or screwdriver). Toys with many permanently attached parts make less demands than toys with a few parts designed to dismantle and reassemble. A mechanical toy may be intricately designed but not be intended to come apart the way a wooden tractor held together with five big wooden bolts and nuts is.

Complexity must always be evaluated in the context of the uses to which a toy is likely to be put by an age and skill range. A miniature road roller with many pieces is, for the preschooler, usually a toy to explore and operate, not an interesting object to take apart or modify by attaching a wire hook to tow a car as a school age child might do. Complex uses and tricky mechanisms (for example, a wind-up toy or a rubber band-driven airplane) cannot be exploited as well by younger children.

Various features and mechanisms of materials make them difficult in different ways. Peg boards and handles on toys may be too small for an infant's motor skills, but a knob that is much larger may be too complex because it requires the concept of turning a knob in a constant direction, which the infant lacks. Screws, nuts, screwdrivers and all such single-direction turning devices are difficult to master before the preschool period. Size, weight, and strength required are additional complicating aspects, as in building with large, heavy, hollow wooden blocks or large wooden boards, or in performing carpentry tasks. The child's general knowledge may also influence his or her success. Two sets of puzzles may be equally complex (may have the same number of pieces with similar interlocking mechanisms), but the one with unusual pictures will present more problems for the same child to solve.

Naturally, we should vary the complexity of jigsaw puzzles and other specific-purpose, problem-solving toys with the child's competencies. On the other hand, a complicated miniature replica of an animal or of a crane with moving parts may have value even for an infant, even though she is not capable of experimenting with all of the toy's uses. As long as a toy can be used in some interesting way appropriate to the child's age, and will not injure the child easily or come apart at the wrong moment, and if the child is not expected to learn beyond her level, an intricate design frequently offers an enriched framework for learning more details and labels. Not everything is learned with equal depth.

Although open-ended materials vary in complexity of design, they do not present as complex a structure as do specific-purpose, instrumental toys. Puzzles and other fixed-solution, problem-solving toys focus on tasks that lead the child into predefined cognitive activity graded in difficulty by the complexity of design. Jigsaw puzzles and toys put together by screws, for example, generally come in graded series so that children can progress in steps from simple to successively more complex examples. With modular materials and free form materials, on the other hand, the child must design his or her own structure, and thereby controls task complexity to a considerable degree. Simple cubes and blocks can be placed in rows and towers by older infants, but more elaborate structures must await the development of more skill.

Free-form materials are even less bound by structural rules that require high skill levels. Clay can be molded, and paint and crayon smeared in some manner, long before the child learns to create structures on some intentional basis. This is one of the particular values of open-ended, and especially free-form, materials; they are useful regardless of age and skill. Fewer teaching errors will be made if these materials are properly prepared, however, and if a friendly and constructive play environment is established. Even free-form materials can be worked only according to certain structural rules which take time to learn and which produce more satisfying and complex creations as mastery of the rules becomes refined. For example, only one end of a brush holds paint; wide and narrow brushes produce different effects; clay must be soft and in small pieces before it can be rolled by the young child. In these and all other play and problem solving activities, play will have a greater value if the materials and tasks are selected to fit the developmental competencies of the children.

Two Dimensional versus Three Dimensional Materials

Many of the types of play materials that are found in three dimensional form have their counterparts in two dimensional form. Both puzzles and open-ended construction and creative materials can be found in both two- and three-dimensional form. Certain specific-purpose puzzle materials are *not* represented in two-dimensional form. Assembly mechanisms and structural concepts that can only be operated in three-dimensional space obviously have no counterpart in two dimensional materials. Among such structural toys are shape *interrelating mechanisms,* such as rings-on-pegs, peg boards, screw-bolts, and rod-in-hole connections (like tinker toys); *containment principle* toys, like nesting cups, dolls, and boxes, drawer or lid opening apparatus, and form insert boxes; and *interlocking mechanisms,* like latches, hooks and eyes, buttons, zippers, snap-on toys, padlocks, and barrel bolts. The rules belonging to the structure of these materials are intrinsically those of a three-dimensional world. One cannot, for example, insert any form in a container that has no depth.

In the realm of construction and creative materials as well, many structural principles cannot be displayed on a flat plane. Some represent *the fact of a third dimension* in a structure, the qualities of thickness, depth, volume, space, mass, and various sculptured qualities. *Construction rules* that involve balance and the effects of gravity and weight distribution, like bridging, cantilevering, and centering, also cannot be demonstrated without a third dimension. Similarly, the problems of the friability (tendency to crumble) of plaster, or sand erosion, have no place in painting and drawing which, for practical purposes, have no depth.

There are two comprehensive differences between the rule systems defining the structures of two- and three-dimensional worlds. The first and the most general is the fact that the principles of organization for two dimensions relate to surface area problems of flat plane design, and for three dimensions to problems of mass, space, and volume. The second concerns the matter of representing objects, of coding real objects like clocks or trees in some simplified form. For two-dimensional materials this means representing things in pictures or diagrams; for three-dimensional materials this means representing things either by using the object itself (when, like a coin, it is convenient to handle) or by making some three-dimensional replica of the object, as a toy truck or animal. Since the essential coding rules for pictorial and object representation are covered in Chapter 2, we need only point out here the importance of teachers' keeping in mind the different rules to aid them in guiding children in looking at pictures and using replicas. We shall also illustrate a few play materials which make use of pictorial coding rules, as well as design concepts on a flat plane.

Surface area materials are designed and used in two dimensions by using rules about color; those about points, single lines vertically, horizontally, diagonally, and straight, zigzag, curved, broken; rules for geometric organization in two dimensions (circles, ovals, squares, triangles); such constructing principles as building and taking apart and adding and subtracting parts (as in mosaics); and various other pattern or organization rules like repetition (of points, curves, parallel lines, concentric circles), balance (one side of a puzzle doesn't have all the parts) and part-whole relations including subsystems, (two or three parts of a jigsaw puzzle fit together to make a picture of a trailer which is connected by a single piece (a tow bar) to three or four more pieces that make up the truck). All of these rules are structural counterparts of the rules of a total space world; for example, circles and squares in form boards are like cylinders (or spheres) and cubes in shape sorting boxes. There are no rules of surface area that are not encompassed in three-dimensional structures, since area organizations are based on two of the three dimensions, but there are, as we have already indicated, additional design rules that the third dimension makes possible.

Flat plane play materials do incorporate a third dimension (no material basis is possible without it), but the thickness involved merely gives the materials substance, and does not allow use as a third dimension. Painting and drawing pictures involve surface design problems and collage employs spatial arrangements of flat forms far more often than they involve building upward from the flat surface of the paper. When construction on a surface is employed, the medium changes to include rules for a third dimension, as in dealing with problems of constructing walls and a roof for a miniature building and gluing them onto a city scene drawn on a slab of cardboard. Although geometric construction puzzles, flannel board materials, jigsaw puzzles, and form board inserts and slots often have thicknesses ranging from $\frac{1}{16}''$ to as much as $\frac{1}{2}''$, it is still by the rules of linear and areal (flat surface) fit and arrangement that the tasks are structured, not by those of dimensional depth and organization. The match in a form board is, for instance, between the two-dimensional surface values of a triangle and a hexagon with the *areal contours* of the triangular and hexagonal slots, not with the depth of the holes. Depth (or thickness), in other words, is used only to give substance to make handling easier, to anchor the insert form, to provide physical feedback, but not because the child builds out or matches in a third dimension—though the child is involved in rules of spatial fit and partial containment (because the form fits part way into a hole).

Design versus Content

Not every piece of play material includes content—that is, represents some common object—by its design, but no toy can be made without some form. Learning about the form and functions of physical matter is, as we have repeatedly observed, what much of children's play and learning is all about. But just how does content differ from form?

We usually speak of *content* in the sense of a toy either (1) *representing* (symbolizing) something else, as a block with a picture of a horse or a letter on it, or (2) in terms of the *function* it is intended to serve. In the second case we probably include as content the parts of the toy that are shaped to perform functions, such as the prongs and handle of a toy rake. *Design* materials neither look like (represent) anything nor do they serve any instrumental function (*do* something). It is their *pattern* and organizational structures alone that are used, without regard to any instrumental function. Construction toys, geometric designs, non-pictorial form boards and assembly puzzles fall into this category.

It is in some ways convenient to recognize, however, that design toys *do* have a content, even apart from the way children often use them symbolically in sociodramatic play or functionally as when they construct a house with blocks. The *content of design toys* is to be found in the rules for how physical structures are designed and used, the rules for two- and three-dimensional materials of circularity, part-whole relations and so on, discussed above.

However, although obviously vital for children to learn, the formal structures of many play materials assume a different type of content, *separate from the nature of their structures,* when they are used to represent some natural or human-made thing. In this case the construction follows various design rules to make parts of the toy serve particular representations or instrumental functions. The circular rule is applied to make the wheels and steering wheel of a toy car; the cylindrical rule to make the axles and steering column; the enclosure rule to form the interior; and where parts are put together (e.g., axles fitted into hubs of wheels), insertion, locking and assembling rules are followed.

Content can thus be classified in several ways according to the fidelity with which the toy reflects real things. At one extreme, a toy may be a real object, such as a cup, a lamp or a table. If intended for children's use, the object is likely to be smaller in size but otherwise complete in functional detail. At the other extreme are highly condensed, abstract pictures and replicas of scenes or objects that distort or omit many features in the interests of stylization or summarization. Many children's picture books and even some miniature toys are constructed in just this way. Fish, for example, may be drawn simply as elongated diamonds, with a triangular indentation at one end for an open mouth, a triangle tacked on the other for the tail, and perhaps a plain circle for the eye, as in Figure 7–4. Children's toy figures (people, vehicles, animals) are typically constructed with many parts missing, few of the parts actually functioning (toy car headlights usually don't work), to say nothing of the fact that animal and people figures are not alive.

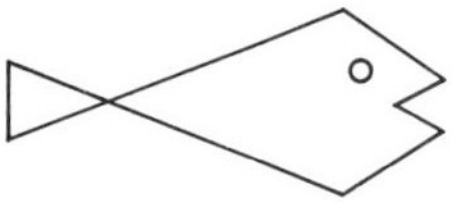

FIGURE 7–4

In between these two extremes are many combinations, but some *distinct types* can be identified. The difference between pictorial and three-dimensional replicas has been amply discussed, but there are also at least two distinct classes of replicas. In one, the copy is illustrative, informative, and designed perhaps for aesthetic or sensory purposes (a cuddly, furry bear or rabbit), but is not intended to be employed according to the functions of the original object. Pictures, obviously, all fall into this category, as do fragile porcelain figures that are meant to stand on shelves only to be admired. Many contemporary stamped-out plastic or metal toys are also so poorly made that they cannot be moved around (toy cars with immovable wheels and boats that cannot float). Similarly, abstract design toys, usually of wood and often designed with artistry, show only the vaguest contours of shape (a block for the shape of a truck) and one or two essential features (wheels and cab in simple block form). These items can at least be employed functionally in play, since the wheels will move like those of a truck to simulate travel along a road constructed of blocks. They are simplified for aesthetic and economic reasons but also with the intent of fostering sociodramatic play in the microsphere, rather than encouraging concentration on the instrumental functions of objects.

The other major class of toys is designed to develop interest and skill in the functions of things employed in the real world. Woodworking tools—saws, hammers and nails, screwdrivers and screws—are often examples of our first real objects used as toys. Older infants (18 months or more) can use well-designed, simulated tools of wood, to hammer wooden nails, screw wooden screws into precut holes, or turn wooden nuts with wrenches. Using genuine tools, preferably reduced in size, many three- to five-year-olds can learn to fabricate crude boat models, tables and boxes. At this level, instrumental play with tools is work in every sense except necessity. Toy tow trucks, dump and cement trucks, and station wagons with movable parts that operate effectively, and the whole world of domestic social role play equipped with doll carriages, baby clothes, washing machines, stoves that sometimes work are all also in this category of simulated adult instrumental activity.

Problems In Toy Design

Special Problems in the Design and Use of Content Dimensions in Play Materials

Because the two forms of play have quite different purposes, instrumental and sociodramatic play materials should, for the most part, be assigned to separate zones of a playroom. Instrumental play is useful for learning about the specific means-ends structures and functions of real life tasks. Materials designed for instrumental play should therefore be chosen and arranged in a setting in the playroom in a way that is more business-like to encourage specific task activity.

Sociodramatic activities thrive on props (including work tools) and arrangements that *suggest* but do *not* necessarily literally *represent* functions and details of the activities. Because the aims of sociodramatic play are far broader and are generally directed to encouraging fantasy expression, materials and settings that are too literal tend to anchor children in task reality rather than foster the elaboration of imaginative activities and social role relations. For example, a real monkey wrench is often too heavy and its parts so precisely made that it requires more skill than a four year old can manage—at least without diverting the child from the social aspects of the play. Tools and other props are usually only suggestively used (the child pretends to use them) as part of a series of actions incidental to carrying out the social dimensions of a role. The child wants to *appear to* carry pipes, screw them together with wrenches, talk about the problem, push buttons and do lots of things that show she is a plumber. The important task is not real plumbing repairs, however, but relating to others and imitating adult social role behaviors. For this reason, toys with a stylized structural design are usually better for socio-dramatic play than for instrumental learning.

Ambiguous Articulation of Parts

Many toys that are designed poorly simply because of cheap manufacture present a major problem of relating form to content. Stamped-out plastic toys (vehicles, boats, animal figures, dolls) often have features that are indistinguishable, a single unrealistic color (commonly garish and luminescent or washed-out and pastel) and no moving parts, thus adding very little to either the child's knowledge or his aesthetic development. Nor do they really serve sociodramatic play well. Few of their structures suggest any meaningful function, nor do they operate well; and they do not possess the social or aesthetic attributes intrinsic to the form of well-designed toys (there is often a diminutive, endearing quality in well-made little figures).

Materials

Plastic construction need not sacrifice instrumental realism or, according to purpose, good abstract design. Many modern plastics no longer suffer from easy destructibility (unlike, for instance, many metal cars) and are in some ways more adaptable to the articulation of form than either wood or metal, the traditional materials—though plastics may cost at least as much. There is no problem of color either. The general problem is simply to design materials and choose colors adequately in the first place. Plastics present *different* aesthetic possibilities, such as uniformity of high gloss, surface texture and dimensional precision in the hard variety, and pliability and color shading in the soft. There are well-designed form boards, nesting cups, and other precision toys of hard plastic; and good miniature replicas of people and animals of both hard and pliable plastic. In the end, it is probably preferable to continue to have access to the good—if different—design, structural, and aesthetic properties inherent in both wood *and* plastics (and other materials, old and new).

The one potentially serious problem with many hard plastics is their brittleness; because they break easily, often into pieces with sharp edges, their use needs more supervision. Obviously, all toys should be as sturdy as possible, but if sturdiness is made too dominant a criterion, qualities of aesthetic design and complexity needed for learning values will be sacrificed. Miniature metal vehicles may break easily (though with less risk of injury); toy tires and jigsaw puzzle pieces are easily lost; pages in picture books are readily torn and marred. Part of social learning is respect for order and materials. Some degree of fragility needs to be planned for, but this does not mean tolerating shoddy construction in toy manufacture.

Color Coding

Though widely used, color coding is inappropriate to the purposes of toys designed to teach dimensional concepts like those of size, form, or number. Stacking rings, nesting cups, size graded form boards, or Cuisenaire rods for pre-schoolers, for example, in which size gradations also vary in color, confuse color with size. The toddler tends to be drawn to the obvious difference in color between the objects, rather than the more abstract relational dimension of size. Since it is size we are trying to teach, the infant needs to have size stand out as the *only* characteristic by which the objects in a series vary.

Similarly, in form boards and other materials designed to teach geometric shapes, if every form and matching slot is colored differently the child has only to match concretely by color without learning much about the more complex rules about shape (angles, corners, curves, straight sides). Shape is less affected by color coding than size, however, (except for size graded form boards) because of the fitting principle of form board tasks. *Having* to fit each shape into a hole of identical shape provides an automatic correctional control (feedback) that signals the child when he is completing a task correctly. Using a separate color to set off all shapes and slots from a uniformly colored background of a form board or shape sorting box, or rings from pegs would be one way of using color effectively—but this is not color coding, since the shapes themselves (or size graded objects) vary only by the concept being taught, shape (or size).

Imprecise Shape Designs

Forms cut with loose fitting dimensions have both advantages and disadvantages. American designers, in contrast to Europeans, are inclined to construct geometric form boards with loose fits, and blocks with rounded corners and edges, presumably to reduce the risk of injury (particularly if blocks are thrown), but also because less precise fits are cheaper to manufacture. This

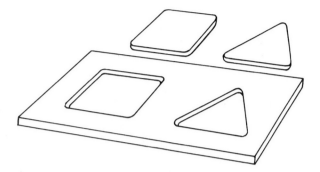

FIGURE 7-5

loose form board construction simplifies the task of fitting for the infant in the early stages of learning shape concepts, as shown in Figure 7-5. Because the shapes fit more easily, the child obtains knowledge of correct matches (feedback) more easily. Many designs are also built with the form board pieces raised slightly above the level of the form board to further ease problems of little hands placing and removing pieces.

Once preliminary skills are acquired, however, it is better to provide children with form boards and other sensorimotor materials, including blocks, with comparatively precise fits and exact dimensions. Rounded corners, edges, and planes only serve to retard the infant's understanding of the cognitive rules about angularity and flatness. Building with blocks of less than exact dimensions is a frustrating experience; structures topple more easily and intricate and aesthetically well-knit structures cannot be constructed because of the greater balancing and fitting problems. As for the possibility of injury, thrown objects of *any* shape are missiles, underscoring again that care involves supervision and that almost any learning involves the socialization of values and respect for both people and materials.

Graded Learning Designs (Sequencing)

Children learn shape concepts more easily when materials are graded in difficulty, the first board starting with a single form, a circle, to fit in one circular slot. Circular forms can be inserted in any orientation, while squares can only be inserted from four positions, equilateral triangles from three, rectangles from two, and any other triangle and asymmetrical figure from only one. If toys are well sequenced, babies well under a year can be started on form boards and other manipulative toys. As they develop skills with circles in a one slot board, two slot boards (still both circles) can be introduced, then a single slot board with a square, followed by a triangle, in a sequence something like that in Figure 7-6. At about the last step in this series, form boards varying in other combinations of shape (including irregular shapes) and number can be introduced, depending on how well the child's confidence and skill are developing. There are many form board designs but few sequential series, except in Montessori materials, few of which are sufficiently graded for beginners, particularly infants.

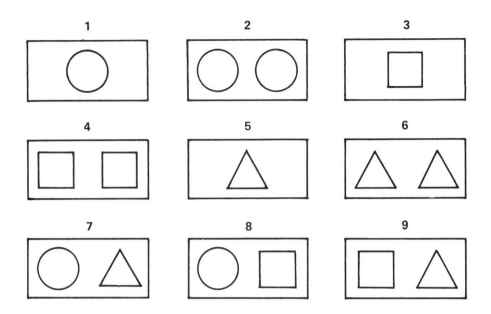

FIGURE 7-6

Distorted Social and Aesthetic Values

Commercial toy manufacturers frequently choose subjects for toy designs that are inappropriate for the age group or, more often, represent subjects thematically in questionable if not harmful ways. There is, in the first place, the widespread manufacture of war and war-related toys such as soldiers, tanks, warships, bombers and miniature replicas of weapons that all but shoot real missiles. The fact that a common soldier (GI Joe) has been developed and outfitted elaborately with removable uniform and equipment to adapt to the patterns of young children only makes the theme more insidious. The subject is aggression and killing, legitimized as a social form by obscuring its horrors.

Aggressive themes are not always so explicitly represented. Many dolls and animal figures on the commercial market portray human characteristics, often in caricature, in the form of competitive facial expressions and physical postures. Many cartoons (TV programs as well as movies) portray an endless contest, in which the protagonists make use of an endless variety of devices of physical violence. The fact that the theme is frequently developed through an underdog who wins through the superiority of his wiles only serves to justify physical violence and manipulative competition as a way of life. In many doll forms, the bold, brash postures and aggressive smiles are usually covered with a veneer of sweetness and sentimentality. There is a surface friendliness enhanced by bland or bright colors and cuddly furry textures that attempt to mask unrelieved individualism and meanness.

Pseudo-sentimental toy designs and *stereotyped social figures* are a second distorting tendency of toy manufacturers. There is a tendency to present all figures in idealized or at best completely bland forms without personality or emotional expression. Baby dolls, animal and family figures are pleasant and smiling, more often than not; doctors, letter carriers, police and other professional and service occupations acceptable to the world of social convention typically wear expressions of bland friendliness or exhibit a kind of masculine strength and goodness; women—who are seldom anything but members of a family, nurses, or possibly stewardesses—are feminine and sweet as well as friendly and wholesome. Such figures may not interfere with the child's attempts to create dramatic images and interrelations in play, but they are, among other things, biased against diversified development and do not serve to develop children's understanding of social life through encouraging more realistic and varied attitudes.

Without expecting low-cost, mass-produced figures to embody complex personality studies which, in any case, would be somewhat beyond the comprehension of most preschoolers, it should not be difficult to show some of the variation in the range of human emotions and attitudes that is found in real life. This would, for example, enable the child in play to select the doll figure who best represented his current mood or the feelings appropriate to the situation he is creating. Some of the depictions would remain stereotypes, but would at the same time impart some of the diversity of social living; children would be helped to recognize that mothers and mailpersons vary in their personality characteristics. Self-assertion and active striving, even mild anger (as distinct from the unrelieved arrogance and aggression of many cartoon characters) could be usefully portrayed, along with gentleness, sensitivity, fatigue, and many other characteristics. While aggression implies attack on others, anger is more of an emotional reaction to injury without necessarily implying attack.

Neither a uniformly optimistic nor a strongly violent approach to life helps children learn how to deal matter-of-factly with people as they are. The fact that the world is loaded with competition and violence is no argument for showing the extremes of realism or for making a uniform cover-up of sugar and cream. If our modes of socialization in preschool institutions are to have any justification, they need to reveal to the child a degree of realism and variation on a level that will stimulate but not undermine his ability to cope.

A third problem is the need for wider occupational and cultural selection in toys, books and other media. A great range of occupational types is essential. Factory workers, lawyers, storekeepers, union leaders, and architects should be shown, and somehow situationally linked to the characteristics of their working environments. Cultural diversity in toy figures and pictures—without stereotypic exaggeration—is obviously critical. Blacks have recently been more widely included in various children's media, but other minority peoples need more attention.

A fourth questionable value trend in children's toys is the sexualized doll syndrome, epitomized by the "Barbie" doll. It is not only that sexuality has been grafted on to dolls; it is the stereotypic concept of femininity and sexual titillation with which it is portrayed that is open to doubt. The sculpturing of the torso and legs emphasizes the sexual lure of teenage girls to the relative exclusion of their characteristics as persons. The nylon stockings and other items of dress further reinforce this concept of dainty, sexualized femininity.

As a model for preschool children, it not only prematurely thrusts them into the roles and problems of interpersonal sex play, it presents exaggerated images of girls as sex objects, only thinly covered by concepts of daintiness and niceness. As a model for girls and boys of any age it serves to perpetuate traditional values of sex-dominated roles for women, merely dressed up in modern form by the inclusion of sexuality. The male counterpart of Barbie, Ken, is as steeped in a highly overmasculinized style of cool, muscular tautness and arrogance, as Barbie is sexually feminized.

The presentation of doll figures in stereotypic sex-linked occupational and social roles, referred to earlier, is little better. Masculine and feminine stereotyping serves the traditions of male dominance, as well as narrowing social development of both boys and girls. At the very least, when occupational roles are ascribed to toy figures (or to pictures in children's books), women need to be shown in a variety of occupations to aid in breaking prejudices and barriers for women in the coming generations.

Gross versus Fine Motor Activities

Fine motor activity makes use of the hands and fingers primarily, with the body and arms employed as leverage and for postural purposes. Gross motor activity embraces the movements of the entire body apparatus. During gross motor play (and later in many physical sports), the refined control of fine motor actions come into play less often and only for certain tasks as secondary to whole body activity.

Cognitively, these differences implicate different worlds of physical and psychological space. Gross motor activities relate to the object world on a larger size scale (i.e., a world of larger objects) and the role of the physical self on the scene is both as actor and object to which the self orients. In fine motor activity, the smaller object world tends to generate the self picture of a "giant" on the scene. The distinction here is related to the one defining the microsphere and macrosphere in sociodramatic play, except that gross motor movements often serve only a secondary supportive role in sociodramatic play. Some of the sociodramatic play that develops on climbing apparatus, which stimulates children to imagine they are climbing mountains or traveling on space ships, is an exception.

The materials employed for gross motor play vary along the same dimensions we have described for fine motor play but also differently. Thus some equipment may be designed primarily for a specific use (such as seesaws, spring horses, suspended ropes or swings) or it may be more open ended, such as climbing apparatus, large building blocks, or an open area for running games. Except for building blocks, most of the apparatus tends to channel activities into specific skills to some degree, such as climbing, running, tumbling, or swimming. There are fewer types of manipulatable or modular gross motor play materials than fine motor materials, and almost no free-form gross motor materials (except perhaps snow sculpture or oversize sand sculpture). Gross motor play usually concentrates cognitively on the production of highly transient forms (sequences of body movements) using the body itself as the manipulated agent. Fine motor activity, on the other hand, is usually concerned with the manipulation and creation of external objects to produce relatively permanent structures. (Musical performance is an exception to this.) Although cognitive processes and motor skills are essential in both domains, the foci and outcomes are fundamentally different.

Gross motor apparatus varies in complexity, but the range for young children, from the simple forms of spheres (balls) and blocks (building blocks) to comparatively complex climbing equipment (jungle gyms, trees), wheel toys (skates, bicycles) and other apparatus (badminton sets) is not so great as for fine motor activities. The focus on whole body movements, however, results in the interesting contradiction that many of the more complex gross motor activities make use of equipment that is simple in structure. For example, a ball, largely used for limited purpose concept identification, insertion, and rolling tasks in the fine motor domain, gives rise to a whole host of cognitively complex ball playing games in the gross motor domain; a flat open surface area is employed for complex running and tumbling games and activities; and a pool allows for swimming and diving. This can sometimes be true in the fine motor sphere in that a plain ball of clay or a set of small cubes are the basis for creating an infinite variety of structures. There are, however, ordinarily fewer gross motor toys of complex design, such as puzzles and mazes (despite the occasional garden maze).

There are hardly any two-dimensional materials employed for the gross motor sphere, because movement through three dimensions is intrinsic to the operation of body apparatus. One may perhaps count an open running area or a hopscotch pattern as two-dimensional materials because movement orients around a flat plane. In hopscotch, the key progression is across a horizontal design; but running, tumbling, and games such as tag derive their structure more from cognitive rules about body movements than from how the external structure (i.e., the ground) is contoured. Tunnels and garden mazes, however, if designed along a horizontal plane, channel the main cognitive activities in a two-dimensional way, although of course movement (whether walking or crawling) takes place three-dimensionally, even as jigsaw puzzle movements do in the fine motor domain. It might be argued that rope climbing defines cognitive problems principally along a single linear spatial dimension, namely progression up and down the rope; but again, use of the body and appendages is the key aspect.

The problem of design versus content is much less prominent in the gross motor sphere, because most devices are physical structures designed to encourage certain kinds of physical skills, not thematic development. Many contemporary playgrounds, however, are planned by professional designers who deliberately employ design principles to make climbing apparatus more aesthetically appealing in color and form. The placement of the climbing rungs, steps, sliding ramps, etc., is often considered from the point of view of both design and functional considerations, to make interesting physical challenges aesthetically pleasing. Unfortunately not all designers take the trouble to study the gross motor developmental needs of children, but may get carried away by the design possibilities. A children's playground may be filled with many visually appealing, wooden log structures piled in different ways and one or two fancy tunnels, but climbing, crawling through tunnel mazes, and limited sociodramatic play, while important, become greatly overrepresented at considerable cost, to the exclusion of other important skills and interests. On the other hand, traditional structures may need reevaluation in the light of variety of function, recent knowledge in child development, and aesthetic principles.

One problem peculiar to the design of gross motor equipment is the risk factor. Poor design principles, garish color, and cheap plastic materials may all affect children's aesthetic development, as they do in the small toy sphere, but there are more injury problems inherent in the use of such playground equipment, both in and outdoors. Sharp-edged designs, cheap materials, and shoddy workmanship may not only lead to cuts and broken toys, but also to broken limbs and concussions from falls. Climbing equipment, seesaws and swings, for example, must be made of strong and durable materials (usually hardwoods or metal; most plastics will not stand up under heavy use or are too expensive) and must be well constructed. They of course should be located over comparatively soft surfaces, like earth, grass, tanbark, sand, or mats, *not* over hard surfaces like asphalt or concrete. It is not always the designer or manufacturer who is at fault, however. Well-designed equipment must be assembled and placed in a safe location by local day care center personnel, who do not always take adequate care even when assembly mechanisms are safe ones and instructions are clear. Unfortunately, too many North American municipalities, agencies, and commercial operators are prone to cut maintenance in grass and flowers by asphalting vast areas of the playgrounds. In many other regions like Europe and Japan, well-maintained lawns are widely used for all outdoor areas except where hard surfaces are specifically preferable (e.g., for using wheel toys).

The quality of design in gross motor equipment is shown in many ways. Construction should above all be scaled to the physical size of the age group. Apparatus that is too small and simple or too large and complicated may result not only in boredom, frustration, or broken equipment, but small children may not be able to do anything at all with oversize equipment, or if they can, the risk of injury increases sharply. For example, if a climbing apparatus designed for elementary age children is installed for preschoolers, the climbing rungs will be too far apart and too large in diameter for the children to grip firmly. Seesaws, swings, climbing ropes, wading and swimming pools, and wheel toys work better when scaled accordingly. *Size* is in fact the salient dimension for developmental age grading for gross motor equipment. Unfortunately, there is a particular dearth of age-appropriate equipment for infants (12 to 30 months), and there is insufficient scaling for size and height differences throughout the preschool age range.

Significance of Physical Dimensions

No one of the dimensions of play materials is more significant for children's learning than any other. Each in its way builds a play environment, because each contributes in some different way to the child's pleasure and development through play. The forms of play children develop—exploratory, instrumental, creative and sociodramatic—depend as much on physical media for experimentation as on a facilitating social atmosphere for their expression and a background of cognitive guidance to help the child to acquire the rules for any forms of play at all.

There are several such basic dimensions, each of which would be hard to do without: gross and fine motor activities are the two basic physical modes for environmental manipulation and problem solving; the social and non-social dimensions merely reflect the fact of two worlds of physical and social existence; the child relates to small and large scales of materials as a simple matter of the child's size in relation to things (macrosphere-microsphere); materials can be designed to work and to be used as they are, or designed to be employed as units to reassemble or shape in creative combinations, according to their substance; objects can be played with for themselves or be used to stand for symbols of other things; and of course toys can be designed to represent different themes (content) and be well or poorly made to serve instrumental or aesthetic purposes.

8

The Play Environment

A natural setting

Young children spend so much of their waking day in play that a good deal of effort in day care is devoted to establishing workable play environments. Time spent in basic care routines is considerable but, even in early infancy, seldom matches the time spent by children in play. Typically, a six-month-old child is awake for ten hours each day, three to four of which are taken up with feeding, changing, washing, and going to sleep routines, a proportion that declines gradually with age. Except for perhaps another hour or more of attention from adults in guided learning and related activities, the rest of the child's day is regularly passed in the exploratory-experimental activities we characterize as play.

187

Since the focus in play is self development, we design environments to stimulate the child to engage in imaginative and constructive activities on his own. The first section of this chapter will sketch the design and arrangement of indoor play areas, and a final section will discuss outdoor play environments.

Indoor Play

Play Room Design

At home, the child is likely to have at least a partial run of the house, at first preferring the proximity of his mother, father or other adults as they go about their household activities. As his world widens with development, his preferences will depend on a number of things, including the availability of a playroom or play area of his own, the consistency of adult guidance in directing where he plays, and the presence of interesting toys, siblings, and playmates. Day care and nursery schools, on the other hand, are structured essentially as environments for the child. The basic part of any center is its playrooms, arranged and equipped specifically for this purpose under the supervision of caregivers or teachers who have few competing demands on their attention. There are specific ways of organizing play areas to stimulate play and facilitate supervision.

Zones for Play Activity

Whether the indoor play facilities of a center consist of a suite of rooms or a single large room for each play group, some organization of space by type of activity is desirable. The total play area should be arranged into a number of areas, each equipped with furniture, materials and equipment appropriate to the type of play to be encouraged in the area. These play zones correspond only partially with the cognitive developmental forms of children's play as defined in Chapter 7 on the development of play. Exploratory play, language play, and sociodramatic play are likely to occur in any setting according to the developmental level, personality characteristics, mood, and problems of children at play in an area. Nevertheless, certain materials can be selected and arranged into sets in a way that will encourage some types of play more than others.

Arranging the play environment into specific areas encourages children to concentrate on each type of activity for longer periods. Putting different materials in each area establishes a minimum order to the environment, in which play of a certain type is fostered by the types of materials at hand. There is value to mixing materials at times to stimulate the child's exploration of interrelations between concepts of all kinds. The details of how concepts are represented in materials will be more thoroughly explored, however, if children frequently play with materials that channel their explorations into a set of closely related concepts. Building blocks, for example, focus on rules for interrelating objects in space to form physical structures—the organizational rules discussed at length in the previous chapter. Children will become more knowledgeable of the various types of concepts, like building concepts, if each type of material is located mainly in one area, where children can be encouraged to experiment with them for substantial periods of time. The development of deep interests is based on detailed familiarity with sets of common concepts. Thus, ordering the environment draws the child's attention to the underlying conceptual order of the world, develops his thinking processes in greater depth and tends to increase his attention span for problem solving.

There is also a need to provide limited physical boundaries between clusters of children working at a common activity in order to facilitate concentration and minimize chances of conflict. Area definitions and partial barriers between areas give a focus to each activity and make it easier for teachers to control social density and traffic flow. Also, children sometimes need to be able to play in a room entirely alone (though within sight of a caregiver); the opportunity to play alone develops intellectual autonomy in mental reflectiveness important to the creative mind. Hence the value of having a variety of rooms of different sizes.

The organization of zones defined below is by no means the only or complete set of play areas that can be identified. Amid the maze of possible combinations, nevertheless, there are standard clusters of materials and rules that "go together". Some arrangements of play zones are also more convenient and conducive to children's concentration than others.

The two basic forms of perceptual-motor involvement in play, the use of the entire body in gross motor activities, and the use of the hands and fingers in fine motor activities, require special treatment. The space and equipment required for each of these vital activities are so different that some provision for their separation is essential.

Gross Motor Activity Zones

Gross motor play is designed to develop concepts, skills, and muscle strength in the body apparatus as a whole, and is vital for maintaining the respiratory and circulatory systems and general health of the child. Gross motor play embraces many activities, ranging from individual gymnastics and related skill activities in different physical media (e.g., swimming, diving, climbing, sliding, swinging) to group activities of all kinds, and later to complex games, team sports, and aesthetic activities like dance. Contrary to much popular opinion, cognitive rules and strategies are extensively implicated in gross motor activities, from the simplest action of reaching to the intricacies of ballet and gymnastics. Every set of movements is constructed of a set of cognitive rules for analyzing, organizing, sequencing, and coordinating the dimensions of the tasks involved. Once a child has mastered a skill like climbing, of course, he can pay much less attention to the various rules for positioning, reaching, grasping, ordering and coordinating the movements of his arms and legs. He is able to do them more or less automatically without thinking, until he encounters a special problem, such as how to reach a very high bar.

Gross motor play thrives best in large scale environments outdoors, with a variety of equipment designed specifically to demand use of the arms and legs. There are few limits to the variety of skills and muscle strengths that different specialized equipment (weight lifting bars, gymnastic equipment of all kinds) can develop, and most of them are useful in some way.

Facilities for the group care of young children are likely to include some indoor provision for gross motor play. The number and distribution of activity zones in an indoor gross motor playroom are defined by the types of equipment, activities, and the amount of space available, and the number and age of the children who must use the total area simultaneously. Differences in available resources and their allocation in large and small institutions will be dealt with in more detail later in the chapter.

The maximum set likely in a large indoor area, especially a gymnasium, may consist of as many as 8 or 10 more or less distinct areas of play. Since not all types of activity are necessarily engaged in every day, the number of areas is usually subject to fluctuation and equipment can be moved around as space is needed for separation. At all times gross motor equipment, both indoor and outdoor, must be placed far enough apart and in such a way as to prevent injury and interference between activities. If running areas are close to swings, for example, collisions between runners and swingers are likely.

Open Surface Area.   This would be an area large enough for free body movement activities like running, jumping, and hopping; group game activities like tag, ball throwing and rolling, and possibly even badminton or softball. Even these less equipment-bound activities will usually need defined areas to prevent injury from thrown or hit balls and intrusion into other games.

Gymnastic Areas.   There can be several well-separated zones for gymnastic activities, depending on the types of equipment in use, such as parallel bars, trapezes, and trampolines and tumbling mats.

Demarcated Area for Wheeled Vehicles.   This is likely to consist of an area at one end of the room, with a well-marked course or network of pathways (using masking tape or rope-connected movable posts) on which children can ride bikes, roller skate, and pull wagons. Part of the course can wind through other activity zones and equipment. Floor vehicles like wagons and large trucks can be used for transporting cargo, and bikes, cars and similar vehicles can be used for transporting people in conjunction with sociodramatic play. The block building area and any designed play structure, like a simulated boat-dock area, lend themselves to play with vehicles in this way, as long as the vehicle path is not designed so that the vehicles crowd the play area.

Block Building Area.   A comparatively small area is sufficient to allow creative building with large hollow blocks, building boards, cardboard cartons, etc. Constructions of all kinds, from plain "houses" to tunnels, ships, "skyscrapers," and airports serve two purposes: strengthening of muscles and sociodramatic play, both of which will be described in greater detail in the section on outdoor play.

It is well to have a subzone for block building with smaller and lighter-weight blocks where infants under three can play in the same room with, but free from the dominance of, older children. Special periods of guided play may be valuable to encourage older children to play cooperatively with younger children. Large hollow blocks are also useful for toddlers for stair climbing practice, for crawling in tunnels and for simple sociodramatic play under close supervision.

Other Special Purpose Activities.   Wading and swimming in pools, and carpentry (which combines both gross and fine motor processes) need their own defined zones. A variety of gymnastic-like apparatuses to ride, such as swings, suspended ropes, slides, and rocking and spring horses also need to be well separated for safety reasons. Nearly all such equipment, particularly the pool and carpentry areas, need close supervision because of the obvious risks of drowning from water and injury from saws, chisels and other tools.

Special Purpose Activities Requiring Less Separated Zones.   A variety of activities, using walking boards, mazes, large empty cardboard cartons, and other equipment for sociodramatic play can be allowed to spread into one another since they involve less vigorous movement and less dangerous equipment.

Fine Motor Activity Zones

The purpose of fine motor activity is to develop the child's concepts, skills, strength, and speed by making use of the refined movements of the fingers and hands. Fine motor play extends over a wide range of materials and activities, including clay, puzzles, building, molding with plasticine, stringing beads, and drawing. Since most cognitive activities in everyday life at any age (including many parlor games and school tasks) involve fine motor components, play environments need to be designed carefully to foster their development in many ways.

Most of these activities can be carried on indoors in moderate or small-sized rooms. Equipment and materials can be placed fairly close together, clustered according to the type of activity. Indeed, large distances between play areas only encourage stimulation of gross motor movements better suited to alternative settings and time periods. Fine motor play materials are essentially small, manipulable objects to be experimented with on limited surface areas, such as child-sized tables accommodating three or four children, or floor and rug spaces of a few square feet.

Below are defined a set of zones that might be found in a spacious nursery school. Keep in mind, however, that various combinations of activity will occur at different times according to program aims, convenience, and the interests of staff and children.

Microsphere and Macrosphere: Sociodramatic Play

Most sociodramatic play is fine motor in focus, although certain activities in simulated environments (play houses, boats, cars, and trucks) and block building with large, hollow blocks, involve varying amounts of whole body movement. These are usually set up outdoors or in gross motor playrooms. In the quiet, indoor playroom, however, where fine motor activities predominate, few broad movements are used in either of the two characteristic types of sociodramatic play (microsphere and macrosphere) defined in the chapter on toys and materials.

At least one distinct zone is desirable for *macrospheric play,* where the children act out roles in a setting scaled to their size, and two are needed for the *microsphere,* where they play with miniature blocks, vehicles, people, and other replicas. One macrospheric zone is needed for domestic role activities, complete with kitchen appliances, household furniture, eating utensils, and adult clothes, for play at cooking, eating, sleeping, and interrelating in family life. Occupational role play can also be freely encouraged in this zone, or, where space is available, a second zone established to allow more varied forms of job play to regularly take place. This zone needs to be plentifully equipped with a variety of suggestive props (clothes and tools) of many different trades and professions (carpenter, plumber, engineer, surveyor, doctor, factory worker, sailor), which are changed around from time to time to encourage variety and to follow the interests of the children.

In the microsphere, one of the two sociodramatic zones might consist of a floor play area, equipped with multiple unit blocks of the basic 2½ inch square by 1¼ inch thick modular unit and toy replicas scaled accordingly. The second zone would contain small tables with building blocks and replicas scaled to a smaller size appropriate for the more confined area, stimulating a finer perceptual-motor focus. In these areas model houses, garages, stores, gas stations, and fanciful structures (castles, Noah's ark, troll houses) might be included to encourage many types of sociodramatic play.

Fixed Form, Means-Ends Play versus Open-Ended Play. Several separated zones will be necessary for the range of activities typical in these two categories. For instance, puzzles, nesting and stacking toys, form boards, and similar materials which depend essentially on fixed or direct-line solutions for their operations (that is, can be solved in only one way), stimulate learning quite different from the open-ended solutions demanded of free form (painting, clay) and modular (blocks) materials. Although there are some advantages to mixing up materials now and then to additionally stimulate open-ended thinking styles, because each of these two basic approaches promote distinctly different forms of learning they are best presented separately.

Each of these basic categories may often be further subdivided into specialized play zones, depending on space and the number and ages of the children. Creative art and craft activities, like painting and clay modeling, for example, are quite different from and are likely to interfere with and even mess up block building and other modular construction activities. Different types of fixed-solution materials similarly follow different rules, two-dimensional form boards and jigsaw puzzles are solved differently from three-dimensional block and assembly toy puzzles. The number of subdivisions to make is in the end a practical decision, influenced by the amounts of materials in different subtypes. Large amounts of materials will result in more confusion and sorting when the activities and pieces mingle together. Usually subdividing can be limited to two or three distinct play zones by monitoring the number and type of materials according to the number of children and amount of space available.

It will be noted that some of these zones overlap with the zones defined for sociodramatic play, both in the macrosphere and microsphere. Some of the same materials are the stimulus base for both building and social play. This need not be a problem, for teachers can encourage the two forms of play to proceed in parallel with slightly separated groups, encouraging children to move around occasionally to insure a diversity of experience.

Both fixed and open-ended materials can be used with advantage on tables, because their confined surface areas tend to concentrate the area of activity by corralling the material within the visual and manipulative field of the child. Working on tables does add the problem of small pieces dropping and rolling around the floor. Some children like to work standing up part of the time, because the position enables them to move around freely to reach different parts of a structure and see things at eye level. Working at eye level may also encourage closer personal relations and cooperation because children can see one another's faces as they work across a table. Small tables make separation between the different types of materials easy to maintain and foster closer relations between two or three children. Large tables, on the other hand, may be advantageous for spreading puzzles with more pieces; for building extensive block structures; and for working singly or cooperatively on large-scale drawings, paintings, or collage.

Children of all ages enjoy the informality of working on the floor, especially when there is a soft textured rug with thick pile which is sensually pleasant. Using a small square of rug (three or four feet on a side) will help to focus the activity and limit the number of children to a constructive play group of three or four. A smooth, waterproof floor surface and close access to a sink make water paints and other sloppy creative activities easy to service and clean up.

The floor does not provide the best angle for eye level work and arm-hand control for fine motor skills like drawing and painting. Easels are advantageous for brush painting or charcoal drawing, because they prevent the child from leaning on the paper and smearing the work. Each child stands and paints or draws on a paper placed at an angle. Keeping the angle of the easel at about 45° and properly mixing paints will prevent them from running on the slanted surfaces. Two children can paint cooperatively at each easel, and more can be involved if a single sheet of paper is spread across two (or more) easels. Finger painting, on the other hand, is easily managed on horizontal surfaces, either on tables or the floor, because leaning and smearing are part of the process. Children will persist more in crayon drawing when they are seated comfortably at a table.

Play with Symbolic (Language) Materials.   Activities involving books, pictures, language games, music, and number symbols may be arranged for a single zone in a room or distributed among several distinct zones or rooms. Even where space is extremely limited at least partial separation helps children to concentrate in using these abstract materials. Music, in particular, is likely to divert children from looking at books and other visual and measurement material. The sheer quantity of symbolic play materials in a well-equipped center may need further separation to minimize conflicts and encourage persistence with single activities.

In a small school with only a single activity room for each age or play group, music can be handled by regulating the times when records are played, especially records of a more appealing kind such as catchy folk and children's songs. Ideally, there should be a separate room for musical activities, equipped with a record player, and simple instruments with which the children can experiment with rhythmic patterns and tones. Other language activities can be

managed by placing sets of materials on different shelves or positions along a
shelf to facilitate a degree of separation.

In a spacious day care center it is possible to allocate a separate zone for
each of a number of types and subtypes of activity, lending to the play in each
zone a special flavor uncluttered by concepts from another type. Guided learning in special programs (see Chapter 10) is preferably conducted in separate
rooms, or least blocked off by movable walls. It may even be useful to set aside
additional playrooms for different types of free play activity, relieving the
problem of frequent playroom rearrangement for different combinations of
activities.

Play in a small center, in contrast, may have to be conducted entirely in a
single large playroom, even, in some cases, without enough space to section off
all age groups. Under such circumstances, zone divisions, though limited in
number, are likely to be even more important than in a large center where a
generous amount of space often permits a certain amount of activity separation spontaneously. Instead of dividing the playroom of such a small center by
age groups, space may sometimes be more efficiently used through activity
zoning alone, children from all age groups playing together in all the zones in
an extended family type group. For certain purposes, subgroups of children
with special needs (infants, children with special interests or problems) could
be confined to specified sections of the playroom at definite periods.

A combination of activity zoning and family grouping is more likely to be
the solution when sectioning a center limited to a single large playroom. If, for
example, an enrollment of 20 to 25 children were divided into two extended age
groups (birth to age two and three to five), each might enjoy its own separate
two or three zones for certain activities, but share zones at certain times, such
as a music or gross motor play period.

In order to describe the functions of structuring play space, we shall present a series of diagrams illustrating a number of solutions to different problems. Figure 8–1 shows a scale diagram of a major day care center followed by
more detailed drawings (Figures 8–2 through 8–4) of the components of the
play and learning areas for one of the three major age groups for which the
center is designed. An additional diagram (Figure 8–5) illustrates the space and
equipment arrangements for a smaller day care center with minimum facilities.

Designs for Indoor Play: Spacious Facilities

The elaborate day care center shown in Figure 8–1 services three basic groups
of 20 to 40 children each, ranging in age from a few weeks old (usually 2 to 6
months at entry) to about 4½ years of age. The children are all located in two
wings (the base and right wing of the "T"). The service and adult supporting
activity rooms are in the center area and the left wing of the "T," including
administrative and clerical offices, seminar rooms, library, teacher offices, testing and observation rooms, kitchen and diet kitchen, clinic, adult eating and
lounge rooms, and space for storage and a furnace room. This auxiliary space
should fit the requirements for a total staff of about 30 to 60 day care workers
and supporting staff (including a director, secretary, two or three cooks, one or
two janitors, a psychologist, a nurse, and students in training). Such a center

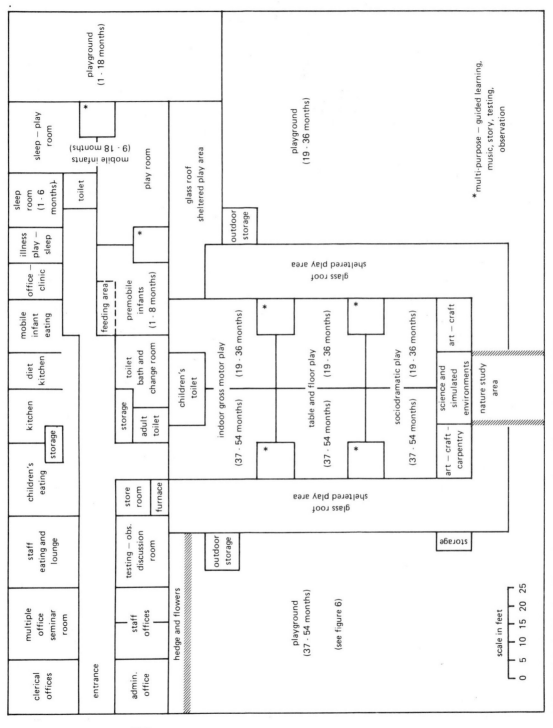

FIGURE 8-1. *Design for a day care center with spacious facilities.*

195

might well have teacher-child care ratios of two teachers for every three children (average overall) for the infant group; one teacher for every three children for the toddlers and younger preschool groups; and one teacher for every four or five children for the older preschool group. Such ideal ratios could probably only be realized through student training programs (see Chapter 3). Activity space for each of the three age groups is equally extensive and divided to facilitate activity concentration but arranged so that communication between areas and to outdoors flows easily.

The center is structured with glass walls on top of four foot tall, solid base walls, that divide the children's activity areas. The glass at the top of the wall distributes light effectively and encourages the flow of adult observation and communication among the different activities and ages, while the solid base walls minimize interference for children. Sliding doors between activity rooms permit children from different age groups to play together easily, and to share teachers and facilities as conditions and the children's needs suggest. For example, there are doors connecting the infant group and the 19 to 36 months group. There are doors between each of the two main activity rooms for gross motor play, table and floor playrooms, and sociodramatic playrooms for the two older age groups (19 to 36 months and 37 to 54 months), enabling younger and older children to move easily back and forth for special activities as their shifting abilities in different skill areas suggest. Each of the large playrooms for all three age groups, plus the art-craft and science rooms, opens directly on the outdoor playground. To make play outdoors possible during inclement weather, the area immediately adjacent to the playrooms is slightly raised and sheltered by a glass roof which allows light indoors.

The infant group has additional facilities, such as a special sleep room to cater to the irregular sleeping patterns of younger infants and those few older infants who require irregular napping. Older infants also have a sleeping area, which converts to an extra playroom. A separate small room contiguous to the clinic office is designed for children who may become ill in the center. It may be used under ordinary circumstances as an extra activity room for guided learning or to separate children whose crying or restless sleep patterns disturb other children.

There are toilet and washing facilities for all three age groups and adults in the center area to reduce plumbing costs. One large washroom unit serves the two older age groups, while the infant group washroom includes a change room. There is also a small toilet next to the toddler playrooms to facilitate toilet training.

The two older groups eat together in a room between the kitchen and the staff dining room and, on the other side of the diet kitchen, there is a room for the babies. An additional corner of the premobile infant playroom is designed as a feeding station to store and prepare bottles for the younger infants, although infants who sit well may eat their main meals with the toddlers.

The indoor play areas provided for the older age group (37 to 54 months), are virtually identical to those for the 19 to 36 months group as shown in Figure 8-1. There are large separate rooms for indoor gross motor play, all kinds of sensory motor and symbolic play activities, and sociodramatic play, along with small special activity rooms for guided learning, music, story time, and arts-crafts-carpentry. Another room (ten by twenty feet) serves both preschool groups for science and nature activities.

The infant area includes two small special activity rooms (for guided learning and music, and stories) but does not have as many separate rooms, since infants follow fewer different activities and are less distractible at shorter distances. For example, since infants' sociodramatic play is essentially limited to a few simple acts related to household settings, there is little need for an occupational play setting.

The social density for each of the three areas is unusually ample, allowing 2025 square feet of total indoor play space for each of the two preschool groups, or approximately 80 to 100 square feet per child (depending on the amount calculated for built-in shelf and cabinet space) for an enrollment of 20 children per group. The infant space totals 1800 square feet, in keeping with their slightly lower space requirements. Since the total set of rooms is likely to be used during any free play period, enrollment of any group could easily be expanded to 40 children per age group and still allow nearly the recommended 50 square feet per child for the two older groups and slightly less for the infants.

The indoor activity areas for the older preschoolers are pictured in detailed diagrams (Figures 8–2 through 8–4) because of the greater diversification of activity.

In Figure 8–2 we see a scale diagram of the large playroom provided for table and floor play, together with two small, contiguous rooms for specialized (guided learning) activities. There are nine distinct areas of concentration in this spacious playroom (525 square feet), which, after eliminating shelf space, easily provides over 40 square feet of play per child for as many as 10 children. Fifteen children should be able to play here comfortably and also remain within minimum standards (30 to 35 square feet per child). Although it is desirable to keep children distributed among the activities to control social density, there are times when play groups and program demands may increase the number of children in certain areas at one time with much advantage, if these periods are not prolonged.

The playroom is furnished and arranged to provide ease of communication and cluster similar types of activities. Using small tables, scatter rugs, and toy shelves to partially enclose areas provides activity zones to encourage concentration, while the general openness in the room provides ease of communication. Clustering is shown in the diagram by the placement of the two play tables (or rugs) in the half-bounded area between the two small activity rooms. The two rooms and the play areas between are designed for language-math type activities, though perceptual-motor learning materials usually also accompany these activities in early childhood. Similarly, the extended play room on the right is designed to encourage two forms of sociodramatic play. One includes more blocks to encourage construction (in the main floor play area in the corner) and the two others include miniature buildings and furnishings (a doll house and store) to be used in table play. Further clustering is observable in the four table and floor play areas designed for fine motor play with problem solving, construction, and sociodramatic materials. This table play area uses the tiniest replicas of people, furniture and animals to fit with tiny blocks.

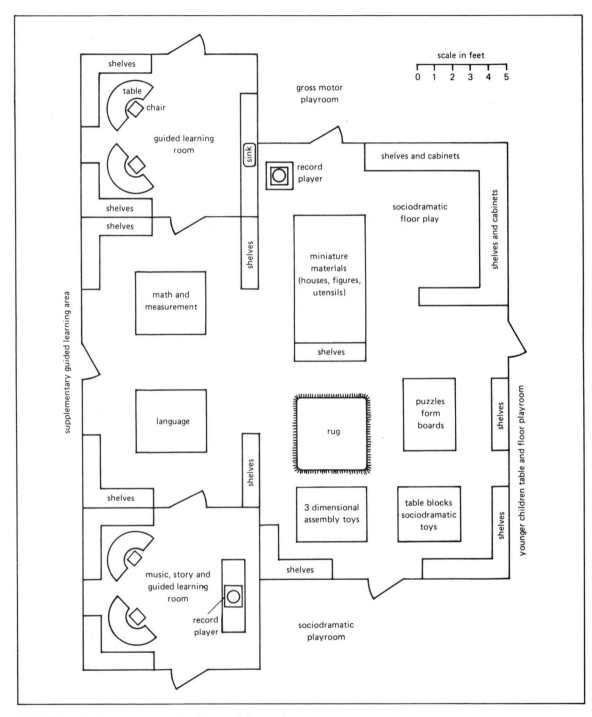

FIGURE 8–2. *Language, and table and floor play areas.*

198

Sociodramatic materials may be removed from time to time in any of the areas to encourage children to experiment more with block building.

Toy shelves are distributed freely around the room. Each set is placed close to the corresponding table or rug area it is designed to service to provide easy access and to avoid conflict between activities. Shelves should be broad, deep, and separated enough vertically to make the toys highly visible, inviting, and easily accessible to children. Although some built-in shelves may be useful, movable shelves make for greater program flexibility and more possibilities of stimulating interest in play through change. Movable shelves with castors and locks minimize unwanted movements.

The arrangements for the two small activity rooms shown in Figure 8–2 are basically much the same, having two half-round tables in each of two corners with shelves for books, records, toys, and other learning materials placed against whatever wall space is convenient. A chalkboard might be preferable on one wall of the guided learning room, and the music and story room has special functions, but in fact both rooms are equally suitable for the guided learning activities we shall describe in later chapters. It will be noticed that the music room has one record player and the main playroom another. The one in the main playroom should be inexpensive and durable for the children to use, giving them experience in exercising their own choice and in the mechanics of operation. Some prescreening of records and background supervision is never-theless important, to develop taste standards and to regulate volume.

A higher-fidelity record player and a more extensive set of quality records in the music room is used for specialized listening, with closer supervision and more instruction. There will be times when it is desirable to involve groups of children too large for the small music room. For this reason, location of the machine near the doors of both the main playroom and the sociodramatic play-room will make the sound carry easily to the larger rooms. Alternatively, stereo speakers can be set up in one (or both) of the rooms to be used for certain planned activities. Listening to records when lying on rugs is a good way of engaging children's interest, and dance, rhythm, and marching activities are easily set up in either room by moving furniture and shelves aside.

Sample arrangements for the sociodramatic playroom and the arts and crafts and science activity rooms are displayed in Figure 8–3. The large socio-dramatic play area (450 square feet) is well suited to a variety of activities which are again clustered through the way in which furniture is arranged. It communicates directly with several other activity rooms, including the shel-tered outdoor play area, which permits play to spill outdoors in warm weather. Communication between age groups is also direct to permit children to migrate back and forth to enrich play themes through mingling the different ages, sta-tuses, and interests.

The sociodramatic play area contains furniture and role playing materials, along with shelves, tables, boxes, and blocks to support the play. The room is arranged into four basic areas with one small additional area containing, for instance, a simulated fire truck and a space ship to stimulate casual play. The four main areas are amply furnished with materials to stimulate family life play, activities in and around docks and ships, a combination store and post office and a work shop (which might be, alternately, a plumber's shop, a repair garage, or even an auto assembly plant). Each area is arranged to suggest the

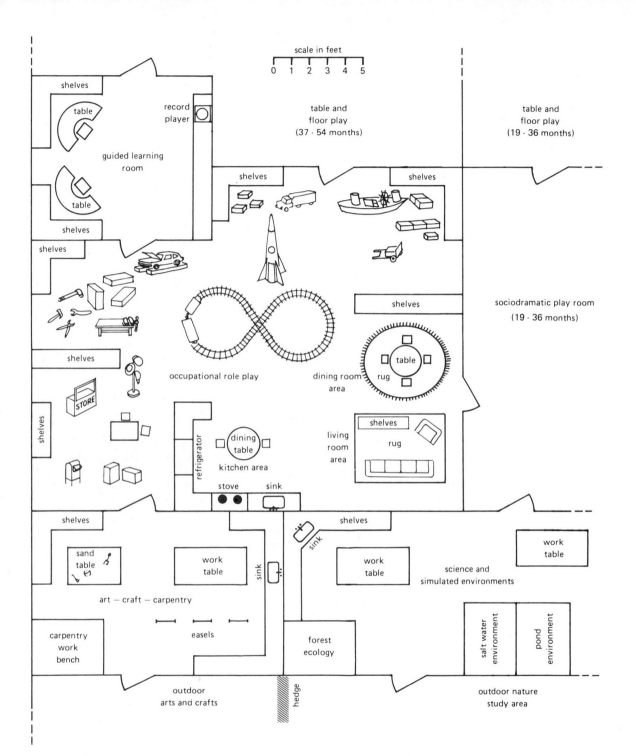

FIGURE 8-3
Sociodramatic playroom and additional activity rooms.

appropriate setting and is furnished with tools and clothes to fit the roles and tasks of the activities. The family life area is the most complete because of its greater familiarity to young children. The family play area has a sink with running water and a child-size stove, oven, and refrigerator that work on demand, *subject to close control by staff.* (These fixtures share a common plumbing network with the art-craft and science room sinks to hold down installation costs.) Rugs are included where appropriate to add coziness to the atmosphere.

The occupational role areas could easily include several cardboard cartons of different sizes, painted and arranged to suggest background and props (the children may design some of these in the art activity room), and possibly a set of hollow blocks (wood or cardboard) to simulate work benches, doorways, and storage cabinets, as well as store supplies, cargo, forked trucks, and other items to stimulate and diversify the play.

The arts and crafts room is equipped with tables, chairs, easels, shelves, a sand table, and a carpentry work bench, along with the necessary stores of art and carpentry tools and supplies. Some of these activities can be shifted to any of the other three playrooms. The main sensorimotor playroom, for example, is already used for other creative activities with "dry" construction materials which do not make a mess, while the arts and crafts room is designed to handle the spread of water, paint, clay, and bits of paper and paste for collage and papier maché. They are thus more easily supervised in a relaxed manner, without inhibiting the children's creativity, in a room that can be left in disarray (if necessary) without interfering with other activities. In warm weather, these activities can be pursued outdoors, though generally confined to the raised, sheltered area close to the room to minimize control and cleanup.

There is only one science room for the two preschool groups because of the expense involved, especially in the design of sealed, miniature ecologies (of forestry, ponds, deserts, etc.). Separate nature study areas and work tables for children to explore and be guided in experimenting with natural science materials might well be set up in one of the other playrooms, perhaps near a guided learning room, to be convenient for use in planned learning projects. Most physical science learning for preschoolers comes, in any event, through play with the various puzzles, containers, blocks, and similar sensorimotor materials. But older preschoolers, particularly, can benefit from using a special area, equipped with a wide variety of natural materials and the tools with which to explore them. Rocks, plants, cardboard and pins for mounting insects, jars for pickling specimens, and dissecting pans and even knives, will help children acquire a basic idea of the structure of plants, animals, and inanimate materials.

Figure 8–4 shows indoor rooms for gross motor play for both the two older age groups of the same large center. The playrooms have been arranged for joint use, to give the children a greater range for movement and more activity choices. On the left, gymnastics equipment (trampoline, high and low parallel bars, trapeze and swing) is set up along the window. Tumbling mats, a large climbing apparatus and a pool are placed along the right side of the same room. The pool draws on a common source of plumbing with the contiguous children's toilets and is bordered by a waterproof vinyl tile area to catch the splashes, and has a rail to prevent accidents.

The entire center area of the room is left open for running, ball playing and

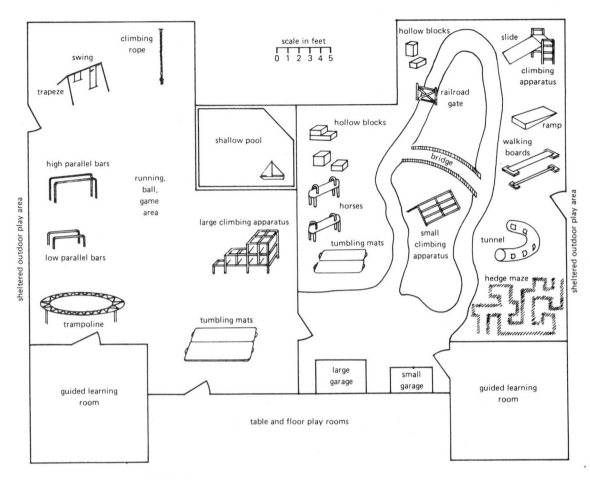

FIGURE 8–4
Indoor rooms for gross motor play (combined preschool age groups).

general movement games. The room on the right contains a wheel toy pathway circuit (including garages for small and large vehicles to fit the two age groups), small and large hollow building blocks and miscellaneous pieces of climbing, balancing, sliding and maze type equipment (a complex maze and a cylindrical tunnel), along with some additional mats and spring horses.

Equipment more suited to the younger group is in the room on the right and that for the older group in the room on the left, but much of it (the pool and vehicle course, for example) is likely to present a challenge to all children.

Designs for Indoor Play: Limited Facilities

The facilities of a smaller center (Figure 8–5), which accommodates two basic age groups, provide fewer choices and less separation of play areas, but are

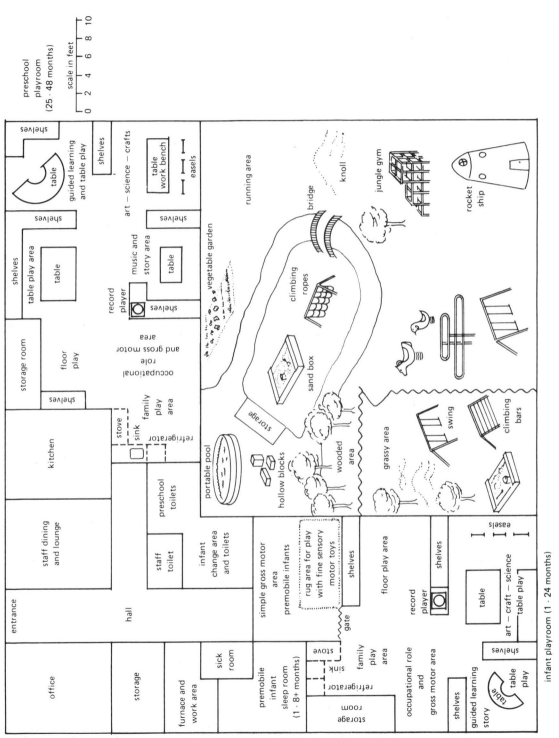

FIGURE 8–5. *Design for a day care center with limited facilities showing general layout, playroom, and playground facilities.*

203

nevertheless ample in many ways. The layout displays two undivided large playrooms, one in each of two wings of an "L"-shaped structure, with needed supporting facilities, including an office area, kitchen, and staff dining room and lounge, adult toilet, storage, and furnace and workroom. None of the supporting rooms is large, but together they can accommodate the expected thirteen day care workers (a director, eight baby staff and four preschool staff) and provide the necessary clerical, storage, repair, eating, and other services. There is even a separate sleep room for younger infants and a small isolation room. There is no separate diet kitchen and an obvious shortage of office and discussion space for teachers, for which the staff lounge and the office would be utilized on an alternating basis. The staff-child ratios are a generous 1:2 for infants and 1:4 for preschoolers.

Each of the playrooms is designed according to the same clustering and communication principles described for the spacious center. Each accommodates about sixteen children, allowing a comfortable 40 plus square feet per child, or a total of 668 square feet for the infant room and 724 square feet for the preschool room. This does not include the built-in room storage closets nor the premobile infant sleep room, which would be expected to be in nearly constant use. In both the infant and preschool playrooms, shelves for toys, learning materials, books, and records serve as boundaries for the various play activity zones, but there is also easy access between areas. Visual distraction for children is also minimized by using shelves higher than the children's eye level, yet much lower than the adults', to permit easy visual survey control and communication by teachers.

The chief distinctions between these playrooms and those in the larger center are that none of the play zones are separated by complete walls, and that virtually all must be employed for multiple purposes. In both the infant and preschool playrooms, the sociodramatic area is combined with a gross motor area. On occasions when the latter play is encouraged, the limited climbing apparatus, wheel toys, etc., must be taken from reserve storage areas, and shelves and tables must be moved back to other areas. Arts and crafts, science, and even carpentry (the latter for preschoolers only) would take place in a single zone, and much of the table play would be set up in one area. There is nevertheless a separated floor play zone for block construction and related microspheric sociodramatic activities, and for a music and story zone, though neither is marked out nor walled off. The guided learning zone and the music and story area could be used sometimes for various sorts of sensorimotor puzzles, blocks, and similar toys.

Space sharing is planned in other ways as well. Younger infants would eat in their own area, fed with bottles and solids in caregivers' laps or from feeding tables and high chairs. (Feeding tables make excellent settings at other times for individual play learning sessions with staff.) Premobile infants also have their own sleep room equipped with cribs, but cots and folding cribs for older infants would ordinarily be stored. The four tables in the preschool playroom and the two tables in the older infant area would probably be moved to a common area of the respective rooms for convenience and communication during snacks and meals.

The younger infants enjoy their own area defined by shelves and a flexible fence or gate. The area as shown provides about thirty square feet for each of five babies, assuming that precrawlers require less space and sleep much of the time and that crawlers will occasionally play with the older infants. The entire playroom has ample space for 16 infants. The younger infant area needs to be equipped with a large cozy rug, soft cuddly stuffed animals, rattles, varied shapes of all kinds (such as geometric shapes, and irregularly shaped bits of wood, cloth, paper, metal, etc.), and exploratory toys, containers, self-operating mobiles*, books, surprise boxes, and other appropriate sensorimotor toys, and an open floor area for push-pull toys, infant crawlers, climbing apparatus and mazes. For reasons of cost, there is only one running water sink, built in adjacent to the centralized center plumbing facilities in the preschool playroom. Water would therefore necessarily be offered on a more restricted basis for both the infants' sociodramatic play and the art and science area.

Outdoor Play

Playground Design

The principle distinction between outdoor and most indoor play is the stress upon whole body movement in place of fine motor and symbolic activity. Outdoor play is also intended to provide opportunity to sample fresh air, sunlight, sky, clouds, a little rain and snow (where possible), earth, rocks, grass, straw, trees, and other plant and animal life. Good playgrounds are designed on a broader, more natural basis than indoor areas as well as in an aesthetically pleasing fashion. They also need a variety of hard and soft surfaces, and regular and irregular terrains, suitable for different purposes.

Playgrounds make use of play activity zones but in a less definite fashion. There is little need to worry about concentration in the vigorous, often less complex mental processes of gross motor play. Zoning is largely necessary for reasons of space distribution and safety. Pieces of equipment placed too close together allow no opportunity for movement between them, and swings, climbing ropes, see saws, and wheel toys may endanger children playing nearby. It may be a worthwhile precaution to install low fences to define the boundaries of zones with moving equipment or other dangers, such as pools, ponds and streams.

As in indoor gross motor play rooms, large hollow building blocks and props for different types of sociodramatic play, such as tools and clothes of a trade or a setting for a store, are used together in a simple zone. Tricycles, roller skates, wagons, street signs, and a few large blocks (for cargo, buildings or garages) will, for similar reasons, preferably use a common roadway network. In addition, islands, boats, stepping stones, water, bridges, and water plant life can be available in a pond or pool. Running and jumping activities and tag games usually require outdoor space, and nature study will be found to occur in a number of outdoor settings, such as garden areas and ponds.

There are also reasons for separating quiet from vigorous types of activity outdoors. In fine weather it is pleasant to move some of the art and craft and carpentry activities, sociodramatic play, and even a few of the sensorimotor play materials outdoors, especially if the communication between indoors and

* Those with long strings with appealing toys attached that attract an infant. When he grasps the toy the mobile is activated—which leads him to repeat the process.

out is not too difficult. Children will attend more to these activities when they are protected from the noise and movement of bycicles, running games, and other active forms of play.

Climbing is most readily encouraged when several types of apparatus are clustered for children to use in groups. Some pieces are better spread among other sections of the playground, however, to attract spontaneous interest, encourage practice, and complement sociodramatic play in various settings. The child can become more of an explorer, meeting up with relatively unexpected tasks, situations, and combinations of playmates when much of the playground equipment is spread around in different settings.

Types of Equipment

There are many types of equipment likely to be found in a well-furnished outdoor playground.

Vehicles. The vehicles and related equipment a day care center might have usually include tricycles, possibly bicycles (with and without training wheels), wagons, kiddy cars, cargo blocks, street signs, traffic lights, simulated garages, gas stations and houses, roller skates, skate boards, and others, operating in a core, hard surface area (usually asphalt or concrete). There is preferably a network of pathways, wide enough to permit two tricycles to pass, which winds around other areas of activity. Separation of roadways from other moving equipment (like swings) is important. Some of the roadway may be bordered by a low fence and divided by a median to control traffic and allow easy teacher access. Bridges (over streams, tunnels, and underpasses) are possible if the slope of the grade is not too steep.

Moving Equipment. Swings, trapezes, swinging ropes (from bars or tree branches), see saws, swinging rings, small merry-go-rounds, rocking boats, outdoor trampolines, and horses on swings all have in common the fact that their operation moves the equipment. They must be set far enough apart to minimize danger and allow a free reign for action.

Construction Equipment. This consists largely of large, hollow blocks, and related building materials, essentially the same as described for indoor gross motor activity. It often is used in a sheltered area outdoors (see below).

Stationary Equipment (for climbing, sliding, balancing, maze following, problem solving, and sociodramatic play). Equipment such as walking boards of different widths, logs and low fence rails to balance on, and various pieces of climbing apparatus can be sprinkled around in different corners of a large playground to arouse interest at odd moments and stimulate different forms of climbing and sociodramatic play.

The design of climbing and balancing equipment can easily vary from the traditional slides, jungle gyms, and walking boards, whose functions are direct, to interesting sociodramatic devices, abstract forms, and modular structures. Among the latter types, apparatus may take the form of ships or rocket ships to climb on; soaring, abstract forms to crawl over; and structures made of many large cubes and rectangular blocks to climb around. Curvilinear and angular shapes with various holes to enter, curved slides and multiple platforms at several levels, and rough hewn log structures in different sizes and arrangement lend variety to children's climbing skills and imaginative play. Natural and human-made objects, like a series of stumpy logs of different length placed on end as stepping stones, large water main pipes, or simply a pile of old logs or boxes (fastened down) may be introduced. Care must be exercised to minimize the hazards of sharp edges to bump against and hard surfaces to fall on.

Tunnels and mazes form a related category of stationary equipment, drawing upon children's exploratory, navigational, and spatial relations abilities. The problem solving is more abstract in child-size mazes than in finger or pencil mazes because the child is "buried" in them and cannot see what step will come next. In small puzzle mazes, the child can not only see the next step but can visually survey all of the possible succeeding pathways.

Mazes and tunnels may be made of wood, cloth (supported with wire supports), cultivated hedges, or other materials. While permanent hedge mazes have a continuing value for each successive generation of preschoolers in a center, portable modular mazes, which can be restructured in many ways, have the advantage of variety in problem solving for learning spatial competence.

Sociodramatic Play Equipment. The playground is a suitable location for child-size structures simulating certain settings of everyday social life, and will contain, if possible, a number of compartments, passageways, stairs, or ladders; and operating controls (steering wheels, throttles, bells) and decorations, suggestive of tugboats, jet planes, play houses, theatres, tree houses, dock areas and warehouses, space ships, submarines. Three to four such items in different sections and settings are usually ample to stimulate endless hours of enjoyment for many children. A miniature theatre may be used for puppetry, story area, and other dramatic play. Boats set in or adjacent to a pond along with a small loading dock involve children in a host of related play activities involving loading, operating, and travelling on ships, climbing, water play, exploration of pond life, and swimming. It is helpful when each piece of equipment is placed in an appropriate physical setting to complement sociodramatic play, which may be stimulated by the teacher. For example, a tree house can be related to stories and pictures about people in different cultures who live in raised houses over water (as in parts of the Philippines), or the children can be asked to imagine the experiences of mountain people.

Types of Play Areas

Open Areas. Every playground needs a sizeable area without any equipment for activities involving free leg movement, such as circle games, ball playing, tag, hopping, romping and running. Most of these activities also involve language play, and only need open space; but organized broad and high jumping activities may be aided by a sand pit. A "home plate" and at least one base makes softball for older preschoolers more enjoyable. Modified forms of badminton and volley ball, using a very low net, can also be fun.

Heavy play will need to be moved from time to time to allow regularly used grassy areas to recover from wear. Adequate foot wiping and cleaning facilities at the entrance to the building will at least ease the problem for teachers in wet weather. A hard surface area can also be covered with outdoor carpeting (where sizable soft areas are lacking) for activities like softball that produce selected wear, yet require some protection from falls. Open running areas can also be surfaced with tanbark (over dirt), very fine gravel, or sand, all of which offer a certain amount of resiliency and considerable durability.

Lounging Areas.   Small grassy areas provide children with a kind of sensory pleasure and relaxation. If the weather often becomes hot and sunny, shady areas, particularly under trees, are desirable. Pine needles, moss, old leaves, trees, and twigs or just plain ground complete the closeness to nature. Natural areas, even if partially cultivated, are particularly important for urban children who have little contact with nature. These areas are designed for quiet and repose, and provide a mental outlook of tranquility and rest from vigorous play.

A soft grassy area is particularly inviting for infants and toddlers to play on without fear of injury. Infants reared in an apartment environment with no continuing contact with the earth may show signs of distress on first encounter with dirt or the tickling sensation of grass. However, if they are gradually exposed to dirt and grass they will soon feel free to explore nature with interest.

Sheltered Play Area.   A roofed-over area, attached to the building and opening from the indoor playrooms for easy equipment interchange, provides the benefits of fresh air on rainy days in selected activities. A number of closely allied gross motor activities (block building and accompanying sociodramatic play), along with many fine motor, art, craft, science, and language activities, work well in an area removed from the distractions of the active playground, in good weather or bad. If the roof is made of glass or transparent plastic, the amount of light reaching indoors will be greatly increased; shades are useful to regulate sunlight and heat on bright, hot days.

Natural Ecology Areas.   Children who live in the country or in small towns grow up with easy access to the natural life of the region. The modern child of the megalopolis, whether from the suburbs or the inner city, has very little first hand knowledge of how plants, insects, birds, and mammals cohabit in different settings of earth and water, though the suburban child has at least seen a few trees, flowers, a well shrubbed lawn and perhaps something a little more elaborate on vacations. In any case, neither child will probably have been exposed to much careful guidance about nature in real settings.

In addition to the miniature ecologies of indoor aquaria and terraria, playgrounds can be landscaped to provide gardens with hedges, flower beds, bushes, trees, and rock gardens, and other areas can be planted to grow in natural ways. Depending on the climate, regional plants can be placed in planned settings of miniature hills, swamps, ponds, rocks, and dry areas. These will soon attract small insect life and worms, and some birds may also appear.

Several such settings in an extensive playground serve many purposes besides that of exposing children to variations in nature. They are aesthetically satisfying and furnish an atmosphere for exploration and mild adventure in the different natural worlds, particularly if each area of the playground has a boundary of trees, rocky walls, ponds, copses, miniature hills, or even wood fences to lend definition and a hide-away quality for each zone. Hills and irregular rock formations with crevices and caves add to the possibilities of adventure and the added inducement and experience of climbing. Ponds are useful for wading and swimming, and a large pond can be stocked with fish.

Vegetable gardens also provide wonderful natural life and learning experiences for preschoolers, may help cut food budgets, and can provide food free of pesticides. Among other things, children are introduced to concepts of growth, development, and the life cycle through the short growing cycle of plants. The concepts of work to sustain life and the cooperative division of the children's and staff's labor in a group project to maintain the garden are basic to this experience.

Planned study and use of natural processes can be extended to raising appealing animals such as rabbits, guinea pigs, chickens, or ducks. These creatures are ideal because they are comparatively easy to manage in a small space. They offer possibilities for studying the complete cycle of higher forms of life in a short span of time; and they can be used to teach children about sources of food. This is, moreover, an invaluable natural way of teaching children concepts about the balance of nature in some of its harsher aspects, including concepts of life and death, to avoid the artificial separation that characterizes so much of our plastic modern world.

Sandbox and Digging Areas.   Both activities serve similar experiences in digging with tools, shaping materials, and sociodramatic play. Wet sand lends itself to the construction of more elaborate structures for concept learning and creative purposes (sand castles and communities); while digging in the ground demands greater tool strength, offers the possibility of deep holes and large tunnels (to be watched with care) for exotic imaginative play ("journeys" underground), and often leads to the discovery of animal life like worms and beetles.

A good variety of digging and shaping tools is important, with enough to go around to minimize conflict. Containers such as pails, boxes, pots, and pans are indispensable, along with cookie cutters and other molds for shaping sand, and other kitchen and eating utensils to stimulate social play.

Sand boxes are generally covered when not in use to prevent contamination by neighborhood cats. Sand needs to be replaced at least once a year because of the dust and dirt which accumulates, and the amount which drifts away. A sandbox placed in a sunny area avoids continuing dampness, but it also needs to be equipped with a parasol or moved into the shade in hot weather. In large playgrounds, two separated sandboxes are useful to permit the development of different age and interest activities; for example, one for building structures and the other for pouring and shaping activities.

Pools and Water Play.   Every playground needs a ready source of water, if only a tap and hose for wetting sand, mixing water paints, and sprinkling children running on the grass. Wading and shallow swimming pools are also pleasant and instructive for children from six months up. Day care centers with restricted budgets can generally manage some kind of plastic wading pool, while large centers may find two or even three separate pools useful, each one varying in area and depth for children of different ages.

Pools are good for swimming and frolicking water play, but tubs or outdoor sinks are better for experimental play with the properties of water (floating and sinking, currents and waves). Natural-looking streams and pond environments full of rocks, logs and other natural irregularities, generously planted with water plants and fish life, furnish essential experiences with water in nature. Water, however, is an inherently dangerous medium. Group care demands constant alertness and knowledge of the particular forms of danger with the different age groups. Infants can drown in a few inches of water because they are unable or too frightened to move their heads when they slip into an unexpected position, and older children may inadvertently pile on top of some child whose face is under water. Without minimizing these dangers, water is not only a great deal of fun, but is an important medium to learn about and to learn to use personally; early skill and confidence in its use, including learning to swim, is invaluable insurance against later accidents and a source of continuing pleasure. The danger can be minimized by a few regular precautions, such as fencing-in pools, draining pools when not in use, assigning specific day care workers to "life guard" duty, and teaching children in a planned program to swim and manage themselves with fun and safety in the water.

Outdoor Playground Designs

Selecting and arranging such a variety of equipment and settings outdoors with spatial and aesthetic balance requires as much planning as indoor designs do. The aid of a landscape consultant and naturalist is helpful, but the voice of teachers and parents should never be excluded. It takes designers *and* users to create exciting environments that are also workable.

A Spacious Playground

An elaborate playground design for a group of 37- to 54-month-old children is presented in Figure 8–6. The area usable for play space amounts to 6725 square feet, a size not unlikely in an area of low land cost. This figure excludes the landscaped area along the wall of the office wing and the two outdoor storage sheds, neither of which count as play space. The outdoor science area is additional space, although it is also not counted since it must serve two age groups. The total area will accommodate comfortably about 67 children at the high standards of 100 square feet per child, or 51 children if only actual outdoor play space is counted (excluding the sheltered play area).

The layout illustrates the usual clustering principles; for example, the spring horses and seesaw (balancing), the hedge maze and tunnelled climbing apparatus (tracking), and of course the vehicles, while a few items are distributed in different sections. The variety of equipment illustrated is considerable, yet there is ample space between items to minimize danger. A fence, for example, surrounds the pond but not the stream, which is shallow enough to be of small risk for the age group.

Most of the main categories of outdoor activity are well represented. There is a sizeable open area for running and cavorting (shown with an irregular border to delineate the area), which amounts to about 400 square feet (about 20

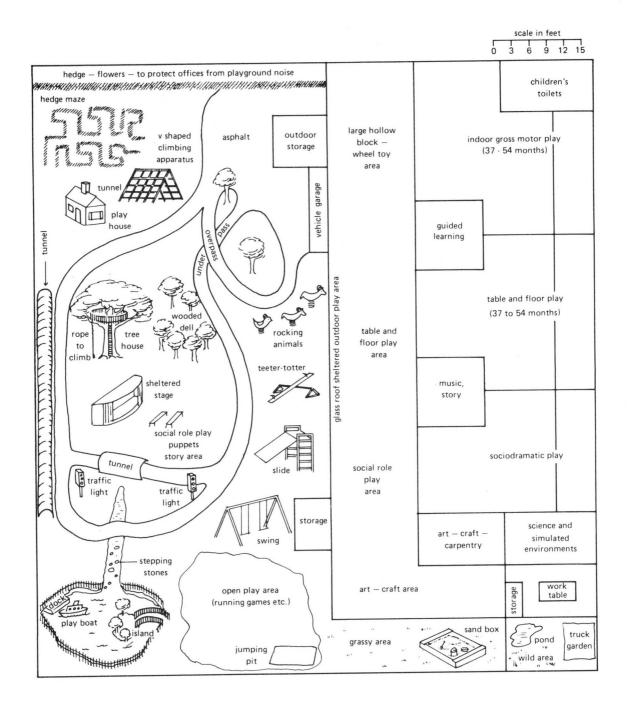

FIGURE 8–6
Outdoor playground for the 37 to 54 month age group, for a center with spacious facilities.

by 20). Some planners might wish to expand this considerably by clustering further or eliminating a few items of equipment; for example, cutting the generous amount of climbing equipment and roadway provided. The open area includes a jumping pit (sand) and might be furnished with two sunken cylinders to hold poles for a badminton net, which would be plugged with some soft material when not in use to prevent injury.

Sociodramatic settings are designed in several ways. There are, first of all, several types of climbing equipment to lead the children's imagination in different directions—from the box shaped jungle gym, to simulate any number of scenes (ship, airplane, house, high rise construction), to mazes and tunnels for exploration, and in inverted 'V'-shaped apparatus, to suggest mountain climbing. There are several building structures—play house, tree house, play boat, outdoor stage—which provide more detailed definition of types of activities, but which children will readily put to many different uses. The play stage (sheltered for use in damp weather) may be used for puppet play, sometimes led by a teacher, or may serve as another dramatic setting. Again, much of the rest of the equipment on the playground, including the sandbox, wheel toys, the wooded dell and island, and the swings, will also stimulate dramatic play.

The vehicle area, which is once more close to the hollow block construction area, consists of an expanse of hard surface, designed with "garages", for concentrated play with bikes, skates, wagons, and other wheel toys. There are two roadway systems leading from the main vehicle area, one a short circular course around a tree, and a second which follows a long winding course around other areas in the playground to give a sense of real travel. The roadways are equipped with road signs, traffic lights, over and underpasses and a tunnel. Roadways are wide enough to permit two large tricycles to pass and are bordered with a low fence.

The sheltered area, following the contours of the building, is designed to permit children to play outdoors in all except very cold weather (less than 10° to 20°F, or −12° to −6°C). Each activity is placed next to a section indoors where the corresponding type of play takes place. For example, play with hollow blocks (and occasionally a few wheel toys) is set next to the indoor gross motor playroom.

Two outdoor sheds are located at opposite ends of the sheltered area to store miscellaneous materials, such as some of the wheel toys, collapsible climbing apparatus, trampolines, walking bars, sandbox toys, sets of balls, and badminton and other game materials.

The extensive landscaping in the playground serves several purposes. The hedge and flower bed area along the wall of the office wing of the building is aesthetically pleasing, a source of additional observation on plant life for children, and reduces the volume of playground noise reaching adults working inside. The pond and stream areas are used for swimming and wading, for boat and water play, and as an additional resource for nature study. There are a number of trees and many different shrubs around the playground, especially around the pond, tree house, outdoor stage, and a small wooded hill, providing variety and an additional climbing and dramatic play area. Grass could be planted in most of the spaces between areas and between pieces of equipment, but some resilient material like tanbark (though sometimes splintery for bare feet) or sand will wear better and drain moisture faster in wet weather.

A Modest Playground

A playground design for a day care center with *limited facilities* is illustrated as part of Figure 8–5. While abundant in play equipment, it is restricted compared with the larger playground. There is less square footage per child, play areas tend to be smaller in scale, equipment is crowded closer together and the single playground for two age groups means sharing its use on a staggered schedule.

The total area is 1672 square feet, of which 280 feet is set aside for younger infants. At 80 square feet per child the main playground will accommodate about 17 children and is thus easily suitable for the 16 children in either of the two age groups at any one time. Moreover, the additional protected area is available to meet the irregular schedules of younger infants at any time without interfering with the outdoor play schedules of the preschool age group.

The same principles of clustering yet distributing types of equipment among several play areas is followed in this playground. Thus, wheel toys are used on the hard surface area and roadway circuit; moving equipment, like swings, teeter-totters, and spring horses, are all located in one general area; while climbing equipment is placed in at least two areas to add diversity.

One of the special features of a compact play area is the fact that the equipment must usually suit a broader range of developmental skills. The main method of meeting this demand in this design is through fitting the smaller infant area with scaled-down equipment. Thus the climbing apparatus is lower, shallower in slope, and has the rungs to climb spaced closer together. The swings are similarly lower to the ground and make a smaller arc. Also, some of the equipment on the main playground is adapted for younger children. One seesaw and one spring horse are smaller; one of the pieces of climbing equipment (near the rocket ship) is constructed on three levels; and there should be two or three sizes of vehicles to ride.

Despite the limitations of this playground, there are plenty of things for children to do and observe. There are even natural settings (woods, trees, vegetable garden) for science study and play. There is no roof shelter, but the proximity of indoor-outdoor play areas makes it comparatively easy to move art materials, tables and fine sensorimotor toys outdoors in fine weather. Lack of equipment can be compensated for by rotation, as in the case of the portable pool. Teacher ingenuity and assistance from parents, moreover, will yield ideas for building or finding equipment to be employed on an alternating basis, for example, a makeshift trampoline, walking boards, slides, climbing apparatus, and even a playhouse, theater, or boat. Despite compactness and cost restrictions, small playgrounds can also be stimulating and enjoyable places to play.

Developing a Free Play Program

Making friends

The quality of adult attention is as important as the characteristics of the physical environment in developing the quality of children's play. The chief problem of developing a free play program is the problem of how to stimulate the children's imagination into constructive forms of experimental activity without over-regulating the activity.

Goals of Free Play

Free play, as a program activity, uses certain techniques to realize certain goals. Among them are engaging every child in activities throughout the span

214

of time allotted for play; facilitating social harmony and learning; and providing experience in experimentation with materials, both alone and in collaboration with peers.

The overriding aim of these play periods is to allow the child to act creatively on the scene of reality, facilitated by the background efforts of teachers. The child is the doer; the caregiver or teacher, the organizer in the background, who prepares the environment and works in small ways to anticipate and solve problems. Free play programs enjoy a special place in day care because few homes are so well equipped with the toys and facilities, and few parents have the time, training, numbers of children, and inclination to match the quality of a good day care center or nursery school.

The Role of the Teacher

Play is "free" in the sense that a significant proportion of the choices, both among activities and among the means employed in activity, are made by the child herself. The types of play are limited, however, by the variety of materials available, the child's imagination, the needs of and relations with other children, and, especially, the effectiveness of teachers in maintaining a nurturant and stimulating atmosphere. An interesting and diversified environment for the child to learn in and enjoy cannot be maintained unless a great deal of thought and effort is devoted to its organization and management. Children cannot be free to develop, to experiment with a toy, communicate with a peer either verbally or nonverbally, or to pursue a task in comfort unless there is sufficient order for them to do so with a minimum of interference and conflict. This condition of necessary tranquility cannot be realized without careful attention to techniques of control. Some degree of structure, in which a balance is maintained between permissiveness and tightness of control, is essential.

Permissiveness in groups may lead temporarily to *some* increase in experimentation on the part of *some* children. This is usually at the expense of other children, however, who withdraw from the assault of their more assertive peers. Without rules, the more active and self-confident children get their way, since young children are not developed enough to establish fair play on their own. But even these children are not free to persist constructively at play. There are always several children, some more insecure and aggressive than others, who cause constant disputes over toys and frequent disruption of everyone's play. Thus in the long run, without adult regulation, children use materials and follow activities erratically, and seldom in depth. Competition and chaos are likely to overshadow occasional acts of spontaneous cooperation. Tension is by no means absent in the presence of permissiveness, since the general disorder and rivalry leads to emotional conflict, frustration and anxiety.

At the other extreme, severity and tightness of controls lead to fear, resentment and a general stifling of creativity and expansiveness in play and interpersonal relations. Children tend to stick to their own little corners, feeling no right to initiate play with others without the direction of a teacher. Only teacher-directed activities, either individually or in groups, become the rule. The child becomes timid and ritualistic about his or her own play, anxious at exploring or working with a toy in a different way for fear it might be the "wrong" way and will meet with the disapproval of a caregiver.

The problem is, then, how to obtain only the degree of structure necessary to encourage both order and spontaneity. Creating a social environment through adapting guidance to the situation and the styles of different children, with minimal intrusion, is the essence of the caregiver's role; it is a process that takes time to develop.

There are many steps in the process of creating a play program, starting with organizing the adult social structure; selecting children and defining play groups; preparing programs, scheduling and coordinating activities, working out teaching roles and methods; and stimulating the play itself. Since the role of a democratic adult social structure as a model influencing children's development has been discussed in Chapter 3 on the social environment, we shall begin with the process of selecting children for play groups.

Organizing Play Groups

Play, by its loose, free-flowing nature, would seem to thrive easily in almost any group of children. But play among little children prospers better in some relations than in others. Among the factors to consider in organizing constructive play groups are methods of admitting children to day care, distribution of children according to interest and personality, and the type of developmental grouping.

Unlike a learning group, a play group does not require a careful balancing of ability and personality characteristics among the children (Chapter 14) to maintain its functions week after week. Yet it is useful to pick children who will play well together and who will bring different styles and skills to enrich the play of all. Where choice is possible, a well-balanced play group can best be organized at the point of admission, using personality matching techniques and sociometric analysis, as discussed in Chapter 5. Even where choice is limited, it improves children's play experiences and development to diagnose and guide patterns of play.

Admissions

The first consideration in organizing play groups is the possibility of admitting children gradually, a few children each day until all attend every day. It can also be useful for new children to attend only part-time, and for parents to remain at the center with their child to provide emotional support during the early part of the adaptation period. There are two conditions in which gradual admissions can be used: (1) on those few occasions when it is planned to admit an entire group of children (new center, fall enrollment, perhaps after a long holiday); (2) for new children at any time. Most day care centers serve a heavy proportion of working parents who cannot afford time off from work to attend the gradual admission of their child. If parents can be encouraged to stretch their schedules to allow some flexibility, however, children will adapt more easily, and it is easier to start off with better relations, quality of play, and understanding of the rules.

There is another reason for staggering admissions and for carefully monitoring the adaptation period. Play groups follow a cycle of development, which makes it easier for new members to enter at some points than at others. Children look around for play partners and form new friendships at the time they enter a play group. When a group is entirely new there are many choices open over which teachers can exercise a great deal of constructive influence. They may see that a restless child can be involved in construction building play with two other interested block builders, or they can bring together for number play two otherwise isolated children who show an obvious interest in counting. If caregivers overlook these early opportunities for influencing choice, they may be lost, because play partnerships soon become stabilized and eventually children form relatively permanent alliances. At this point, the efforts of teachers to find someone for a slow child to play with or to break up a tight clique of children who only engage in structural house play meet greater resistance, because a relative social equilibrium is already established.

Fortunately, this equilibrium or balance shifts from time to time, as a result of children leaving or entering a play group, or when children develop new interests or personality traits, which in turn sometimes result when teachers or parents cultivate the new interests or traits from awareness of the need for change. However, children's patterns can just as easily deteriorate from new problems at home, a change in caregivers, or a decline in caregiver efforts, making change likely under difficult circumstances. Sometimes the social balance may exhibit remarkable persistence, moreover, despite the departure or change of one or two children, especially if two or three strong leaders remain. Accordingly, teachers need to be constantly aware of the balance of relations and play patterns in their groups.

The various techniques for diagnosing problems described in Chapter 5 are helpful aids to spotting trends that may be used to bring about needed shifts. A caregiver may note, for example, a moderate lessening of one child's aggressivity or another's increased cooperativeness, which might otherwise go unnoticed. These trends may signal a change in the readiness of a small group of playmates to be more flexible in admitting a new partner, or even for one of them to shift to a different play partner in another activity at least some of the time.

The problem is not only that of ensuring constructive play and a choice of play partners for all children, including entering children and timid or shy children. It is equally making sure that no child is excluded from satisfying relations and opportunities to play for reason of cultural or sex discrimination on the part of other children. The problem may be particularly acute for a new minority group child, such as a black, Hispanic, or Chinese child, entering a center in which the children are predominantly white Protestant in background. The problem is also likely to arise with almost any combination of children when play selections are allowed to develop without attention to every child's needs. Thus admitting blocks of new children gradually to ensure every child finds a place and being aware of potential openings for new children in the various small play groups, are useful admission tools for ensuring adaptation to group care.

In a prospective play group of fifteen children, for instance, both the number of children attending and the frequency of attendance can be limited over the first few days or more of school. Parental attendance with the child until he or she shows signs of enjoying school is an additional key to the process. During the first week, three new children could be added to the total each day until the maximum of fifteen is attained by the end of the week. The children who enter at the end of the week may experience some disadvantage, since by the time the cumulative enrollment reaches nine, subgroup play patterns will have begun to form. Assuming caregiving ratios are adequate, the first patterns are not yet so fixed, however, that new playmates cannot be eased in comfortably through skilled guidance. If children find themselves in a social environment that is warm, friendly and attentive to their personal needs from the moment they enter the strange situation, they will usually adapt very quickly. Assigning a particular teacher to generally look after each child all of the first day and much of every day during the first week will accelerate the process of feeling "at home". There are always a few children who, because they adapt easily or are already at home in day care, will not suffer if a few days of staff attention is concentrated on the needful newcomers.

Pre-admission diagnostic procedures can also be used to identify children who are more or less likely to adapt easily to group care. If enough staff are available, more detailed assignment of children to different phases of the admission cycle may be advantageous. One technique, usually only feasible in part-time programs with families where one parent either does not work full-time or enjoys a flexible work schedule, is to invite parents to bring their children to school for preliminary observation in play groups of five or six. On the basis of ratings made during these play periods, children can then be assigned in clusters of likely play partners to enter at different phases. Among things teachers do is to see that children with little social experience are clustered with a combination of friendly and other less secure children to enter on one of the first two or three entering days (or entering phases of two or three days each). Such children should form relations more easily and be able to identify common interests in smaller groups, and caregivers would be able to provide greater attention during these early periods. The clustering should also consider questions of sex, culture, language, background, interests, and other aspects of personality as they might affect how well children would be expected to adapt and play together, and to establish a good balance of similarities and differences among children. Screening in pre-enrollment play observation is equally useful for setting up the total play groups, regardless of whether or not graduated admissions are used.

The more usual condition of admitting children individually as vacancies occur makes use of many of the same principles. Each child is invited to attend the center for no more than a few hours at a time during the first week, preferably visiting on alternative days. Part time (half day or alternate day) programs may not require such gradual introduction and, fortunately, most children adapt very quickly with full attendance from the start. But certain children, who adapt slowly, sometimes because of overprotectiveness or conflict at home and sometimes because of difficulty with aggressive peers in day care, may need the continued attention of a specially assigned caregiver for as long as several weeks or even months. Many centers may have to restrict severely the number of such children they admit because of the drain they obviously make on limited staff resources.

Because many parents cannot spend the time to help their child adapt gradually, personalized care is often the only solution. Extra alertness to children's needs and idiosyncrasies during the initial adaptation period will strengthen their adjustment and make them easier to handle in the long run.

Obviously, the number of children admitted each month should be limited to minimize distressing disruptions to the ongoing play patterns and to enable staff to provide enough individual attention.

Defining the Play Groups

The second consideration for establishing viable play groups is the method of grouping. To work well, the interests and styles of the children in each group should be sufficiently *similar* (homogeneous) that they will play compatibly together and sufficiently *different* (heterogeneous) to nourish variety in development. If, for example, all children in a group are obsessed with the automobile culture they may play day after day with cars and other vehicles, developing a narrow focus which leaves them quite deprived in other areas. Such overconcentration makes it trying for teachers to encourage imaginative play in other vital areas. It is equally difficult, on the other hand, to develop close associations among children who have few interests in common.

The picture I have drawn is exaggerated, for almost any group will be found to have some range to their interests and some commonality; but what is obvious in the extreme is also important in the minor trends that develop to create problems in play groups. Homogeneity among children is determined by their similarity in interests and matches in personality characteristics, either directly, as in their speed or concern for detail in doing things, or through complementing one another's styles, as in dominant-submissive relations. (For a complete list see the diagnostic method in Chapter 5 and Appendix B.) Age, sex, sibling position and such social characteristics as ethnicity, social class, and parental occupation and education all exercise some degree of influence. Heterogeneity is found in proportion to the number of differences among all social and individual characteristics of children. But how can homogeneity and heterogeneity be maintained in each of the play groups?

Age Grouping (Developmental or horizontal grouping)

There are two main methods for grouping children, horizontally by age or vertically in "family" type groups. Each has different advantages and disadvantages with respect to the problem of balancing similarities and differences among the children in a group. Age, which is the traditional method for grouping children, maximizes the number of likely playmate choices, since age makes for a similarity of outlook that transcends many other differences. Age mates may vary markedly, however, in social, language, and other competencies and interests that affect their enjoyment and success in playing together. Most day care centers use age only as a rough index of development, therefore, admitting and promoting children according to a broader clinical consideration of their social adjustment and competence development. Centers following this practice are likely to have each age group cover a span of 12 to 18 months and to allow the groups to overlap slightly in age (usually by a few months), depending on the current characteristics of the children.

The chief problem with this method is that, except in large centers having more than one group at each age level, even when age grouping is not rigidly followed, it is not easy when promoting children to take account of differences

Age Grouping   Family(Multiple Age) Grouping

FIGURE 9–1
*Methods of grouping children for free play. Children find more
congenial playmates in groups organized by age, but may also compete
more. Children gain more leader-follower experience and often compete
less in cross-age family groups, but usually also find fewer congenial
playmates and develop less elaborate construction projects.*

in personality and social characteristics to maintain heterogeneity. At some
point, the immature child must be promoted, if only to make room for new
entries or promotions from the successively younger age groups; while the
bright, well-adjusted child can hardly, under this policy, skip an entire age
group, when eighteen months is such a large percentage of the life span in early
life.

Family Grouping (Vertical age grouping)

This method further extends the age range in which children are grouped, often
by several years, in order to recreate the advantages of the varied age relations
of the home. Because of the increased age range, which substitutes parenting
and dependency ties for rivalries between equals, relations between children
and between caregivers are supposed to resemble closely the informality of
family life, attachments, and control, as I shall describe shortly.

The chief advantages of this method are the expanded opportunity (1) for
including personal and social characteristics as criteria for admitting children
or shifting children between groups, and (2) for leader-follower experiences. A
center of 40 children, for example, might set up two broad groups, one encom-
passing children from ages one to three and the second from two to four years.

There would thus be no difficulty under this arrangement in occasionally shifting two- and three-year-olds back and forth between the groups to keep the groups balanced and solve adjustment problems.

It is also an advantage when each play group encompasses a two- or three-year spread that differences between social and intellectual competence in all areas become so great that older children are almost inevitably the leaders and models for younger children. By encouraging older children to set an example (modeling) and younger children to follow this example (imitation) a different form of give and take in play and caring between children predominates that may temper the extremes of competition characteristic of our achievement-oriented society. The dependency of the younger child draws out the competence and appeals to the caring attitudes of the older child, rather than challenging anyone's status through rivalry as a peer. The younger child is inspired to learn, to follow instructions, and to accept help, while the older child learns to set an example, teach, lead, and give help, thus furthering his or her autonomy and social responsibility. Only those children who attend a center which uses this method over a period of at least two or three years will share in both leader and follower role experiences, however.

Family grouping faces a chronic problem of ensuring enough peer playmate choices for each child, however, because abilities and interests *are* partly tied to age. Even in large groups there are somehow never quite enough companions for each level of competence. For example, a typical group of twenty boys and girls of many interests and types, spread over no more than two years, provides a reduced set of 10 age peers among whom to choose playmates. Since children's skills and interests often break down further into younger and older half-year spans for playmate preferences, a certain amount of ingrown relations and peer social isolation is difficult to avoid without enlarging the total group beyond manageable size.

Selecting Children for Groups

Once the methods for defining play groups are chosen, either of two ways of organizing well-balanced play groups can be used, the first by fitting children to groups as they are admitted, and the second by arranging play activities that bring together children in different combinations. An hour of observation of each child during free play at the center as, or just before, the child is admitted, in combination with information from a parent on the child's characteristics, provides a good basis to decide which play group best matches the child's needs. This procedure is obviously only applicable in large centers offering a choice of play groups. Information from parents should include a few details, obtained through an interview or from an application form, on the child's developmental history and current characteristics and problems. If children are observed and their characteristics rated by two teachers independently, a more balanced decision of their patterns can usually be arrived at.

It is obviously important to have in mind the characteristics by which existing play groups are defined at the time of the observations in order to make practical decisions of how and where the child will fit with other children. Thus, such questions as the age range of the various groups, the balance of girls and boys, the diversity of social and cultural backgrounds represented in each group, the balance of leader-follower types of children, and other characteristics are preferably worked out in advance.

Because it is virtually impossible to maintain well-balanced groups, it is advisable to also plan on putting children from different play groups together in different combinations for various activities. For instance, different age groups might share sociodramatic play or art activities. The appropriateness of hierarchical roles (parents and children, supervisors and workers in a shop) in the former activity, and the separateness of children (easel painting) in the latter, make both activities adaptable to a broad range of ages. On the other hand, puzzles, block building, and story reading might be more suitable for children similar in age and ability, because of the problem of avoiding frustration in children or preventing chaos when materials have many small parts. We have seen earlier (Chapter 8) how children of widely different ages can play together in the same setting in gross motor activities.

There are other reasons for switching play subgroups around, such as varying leader-follower experiences; avoiding social isolation; ensuring that timid children get special opportunities to play with other gentle children who will encourage them to assert themselves; finding enough partners for both girls and boys to learn about both "boy" type, mechanical activities and "girl" type, interpersonal play; and exposing children to others of different ethnic and cultural backgrounds. It is essential, on the other hand, that flexible subgrouping does not lead to a loss of continuity in attachment relations and play interests with valued caregivers and playmates.

The Free Play Program

Program
Preparation and
Theme Planning

The essentials of free play programs are in large part defined by the types of materials and activities, and their arrangement, which we have discussed in the preceding chapters. Preparing programs is, however, a continuing process composed of several features needing further discussion: preparation of the daily program; daily activity cleanup; program perspectives, development, variation, and cyclical rotation; and involvement of children.

Once a healthy diversity of materials and equipment have been selected and a basic set of zonal arrangements has been laid out, work on the program proper begins. The two main dimensions of *daily preparation* and *program planning* should, under the best of circumstances, be interrelated. Many day care staff, staggering along with poor staff-child ratios and scattered bits of equipment, may feel lucky if they can find any advance time for daily preparation. But if children's play is to have any depth, long-range planning is essential. The long-range functions of play are to foster the child's development in important areas of life, with the use of materials in each type of activity planned to this end. Planning needs to occur in two directions—vertically, graduating the use of materials from the simple to the more complex, and horizontally, through coordinating the use of materials in different areas to interrelate the child's understanding among concepts in common *themes*.

Free play programs are generally planned more broadly than guided learning programs. Play is a much looser type of activity than the detailed sequences usually programmed for guided learning. But although play offers children more choice in type and use of materials, especially in sociodramatic play, materials must still be selected, arranged, and varied from week to week according to the rates at which children's competencies develop in different areas. Presumably a wider range of difficulty and variety should be represented in the materials used in play than in those for guided learning, not only because materials are used more creatively and in many more ways, but also because the spread of competence in children's play groups is typically greater. Yet in the end, *thematic planning* weaves together the two sorts of activities in many ways.

A *theme* stressed in sociodramatic play areas, through material selection and teacher suggestion, which is paralleled with specific teacher guided learning activities around the same theme over the same period, may spontaneously appear in the children's free play. For example, if the theme is size concepts, children are likely to be found attending to size variations in free play with puzzles, form boards, stacking and construction toys. Interest in size variations would also appear in painting, drawing, and carpentry activities.

A year's program plan can include several topics, each with a number of themes, which can be linked together by similarity in concept category or content. A topic on shape moves easily to color, then size, number, and other dimensions of things. A topic on size leads logically to others on length, width, height, and other size variations, while process concepts of means and ends, cause and effect, and speed are similarly closely linked. Or again, topics can be related around a common content, such as studying the size, shape, and other characteristics of different toys, different clothes, and then different dishes. Teachers can prepare *kits of material* for children to use during play periods and make suggestions for using them to encourage additional focus in the current theme concept.

Planning an interrelated program over a long time period ensures that basic areas of knowledge are systematically covered and that experience is planned to ensure that the various rules and examples for each concept are well exposed. This method also permits extensive review by weaving previous themes into subsequent activities as the program develops. Concepts of number, for example, need not wholly disappear when new themes on size or time are taken up. Counting is easily brought into the concepts as in counting the number of objects of each size, or counting the number of minutes it takes to fill a bucket with water. It may also be useful to develop a kind of *spiral curriculum* approach by returning repeatedly to a limited range of selected themes of value, each time with somewhat greater depth and abstraction. The latter approach maintains enthusiastic interest in children in each of the areas, because of the freshness they feel in changing themes while maintaining the sense of familiarity and accomplishment they experience in picking up former themes at ever-advancing levels.

Once a basic outline of such a program is constructed, much of the subsequent preparation can be done from theme to theme and from day to day. The basic unit for planning and preparation becomes the theme or topic for the period. Packages of pictures, miniature replicas, sociodramatic play props, and other materials of the type outlined in Chapter 7 can be prepared in advance of each two- to three-week theme period, and a schedule of excursions drawn up. This reduces daily preparation to a process of arranging and rotating materials, and preparing those arts and crafts materials which cannot be wholly prepared in advance.

Toy Arrangements and Use

Toys are learning materials that fall into two types—those that are readily accessible for play at all times and those that are rotated. A *basic repertoire* consists of a broad set of fine motor toys, gross motor apparatus, and art, science, construction, and sociodramatic materials with multiple uses that children rarely tire of. A *rotating repertoire* consists of materials with more specifically defined uses, and thematic program-related materials. There is not always a sharp division between these two categories, since miniature replicas of people, vehicles, and animals, for example, are generally at hand in block areas, while not every set of blocks, assembly toys, or art materials is set out for play daily. It is best to err on the side of a small basic repertoire, rotating a substantial reserve of toys taken from storage closets or high shelves which are easily accessible to adults; this sustains the children's interest through novelty.

Not only sociodramatic and related theme materials, but all types of toys, books, records, art, and other materials need periodic circulation to ensure that a good variety of materials is regularly covered. Shifting toys according to the interests and learning patterns of the children is more productive than using a fixed schedule of toy rotation. Since children often spend the first day or two re-exploring the dimensions of materials they have not seen for a period, it may take a week or more for children to build up interest and use the toys in complex ways. It helps to introduce alternative toys at the point when children's interests are beginning to flag.

Daily and even morning and afternoon preparation of free play programs is an important process. At the beginning of each period, display toys visually in sets in the zones where children are to use them and in a manner to invite interest and quick access. Toys with many small pieces can be stored in open boxes or baskets for easy transfer from shelf to table. Puzzles, form boards, and records can be stored in cabinets designed for accessibility and easy inventory. Modular toys like blocks and assembly toys can be arranged in sets to draw attention to their unit characteristics and provide easy access, as in Figure 9–2.

Unless toys are inventoried regularly, many of them are likely to remain unused for long periods, leaving the children with insufficient exposure to a variety of activities. There is no point in letting a toy which consistently arouses no interest to take up space. However, if certain good toys remain unused or some children lack interest in certain types of activity, a rearrangement of materials, play groups, or even the methods and circumstances of introducing the toys may change the patterns of play.

In addition to checking on the readiness of the basic toy repertoire and setting out the rotating and theme materials in the play zones, daily program preparation includes setting out the creative art and craft materials ready for immediate use. Clay, for example, needs to be removed from its protected, moist environment ready for use; paints need to be uncapped or mixed; crayons, paper, paste, and collage materials need to be placed in position on the tables. If any of these preparations are left until the free play period actually

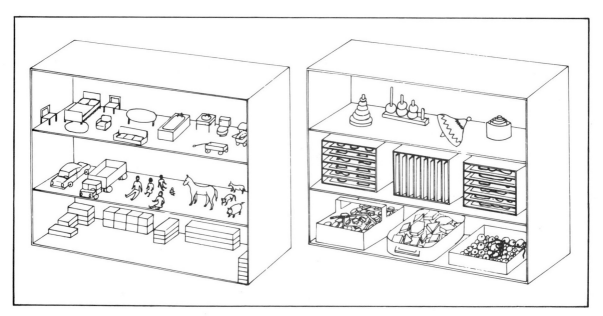

FIGURE 9-2
*Different types of play materials should be stored and displayed
differently.*

begins, they might be the responsibility of a floating teacher who is not needed
for continuing supervision of play. A good choice of several types of materials
prepared in advance nevertheless avoids conflicts and prevents the children's
play from falling apart. In addition, various special sensory exploratory activities usually need last minute preparation; flowers, food, and liquids for tasting
and smelling are particularly demanding in this way.

**Involving Children
in Preparation and
Cleanup**

Preparation

Program preparation is a more complex process than cleanup; it requires thinking about the uses of materials and the match between toys and the play needs
of the children. Nevertheless, some involvement of children in preparation is
possible, usually more in terms of setting out materials than in planning. Older
preschoolers may also be involved in brief discussions of ideas for activities;
this can be a valuable experience in working toward long range goals and
memory development with anticipation of future events and the group process
as motivating aids. Work sessions to make future program materials, such as
filling egg cartons with soil for a later seed planting project or making paper
boxes to hold different leaves for another nature project can also be a part of
free play or special activity programs.

   The major dimension of preparation to emphasize with children is setting
out materials each day. Arts and crafts activity is a good example. Children can
be assigned to day care workers responsible for preparation. A small group of

Preparation   Cleanup

FIGURE 9–3
*Teaching the value of work: Involving children in play preparation and
cleanup. Preparation is often learned and accomplished most easily by
early arrivers in the morning or from outdoor play on a rotating basis,
while cleanup is an extensive task easily learned and accomplished
when everyone pitches in.*

children can be scheduled to work with the teachers when duties or play activity can be left without conflict. Taking turns daily or weekly will ensure that
little time is lost from the playground or other interesting activities and that all
benefit from an important work experience. Scheduled rotation is usually preferable to casual invitations, since the children will be prepared to come instead
of facing a last-minute conflict between leaving some interesting play in progress and missing the opportunity to be a "teacher helper". It also avoids the
danger of playing favorites.

The term "helper" points up the value of presenting work tasks so that the
child recognizes the social importance of chores. When it is her turn, a little girl
will see the opportunity as a prize and take pride in her contribution to the
program for the benefit of her group and the center. Such an orientation will
not succeed, however, unless the teacher involves the children in a patient and
interesting way. He should ask them to do small things at first and only work
for short periods, depending on the scope of the chores they have been expected to perform at home. The child may need frequent demonstrations and
help over critical points, such as pouring paints without spilling them. The
entire process can be made more productive and interesting if the teacher occasionally leads a discussion about the duties and the difficulties encountered,

and if the children themselves help in assigning the tasks. Following the completion of preparatory duties, a brief inspection by all members of the group of all parts of the task will heighten involvement, social responsibility, and a sense of standards. How well did Susan place the drawing papers around the table, or Henry set out the paint jars and brushes? Did they bring out enough pieces, were the crayons there, was the paint too runny and did they have enough help? These and other questions lend a sense of importance and excitement to what the children do and raise their consciousness about doing tasks well to help one another.

Setting tables, serving food, folding diapers and even some of the office routines (getting supplies from the closets, filling a few envelopes, possibly turning a hand mimeograph) can also be valuable preparatory activities for the children. They teach something about the scope of adult work, give first-hand experience in adult social roles, and, above all, provide the beginnings of concepts about work, its standards, and functions in social organization.

Cleanup

Cleanup is a more focused, concrete activity, but the sorting necessary in putting things away teaches the children the beginnings of classification; it can be made easier for the children by marking shelves and boxes with outlines or pictures of the toys to be placed there. Individual children or small groups usually take turns in different tasks following the same system of social involvement and regulation as for preparatory activities. Putting toys away is the main activity, but clearing lunch and snack tables, emptying wastebaskets and diaper pails, and light sweeping or mopping can also be done by the children.

When the practice is started early, graduated according to the expanding skills of children, and embedded in a positively rewarding group process, the basic attitudes, expectations, and initial skills will be launched as a matter of course. Taking turns and organizing the tasks so that small groups of two or three work together at each set of tasks in a friendly atmosphere with short, well-defined objectives will go far to make the experience simply another pleasant routine. Three children setting the table each day, one child the spoons, a second the forks, and a third the napkins, and trading around from week to week, makes a quick and friendly social routine providing both variety and a sense of achievement. Active participation by adults is also vital to establish norms and expectations. The teacher who works along with the children, making sure to do neither too much nor too little, is more fun to work with than the teacher who just stands over them and reminds them what to do.

Cognitive Guidance and Stimulation in Free Play

The role of adults in free play is not limited to care, settling conflicts and enforcing rules; attention to guiding children's learning in free play enjoys equal importance.

Children learn more rapidly and play more constructively when they are regularly instructed in concepts, tasks, and the use of materials. Guidance of this type should be regular, but brief. A teacher should watch each child in turn, looking for opportunities to suggest alternative toys, furnish help, or comment as needed. No child should be neglected, but help should not be given too often; some overdependent children magnify their helplessness to get more attention. It is particularly important to compliment any efforts at independent problem-solving, however feeble, which overdependent children display, to reward them for autonomy and encourage its further development. A little boy whose family has always done things for him, needs more praise at first just for trying to find a piece to a puzzle than the child who always goes ahead alone with all of her puzzles because she has been routinely encouraged to do so at home.

On the other hand, however well play materials are matched and sequenced, there are always unexpected difficulties, making guidance on difficult problems essential at certain points. A complete demonstration of an entire task may be helpful for the child to gain an overall picture, but isolation of the one or two parts of a task that present the most difficulty will usually ease him toward mastery.

Cognitive guidance consists mainly of labelling and pointing out key features of a task to which a child is attending. For example, when a child is in the process of trying to make a bridge with a block that is too short, a teacher can demonstrate the advantage of a longer block. On other occasions she can point to and turn the handle of a jack-in-the-box; point out and identify a jar of orange paint the child has overlooked; or suggest a relation between a pointed piece in a puzzle and several angular holes in which the piece may fit. Note that the caregiver is teaching language as a tool for problem solving, as well as helping the child to improve techniques in problem-solving.

Children will value solving problems in proportion to the pleasant emotional experiences they enjoy in problem-solving activities with adults. Enthusiasm and warmth are essential. Tension, coldness, and impatience will only discourage children, reducing their self-confidence and efforts. On days when an adult cannot be warm and friendly, relaxed and easy, he or she should minimize the cognitive guidance he or she gives in free play.

As the complexity of their problem-solving skills improves in an area, children become more confident, autonomous, and able to enjoy an activity for longer periods. When they first enroll in group care many children, because of limited competence, are inclined to skip around superficially among tasks almost regardless of age. Some children have hardly had any opportunity at all to play consistently with toys. They may need special encouragement in learning how to play constructively and with persistence. Such children usually need initial attention and support to help them perceive the significant parts of the new tasks before they can begin to work independently. When things go well, gradually, over a period of days or weeks, a teacher will become aware that a child has learned to spend more time on his or her own in one area, with only the occasional need for encouragement or guidance to solve a new and more challenging task.

There is probably no time when guidance is not necessary, although any day care play group usually produces a core of inexhaustible, imaginative players who are a source of constant stimulation to the others, children who presumably have been cognitively well-nourished at home. But even these children will advance more rapidly, and their play will be enriched, if encouraged by suggestions from teachers. If their play begins to lag, it is probably largely because the range of activities (and new ideas) offered is not sufficiently challenging. They often need new materials, like more complex jigsaw puzzles and assembly toys, and new themes (about different trades, for example electricians, sailors, veterinarians), stimulated also by stories, guided learning programs and excursions, to keep them interested in different aspects of play.

A method of rating the effectiveness of teachers in supervising free play activities is shown in Table 9–1. The method is designed to provide a quick overview of teaching and caregiving skills important to organizing the play environment, and promoting healthy social relations and cognitive learning in play. Ratings are designed to be used over a thirty to forty-five minute play period, but could be easily adapted to longer periods.

The ratings are most useful for spotting particular areas of strength and weakness and, like the other ratings described in Chapter 5, probably enlist teacher support better when the teacher or teachers themselves are involved in making the ratings, through checking off items at the end of a period or by videotaping sessions. The method is also well-suited to repeated use over a series of observations to assess how well a teacher is progressing or maintaining skills.

Techniques of Supervision

| I. Direct Methods of Control | Establishing Play Group Rules and Consistency of Methods |

One of the basic principles of effective playroom supervision is consistency. If a playroom is well arranged and rules are established from the very first day of each child's participation, the need for intensive adult guidance on these elemental matters is greatly reduced.

Rules and methods are more effective when the entire staff defines and agrees to them from the beginning; without staff agreement any system will soon suffer or break down. If one teacher lets children climb on the window sills while another doesn't, children will climb when the latter teacher is not looking but in any case will tend to resist her enforcement, which will undermine children's acceptance of rules. Too few rules lead to disorder, while too many rules restrict spontaneity. If no more than one or two new children are enrolled each week in a center, the original group provides a good example for new children to learn to accept the basic rules of the program. Too many new children at a time may provide too many examples of children breaking rules (however unknowingly) and will undermine the acceptance of all rules by the children, particularly the less popular but still important rules, like not shouting or running in the halls. Graduating admissions as described earlier will ease the acceptance of key rules from the beginning when an entire new group is to be admitted.

Few new children have fixed ideas of what to do or what is expected, and are therefore comparatively receptive to a wide range of social rules. Building

TABLE 9-1. Monitoring free play activity: ratings on teacher supervisory behavior

Physical Environment

1. Play area divided into 3–5 zones of play.   Rating_____
2. Each zone equipped with 4–6 different types of toys.   Rating_____
3. Teacher regularly checked each zone of play (saw enough toys available, controlled social density, ensured agression channelled to constructive activities).   Rating_____

Remarks:_____

_____

Socioemotional Care

1. Teacher regularly set up collaborative play experiences.   Rating_____
2. Teacher cuddled, hugged, petted or smiled at each child.   Rating_____
3. Teacher attended to children without scolding, threatening, or punishing.   Rating_____
4. Teacher gave reasons or suggested alternatives when using ''No.''   Rating_____

Remarks:_____

_____

Play Stimulation and Language

1. Teacher helped initiate play and encouraged children to play.   Rating_____
2. Teacher helped each child at least once during play, according to need.   Rating_____
3. Teacher arranged and introduced a variety of toys and materials within each zone of activity (including some ethnically diverse materials).   Rating_____

Remarks:_____

_____

Rating Guide: 7. Extremely like.
                        6. Much like.
                        5. Moderately like.
                        4. Neutral: sometimes like, sometimes unlike
                        3. Moderately unlike.
                        2. Much unlike.
                        1. Not at all like.

clear definitions over the first few weeks is easier for teachers and children alike. A few basic rules clearly defined and enforced from the start gradually disappear as points of friction, thus freeing children to pursue their play constructively and with enthusiasm (see Chapter 5).

Constructive Direction and Positive Social Attitudes

When direct instruction and control seem necessary, positive social attitudes contribute to children's acceptance of rules. Practice simple directness and clarity of instruction in a tone as free from tension and hostility as possible. When a child is asked to help put out the crayons in a friendly way, cooperation is much more likely than if asked, vaguely, to "put out the materials," and in a cold or impatient manner. If instructions are usually phrased in a positive way (to *do* something), rather than as a prohibition (*not* to do something), the child will learn how to actively cope rather than simply inhibit his behavior. Ask the child to please keep his food on his plate; when feasible, avoid asking him to *not* put it on the table. Children, even badly misdirected ones, usually *want* to do well and can learn to understand.

Find occasions to reward each child warmly with praise and approval when he or she performs well and cooperates with others. Repeated criticism of undesired actions will tend to make these "naughty" ways exciting to children; not only may the actions themselves be interesting, but because they are forbidden they become a means of challenging authority and a method of getting attention. An unthinking adult can actually set up a cycle of antisocial behavior in a child by combining insufficient attention to constructive behavior with overattention to destructive play. From the child's point of view it is more satisfying to challenge an "unjust" pattern of lack of attention, than to do without attention at all. Constant nagging at a child to stop teasing other children, without ever showing interest in the child when she is playing well, usually reinforces her desire to tease all the time, as the only way to get any attention from the teacher in ordinary play every day (see also Chapter 5). Constant teasing is probably rooted in insecurity and competitive home practices, but in any case nagging reinforces it, while constructive attention may temper it. For serious problems, outside help may of course be necessary.

Constructive direction should not be confused with negative criticism, however; if the latter is to be avoided, the former is sometimes essential. Given with a minimum of tension in a friendly manner and with an expectation that a child—in the long run—understands and wants to behave, *direct* and positive guidance will lead to desired social habits. Repeated enforcement of a few clear rules of "dont's" as well as "do's" will not produce much rebellion or resentment, provided that overall positive guidance outweighs negative criticism and that the program and the social climate are enjoyable. Thus it is sometimes clearer to focus on the fact of *hitting,* for example, and talk about its meaning, rather than dodging the issue by saying "positively" to play with this or that toy when it is the aggression that is of concern. Dodging the issue fails to deal with the child's need to understand the nature of his or her actions and their consequences.

II. Indirect Methods of Control

Once understood, repeatedly making an issue of negative behavior only promotes conflict and retards learning. Thus, whenever conditions permit, it is preferable to use indirect methods to guide children's choices and behavior. Establishing zones for block building, puzzles, art activity, and other forms of play through placing some physical barriers between them (see Chapter 8) is perhaps the most basic application of indirect principles for regulating children's behavior during play, because their activity is channeled with a minimum amount of human authority over their behavior. The child makes choices according to the physical circumstances, not just because of the authority of the adult. For example, a child will not extend a block building beyond a certain distance because a toy shelf blocks the path, not because the teacher says not to. Even if the child understands that the physical conditions were arranged by the adult in the first place, barriers and area definitions seem to elicit children's cooperation through their obvious purpose and the concreteness of the reality they establish. Children are not "naturally" opposed to structure when it is fixed, simple and has an evident purpose. Bounded play zones, which regulate their choices among a variety of interesting activities, tend to produce cooperative behavior because conflict is minimized. Given minimal boundaries, choices are consistently and concretely defined for them by the physical arrangements without the constant tension of adults telling them what to do.

Zone Assignment of Teachers

Well-arranged play area boundaries bring us more than half way toward effective control of traffic, noise, and social density. They prevent children from running around and disrupting the play; they discourage noisy shouting across the room; and they prevent any one area from becoming crowded with more children than can be managed or than can profit from the toys available.

Aside from physical boundaries, there are other ways of encouraging children to persist quietly in play, and of controlling noise and traffic as children move from place to place. One technique is to assign staff to the *zones of play activity,* each staff member being responsible for one area of the playroom and for the behavior and regulation of all the children in it.

One of the chief advantages of this technique over that of assigning teachers to specific children is that *no area is ever left unattended.* It is not that teachers should constantly hover over children. It is simply that without continuous responsibility, problems are not attended to when they arise. A fine block building or painting, which may have taken several children a long time to accomplish, is easily destroyed in a moment by a thoughtless or envious child when a teacher is absent. Such destruction and similar upsets, or even injuries to infants from grabbed or thrown toys, are easily anticipated and prevented by alert teachers watching for signs of approaching conflict.

When moving a group of children from one room to another, the child responsibility method may be preferable, to see they all get there. Upon arriving in a playroom or on a playground, however, an immediate switch, planned in advance, to zone methods will allow greater flexibility in activity choices for children at no sacrifice of supervisory control or of individualized attention. On any day when there are too few staff members available, areas which cannot be effectively controlled by the zone method can be completely blocked off. Otherwise children will play in these areas without sufficient supervision and disturbances will inevitably occur.

As an alternative to closing off areas, well-designed playrooms lend themselves to the management of two and sometimes three connected play areas by a single staff member, if there are not too many children in the group. The success of dual or triple zone control also hinges on how well zone definitions channel the children's play in functional play groups, while enabling the teacher to visually survey and move freely among the zones with little effort. If children constantly play on the border between two floor play areas, for example, because both zones contain blocks the children want to build with together, these children may be overlooked by the caregivers from both zones. Perhaps one of the areas should be enlarged and all the blocks placed in it, or one combined zone be created for which both caregivers become jointly responsible.

Supervising children in these circumstances should be as gentle and personalized as in any other control system. Some sensitivity to differences in personality style may be lost, but in any case is more than compensated for by the reduction of confusion and increase in children's concentration, enjoyment, and learning. Where a certain child needs closer care by an individual caregiver because of recent entry to day care, difficult problems at home, or for any other reason, the child can be encouraged to spend more time in that caregiver's play zone, until he or she develops greater emotional security and autonomy. More often, it will be enough for designated teachers to be assigned responsibility to keep a general lookout for children with special needs, even within the framework of zonal control. In the long run, responsibility and independence are fostered through encouraging children to move from place to place by their own means and to make their own play decisions in all types of activities.

Floating Teachers

It is useful to structure a variety of different supervisory roles for teachers. Most teachers can be assigned to control zones for particular activities, but in any large playroom the presence of at least one floating teacher will increase the smoothness of operations throughout the play room. She can easily anticipate, spot, and assist with the difficulties that a zone teacher, temporarily occupied with problems in one corner of an area, may overlook.

This role may be defined as supervisory, which would involve making decisions or suggestions to shift staff and children when necessary, closing down play areas, and bringing out new or putting away old materials, as well as seeing to the general state of activities; or the role may be limited to coordinating and troubleshooting, in order to avoid adding an unnecessary level to the status hierarchy among teachers. Coordinated planning, free discussion, group decision making and other democratic processes at all times are, in either case, essential to avoid destructive feelings and competition between teachers.

Assigning a floating teacher serves as a means of distributing staff energies where they are needed, for example, when conflict arises in two or more areas at a time. Without an additional hand, one staff member might have to leave her zone totally unsupervised in order to help a teacher in another zone if several children started throwing blocks. Floating supervision is so valuable that even when staff is limited, it may be advantageous to restrict the number of types of play, or at least the number of zones, to free at least one caregiver for general supervision and troubleshooting. The variety of play might be maintained by rotating the availability of activities during different days or periods of the day. Floating teachers are also a convenient device for providing temporary substitutes for staff breaks, since the short absence of a floating teacher is not likely to be critical.

Diversion

Diverting children is another indirect method of regulating children's behavior. When a child damages or displaces a toy or disputes with another child it is usually best to divert the child's attention. Instead of scolding, correcting or forcibly stopping the child, show a constructive way to use the toy or present the child with a substitute toy; conflict and tension are minimized by arousing a new focus of interest. The child learns social rules through indirect methods, which decreases positive feelings toward undesired behavior by engaging his or her interest in constructive forms of behavior (see Chapter 5). Children learn *how* to make interesting crayon marks on paper, instead of the wall, first to please the teacher, but as they practice they see the rewards that come from skill, and end up by pleasing both themselves and others.

It helps, of course, to comment occasionally on the child's behavior, perhaps mentioning, for example, how crayon marks damage walls, but make interesting pictures on paper, and thus explain the rule in question. But remember that language is not the strong point of young children and that much social rule learning takes place through observation and understanding acquired over long periods. Too much direct control will stifle spontaneity and self-direction, creating more anger and resentment of authority than will indirect methods of guidance. Often a child becomes more preoccupied with relations with authority or conflicts with peers than with constructive play and cooperative relations with peers.

Alertness and Anticipation

Among the most useful techniques promoting smooth operation of a playroom are teacher alertness and anticipation of problem situations. The practice of zone responsibility combined with the presence of a floating teacher is particularly effective for spotting potential sources of difficulty and employing preventive measures before play becomes disrupted. Staff need to keep a constant lookout for problems children may encounter in working with a toy; watch for lagging interest in play; and notice the need for additional or alternative materials, arrangements, methods of problem solving, play partners, interest areas, and themes to revive flagging sociodramatic play. The moment to control conflict situations in order to maintain stable play patterns and cooperation is *before* a conflict occurs.

To avoid conflicts, a teacher needs to be thoroughly familiar with the children's play patterns and the functions and purposes of the toys in the area. An obvious instance arises when a child repeatedly builds a high tower with blocks. Building high towers can be fun, but can often turn into a noisy and disturbing interest in falling objects, particularly in a hyperactive child. It is useful to watch for this shift of interest *before* it occurs. Suggest limits on height as a structure begins to totter, or shift the child's focus by adding blocks horizontally or alongside in a second tower, or by making a bridge. (Occasionally, an interest in falling towers and other objects can be encouraged as a means of promoting curiosity about gravity, but generally only in planned circumstances when other children will not be disturbed and not as a means of destructiveness for its own sake.)

Additional things to watch for as potential sources of conflict include: an occasion when two or more individualistic children head for the same corner or toy, to guide one of them to another task; that one child who wants to roll her truck, and another who wants only to build, do so in different floor areas from the moment they begin; and that there are ample blocks, trucks, toys of all kinds, and art materials to go around.

As an alternative to shifting children from a common area of play one can (according to the developmental levels of children) suggest complementary roles in building with blocks or in other types of play. For example, one child can be encouraged to build a road and another to operate a vehicle on it. Younger and less cooperatively developed children may get along better just building roads side by side without interacting, each operating trucks on his or her own road, with the teacher, in time, gradually bringing them together in cooperative play.

The continued surveying and detachment required for effective supervision need not prevent a teacher from personalizing relationships with the children. It is possible to balance the two orientations, alternating concern for the individual with management of the group as needed. The most effective means for supporting this duality is to limit the number of children and the size, type, and number of zones for which a teacher is responsible, but there are also other ways to handle these problems.

Scheduling and Coordination Problems

Two principal questions in scheduling free play activities are how to coordinate the movements of groups of children from place to place, and how to schedule a variety of activities within and across blocks of time.

Perhaps the major form of scheduling is to set a definite period within which both teachers and children can expect to engage in activities of a certain type at a given place. For example, a program may call for free play in a quiet playroom for a forty-five minute period each morning (as well as at other times in the course of the day). For children to gain the most benefit from this period, the staff must agree upon a definite room arrangement and system of zone control, as we have described, and some rough plan of the type of activities in which each child should participate in this (or any other) period. Initially, encourage children to settle in groups of two and three in the several zones of a playroom, then gradually, when desirable, encourage them to move among the different zones of the playroom. It takes some time before infants develop a clear mental map of the choices and arrangement of activities in a playroom. Even when they walk, many children need encouragement to move from place to place at appropriate times, sometimes by leading them, sometimes merely by reminding them and pointing out alternatives and pathways.

If children are not moved around in play to some degree, at least two things tend to occur. Children pile up in confusion in one or two activities, and teachers gain little understanding of the degree to which each child's experience is distributed among the different types of play. Schedules should *not be rigid, nor the order fixed* but someone needs to keep track of the range of activities in which each child is engaging over the course of every week (either each teacher for his or her designated children, or perhaps a floating teacher whose surveying role keeps him or her informed). It is not enough to let interests develop where they will; during the formative years continuous opportunity to explore all types of activities is necessary to guarantee rounded development. Too often girls spend much of their time in house play or art activities, to the neglect of problem-solving toys, block building, wheel toys and vigorous climbing and running activities. Conversely, some boys never get to the sociodramatic play areas or into art activities. Specialized interests like art or building skills should not be sex-role stereotyped, nor developed at the expense of cultural enrichment and broad preparation for the varied demands of later school learning and the many skills adults are expected to know in our complicated world.

From the point of view of supervision, moving children among several activities every day, or at least over the course of a week, helps to prevent pile-ups, distribute the supervisory load, and minimize attentional interferences. Minimizing these problems will, in turn, encourage children to develop themselves more deeply and seriously in each individual activity. Circulating children from time to time also sustains motivation and decreases fatigue through recurrently introducing novelty.

A scheduling pattern for any time block (often forty-five minutes or an hour) need not be divided literally into equal periods, say, three distinct fifteen minute periods, each devoted to a separate activity. It is equally important for children to learn to pursue their interests and become deeply immersed in particular activities over long periods. It is sometimes preferable therefore to allow or even encourage a child to stay in an area for as long as a half hour or more, perhaps engaging in only one or two activities in that period each day. Developing a child's interest in a variety of activities can be accomplished by seeing that he or she is led to alternative activities at other periods of the day or on other days over the course of a week. As in all things it is the *total balance* of time which counts—but without a *definite* record and planning schedule a healthy distribution is unlikely to occur. Many factors bring a child to a given activity, including just plain physical confusion or the knowledge and preferences of teachers for certain activities like music, gymnastics, or the study of fish life.

One of the small difficulties that occasionally plague teachers is children choking passages in transit from one activity to another. This minor source of temporary confusion is sometimes better tolerated rather than trying to enforce rigid rules for movement. Yet children can be taught to move in an orderly fashion most of the time as long as there is plenty of opportunity for vigorous and noisy gross motor play at other times. A prearranged plan for coordinating changes will keep down the amount of movement in passageways or in entries to the play areas. Another plan is to coordinate the movements of two teachers by prearranged signals, often best carried out through a supervisor or floating teacher. Gestural signals (since voice communication is usually muffled by the noise of play) can be used to indicate when children are getting bored and to suggest a switch of selected children among desired areas. It is occasionally desirable to shift a number of groups simultaneously, which temporarily increases confusion but minimizes the number of transitions over a period.

Flexibility in scheduling is essential if one is to individualize and vary the amount of time that children spend in different activities in any free play period. Informality, casualness, and avoidance of rigid scheduling are also important if a friendly and relaxed atmosphere is to prevail. It is possible to realize both major educational aims—on the one hand, broad and concentrated participation of children in all activities, while, on the other, preserving relative tranquility and enjoyment—by laying out ground rules in sensible ways. Tension usually arises when plans are either too vague or worked out in unnecessary detail. In the end there is no substitute for staff understanding, agreement, and coordination, but the development of smooth staff work requires time as well as continuing analysis.

External Interferences to Play Activity

Observations of visitors, other teachers, and researchers in a playroom can be accommodated easily and informally when kept to reasonable numbers. Reasonable is defined in terms of program objectives, space, number of children and staff, and the convenience of the facilities for observation without interference. If advance arrangements are made and the staff agrees on what role observers and visitors should play, it is easy to manage the time and place in which visitors can either participate or remain in the background to avoid distracting children from play.

Fostering Cooperative Relations and Group Processes

Much of the discussion on free play has centered on relations between teacher and child. Some attention has been given to conflicts between children but little has been said on how to foster cooperation and, expecially, how to encourage collaboration between children as a means of social control. This is not cooperation's only purpose, of course, since we are as interested in teaching children how to cooperate in the interests of their social development, of social harmony, and as a means of sharing the playroom chores.

We cannot expect children to work together in more than pairs until perhaps the latter part of the second year, and then only in the simpler forms of play for brief periods (see outline on development of task cooperation, Chapter 13). Until this time they tend simply to play alone or side by side, depending on their social learning, occasionally glancing at each other or reaching to explore or take the other's toy. Some time after the age of two and certainly by the age of three and four, however, we need to institute extensive opportunities for group participation in working a jigsaw puzzle, bringing out the rhythm toys, and carrying out other similar tasks together at work and play. By this time children can learn to work for fairly long periods together at surprisingly complex tasks with little adult guidance. The work periods will vary in length with the concentration spans and the experience children have had in group work, which will be discussed at length in Chapter 13. The peer interactive method of teaching children in small groups is likely to enhance their ability and interest in cooperating during free play.

Task Rules and Social Rules

There are really two distinct sets of ideas that children need to acquire in order to cooperate well together. They need, first, to know some elements of part-whole relations and how to perform tasks. They need a clear picture of the fact that a toy has more than one feature, leading to awareness that more than one person can work on a task at the same time. That, for example, there are several pieces in a puzzle and different areas of the puzzle which need to be filled in, or that large sheets of paper offer enough space for others to paint in different sections.

Often, as work progresses on a task, children reach a point where their efforts overlap and conflicts ensue. This brings us to the second major problem, that of learning such social concepts as taking turns, awareness of others in a situation, and the social roles involved in group collaboration on a project. The skills for both of the basic sets of ideas vary from the simplest to an intricate network of coordinated efforts.

The social rules of genuine cooperation, unlike the directed cooperation of relations between adult and child, are learned mainly through give and take of peer experience, which many children, raised singly in the home, do not get a chance to learn until junior kindergarten or even school age. The premium on individual achievement and competition in American life, moreover, tends to make it difficult for many children to learn to cooperate. Exclusively home-reared children sometimes come to school well equipped to play at tasks but quite unprepared for working together with other children on a joint project. They may be aware of the fact that tasks are complicated and that it takes time to complete a project, but they are used to being guided or to carrying out a whole task by themselves at their own pace, several steps bunched together or one step at a time. Children must acquire familiarity with *methods* of coordinating their actions with another person in an activity, and they must also acquire the willingness and expectation to contribute equally and together. They must learn to stick mainly to their own side of a puzzle or place only their own cards in a lotto game. If they see where another child's puzzle piece or lotto card might fit, they must learn to ask if they can help, not always try to do it for the other child. And in turn, if they are stumped, they must learn to ask for help and accept it, not hold up everyone else for long periods, trying to persist alone. They must, in short, concentrate on both the rules for getting a task done *and* the rules for working with others, considerately and efficiently.

It is, accordingly, much easier to start with babies one or two years old. This is not to say that children should not learn to strive and work alone; privacy for play alone is important to develop reflectiveness and self-reliance.

A good portion of play can be encouraged with this aspect of individual development in mind.

Developing
Cooperation
through Play

With infants under a year or two, social participation is so simple that adults may not be aware of its occurrence. Occasionally, we may observe one child hand another a toy or relinquish a sought-after toy with good grace, but much of the social activity of babies is no more than playing happily side by side, each child with a different toy. A certain amount of parallel play is characteristic throughout the preschool years, but its gradual replacement by more direct and complex forms of social interaction depends a great deal on how much social experience and effective guidance a child experiences.

The Role of Problem-Solving Toys

If we begin to sit babies side by side at a table with two and three-piece puzzles and help them to work together fitting pieces, we are leading them toward more complicated forms of cooperative play. Form boards, peg toys, and similar fine motor problem-solving activities can all be used to develop group work over the entire preschool period, but it is best to have children cooperate in pairs until group work skills are well accepted. Many of the joint tasks they can understand offer too few parts for more than two children and protracted waiting for turns creates frustration and friction.

The Role of Construction Toys

Building blocks and similar toys are suitable for three or more children to use together to build elaborate structures. When blocks are used with miniature wheel toys and figures, children frequently work on quite separate aspects of what, in their minds, is a group project. One child builds a garage, another a zoo cage, a third runs a road between, a fourth (or usually all the children intermittently) operates the wheel toys and sets up animal figures. Those children who develop keener social and task perception will, by three or four years of age, work together quite constructively to build a single, rambling, intricate community structure. This requires a certain harmony of personality among the children, sufficient community of interest, and a solid understanding of rules, both for the task and for cooperating; all of which usually come out of a background of much well-guided experience in social play with other children.

The Role of Sociodramatic Play

Social role play (as doctor, nurse, mother, father, teacher, letter-carrier, factory worker, firefighter, etc.) is another area which rather naturally teaches children to cooperate. Cooperation becomes part of social role play as soon as the child develops any awareness of a social scene or situation. The first awareness of dramatic play may be limited to the use of a toy car or chair to sit a stuffed animal in, but the social basis is indicated by the child "driving" the car and the animal "sitting", which quickly extends to using many things as symbols, for

Problem Solving

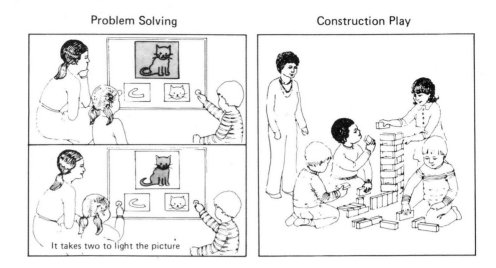

It takes two to light the picture

Construction Play

Gross Motor Play

Art Work: Common Themes

"Remember all the boats we saw in the harbour?"

Sociodramatic Play

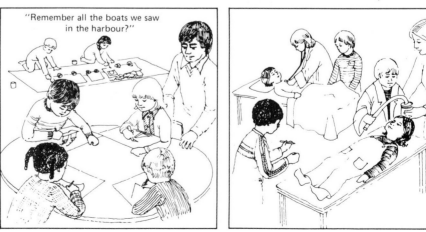

FIGURE 9–4
*Children can learn
cooperation
through different
types of play.*

example, a block as a piece of meat to feed the bear. Soon the child is playing with another child, then a third in symbolic play, each feeding the bear, then sitting in chairs at a table, then setting it and going through an elaborate ritual of an entire meal, which of necessity is based on continuing, complex, cooperative give and take to carry out the roles in play. Every child has a part to play since all that is required is to say which family member or worker one is and create with the others cooperatively an imaginary scene which copies or reflects everyday life.

At first role concepts are fluid and simple, consisting of little more than identifying oneself as one or another family member or worker common in the culture, and perhaps putting on an apron or coveralls and holding a broom or tool. Learning the duties and relations of the various roles usually develops most rapidly in the home scene with which children are most familiar. They see the apartment or house cleaned, the meals prepared, and hear family problems discussed almost every day. They usually need more exposure to the jobs people do, however, through stories, visits, and discussions, in the way we have described in chapter 7, and of course plenty of clothes and tools available as they are needed. On the other hand, many children already know more than many caregivers realize about bus or subway conductors, truck drivers, carpenters, plumbers, auto mechanics, building construction workers, sales people, and many similar trade and service workers whom they see from time to time when accompanying parents en route to and from the school or center, or in shopping errands and other trips around the city.

The Role of Art Activities

Although some art activities lend themselves to group work, social interaction in this medium usually takes the form of working in parallel in a common setting, around a table or at easels side by side. A sense of group awareness will arise if the teacher proposes a common theme to the children as they work on individual projects around a table. For example, she can suggest making animals or buildings when the children are working with clay, crayon drawings, or collage, each child continuing to use his or her own materials and section of the table. Interest in their creations and social relations will heighten as they show each other how they are representing the theme. A sense of cooperation also arises when children's drawings and other art work are put on display for the purpose of day to day decoration and occasionally for a parent evening or other visitors. In these cases it is essential to talk about these purposes with the children, to discuss how their designs and drawings of things brighten up the room and are interesting for all to see, and to make sure that contributions of every child are represented.

The Role of the Teacher

The role of the teacher in developing group participation demands a clear understanding of the possibilities of cooperation in the types of activities involved. There is, for example, very little problem in inducing cooperation between suitably-sized children on a teeter-totter; one simply guides a child to each end and the balance mechanism of the teeter-totter almost teaches the rest by itself. In this instance the children need little preconception of any necessity for cooperation or of opposing interests. Jungle gyms also permit collaboration in social role play, such as pretending the jungle gym is a ship on which they are sailing, one child being the captain, one the engineer, another a sailor.

Persistence and detailed instruction are needed to help two children to learn the joint use of many toys. Patient, repeated, gentle, but precise demonstrations over a period of days and sometimes weeks, along with the simplest of explanations, are necessary to show children how to play and work together. We must recognize that children who may be receiving more than their share of indulgence at home may find it difficult not think of every object and task as their very own possessions. It is often useful to try to match children in personality and style; for example, a somewhat tolerant and not too passive child may cooperate well with a more active, demanding one, who provides needed stimulation for the passive child. One must watch, however, that the interests of the more accepting child are not systematically down-trodden. On the other hand, it is easier for a demanding child to work when he or she is not required to adjust immediately to an equally demanding child; this might be quite beyond the child's initial capacities. In contrast, two passive children may not provide enough demands or stimulation for one another to get a joint activity going at all, as in the case of moving a truck, rolling a ball back and forth, or building a wall with blocks.

The Importance of a Group Orientation

The foregoing illustrations point up the value of a group orientation in handling children, a concern for relations between children rather than merely concern for each child's development individually. Both a passive and an overactive child will accept stimulation from and tolerate a child at the same level, while often not understanding or accepting the same demands made by an adult. Somehow the relative greatness of adults in size and skill, perhaps together with a history of problems with the authority of parents, magnifies the difficulties a child has in understanding or accepting adult guidance. While this point should not be overemphasized, since most children enjoy and learn from adults even when the adults are not particularly either warm or skillful in the way they teach, learning through peer relations has its own values. Moreover, learning that takes place in peer relations not only multiplies the number of opportunities for children to learn, but takes place in a context of learning to get along with others as equals, an essential basis for social life.

It is important to *work on the level of each child* in terms of social understanding, willingness to share, and understanding of and interest in different types of toys. Success in stimulating children, maintaining their willingness to work together, and helping them develop to more advanced levels requires a great deal of attention to the proper match between children's personalities, and between children and toys. Two children who both like carpentry, for example, might be helped to get along better while sawing and nailing wood than in puzzle play, especially if only one really likes puzzles.

The rewards of devoting time and patience to group processes in projects are ultimately considerable. As children develop in social and task understanding they will tend to play constructively for longer periods. Conflicts between them will diminish and guidance can come less from the teacher and more from interactions between children themselves as teachers of one another. In a smoothly working group of children at play, building with tinker toys, or playing "gas station", for example, the ideas, suggestions and responses to one another pour out in an endless stream with little friction and intense concentration. The basic motivation for children to play with and learn from one another is really very powerful. Children *want* to work and play with other children as soon as they are able to perceive other children as being similar to themselves. A group of children provides standards and norms for doing things with which each child can realistically compare his or her own skills and interests. Because adults don't normally engage in sociodramatic play or work simple puzzles, or do so only to teach children, they provide no real basis for comparison.

Solving Children's Problems through Peer Play

Among the special, continuing problems of social relations in free play that are best handled through regulation of peer groups is the problem of social isolates. There are ordinarily some children in any play group who, for a variety of reasons, fail to relate easily or establish stable relations with any of their peers. They play alone most of the time, seldom playing for any length of time with even one other child. These may be "only" children, reared at home past infancy without the peer experience necessary to learn the rules of give and take of feelings involved in interpersonal relations. They may be over-indulged children, or ones with a history of illness which caused parents to become habitually overconcerned about the children's welfare. They may have been babied so much that they expect others, including their peers, to constantly nurture them. Whatever the reasons, children with these emotional problems need extra support and guidance to cope and develop socially in nursery school or day care.

It is during free play that help is most needed. Guided learning and routine caregiving activities necessarily provide withdrawn or underdeveloped children with plenty of attention from adults. The small group types of guided learning we shall discuss in Chapter 13 also bring them into constructive relations with their peers in a structured work situation which enables them to function with other children. These group experiences in guided learning activities may provide isolates with their first real relations with other children. Because there is a definite task, like comparing leaves from different types of trees, in which an adult engages all the children together, the child more easily forgets himself, losing his self-conciousness as he shows an example to another child at the teacher's request.

Free play, on the other hand, is relatively unstructured. The teacher's role is principally in the background as a resource person helping and guiding only occasionally. The shy child does not know how or is too afraid to ask to play or to start playing with another; to sit alongside the second child, turning the pages and looking at a book together, or working on interlocking toys together; both of which soon lead to talk and often joint action in outgoing, socially skilled children who meet for the first time. In free play every child must at least in part initiate and sustain a partnership in play. This is unlikely to be helped spontaneously by other children, who usually do not feel the problem, but seek relations with others who already know how to work and talk together freely in play.

Occasionally a child who enjoys dominating others may use (and abuse) the isolate in some joint project, but even here the isolate provides insufficient response to make the domination challenging. The problem often becomes chronic when, after a few days or weeks of unsuccessful relations, the socially underdeveloped child gives up, withdrawing behind a kind of self-made barrier which effectively repels others. Adults must intervene early to prevent the development of such patterns.

The first thing to do is to be aware of the children's personality trends and how they are faring in their relations with one another. Avoid simplistic labelling, calling one child aggressive, another child shy, and a third a "problem" child, before careful observation and analysis establishes that a given child acts the same in all situations. Staff discussion may disclose that a so-called problem child is in fact quite well-behaved and relaxed at meal time, or that an apparently timid child plays quite well with one or two others whenever they work in clay. In some cases, there may be a certain teacher whose presence or special techniques—which might be observed and adopted by others when working with the "problem" child—brings about the change. The developmental monitoring procedures (Chapter 5 and Appendix B) can be usefully applied to day to day free play situations. If this type of analysis is utilized from the first days of any child's entry, children's trends towards passivity, withdrawal, and isolation, or aggressiveness and hyperactivity can be identified and plans worked out for modifying them before they become too fixed.

Once a plan is formulated, the second thing to do in helping the withdrawing child is to lead the child into relations with other children, persistently but a step at a time. The day care worker will need considerable understanding of group processes and sensitive understanding of the particular patterns of the subgroups in his own play group if he is to make any headway. A sociometric analysis (see Chapters 5 and 14) of which groups are more open to change (because their interrelations are less tightly knit) may be useful. The essential approach is to bring the withdrawing child into close relations with one or two other children, who will not summarily reject him or her in activities where some common interest is (or is potentially) shared. Children who are more reflective, sensitive, and gentle are the type to look for. Initially, it may be necessary for a day care worker to initiate a social situation each day by participating in the group play. Developing the child's interest in a new activity may provide a point of contact with other children not previously experienced. A special experience, such as a visit to one another's homes or an excursion, which others in the general play group do not share (at least until later), may similarly lead toward the nucleus of a relation and thus a new subgroup formation in the larger play group.

Socially underdeveloped children are not the only ones who need to be aided in their approach to peer relations. Rigid children who want everything their way can perhaps learn to loosen up through playing with a flexible play group. Children who dominate excessively and destructively may benefit from experience with equally strong and individualistic personalities who teach them how to interrelate on a more equal basis. Teachers may need to try many combinations before finding viable ones that effect change; they should be constantly observant of peer patterns to note which relations are socially healthier and which ones need a shift in direction. Patience is also required, along with awareness of when a play interaction, encouraged for the purpose of forming new relations, is likely to work out.

When a teacher works through peer relations to solve individual children's problems the social orientation shifts from a predominately teacher-dominated, teacher-child interactive approach to a group-centered framework, in which all work together even though the teacher may still have a central leadership role. Should the group at Tinker Toy or "gas station" play appear to be running out of steam, the teacher may make a suggestion to build a windmill, for example, knowing the children's recent interest in a book on windmills, or she may even play a role as customer with a flat tire for the gas station group to reactivate the play. Or again, in the process of shifting her attention from child to child to give individual guidance, but in a way that shows children how to work with one another (such as suggesting how one child can fix the "motor" of another child who is a customer), the teacher is recognizing and building interpersonal relations. As the skills and understandings of children develop, play groups will form and re-form in constructive relations, with less supervision, for gradually longer periods. During intervals when a teacher is not actively supervising a group, certain children may spontaneously assume (or be assigned) leadership, depending on the child's competence with the problems a group faces. To witness this kind of development in young children can be a very satisfying experience for a teacher.

Bibliography for Part III

Almy, M. *Early childhood play: Selected readings related to cognition and motivation.* New York: Simon and Schuster, 1968.

Arasteh, J. D. Creativity and related processes in the young child: A review of the literature. *The Journal of Genetic Psychology,* 1968, *112,* 77–108.

Bruner, J. S., Jolly, A., & Sylva, K. (Eds.). *Play: Its role in development and evolution.* New York: Basic Books, 1976.

Butler, A. L., Gotts, E. E., & Quisenberry, N. L. *Play as development.* Columbus, Ohio: Charles E. Merrill, 1978.

Di Leo, J. H. *Young children and their drawings.* New York: Brunner/Mazel, 1970.

Eckerman, C. O., Whatley, J. L., & Kutz, S. L. Growth of social play with peers during the second year of life. *Developmental psychology,* 1975, *11,* 42–49.

Eisner, E. W. *The Kettering project of Stanford University.* Stanford, Calif.: Stanford University Press, 1972.

Fowler, W. On the value of both play and structure in early education. *Young children,* 1971, *27,* 24–36.

Fowler, W., & Swenson, A. The influence of early language stimulation on development: Four studies. *Genetic Psychology Monographs,* in press.

Furman, W., Rahe, D., & Hartup, W. W. *Social rehabilitation of low-interactive preschool children by peer intervention.* Minneapolis: University of Minnesota Press, in press.

Garvey, C. Play. In J. Bruner, M. Cole, & B. Lloyd (Eds.). *The developing child.* Cambridge, Mass., 1977.

Goldberg, S., & Lewis, M. Play behavior in the year-old infant: Early sex differences. *Child development,* 1969, *40,* 21–31.

Goodnow, J. *Children drawing.* Cambridge, Mass.: Harvard University Press, 1977.

Hartup, W. W. Peer relations: Developmental implications and interaction in same- and mixed-age situations. *Young children,* 1977, *32,* 4–13.

Herron, R., & Sutton-Smith, B. (Eds.). *Child's play.* New York: John Wiley & Sons, 1971.

Lewis, M., & Rosenblum, L. (Ed.). *The origins of behavior* Vol. 3: *Friendship and peer relations.* New York: John Wiley & Sons, 1975.

Lieberman, J. N. *Playfulness: Its relationship to imagination and creativity.* New York: Academic Press, 1977.

Lowenfeld, V. *Creative and mental growth.* New York: Macmillan, 1970.

Millar, S. *The psychology of play.* Harmondsworth, England: Penguin, 1968.

Mitchell, E. The learning of sex roles through toys and books. *Young children,* 1973, *28,* 226–231.

Mooney, R. L., & Smilansky, S. *An experiment in the use of drawing to promote cognitive development in disadvantaged preschool children in Israel and the United States.* Washington, D.C.: Office of Education, U.S. Department of Health, Education and Welfare, 1973.

Nilsen, A. P. Alternatives to sexist practices in the classroom. *Young children,* 1977, *32,* 53–58.

Piaget, J. *Play, dreams and imitation in childhood* (C. Gattagno & F. M. Hodgson, trans.). New York: Norton, 1962. (Originally published, 1952.)

Smilansky, S. *The effects of sociodramatic play in disadvantaged preschool children.* New York: John Wiley & Sons, 1968.

Smilansky, S., & Boaz, T. Advancing language and cognitive performance of young children by means of earth-clay modeling. In M. L. Hanes, I. J. Gordon, & W. F. Breivogal (Eds.), *Update: The first ten years of life.* Gainesville, Fla.: Division of Continuing Education, University of Florida, 1976.

Yarrow et al. Dimensions of early stimulation and their differential effects on infant development. *Merrill-Palmer Quarterly,* 1972, *18,* 205–219.

IV

STIMULATION: THE COGNITIVE BASIS FOR EARLY DEVELOPMENT

Guided Learning:
A Model for Stimulation

Guiding infants

Whatever the age or intentions, any interaction between two individuals is a teaching and learning situation. And whatever the methods employed, teaching-learning situations have a structure. Interactions teach by providing information from what each person says and does, some—though not necessarily the same—part of which will be learned by both parties involved. Each person learns mainly from what the other person does and says, though trying out an example also teaches. The structure of any interaction consists of several dimensions critical for learning, such as the complexity of information ex-

249

changed; differences in the amount of activity, information, and emotion expressed by the two parties; the degree of rapport; and the frequency and duration of interaction. There are also numerous minor dimensions, like posture and small movements, which only occasionally play important roles in the teaching and learning process.

While information of some kind is usually exchanged in interactions between adult and child, it is the information imparted by the adult to the child that is the main focus in early education. The behavior of the child is chiefly of value in its feedback function to the adult as teacher. It tells the caregiver how well the child is progressing and enjoying himself. It is the role of teacher and the organization of interaction that are crucial to the young child's development. Although every interaction furnishes information to the child, it may be information that is insignificant or even harmful to his development. For example, the mere presence of an adult provides more reassurance than stimulation, and adult hostility of course contributes more to tension than to curiosity.

In the approach I have developed for guiding learning, the child is engaged by an adult (or any competent older child) in a program of learning through play. Several important dimensions of interaction have been found to be productive of learning. The aim of teaching is to bring about regular, significant cognitive transactions throughout development. Attention is centered on the unique ability of informed adults to help children learn concepts through combining language and action in an infinite variety of ways.

I have constructed a general model of tutoring designed especially for guiding the child through planned programs of learning, although it can also be applied in a wide range of situations. Thus, in any communication between adult and child, the application of the principles from this model is likely to enrich the child's learning experience under any circumstances. Since the principles and techniques for interrelating with children in free play and basic caregiving are detailed elsewhere (Chapters 9 and 2), I shall concentrate here on techniques useful in planned learning programs.

Comparison of Guided Learning with Free Play and Basic Care Routines

Guided learning programs are distinguishable from free play and the routines of basic caregiving mainly in the goals of the activities and the role of the child. In free play, the child's autonomy in program planning is paramount. Within the framework of influences determined by the availability and arrangement of materials, the tastes of their peers, and the type of adult guidance, the children are free to select the form of play they enjoy. The aims during free play are to provide maximum opportunity for self-regulation and experimentation. The routines of caregiving have as their chief objectives tending to and socializing such physical needs as dressing, eating, and sleeping. Learning as well as loving should be plentifully engaged in care routines, but the scope of learning in the long run is likely to be greater in planned learning programs, and it should occur without sacrificing good emotional relations. In fact, the guided learning model explicitly also concerns itself with socioemotional processes.

The Strategy and Tactics of Guiding Learning

The discussion of guided learning may be divided into two major categories, strategies and tactics, each of which embraces several topics. Strategies center on the long-range developmental problems of teaching and learning, selection of curriculum and measurement of developmental progress.*

Tactics in guided learning center on the immediate conditions in a learning session. First the selection and organization of the physical environment, the setting and stimulus materials as discussed in Chapter 11. Second is the organization of methods of stimulation and motivation, and teacher and child roles, including both individual tutoring and small group processes. We shall consider tactics first in a series of four chapters as a convenient basis from which to approach problems of strategy in Chapter 14.

Organization of the Learning Task

The organization of stimulation involves *teacher organization of the learning situation*. The organization of program materials by the teacher in interaction with the child ultimately determines much of what the child will learn. Organization has at least two aspects, the way in which arrangements affect perception (what the child sees) and motivation (what the child wants), and how organization of the task helps the child to understand and to learn.

The Demonstration of Cognitive Rules

In order to describe teaching methods we must first recall the process of how a mind acts according to cognitive rules (see also the discussion in Chapter 1). Knowledge ordinarily implies competence to do something; we come to know a person's knowledge of a concept through his ability to perform some task. The performance of a task to reveal competence includes, as a minimum, perceptual-motor actions and, for many concepts beyond those of earliest infancy, an expression of language. The task the child performs, however, must entail more than carrying out the same action every time. *Competence to perform a task correctly* can only be shown by performance of it in some generalized way, that is, following some rule in which the specific procedures employed will vary from situation to situation. The individual relates to the materials selectively and with an organization that reflects the *essential dimensions* of the task, namely those that define the rule(s) for a concept.

If we attempt to teach the size concept "bigness," for example, it is necessary for the child to understand that "bigness" applies to all sorts of "big" things, not just his big ball or a particular big doll he sees at the moment. Since size is a relational concept he must also understand bigness in relation to other things that are smaller, but the point here is that he must see bigness as a *rule* about things in general, in which any set of objects can be compared for size, regardless of their shape, color, number of features or any other characteristics. His first learning of the rule that defines the idea of bigness, will be shown

*Curriculum sequences for the three major categories of cognitive processes (knowledge, language, and problem solving) are presented in the companion volume, *Curriculum and Assessment Guides for Infant and Child Care;* organizing programs and measuring progress are considered in Chapter 14.

when he is able to *indicate in action* (for instance, by pointing) with *any* materials (when size variation is present) which of the objects are big.

In ordinary conversation, many ideas like "bigness" or "redness" are expressed in speech without bothering to demonstrate competence through action, because we are already familiar with the things we are talking about. But our problem here is not everyday communication about ideas that two people already know. We are concerned rather with the problem of *how a teacher demonstrates and guides the child in learning concepts; and then how the child experiments with and performs a task to show that he has learned the rules that define the concepts.* For this reason, concept learning must include physical actions as well as mental operations for both child and teacher.

Knowledge of concepts requires at least two problem solving strategies: analyzing particulars, and relating them (synthesizing) in some way. The significant features of examples (mental analysis) are less difficult to illustrate in action than relations between the elements, however. The latter (mental synthesis) is often difficult to show physically, even with movements linking two elements, though these help. Thus, in the example about "bigness", the child must synthesize (connect) mentally *relations* between all large and small objects to grasp the concept. But his competence in mastering the rule is indicated mainly by his consistency in pointing to the correct choice every time under all conditions. These actions directly reveal only the analytic aspect— that is, pointing to the more significant of the two elements (the "big one" versus the "not big one", which is usually the first way the child understands smallness).

It is more difficult to physically demonstrate the synthesizing process, since this is an abstract and invisible relationship, in this case, between two elements that define polar opposites, the "big one" and the "not big one" (smallness). We can see and say that the "big toy" takes up more space and that increasingly bigger things take increasingly more space, but again it is always the separate toys we see, while the idea of bigness really exists in the *relations* of one toy relative to another, a relation we can only connect mentally. We could ask the child to place big and little things together in pairs, for example (and later, size series in rows of objects decreasing in size). But this task requires the child to select and organize objects in patterns according to the abstract rules he is just beginning to grasp, which is a more abstract task than picking out which of two objects presented is the big (or small) one. In any case, such pair arranging still does not show the mental *connecting* or synthesizing the way pointing to something directly shows the analyzing process. Synthesizing is inherently a more abstract mental process, often greatly aided by the use of language.

Cognitive Rule Learning: Processes of Teacher-Child Interaction

A child can either discover the dimensions of a concept himself, or learn them from others. All methods of cognitive rule learning ultimately require children themselves to identify (analyze) and put together (synthesize) the dimensions of the structures that make up the rule. If the rule is just a variant of other rules they already know, it may be easy to learn; for example, learning about hexagons is easier once one is familiar with squares and pentagons as many-sided figures. Or it may be a rule at a new level, needing repeated observation and experimentation, such as learning about color or algebra for the first time. Whatever the rule, good teaching is essentially the skill of arranging external stimulation in ways that aid the learner *himself* to perceive how a rule operates. Although new concepts are touched on and partially grasped concepts become better understood through the child's own experimentation in play, the adult can do much to initiate and aid the rule-learning process, provided the rule selected is appropriate to the child's competence level.

The child learns from others in any of three ways. First, he learns by *observing* the actions of others, as when a teacher compares a square with a round shape, commenting on and pointing to the angularity of the square against the curve of the circle. The learning is enhanced when he attempts to *imitate* what they do, a process consisting, not of rote copying, but of learning by rehearsing and experimenting with the dimensions of the rule under different conditions. The child may bring another circle next to another square and run his finger around the circle, but the first time forget to look at the feature characteristic of a square. In this way, he works out the problems of understanding to make the rule integral to his own mental processes. In this context, pictures serve much the same purpose as the objects themselves; in either case, we are concerned with the actions of adult and child in a demonstration and an imitation.

He learns, secondly, *through someone guiding his movements* as he experiments with a rule. When a child is working with the rule about square shapes, for example, an adult can guide him by pointing to a square hole, or to the corners and straight sides of both the square block and the square hole, to indicate how they match. In this approach, the child's attention is drawn to elements which, if he attempts to bring them together through his actions, he may be able to synthesize mentally, and thus learn more about the rule.

The child learns, thirdly, through *someone using words to explain* the characteristics of a rule to him. In the example above, for instance, the adult could mention that square things have sharp corners and straight sides. This method is dependent on the child's understanding of language rules; for example, that words like nouns and verbs stand for objects and actions; and that adjectives describe the shape and other characteristics of objects. If he does have some understanding of language, the explanation can lead him to look for, and experiment with, matching objects with square corners and straight sides, and thus to grasp the rule.

For a number of reasons, none of the three methods of learning is likely to be used in a "pure" state. Demonstrations are usually more helpful when the adult follows them up with a few pointing cues when the child attempts to imitate. And language, even when one knows language rules, is of no help without initial exposure to the physical elements themselves (corners and straight sides). More than this, rules require mental syntheses (in our example above, relating corners to sides), which, as we have pointed out, are difficult to help the child understand with physical movements alone. As a result language, used carefully, will help to clarify the demonstration of a rule, even for infants who are just beginning to use words. Fortunately, certain terms like "see", "has", "goes", "here", "and", and "together" are so common in every-day usage that the infant can early (by 24 months and sometimes earlier) be aided by using them to guide him to grasp relations (synthesize). For example, saying "the square has *corners* and sides", while pointing to each in turn; or, "the side *goes* to the corner", in each case stressing the key words as one points to the appropriate picture or makes an appropriate movement, can help the child learn more easily. Language can also define which characteristics are *not* part of the rule (for instance, that color does not affect size), and the complicated interrelations between rules (squareness and roundness); these are both extremely difficult to show in other ways.

Since language is constructed of its own complex rules, however, it must be used carefully and sparingly. The younger the infant, the more simple and concrete the words and phrases required, and the more important it is that each word used be close in time and place to the actual features and physical actions that the teacher is describing. Only when the child is well into the pre-school period can cognitive rule learning begin to take place with language partly removed from physical demonstrations of rules. Even adults generally learn new rules much faster if they are directly accompanied by demonstrations or pictures.

Model for Teacher-Child Interaction

If a combination of the three methods mentioned above appears advantageous to help children learn, then how should a teacher proceed? One likely approach is through the child's own medium, active play. In this manner the teacher can, from time to time in the course of a child's exploration of various number, classification, or other concept learning materials, introduce demonstrations of each rule accompanied by simple descriptions of her actions, and point out cues to help the child in his attempts to work out the rule himself. In teaching concepts of number, for instance, the caregiver may at first simply cluster two shells, then two marbles, calling each pair "two" as she does, and then show further how the rule works (give cues) by contrasting two shells with one shell and two marbles with one, in turn. Figures 10–1 and 10–2 show samples of teacher-child interactions directed toward helping a child learn a rule.

Guided Learning Interaction: Summary of Sequence

Figure 10–1 shows a condensed outline of the main steps in a sample sequence, while Figure 10–3 presents the series in greater detail. The opening situation (Step 1) is an invitation by the adult to the child (or children) to enter a special guided learning area, where the child is offered a few supportive play materials (miniature unit blocks, diverse containers, trinkets, miniature replicas, etc.) and is encouraged to explore and manipulate them in play as he or she wishes. Children slow to take interest may need more encouragement. The teacher should then join the play, simply moving the objects around, putting a trinket in a container, or the like, the way the child does, to establish the interactive form of relationship desired for guiding the child in learning. The main objective in this initial process is to encourage a warm, friendly atmosphere and

FIGURE 10-1. Guided learning interaction: Summary of sequence

Teacher	Child
(1) Introduces materials and interests child in play.	
	Plays.
(2) Demonstrates rule and guides child's experimentation with rule; encourages play.	
	Experiments with rule— imitates—plays.
(3) Remodels rule in different form and aids child's experimentation with it; encourages play.	
	Experiments with rule— imitates—plays.
(4) Inquiry: asks child to perform a task.	
	Attempts task—plays.

Cycle repeats until rule mastered or session terminated.

relationship to develop between adult and child (or children, if a group) and to arouse an active interest and engagement in play activity.

It is during this preliminary phase, moreover, that the boundaries of acceptable social behavior and areas of play may need to be defined clearly. Are the children expected to sit around a table in chairs, around a rug on the floor, or can they move around from place to place as long as they stay close at hand? Whatever the social rules, it helps to make them clear from the beginning, usually first through guiding children to their expected places, then gently reminding the more active children if they move around more or become more active than the limits allow. It is well to remember, however, that limits are no substitute for interest. Well-conducted guided play and learning activities hold most children's interest for extended periods. When a caregiver finds herself reminding children frequently, it is well to ask how well the sessions are being conducted. There is seldom much difficulty with a single child who, unless he is over-directed, will tend to warm to the undivided attention of an adult who encourages his most natural interest, play. Problems of social control with a group of children are described in Chapter 13.

The subsequent steps in the interaction sequence consist of a series of demonstrations of a cognitive rule about a concept by the adult, alternating with play and teacher-aided experimentation with the rule by the child, (such as making up and taking apart clusters of two and three shells, marbles, or other objects, to teach beginning rules about number concepts). The session is terminated with a teacher inquiry, in which she asks the child to perform some action, in the course of which the child's competence in a rule is revealed. If the child shows definite mastery (can easily pick out groups of two and three marbles or shells), play activity can continue with the learning of another rule in

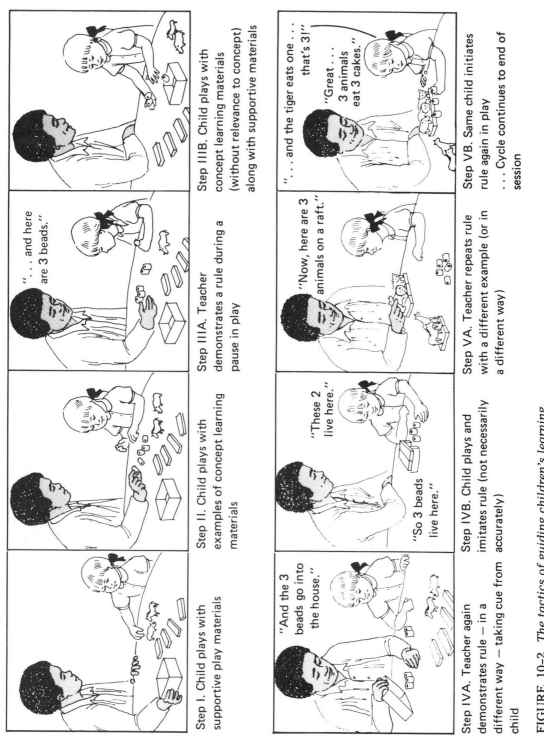

Step I. Child plays with supportive play materials

Step II. Child plays with examples of concept learning materials

"...and here are 3 beads."

Step IIIA. Teacher demonstrates a rule during a pause in play

Step IIIB. Child plays with concept learning materials (without relevance to concept) along with supportive materials

"And the 3 beads go into the house."

Step IVA. Teacher again demonstrates rule – in a different way – taking cue from child

"These 2 live here."

"So 3 beads live here."

Step IVB. Child plays and imitates rule (not necessarily accurately)

"Now, here are 3 animals on a raft."

Step VA. Teacher repeats rule with a different example (or in a different way)

"...and the tiger eats one ... that's 3!"

"Great.... 3 animals eat 3 cakes."

Step VB. Same child initiates rule again in play ... Cycle continues to end of session

FIGURE 10-2. *The tactics of guiding children's learning.*

the program sequence (play with groups of one to four shells and other objects); otherwise the cycle can be repeated with the same rule (with variations, such as using different materials and types of play) a number of times for the balance of the session, according to need, the degree of interest and the amount of time available.

It is essential to remember that the interaction sequence we have described is *not* a fixed order to be followed without variation. The sequence is merely a model, a sample of the type of actions that ought to occur when things go well. Thus in any well balanced learning situation there will be plenty of play and good relations, numerous demonstrations of each rule, guidance of the child's efforts to experiment with it, and some method of determining the child's progress, such as an inquiry. But the exact number and order of each type of play, rule demonstrations, and so on, will always remain open to the teacher's judgment of what the child needs to help him to learn and play freely.

The open-ended, play interaction approach is intended to foster creative orientations to seeking knowledge. Programs are constructed to teach definite rules about the world, because in the course of human history people have developed logical understandings of things the child needs to know (size, speed, number, classification). But praising effort, encouraging experimentation, and searching for *examples and variants* of rules in the inquiry method are necessary to develop *general* concepts and stimulate curiosity about alternatives and creative thinking. Using only one or two examples (shells and marbles) won't teach the general idea of number the way using several kinds of materials (shells, marbles, dolls, paper clips, bits of paper, blocks, etc.) will. And without an inquiry with many alternatives (clusters of twos and threes with many different combinations), in which the *child* must figure out and perform, active curiosity, broad mastery, and creative manipulation by the child will be less stimulated. Cognitive rule learning is in this way flexibly structured as an *active* adaptive process with many possibilities open to the learner.

There are certain principles involved with the interaction sequence which work best when applied adaptively, according to the individual teacher's style. Enthusiasm, for example, arouses interest, and the mystery of a "hide and seek" game or a search for "treasure" lends excitement and drama to the activity. Conversely, a quiet style, which rewards the child's efforts with a smile or a gentle look, may be more natural to the teacher concerned, and will be equally effective as long as the examples are used in play in some flexible way (see Chapter 12), and a friendly relationship and genuine interest in the activities are maintained. Regardless of the teacher's personality, these six principles are useful to keep in mind:

1. Sensitivity to the child's needs and styles
2. Interest in the task as a problem to be solved and a search to be conducted
3. Continuing interest in and use of the play activities
4. Setting up the inquiry in sensorimotor play form
5. Clarity in understanding and guiding the child in rules for a concept, that is, maintaining precision in analyzing parts and pointing out relations

6. Setting up materials and phrasing questions to match the child's probable level of understanding each rule

All of these principles apply to teaching style in all aspects of the guided learning sequence, including the inquiry process. Without sensitivity and interest, teaching becomes at best a mechanical procedure which provides the child with no emotional support or reason to care about learning. Play is the natural style of the child; adults who cannot adapt to it should perhaps avoid teaching or parenting children. Clarity in understanding concepts is obviously much of what teaching is all about, but it must be clarity at a level that can be *communicated* to an infant clearly by word and gesture, through an ability to single out and interrelate critical features in an actual situation.

Many parents have not stimulated their children to develop curiosity and a problem-solving approach toward activity. They may have provided few toys and discouraged exploration, play, and questions about things and daily events around the home. Unless caregivers first engage such children extensively in simple exploratory play to arouse and develop their "curiosity systems," they will turn away quickly from a teacher's efforts to engage them in rule-learning tasks. For those children, an interest in learning, problem solving, and even complex forms of play will come only slowly over a series of sessions, aided by discussions with parents to help them change unproductive aspects of their methods of child-rearing. Among goals to help the parents work toward are purchasing or making a few toys (cutting and painting pieces of wood as boats, trucks, and building blocks; stuffed socks with faces for dolls and puppets); encouraging play with kitchen pots, pans, and empty cartons and containers; encouraging the parents to spend a few minutes of daily play on the floor with their child, comparing and talking about shapes, colors, sizes, and features and functions of objects, putting small objects in and out of containers, engaging in dramatic play, etc.; reading stories from picture books daily; and at least occasionally taking the time to talk *with* the child about the daily activities as they happen and encouraging questions, instead of ignoring or just telling the child briefly to do this and not do that.

Much of the focus with learning projects at school or in day care first needs to center on building strong emotional ties with the teacher and making use of particular forms of play the child understands and enjoys, perhaps just exploring and manipulating and building with the various play and learning materials for a few sessions. As a child's trust, self-confidence and curiosity develops, the informal play can give way to demonstrations with examples of concepts, at first only in passing, still concentrating on the casual play, and for some time weaving the informal play generously into the experimentation with learning, until interest in playing with concepts themselves becomes set. Even then, as with most children, using the concepts in play as shown in Chapter 12 generally remains a key part of the teaching process. Adopting this approach, any person who enjoys play with young children will find no lack of opportunity to introduce plenty of demonstrations and guidance to almost any child without meeting resistance or causing stress.

In sum, the interaction model outlines the kind of methods and course to follow, *not* a map of the territory. With this framework in mind, we shall turn to a more detailed discussion of the characteristics of the model, as shown in Figure 10–3.

FIGURE 10–3. Guided learning interaction: Detailed sequence

Teacher	Child
(1) 1. Invites child to learning area. 2. Offers supportive play materials. 3. Observes and encourages play as necessary.	
	1. Plays. 2. At some point, makes transition, (pauses in play, shifts attention to another activity).
(2) 1. At this point introduces learning materials. 2. Observes and encourages child's play; shows involvement and affection.	
	1. Plays. 2. Transition in play.
(3) 1. Introduces similar learning objects (or uses child's examples). 2. At this second stage, *demonstrates rule through play*—if possible, related to child's form of play.	

	1. Continues playing (whether or not child observes teacher's demonstration, with or without engaging with teacher), and/or
	2. Attempts to imitate rule demonstration
	  (a) successfully—with or without variation in form, or
	  (b) unsuccessfully.

(4) 1. Encourages and aids child with rule experimentation, showing affection and involvement in play. 2. Praises any effort of child to experiment with, or imitate, rule behavior. 3. *Re-models rule task,* using same objects but with slight variation in form, or position. 4. Guides child in demonstrating rule on his own.	
	1. Continues playing as before, and/or 2. Attempts to imitate, or experiment with, rule behavior.
(5) 1. Encourages and aids child with rule experimentation, as before. 2. Praises any effort of child to experiment with, or imitate, rule behavior. 3. *Inquiry:* asks child to point to stimulus or perform action that indicates knowledge of rule.	
	1. Continues playing as before, and/or 2. Performs discrimination task successfully or unsuccessfully.

FIGURE 10-3—(Continued)

Teacher	Child
(6) 1. Encourages play and aids rule experimentation as before. 2. Praises rule behavior as before. 3. *Re-models rule task* with a third slight variation in form.	
	1. Continues playing as before, and/or 2. Attempts to imitate rule behavior.
(7) 1. Encourages play and aids rule experimentation as before. 2. Praises rule experimentation as before. 3. Engages in sensorimotor play with child, *delaying re-modeling of rule task* for half a minute, unless or until child appears receptive.	
	1. Continues playing as before, and/or 2. Attempts to imitate.
(8) Repeats Step 5.	

Cycle of Steps 3 to 8 continues, until rule mastered or session terminated.
(See Figure 10-4 on continuing lack of interest).

Guided Learning Interaction: Detailed Sequence

The first learning materials used to demonstrate a concept may be introduced in two ways (Step 2 in Figure 10-3). Either they can be presented quickly, in the form of some dramatic play movement (hiding the stimulus items, such as two marbles or three paper clips, under an inverted box), or they can be eased into the child's perceptual-motor field, to be explored and incorporated into play. If the child shows no interest after a short period (a few seconds), a dramatic ploy becomes more appropriate. The dramatic presentation of the stimuli in play would, at the same time, ordinarily be a clear demonstration of the rule (three as opposed to four pennies). Children whose attention is difficult to capture, however, may need several such dramatic presentations before they are observed to attend to the rule dimensions of the stimuli and task.

The necessary movement and procedural variations which will occur when playing with supportive play materials makes the problem of providing plenty of different examples of a rule easy to solve. A good variety of the learning materials themselves is also needed, however, to demonstrate the generality of concept rules through providing several examples.

The need for repeated demonstrations of each rule is not limited to inattentive or slow-learning children. Repeated demonstration is built into the interaction model because a rule is seldom learned in one or two trials unless the child is already on the verge of learning the rule. This fact is reflected in the series of steps two through four, and the expected continuation of the cycle over many learning sessions if necessary.* The second and all subsequent demonstrations (Steps 3, 4, and 6) follow much the same form, except for varying procedures and the examples used to teach the general idea. All demonstrations involve as much analyzing and synthesizing of critical elements in a task as is feasible to point out the critical dimensions of each rule. In the number concept example we have been using, the child may be shown how a cluster of two blocks is made up of one block and one block (analyzing), by separating them, then putting them together (synthesizing or relating them) to make two—which incidentally, starts preschoolers in addition and subtraction arithmetic operations.

As a further example, at a moment when the child is paying attention, an example of a concept (a *flat* block, a *garbage* truck) is briefly isolated (analyzed) from other objects and compared (related to) another object which is *not* an example (a *non*-flat block, any *other* truck), pointing out the difference in characteristics (flatness—non-flatness, presence—non-presence of garbage carrier and grinder), to enable the child to synthesize (connect mentally) the dimension of the rule being taught. Similar procedures apply to learning rules for any concept, no matter how simple or complex (functions, ecological relations, class membership).

With each repetition of a rule demonstration, a phrase is used to describe each feature, relationship, and part of the process, as the teacher makes the corresponding action. Again, it is helpful to emphasize each key term ("the *two* shells," "the *green* one," "the wind *blows* the sail to make the boat move") at the same time as the critical feature is being pointed to, or the action performed, by placing voice stress on the key terms. Try to avoid speech that is mechanical or strained; natural and dramatic forms of expression have greater appeal.

It will be recalled that children learn when their own efforts are guided, as well as from observing a model (demonstration) of a rule. Some children can learn mainly through observing another's actions and listening to their accompanying descriptions, quickly demonstrating their knowledge with accurate imitations. If her imitations show that a little girl has grasped the rule by adapting her procedures to changing circumstances (can count three peas on her plate at lunch as well as during the guidance session), she has indeed learned it without the teacher guiding her (perhaps helped by parents or older siblings). But imitations of an observed model are rarely correct during the first one or two trials. Typically, the learner must experiment herself, because she confuses *local* conditions, such as length of a row of pennies in a number learning task

---

* The latter situation may arise in the case of the first introduction of a complex concept, especially one so abstract as number, where several variants, such as "two," "three" and "four" of the basic general rule that "things can be ordered by number," (as well as many examples of each rule) may be necessary before the rule is mastered. In this case, the child will sometimes seem to make no reliable progress for a week or two, then suddenly learn several of the rule variants, such as counting two and three with many different objects (or learning new colors, geometric shapes, letters of the alphabet in programs on color, shape, or letters respectively). Similar learning patterns may occur in children who have experienced little previous systematic instruction. These patterns are discussed further in Chapter 14.

or the color and shape in a size task, with the *general* dimensions of the rule, in this case, the "number" or "bigness" dimension. Remember, it is *not* rote copying we are trying to teach, but competence in performing tasks according to cognitively regulated rules, which is a quite different form of imitation. Such imitation is almost bound to involve experimentation, frequently even when the essence of a rule is understood, because particular, and sometimes unforeseen, circumstances cast the problem in a slightly different form. Color patterns and positional relations, for example, sometimes obscure even moderate differences in size, number, or other features.

Although the child needs to take an active role, and to experiment extensively in order to learn well, it is helpful if the teacher points to a relevant feature and makes an occasional well-timed gesture or suggestion in the course of the child's experimentation. When the child works on a task herself, she forgets, or the objects do not appear in quite the same perspective, a little guidance may help her to pinpoint precisely the relationship she keeps missing when she tries the task herself. This guidance role of the teacher is indicated in Steps 4 through 7 of our model (Figure 10–3).

Guidance follows the same analytic-synthetic process the teacher employs for his own demonstrations of concept rules. The difference is that the *child* is now the performer, and therefore the teacher is "outside" the rule experimentation process. As such, the teacher is an observer who helps best by acting selectively at certain critical junctures of difficulty. The teacher or caregiver moves the pennies closer together, just at the point a child is saying that the row of four pennies contains five, helping to dispel the influence of the length of a row, or points (or moves the child's finger) to the skipped bean so it will get counted too. He may or may not say (as he makes the motion), depending on how recepetive the child is, "See, this row was longer, making it look like five pennies" or "Did you miss this one (pointing)?" Thus, he does not carry out the entire task, but makes an occasional verbal comment and/or performs an action carefully timed to fit the child's performance. His approach is focused on relevant features and relationships, but his actions limited to the occasions when needed.

If the adult intervenes too often, the child may become too dependent and fail to become independent in using her own reasoning powers. In particular, children already inclined to lean too much on others need the encouragement and opportunity to *try different things out themselves*, lest they learn no new rules without initiative from others.

Although the teacher frequently takes the lead, he must be careful that the manner in which he assumes this initiative, and the timing and frequency of his actions, does not stifle the interest and initiative of the child. The teacher must, in other words, constantly keep in mind the need for the child to perform a great deal, observing closely to see how she is responding to what is being presented. If her attention wanders or she tries to leave or disrupt a situation, the chances are that the teacher is not presenting the idea on a level or in a form that will capture her interest to reach her understanding. Unless the child is getting close to capturing the general abstraction about numbers, for example, she may not see at all how it is the length of a row that is diverting her, or only get confused when she is interrupted in counting.

It may take further demonstrations at other moments in the course of play with different examples, comparing them under various conditions, to point up the problem and eventually make the rule(s) clear; for example, lining up several rows of the same number of small objects, each spread out to a different length; also comparing three rows of two, three, and four beans that are all the same length. But *practice* alone for the child is also essential; as she counts more and more objects of all kinds, groups and regroups them in small clusters of two, three, and four, she herself is coming to grip with the problems to iron out the general rules.

It is difficult to define exactly how many times in a ten to twenty minute learning session the teacher should demonstrate tasks to learn. Obviously, the more often a teacher takes the initiative the less opportunity the child has to do so, particularly if there are as many as five or six children in a group. The range can perhaps extend from as few as four or five presentations to as many as twenty or more if there is a lively group of children, well-oriented toward the task of learning, and if the teacher has established good rapport and dramatic means of presentation.

Although a rule-oriented, interactive approach is itself a cognitively adaptive method of teaching rather than a rigid, rote method, there are other techniques we can employ to encourage an open-ended, creative style of learning and problem-solving. Among these are the free-flowing play approach and an inquiry form of monitoring developmental learning.

Monitoring Cognitive Rule Learning

The fifth step in the sequence (Figure 10–3), it will be noticed, is an *inquiry*, designed to assess the child's understanding of a rule. Although something of a test, the inquiry is, like the demonstrations of rules, presented in play. Formal testing, either in form or attitude, is neither used nor needed during teaching sessions. The game-like inquiry and incidental observations of the child's experimentations with the learning tasks will provide plenty of information to indicate his or her progress.

It is better *not to begin* any learning session with an inquiry (unless some test of long-term memory is desired), but to first demonstrate even recently presented rules once or twice. This procedure will freshen the concept in the child's mind, and make success more likely. Some children have been reared to experience any question as a demand for perfect performance instead of an inquiry into problems. It is, moreover, *understanding* of rules we seek first, rather than long-term memory. The latter will come with the frequent review built into programs.

In the inquiry, the action the adult asks the child to perform is, in fact, a demonstration of some part of a rule. Previously, the teacher has relied heavily on the child's natural inclination to imitate the behavior of emotionally supportive adults in order to involve the child in learning. By asking her to do something herself, the teacher captures the child's attention more directly, through conducting an interesting search for a missing item to solve a problem. It is thus an extension of the kind of problem-solving play natural to the child's ordinary sensory-motor activity, encouraged freely throughout the learning activities. The recommended form of inquiry may be illustrated by an example with size concept learning (Figure 10–4).

The purpose of the inquiry is to monitor the child's progress in learning as defined by the sequence of concepts in a program. Although an inquiry task is a kind of test, it should *not* involve "testing" in the sense of a threat to the child's competence. It is for this reason that we set up an interesting game-like problem to solve (a "search"), embed the procedures in play, and reward the child's effort as much as her competence. Avoid persisting in an inquiry that

FIGURE 10–4. Size rule inquiry (Figure 10–2, Step 5)

Teacher	Child
	(Preferably when child has been playing with the same materials or task for a few seconds or pauses in play . . .)
. . . places a large and a small block, separated by a few inches, in front of the child, and says immediately, "Can you find the *big* block, John?"	
	If no immediate effort by the child . . .
. . . then says, "Where's the *big* block?" or, "Let's find the *big* block!"	
	If child points to, or otherwise indicates, correct choice . . .
"*There* it is!" (with enthusiasm)	
	If child makes incorrect choice, either small block or some irrelevant stimulus . . .
"That's fine!" and, "You found the *little* block!" in a positive tone, (identify whatever the child picks from the various play materials)	
	If child has continued playing, with no attempt to engage in search . . .
(After a few more seconds) . . . picks up the block with interest and says, "Here it is!" or, "We found it!" and "It was right over here, it ran away from us!" (avoiding implied censure)	
	If child repeatedly shows no interest in search tasks in response to inquiry . . .
Terminate session: There is probably some general problem of lack of interest, confusion and/or resistance to guided learning activities that needs analysis. This might be caused by over-direction by teacher; use of examples or concepts that are too advanced; unclear demonstrations; rivalry with peers; feeling of rejection by the adult; or emotional upset from problems arising outside of the learning situation.	

brings little response from a child; instead, begin to participate in the search task, thus turning it into another rule demonstration and establishing a cooperative social relationship in a joint inquiry.

The form of the inquiry sets up a task for the child in her natural sensori-motor style and anchors the task itself to a limited, comparatively easy set of choices. By asking the child to *do* something *physically* with the stimuli, we are minimizing the level of abstraction at which we use language. If, on the other hand, we point to the larger one of two blocks, and ask the child, "What is this? or, "Which one is this?" we are demanding an answer in language form alone. This is often a more difficult level of performance in the early years of language development, particularly for children under four.

An easier form of inquiry, though still requiring a language response, is to phrase the question, "Which is this, the *big* or the *little* (not big) one?", while pointing to one of the two objects in question. Instead of having to recall from memory the correct name for an object from all the many names he knows—a huge, abstract, multiple choice task—the child now merely has to match one of the two labels that we have provided with the designated object. Although "bigness," of course, is an abstract, relational rule, and not the name of an object, like "block", this problem applies to any form of inquiry we might make; and it is intrinsic to the rule about "bigness".

The preferred form of inquiry, however, is still the one outlined in Figure 10-3, in which the response asked for is *physical action,* not language. Even the easier form of language has limitations. Because it does ask directly for a language response, it is probably more appropriate when the teacher feels reasonably certain that the child knows a rule well. Used too early in the learning process, it is too difficult a task, partly because it still does not ask the child to search physically to solve the problem as is more natural to her age. But in the second place, she is posed with *abstract alternatives,* perhaps for the first time. In the beginning guided play sessions, the demonstrations and inquiries usually involve only a single label to keep in mind, such as a "big" block or a "little" one, not both, Now, on the other hand, the possibility is put to her that the object pointed to could be either "big" *or* "little" (not big), which is really a more advanced stage of the learning process. Children typically must group the separate rules about *each* end of a dimensional pole, such as big, tall, bright, etc., or little, short, dark, etc., before they can understand and use both together. They also find it easier to learn the more positive one (big, tall) before they learn the lesser one (little, short).

When the recommended type of inquiry (Figure 10-3, Step 5) is employed, on the other hand, the child is not only simply asked to find the correct choice in concrete form (an object), but given a single language label, she only has to match the *one* label with one of the two objects—and she engages in the kind of perceptual-motor search little children are typically good at. For these reasons, this inquiry-action method of monitoring is recommended for use most of the time. Only later on, when a child has thoroughly mastered the separate rules about two poles of a concept (big-little, fat-thin), and is now ready to learn them together, can the child be comfortably asked to deal with alternatives, which necessarily involves language more.

Monitoring through inquiry is not necessarily limited to a search for the choice between the same two objects, however. Like the teaching demonstra-

Phase I
Similar Materials

Phase II
Dissimilar Materials

FIGURE 10-5
*How inquiry expands to increasingly complicated examples and
contexts to further mastery and generalization of concepts.*

tions themselves, many different examples in many different arrangements will
be needed to discover how well the child is progressing. Again, because we
want the child to learn general *rules* about concepts, not rote tasks, we must
ask her to look for the big marble, the big box, the big doll, and so on, when
paired with many different small things, and eventually each small thing compared to many different big things in order to monitor progress in cognitive
rule learning.

At a certain point the child will have progressed enough to have her competence assessed with more complex forms of the task. She can apply the rule
when asked to find the example (the big car) when more than two objects are
in front of her. Confronting her with a big and a little toy—for the moment
separated from the supportive play materials—is the simplest version of the
task, particularly if the two objects are ones with which several demonstrations have recently been made. The task becomes more complicated when she
is asked to choose between different types of objects (a small toy car versus a
large block). It is increasingly complicated by introducing one, then two, three,
and more miscellaneous play materials from which she has to find the example.
Gradually the extraneous materials introduced can also become close in size
(or weight, brightness, etc., according to the concept being learned) to the
example requested. Finally, we can ask the child to search for examples of her
own, first from the materials immediately in front of her, then later around the

FIGURE 10–5
continued

room and in other settings. At this stage, we have not only greatly expanded the complexity of the problem for the child, but we have widened the inquiry to embrace an almost infinite range of alternatives, thus fostering the broadest form of creative problem solving. (Monitoring children's learning over a long sequence of rules will be discussed in Chapter 14 on strategies of learning.)

The form of guided questioning we have described demands active problem-solving on the part of the child, and is thus an *inquiry approach to learning*, as well as a monitoring technique. The child is faced with an interesting problem, and in order to solve it, she must actively engage her mind in learning rules about a concept, which of course is a central objective of the learning program. By presenting learning as an active engagement in problem solving rather than as passive reception of information, we are able simultaneously to accomplish three things: we determine whether the child understands in an active and cognitively broad sense; we obtain a wide, general *measure* of the child's competence; and we furnish the child with a broader experience in learning. If we merely let a child observe the teacher's performance, she does not have to test herself and experiment with the dimensions of the problem to ensure mastery; nor do we have a guarantee that she has, in fact, learned any information at all, unless she happens to perform spontaneously.

It is therefore important that a portion of the caregiver's effort in any learning situation be devoted to guided inquiry, in which he asks the child to perform increasingly broad and varied actions with the material rather than the caregiver himself always demonstrating the actions. When presenting a new object to be learned, or when confusion arises the teacher will, of course, need to continue to label and demonstrate. If he has to do this too often, however, it is probably because he has been introducing too many new rules or examples.

It is useful for a teacher's approach in directed questioning to follow a kind of *joint inquiry*, in which the child (or children) and the teacher perform in turn. Not only does this become a kind of game, but there is a sense of everyone working together, cooperatively, to discover how a concept works. Cooperating in this way also places stress on interaction as opposed to the teacher's role as an authority who simply runs things. The teacher becomes, in a sense, a member of the group at the children's own level, by taking his turn with the others rather than constantly assuming the role of leader.

The world is constructed in terms of many basic concepts people have worked out over many years. Many of these concepts are obviously useful for the child to learn. An inquiry approach, however, always leaves open the possibility for alternatives, and for the child to work out rules in her own way. This potential should be encouraged whenever possible without ignoring the value of learning rules that link the child to the physical and social world in which she lives.

11 | Place and Materials

A place outdoors

The Setting: Physical Environment

Children can be guided to learn almost anywhere in the home, day care center, school, or other places in the community, both indoors and out. However, for planned learning projects and activities certain ways of arranging the environment will sustain the child's attention in directed play better than others.

Spatial
Arrangements

The space available for guiding cognitive learning activities should be large and well distributed enough to enable the children to move and concentrate with little interference from one another. Since most activities take place with a single teacher interacting with children individually or in small groups, small

269

rooms or sections of larger rooms, ranging in area from 50 to 150 square feet, are best. This will permit several guided learning activities to take place separately and simultaneously. Otherwise it is difficult to accommodate all children in the school several times every day.

Children are naturally more at ease when the learning area is organized on a child-size scale, with furniture and equipment arranged to minimize clutter and permit freedom of movement. Because the natural form of expression of the young child is through action, space enough for both large and small motor movement is likely to promote longer attention spans.

Design of Learning Area

Tutoring can take place in many spots in an ordinary playroom. It helps a child to focus, however, if there is a special area, marked by some boundary, like the edge of a table or a small rug on the floor, which fits comfortably into his visual-motor field of activity. Each area requires about two to four square feet for every child. Children group themselves naturally around the edge of a rug or table; the teacher needs only to ensure that each child gets a fair share of the activity area.

When tables and chairs are used, scale them carefully to the average size of the children using them. It is too expensive and too awkward to match chair sizes to children individually, because there are too many variations between children, enrollments change, and different learning groups usually use the same chairs. If anything, then, choose furniture that is a bit small for the larger children, so that every child can easily place both feet flat on the floor in a comfortable position. Since young children's furniture is often designed much too large for their comfort, it may be advisable to cut down the legs of some tables and chairs. Circular tables, cut in quarter or half-round sections, can be fitted together in combinations to accommodate varying numbers of children, as illustrated in Figure 11-1. Circular tables place children in a more equal relationship to one another and to the teacher. This encourages cooperation in learning and enables the teacher to interact with each child at an equal distance. A round hole cut in the center of what would be the total circle enables the teacher to serve the children equally.

Rectangular and square tables will, however, work very well. The dimensions of rectangular tables can be such as to place children at about an equal distance from the teacher, as in Figure 11-1. Such tables provide each child with a larger working area, but are slightly less flexible in accommodating varied numbers of children, in making table combinations, and promoting cooperation between children. The greater division between the children can, however, help a hyperactive or aggressive child to concentrate. Inset cutouts at each child's position will magnify this effect, but also will limit the number of places at the table.

Arrangement and Storage of Learning Materials

The first priority in arranging learning and play materials is the accessibility and display needed to conduct the activities. Regardless of the type of learning program, some materials need to be close at hand for day-to-day use, while others are better kept in reserve. It is usually best to minimize conflicts that arise from children's curiosity to explore reserve materials by storing them on

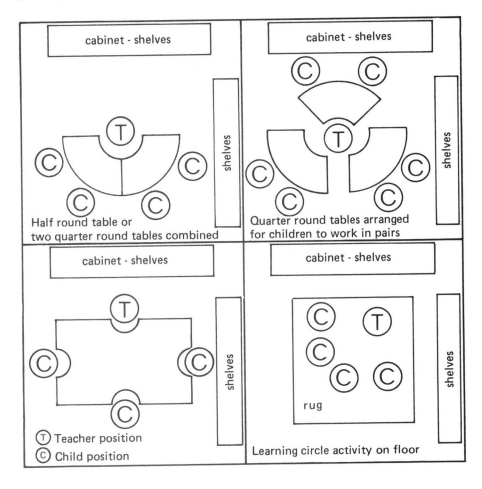

FIGURE 11-1
*Varied types of
table and floor
arrangements for
guiding learning
projects.*

high shelves or in closed cabinets, out of visual or physical reach. Since many preschool learning materials consist of miniature objects and pictures, cabinets with banks of small drawers make a convenient storage and retrieval system. These materials can be arranged into categories in advance to be readily accessible in exact form on demand.

It is convenient to arrange materials in current use in categories defined by the children's degree of mastery (new materials, current materials, and review items) and by the concepts in the program to which they belong (animals versus people, or object features and functions or relations, such as length and width). Additional categories include supplementary play materials, different sets of examples for the same concepts (sets of human or animal figures of different sizes and with different specific features) and sets of similar materials for each child in order to individualize the learning process.

A convenient method of arranging materials in multiple categories is to place them on open shelves divided into several pigeon-holes or compartments. It is helpful to keep some of these categories in miniature drawers to minimize visual confusion among displays, but within easy reach and labeled with symbols (or pictures) providing ready identification by the children. Bulky sets of materials, like games and programs in series, collections with large or interrelated pieces, and educational devices and apparatuses may require special shelves. Figure 11–2 shows one convenient arrangement of materials and furniture in a small center where one room must serve several activities simultaneously.

Timing and Scheduling

Teaching sessions must obviously be timed to fit into the schedule of other activities and routines of daily life in home or day care. It is useful to schedule substantial blocks of time (20- to 30-minute periods) free from interruption by other demands, to allow adequate time for movement to and from the learning area, and for children to become thoroughly immersed in a learning session. Flexible scheduling maintained throughout the program will be more conducive to a relaxed and involving atmosphere.

Children will learn best if the more complex and challenging learning tasks are presented when they are fresh and alert, usually in the early periods of the day or following a nap, allowing time for sleepiness to disappear. Less demanding types of cognitive learning sessions, whose objectives are sometimes more in the nature of quieting or entertainment (looking at familiar books, listening to light stories and records, engaging in rhythm, dance, or circle games) will often work well toward the end of the morning or day when children are likely to be tired, hungry, bored and disinclined to concentrate or play on their own. It is advisable to alternate periods of relatively intense learning with periods of free play and guided entertainment and allow time for active movement. Time for preparation and clean-up also needs to be allowed for.

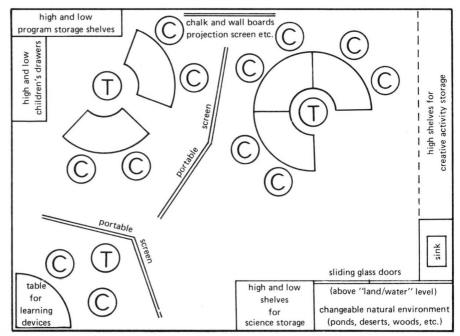

FIGURE 11–2
Arrangement of learning materials and work space in a guided learning room.

FIGURE 11–3
Setting for guided learning activities.

Freedom from Distraction

Learning areas which are located and furnished to prevent distraction from all sources, either inside or outside the room, will encourage concentration on the intended activities. Much of the problem will be solved if facilities are designed and arranged to cut interference from activities outside the guided learning area, as described in Chapters 4 and 8. It is seldom possible, nor desirable, to keep activities in adjoining rooms constantly quiet.

If walls or partitions are thin or incomplete, acoustical tiles, rugs, and wall hangings of heavy materials (blankets, curtain material, canvas) will cut down much of the interference from noise. Uniform light and glare-free color on the floor and table surfaces in learning areas will enhance perceptual focus on the learning and play materials. If the surfaces of learning areas are padded with soft materials (rugs or felt), the pile should not be too thick to hamper the placement and movement of small objects and pictures.

Perceptual and
Aesthetic Appeal

Arrangements that are too simple may be too bare. Pleasant, light, and relatively pure color tones will enhance the psychological atmosphere, here as everywhere in the children's environment. Insipid pastels and cheap luminescent colors contribute little to children's aesthetic development. Lighting can be too bright and glaring as well as too dim. Good lighting is spread around (diffuse) and soft in tone. Wall and non-learning surfaces may be painted with attractive but simple and subdued designs, or punctuated with a few well-spaced pictures and drawings that lend interest but will not distract.

Types of Concept Learning Materials

There are many aspects to be considered in choosing and arranging program materials. Materials may be

(a) about concepts either common or uncommon to the child's local environment;
(b) represent many different categories of concepts, from within the categories of knowledge, problem solving and language described in Chapter 1;
(c) prepared program materials or objects likely to be met in daily experience.

Familiarity of
Concepts

Much of the child's early experience is concerned with learning about *common things* in the everyday world. Indeed children can hardly help learning more about these than about exotic things because they are continually surrounded by them; the frequent repetition from continuing exposure makes them easier to learn. Early experience is filled with endless examples of basic concepts, the various common rules about size, shape, and how wheels roll which abound in daily life.

The most logical and easiest source of program learning materials is thus the common objects and pictures drawn from the child's everyday environment. The child will learn concepts most rapidly using the materials whose characteristics are already familiar in a general way from personal experience. Small common objects, like kitchen utensils and other household items, small tools and desk materials; miniature toy replicas; and pictures, photographs, and simple, clear drawings are all excellent materials to use.

As children move out of infancy, using materials from less familiar categories of concepts will serve to expand their knowledge. Because uncommon materials are by definition less likely to be met with in play and other situations in ordinary life, it becomes more important to introduce such materials in other activities. The organization of the group care experience around themes as described in Chapter 7 becomes particularly important. A theme like ships and docks, or farm life, has little real meaning to the typical urban or suburban child who has never been near a harbor or a farm. A guided learning project on either of these themes less familiar to the child's world will need to be extensively supplemented through excursions to harbors (or farms), picture books about these settings, and sociodramatic play with relevant props to deepen the meaning of the theme for the child.

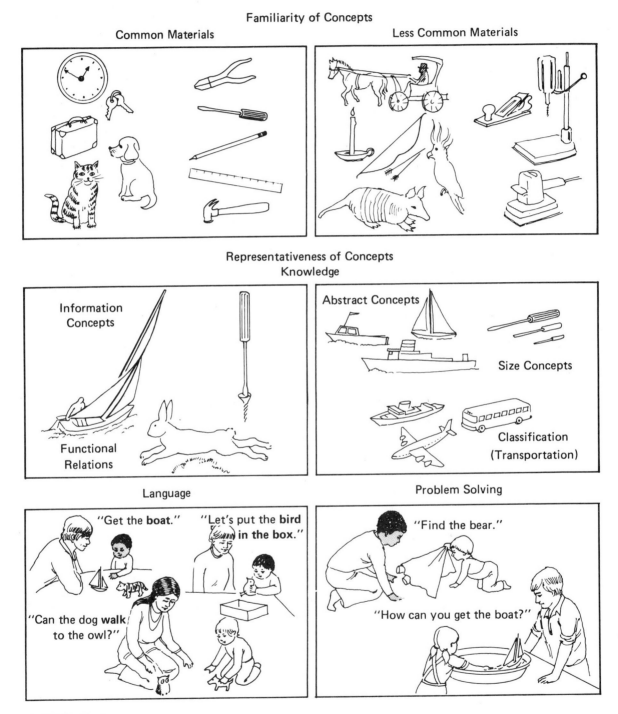

FIGURE 11–4
Types of concepts to represent in guided learning materials.

The choice of concepts to emphasize in early learning programs is, however, partly a matter of preference and partly a matter of value. Themes like those about animals and household activities which are prevalent in the culture will invariably be covered to some degree, but parents and teachers will always prefer some categories to which they will probably give more emphasis. The final choice is usually determined by some combination of the interests and knowledge of the staff, the availability of materials, and the developing interests and competencies of the children. If no teacher likes or knows much about ships or farms and neither harbors nor farms are located nearby, neither theme is likely to be given much attention. On the other hand, assuming sufficient teacher interest and that the environment and materials are available, if children become interested in music (perhaps from stimulation at home), special projects in listening to records and even specific training in singing or learning (by ear) musical notes and phrases might well be introduced.

Representativeness of Concepts

General intellectual development thrives on programs and materials that represent broad areas of knowledge, language, and problem solving (as outlined in Chapter 1). Certain materials will illuminate some rules better than others. In basic knowledge, for example, size concepts obviously require materials that vary in size. In language, fortunately, almost any materials lend themselves to illustrating all the different language rules. Thus every object is represented by a noun and all objects can be used in various actions to illustrate verbs (push, drop, etc.); and sentence rules are simply the means and ends of activity, again using almost any materials in increasingly complicated ways (the doll, the doll sits, the doll sits down, the doll sits down in the chair, etc.). It can be helpful not to introduce different materials too often in order to help the child concentrate on the language rules rather than on the novelty of the materials. Problem solving as well is largely a question of giving attention to how to analyze and organize various materials into new relations to solve a problem. To learn such skills many ordinary materials will do, such as using sticks to retrieve a toy at a distance or selecting and putting together in order the pieces of a puzzle.

It is in the area of general knowledge, then, that the greatest attention to the selection of program materials is needed. A broad variety of program materials, selected and organized to represent the major categories of knowledge (plants, animals, clothes, etc.), and the various dimensions and processes of knowledge, such as the features and functions of things (noses for smelling), that events are caused (water wets paper) and things can be grouped by their characteristics (different toys have the same color), are needed in day care and schools to ensure the general development of children. And even though language and problem solving at first appear easier to manage, representativeness and systematic development are difficult to guarantee without advance planning and preparation.

Prepared Programs

It is easier for caregivers and teachers to work in learning projects with prepared materials than to use whatever comes to hand and work only from day to day. Without advance preparation, it is not only difficult to know what steps come next, but the types of examples necessary to illustrate the concepts in a sequence will rarely be available when they are needed. Teaching about reptiles, for example, will obviously need many pictures, replicas, scenes and other materials involving alligators, snakes and other reptiles in different settings, while number concept learning will need a variety of different small objects to arrange in sets and count, such as blocks, nuts, and spoons.

Published programs may provide materials to work with in a planned series of learning experiences, or they may outline the steps and describe methods and materials, but leave the task of collecting materials to teachers. Since published materials seldom include enough examples or steps to meet the varied needs of children and broaden the variety of concepts involved, some advance preparation is usually needed, if only to go over the program and prepare supplementary materials in advance. Usually preparing about a week at a time works well, assuming some general familiarity with the goals and steps in a program that is expected to last two or three weeks or longer.

The various toys and learning materials employed in free play can often be used for projects (blocks for counting, size graded nesting cups), but the ordinary household and other everyday objects and magazine pictures staff and parents bring from home are among the best sorts of materials to use. Empty cans and other containers of different sizes to teach size and volume (with liquids); different colored yarns; lengths of wood to teach width and length; stones to teach weight and counting; spools for wheels; discardable kitchen utensils, tools, clothes, desk and writing materials, plants, and many other household items can all be used to develop excellent programs of almost any kind.

Characteristics of Materials

Apart from the choice of content and the organization of materials into program sequences, learning materials have structural characteristics influencing what and how well children will learn from them. Although characteristics of materials were discussed at length in Chapter 7, a number of characteristics pertinent to choosing and preparing materials for guided learning programs deserve brief comment here.

Clarity of Designs   Clarity in the design of materials for young children means above all that materials have parts that are well defined, making them easier to perceive and understand. In the case of concepts about the structural dimensions of things, namely their size, shape, texture and so on, the best objects and pictures represent each dimension in precise form. Size and textural differences are substantial, angles are pointed (not rounded off) and boundaries between areas well marked by sharp lines and gross differences in color. In the case of information concepts, the more significant characteristics of the object are clearly in evidence; for example, the hump of a camel or the udder of a cow.

Simplified Examples

Clarity of Design

Variety of Examples

Graded in Complexity

Real Life Experiences

Realistic Designs

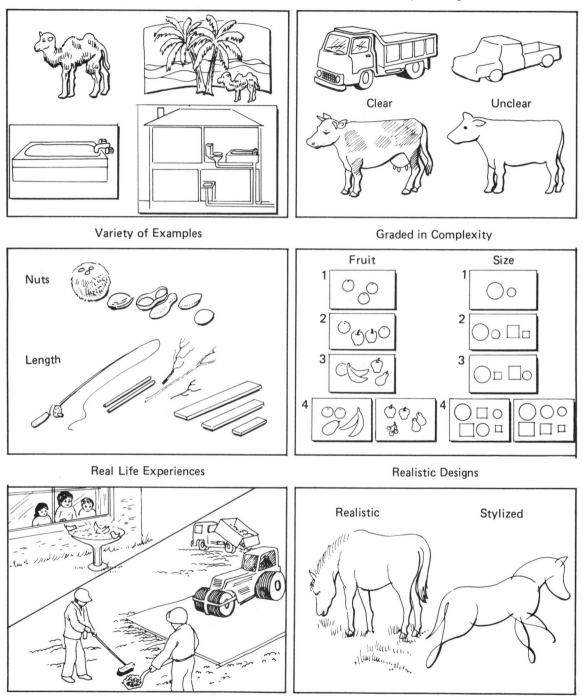

FIGURE 11-5. *Characteristics of well-designed guided learning materials.*

Simplified Examples

Learning materials and drawings that simplify structures represent objects in a realistic (but not naturalistic) way that informs but ignores details of form, color, and texture that are irrelevant to the concept and might therefore confuse the child. There are three characteristic ways in which materials are simplified.

Miniature Replicas

A good number of learning materials for the young child can take the form of miniature replicas of real-life objects. These are three-dimensional in structure, but are usually reduced in size to enable the child to observe and play with them easily in a planned learning activity. They are designed according to a code or set of language rules, but one that makes a three-dimensional, *visual* summary of an object, in which important features are accentuated and others are ignored. The main features of mammals and birds are shown, for example, like the head, eyes, and outlines of mouth or beak, wings, and legs, but seldom the hair and feathers in detail. Better made replicas usually suggest the presence and contours of feathers and curly hair and some even provide feathers and hair.

Pictures and Drawings

Except for highly schematized drawings (like blue prints), pictures also usually make a visual summary of objects, although coded more abstractly on a flat surface. Pictures are a familiar medium, often include more informative detail than replicas (including nostrils of bird beaks and shadings of feathers, scales of reptiles, etc.), and usually represent full scenes as well as single objects. Their advantage for guided learning programs, therefore, is enormous. Precisely sequenced programs covering almost any topic can be prepared and reproduced in quantity at little cost. Photographs can lend reality, while drawings can be made to reveal and throw into relief characteristics impossible to display in the objects themselves (an animal's heart or stomach, the cylinders of an engine).

The control of size and comparative ease of manipulation in cramped learning areas also make pictures and drawings extremely useful. They can be blown up to accentuate small but significant details (key holes), and reduced in size to facilitate handling in play. Pictures are not as easy to handle as solid replicas, but they can be pasted onto stiff cardboard. Photos, slides and magazine cutouts can easily be arranged into learning programs by parents and teachers.

Ecological Scenes and Mockups

Ecological materials are pictures and three-dimensional mockups illustrating the relation of objects to their environment. The structural and functional relations between objects and environments can be regularly demonstrated at an early stage of learning in every information concept area. No realistic understanding of fish, for example, is possible without seeing them swimming in water, watching how they move their gills to breathe and how they move their fins and tail to propel themselves through the water. Large-scale photographs and drawings which can hang on the wall make excellent simulations to enrich understanding. Two-dimensional scenes can be used to depict natural life and neighborhoods, dock areas, airports, the interior of houses, stores, factories and offices. The depth of three-dimensional mockups and, especially, the actual operation of live, miniature environments (aquaria and terraria), however, demonstrate more realistically relations between natural rocks, plants, and animals, and specific environmental characteristics. The child sees how the roots of plants extend into the soil, for example, how rocks may pile up and balance on one another, how butterflies fly and insects move their legs or burrow.

Variety of Examples

At least three to five examples (in replicas or pictures) of each rule in a program is the minimum variety needed to teach rules effectively. A learning program including only one or two illustrations of a house or the color red, for example, will fail to indicate to the child the full scope of the rule—that houses, though all shelter people, vary greatly in form, or that red is a general name for many shades occuring in many places.

It is precisely this variation in details irrelevant to the concept that the child must experience in order to grasp the term as an abstract, general rule instead of merely as a concrete label. Different examples illustrating the concept of length, for instance, need to be wide and narrow, different colors, materials, textures, and used for different purposes. Sticks, poles, pencils, tree branches, and fishing poles, all long, and others all short will effectively dramatize the concept for the child.

Materials Graded in Complexity

The younger the infant and the earlier the stage in a program, the more important it is to use materials that are clear and simple in design. Structurally, stimulating materials for babies under 18 months are very clear and selective, representing a few, well-formed features. Good photographs are better than drawings, which often omit important cues of shading and perspective that the infant needs to be able to interpret drawings as objects. A line drawing of a horse, for example, with no shading to show the roundedness of the body, may not look like a horse even to many two year olds.

Necessarily, infant programs are confined to simple, concrete concepts, such as the characteristics and functions of things appropriate to their level of development. They generally can easily learn to recognize many, many things like goats and trees, their features like eyes and legs, and branches and leaves; and that they are white, have pointed horns or are big, and do things like run or give shade. One-to-two years olds can also begin to learn more abstract concepts about grouping things by size and numbers, time (now, soon) and cause and effect, but only slowly and in limited ways through using many examples.

Examples for infants naturally begin with the simplest forms, so the concept stands out clearly. When the size rule is the focus, for instance, variations in color, shape, and other characteristics are first made one at a time. First two blocks, one big and one small, but otherwise identical; then a pair of big and small blocks, of a different color; then a pair varying only in size and shape (e.g., a big wooden block and a small plastic one). In this way, size as an abstract rule can be taught by simple variations at a rate the infant is capable of grasping.

Neither the infant nor the beginning learner in a program will remain at this simple level long, of course. As a child makes progress in generalizing a rule with simple examples, examples which differ in two and eventually several other characteristics can be learned. As the child is making real progress in size, other dimensional concepts like number and loudness can be introduced in separate activities, again starting with the simplest examples and progressing according to the child's rate of understanding.

A good program of prepared materials is constructed with a sequence of materials graded in complexity to match its intended scope. A full early childhood program extends from the simplest concepts about movement and objects during the first few months of infancy, to a degree of mastery of more complex concepts like time, number seriation (setting up a series of three or more objects increasingly larger in size or lighter in brightness) and classification (grouping sets of things by their characteristics, such as meat and vegetables, digging tools and carpentry tools). The gradient of complexity will naturally be steeper in programs designed for older preschoolers than in those for younger infants, and the concepts themselves will, on the whole, be more advanced (see Chapter 14). That is, the steps are bigger, the child learns more rapidly and the concepts get more complicated (such as learning to count to 15 or 20 instead of only to 4 or 5).

Ideally, however, learning programs need to include different materials of differing degrees of complexity and detail at each level to match the different learning rates of younger and older children and slower and faster learning children. Two children may be able to learn to grade lights according to brightness, for example, but one might need many more examples with light and shades of color to learn than the other.

Use of Real-Life Materials

Programs that include illustrations of rules under "natural" conditions will give children a more realistic, broader form of cognitive development. It is probably not enough to rely on the child's ordinary experiences outside of the planned guided learning programs. What is natural to one child's milieu, richly furnished with objects, books, discussions, and excursions, is likely to be quite unusual to a child reared in poverty. Bridges to reality can be built into concept learning programs in many ways: selected materials, partially simplified in form, can be given to the child to experiment with during play; ecological environments with small, live materials are useful (various small plants and small creatures like grasshoppers, crickets, butterflies and other insects, and garden worms, frogs, fish, turtles, and snakes can easily be obtained to provide detailed demonstrations of how the parts of animals actually work); and especially, excursions can be made so that the child can observe and explore concept examples in real-life settings.

Stylistic Designs

Children learn concepts more easily through guided learning programs when stylized learning materials are used only sparingly. Many children's toys and illustrations for books are designed with unrealistic features, as discussed in

Chapter 7. The intention is usually to portray a quality of sentimentality (enlarged appealing eyes), aggressiveness, or whimsy by exaggerating the harshness or softness of certain features (tightness or looseness of the mouth, jut of the jaw). The background in pictures may be similarly made to look grim (dark and barren) or enchanting (vague and diffuse, multi-green colors). Younger children assimilate more from a selective presentation of such stylistic characterization, since they lack the social experience and ideas needed to interpret it well.

Since early development is a period for learning about the actual characteristics of animals and other things, materials that portray them with the greatest clarity provide better information about the environment. Programs aimed at developing a fanciful interpretation of experience are also desirable, as a basis for the development of creativity, but a great deal of fantasy material is more appropriate for story reading and story telling (with picture accompaniment) activities. Stylistic designs express emotions about people and things, moreover, which children cannot understand until they have seen them expressed in the faces of real people, and felt similar emotions in their relations with people and events. Understanding emotions expressed through stylistic exaggerations also requires the mental development necessary to grasp both the complexity of emotions involved and the special technical rules by which ordinary things are drawn stylistically. Fanciful material needs an expanding base of real life experience, which, like everything else, works better when it is introduced gradually, allowing the child to develop sufficient socioemotional and realistic concept experience for stylistic expression to have a personal meaning. Until the child gathers these understandings and socioemotional experiences, exaggerated styles either have little meaning or appear as vague, silly, or sometimes frightening things.

Be sure, therefore, to provide plenty of pleasant experience with realistically made materials and pictures. When stylistic designs are used, choose ones that are neither too exaggerated nor too frightening. Many traditional nursery rhymes and fairy tales (especially the Grimms' fairy tales), for example, strongly stereotype the characteristics of boys and girls and men and women, and are frequently filled with concepts of violence, which may frighten many children. Such materials also provide models of violent behavior for children which they tend to imitate. Used relatively and gradually, however, as infants develop a healthy, realistic understanding of human relations, the better stylized designs and fanciful stories expand children's imagination, helping them to be sensitive to and cope with the joy, sadness, beauty, and humor of life in all its emotional variety and richness.

Supportive Play Materials and Props

These are materials whose features and uses are not directly illustrative of the concept being learned in a program. Supportive play materials (blocks and miniature replicas) are employed to lend additional interest to a learning situation, while props serve as devices for sorting, storing, and guiding the use of materials in learning tasks. Both often fulfill the two purposes, though with different emphases. Supportive play materials make it easier to use examples of concepts in many different ways so that essential relations can be repeatedly demonstrated without loss of interest, while props help set up or organize a learning task.

Supportive Play Materials

These are materials that can be used for each of the types of play discussed in Chapter 6 on "Play and Development": exploratory, means-ends, construction, and socio-dramatic play. The function of each is to adapt instructional activities to the types of activity young children enjoy. The attention of the child is caught by the sensorimotor play, in the course of which he or she incidentally learns the cognitive rules of the learning task (see Chapter 12 for methods of using supportive play materials). When a child is given several trinkets to explore, for example, along with two examples (pictures) of different fish to learn about, alternating attention between the pictures (pointing out their features) and the trinkets in manipulative play makes it possible to draw the child's attention to each picture several times in the course of a fifteen minute session without tiring or boring the child. The materials suggested below are useful for the various forms of play.

1. *Exploratory Play.* Exploratory play requires few special materials for guided learning activities. Almost any small objects that can be explored and manipulated easily by the child will serve the purpose, both for this and other types of play. Objects varying in color, shape, and texture as well as in complexity are likely to arouse and sustain the infant's curiosity. Colored cubes, small multi-shaped blocks, miniature hardware gadgetry, miscellaneous containers, trinkets, inexpensive jewelry and decorations, bits of cloth, paper, pieces of wood and metal (not too small and without sharp or pointed edges), marbles and pebbles (again, not too small) can all be used.

2. *Means-Ends, Problem-Solving Play.* Many of the foregoing materials are adaptable for instrumental play activity as the infant develops the necessary understanding and skills. Any small objects are easy to use in placement and retrieval play, for example, and most are suitable for insertion and removal play with containers.

There are, however, specialized items needed as tools for problem-solving activity, such as toy rakes and poles (with rounded-off ends) which make good retrieval tools; glass and plastic jars, paper bags, boxes and other containers of different sizes, materials, and means of opening provide endless enjoyment for children for putting (or dropping) in and taking out concept examples and the various exploratory play materials. Flat boards, pliable pieces of cardboard, and box lids all make useful barriers with which to set up both detour and hiding problems. Construction paper, pieces of colored cloth, jar and box tops make suitable targets for placement and retrieval tasks. Lengths of twine, rope, and string can be used for marking boundaries, for retrieving toys at a distance (with a loop or when two strings lead to a distant object, only one of which is tied to it) and for tossing objects (tied to a length of string) into a wastebasket or bucket at varying distances.

Although the variety of problem-solving materials and tasks is endless, certain tasks like puzzles, form boards, and mechanical toys, because of their intricacy, will divert the child's attention from a learning task too long. Materials that lend themselves to quickly arranging simple tasks in many different ways will hold the child's attention well without upsetting the flow of involvement with concept learning.

3. *Construction Play.* These include sets of blocks, building bricks, or other modular materials. It is generally inadvisable to include building materials with interlocking mechanisms, ones that require complex fits, or free form materials like clay or paints in guided learning programs. Such materials again demand too much attention in their own right and generate mess that directs focus away from the learning task. Unless the learning task itself is concerned with learning construction rules or free-form shaping rules, it is easier to use one or two basic sets of building blocks that are few in number and not too different in shape.

4. *Socio-dramatic Play.* Almost any small objects can be used as symbols for anything the child wishes to represent in play. Miniature replicas, however, will stimulate the child to engage in socio-dramatic play better than objects not representing anything. They are particularly valuable with the child under three, whose experience is usually insufficient to enable him or her to develop themes in dramatic play without suggestive materials. Pictures may also be useful—particularly small pictures of individual animals and people, since they are easy to move around in play. Although pictures and three-dimensional replicas of social settings and scenes (gas stations, airports, a doll house, or a community with streets, stores, and houses) stimulate play, they also may divert attention from the course of learning because of their intricacy.

It is better to use no more than a few pictures or replicas and one or two trinkets in combination with a few building materials. This arrangement makes it easier to quickly build, remove, and rebuild simple settings in which learning materials can easily be brought in and out of the play without too much attention to the details of the scene. Simple dramatic movements, like sitting or climbing, can be used, either alone or combined in a chain of events in a story (visiting the zoo or riding in the country), but in any case bringing in examples of concepts easily in the course of the play.

Props

Any object or device whose function is to help organize learning in some activity may be considered a prop. Many of these devices, such as wall or pocket charts for placing pictures or printed words, or lotto games, are included in commercial education programs. Chalk boards, drawing paper, and sorting boxes are similar devices teachers introduce to provide a framework for learning activities. Simulated environmental scenes (pictures, mockups or miniature live nature settings) accomplish the same end, but are designed for specific learning objectives.

Among the most useful props are individual storage cubicles (pigeon-hole compartments or small banks of drawers) or containers (boxes, jars). These give each child a place of his or her own (a "treasure chest") to collect a store of examples, such as pictures, drawings, and replicas illustrating concepts, to work with and review. Containers have the additional advantage of portability, enabling the child to carry materials to any area, and making it easy to change settings to meet scheduling problems or simply to provide a fresh scene.

Other materials set the scene for activity rather than being used in the learning activities themselves, for example, tables and chairs, rugs, dividers, wall pictures, burlap hangings, and display tables. While these are in some sense merely part of the setting, they serve as props in that they help focus or lend background interest to the children's play and learning. Periodic changes in the setting, its arrangement, as well as changes in the types of props and supportive play materials, do much to freshen the child's and—no less important—the adult's interest.

12 Play Techniques for Motivating Learning

Reinforcement

Several types of activity inherent in a guided learning approach arouse and sustain children's interest. First, the pattern and sequence of stimulation bring response through contrasts arising from novelty, complexity, and incongruity. Second, children become involved in learning concepts through a variety of play and problem-solving activities. Third, social reinforcement and feedback are engendered by the teacher and by peer relations: on the teacher's part, through approval, praise, and encouragement however expressed; and among peers, through the pleasures of belonging to a group.

Children thus become interested in learning about concepts like heaviness through the novelty of contrasting heavy and light toys and seeing new examples, the challenge of making increasingly complex comparisons with smaller differences and many examples, and the oddness of large blocks of balsa wood weighing so little; simply through the fun of playing with heavy and light things to do other things, like building with them or dropping them in containers; and through the interest and attention caregivers and other children provide when a child plays with or learns some rule about heaviness (heavy things take more effort to lift than light things do).

For young children, the frequent repetition they need to master concepts thoroughly can be provided by repeatedly demonstrating the concepts in different forms of play with many different examples. Teacher recognition for achievement can be part of the children's play and problem-solving activities. In group situations the children can be encouraged to demonstrate concepts for one another, be friendly, and actively recognize the accomplishments of their playmates. The wise teacher will keep to a minimum corrective feedback that draws attention to the children's errors.

The way in which contrasts, play, and social interaction are used to motivate children, or to interest them in learning, will depend on the developmental level of the children concerned. In general, infants under one year can see contrasts between only two or three objects, or notice the obvious features of a simple object, respond only to the simplest forms of exploratory play demonstrations with objects, and show little peer interaction. Older infants and preschool children benefit from more complex situations, language, social involvement, dramatic play, and a variety of problem-solving activities.

Rationale

Systems for motivating children can be classified according to whether they arouse interest through properties *intrinsic* to (part of) the program concepts, or properties *extrinsic* to (outside) the processes to be learned. In the latter, the child learns programmed concepts presented incidental to his involvement in developmentally normal types of play. In general, activities are designed to fit developmental concepts, with program concepts matched in complexity to the child's progressing interest and understanding.

Intrinsic and Extrinsic Motivation

Learning
Differences

Basic to all learning is recognition of differences. Learning concepts involves learning which differences are important; the wheels and motor of a car are important, while its size and color are not. Seeing and learning about differences—in size, shape, or color; between the simple and the complicated; and especially between the new and the old—draws the child's interest and speeds the process of learning about things. The young child is surrounded by so many new differences, that arousing interest in understanding the basic differences between animals, clothes, and toys; between features like *curved* and *flat* or *red* and *blue*; and between processes like *slow* and *fast* or *dig* and *pour* is fairly easy.

The best course to follow in a learning program is to expose the child to objects that differ in a wide variety of obvious ways, but are neither too familiar nor too strange, and neither too easy nor too difficult. If we surround him with stimuli already familiar and understandable to him and in keeping with what he expects in the everyday world, he has little to learn. Thus deprived homes and deprived group care settings are among other things, places with few toys, books, or other objects, and little attention to anything new. Children as well as adults learn best under conditions of moderate novelty and difficulty. A child will usually show less interest in a new example of a concept which is either extremely different from or very similar to examples he knows well, than he will to a novel design in which he can see both differences and resemblances to what he already knows. In a program about furniture, for example, a child is likely to respond less to a bizarre modern chair or an ordinary chair than to one that is moderately unusual. Curiosity, expressed in a wish to learn, is aroused most keenly by things partially familiar. A middle range of complexity, novelty, and incongruity raises interest to an optimum level. The too difficult or different evokes frustration, fear, or at the least disinterest and avoidance; the too easy or over-familiar produces boredom.

Because children vary greatly in the amount of challenge they like to encounter, however, programs need to be tailored to differences in style. Children who have been encouraged since infancy to explore everything novel and different are far more open to exploring and trying out unusual furniture or other novel designs and experiences than children raised in a monotonous environment where small changes and any efforts to explore or try something different have been actively discouraged or met with distrust. The traditional very "good" or "well behaved" child may be no trouble to his parents and caregivers, but he is also likely to lack imagination and openness to learning. The "problem" child may be—though not necessarily—a curious child because his problems help him see differences.

Learning through Problem Solving and Play

With respect to concept learning programs, problem-solving and play activities are mixed categories; both are intrinsically and extrinsically motivating. They are intrinsically motivating because they involve the child directly in seeking and experimenting with different means to reach goals or to figure out how things work. On the other hand, play and problem solving may initially make only limited use of the properties of the materials and in this sense be at first only extrinsically motivating him to learn the desired concepts. Children naturally explore a new shape sorting box, for example, but first without seeing how each type of shape fits in only one type of hole. In the course of handling, stacking, and poking around, however, and usually aided by periodic guidance from a caregiver, they discover the shape relations the toy is designed to teach. This is the manner in which play and problem solving can be used to arouse children's interest in learning special concepts in planned learning programs. The play is intrinsically part of the young child's natural tendencies to explore and learn, but at first his interest is extrinsic to the more complex use of the concept program materials.

Thus during the early phases of a program a child may explore various clusters of two and three toys, for example, but only briefly. These explorations are useful to familiarize him with the different materials (such as pennies, or marbles) and the fact of clustering, but too limited to build sufficient understanding to maintain interest. The intrinsic appeal of differences between things, while often adequate for initially arousing curiosity to explore, is frequently inadequate to maintain interest in learning in depth. A similar situation often arises with new programs that contain materials too novel and different to arouse more than a passing interest in the child. For young children adding play and problem-solving activities lends continuing appeal to all stimuli whether new or old, easy or difficult, thus encouraging the child to use them freely for a series of learning sessions, and thereby insuring progress. Over a period of weeks an infant or young child will acquire enough basic knowledge of a set of concepts (recognizing differences between two, three and four of something) to want to use his knowledge. But this interest frequently develops only after extensive play experiences, accompanied by repeated demonstrations and comments; pointing out, for example, the differences between two and three of many different things, which are brought into the ongoing play by a caregiver or teacher from time to time.

Children under three seldom lose interest in play, but older children with a skilled, enthusiastic teacher, may concentrate almost entirely on the learning process, as they acquire understanding and thus interest in the concepts themselves. These children develop a general outlook of *learning to learn*, and sometimes come to regard play as an unnecessary diversion. In general, however, even older preschool children value play and incidental problem-solving tasks, which generally continue to enhance both their interest and their progress in learning.

A diversified play approach serves to reduce pressure and make learning more relaxed. Through games and dramatic play, the child is exposed to selected aspects of program stimuli, and can hardly avoid learning the desired characteristics, but is not pressured to learn them. Subsequently, as he acquires more skills in how to learn, more extensive knowledge of content areas, and more general rules about how objects can be organized in concepts, the child's interest in concept learning increases. Correspondingly, the risks from pressure to learn decrease as the child's general skills and confidence can more easily cope with mistakes in teaching methods, or program inadequacies.

As the child gains knowledge, he can use or understand program objects more often according to their intended functions; for example, trucks to transport cargo by road and plant roots to draw moisture and nutrients from the soil. Here he is learning through a system of intrinsic motivation appropriate, not only for the general developmental styles of young children, but also when applicable for the goals of the program. Both intrinsic and extrinsic motivational systems appear to have a place to foster learning in children.

Intrinsic Motivational Methods

The child's interest in objects is heightened by contrast. Color, size, and shape (discussed in chapter 8) are perhaps the most obvious differences, but novelty (unfamiliarity) and complexity play a much more significant role. Ambiguity and incongruity, too, have a contribution to make.

Novelty

It cannot be said that either novelty or complexity is more important. If, at the beginning of a new project, we place before a child miniature replicas of two or three animals, say, a lion, a snake, and a kangaroo, that he has not come across before in any form, he may find them all equally unfamiliar, even though they differ markedly in some specific features. For example, a lion has four legs, a snake has none, and a kangaroo has foreshortened front legs and an extraordinarily long tail. But since these animals have no meaning for him, he will not easily form mental pictures of them and remember their specific parts; he will probably confuse them with animals or other objects with which he is familiar, unless examples of both are placed side by side for visual comparison. He may see the lion as a large dog; and the snake, unless it is alive and moving, as a rope. Contrasting new objects with familiar ones may be a complex task for a young child at the beginning of a program; there are too many new features and small differences for him to grapple with at once.

Complexity

In controlling complexity at least three aspects must be considered: the number presented in any learning situation, and whether they are "old" or "new"; how far the child has progressed in a program; and how well developed he is generally in his cognitive functions. A three- or four-year-old child can handle several objects—maybe eight or ten at a time—in a play situation with little difficulty. He is familiar with many objects of the everyday world, and accustomed to things he can move around and put together in many different ways. He also understands the relations of parts of objects to whole objects, and the functions and relations between objects generally. He has some idea, for example, of why a car is driven into a gas station, even if he does not clearly understand how gas gets into the car or how it is used. Infants of two or younger are likely to have little awareness of the relation between cars and gas stations. Yet even a two-year-old, exposed to several trucks, cars, and boats, soon recognizes a few of their prominent characteristics—wheels, body shapes, steering wheels, and the absence of wheels on boats.

Complexity is a subtle and intricate matter, since objects to be learned often not only have many interrelated parts and functions, but these parts are not equally visible or stressed in various situations. A train, bus, or car, for example, has literally hundreds of parts. The preschool child who has been playing with vehicles for months may have become vaguely familiar with many of their parts and functions, but often can manipulate only a few simple items easily and intelligently. He can usually recognize certain features (the steering wheel and door of a car) more quickly than others (fenders and hubcaps) and can show how some parts work more easily than he can others (wheels versus crane of a tow truck). Also, he will identify a specific car more readily in a group of three or four than in a group of fifteen or twenty even though he knows them all well. Numbers make a difference.

Knowledge is familiarity, and as familiarity increases it makes for rapid perception, understanding, and the ability to deal with more and more elements of a situation. Intimate acquaintance with the child's knowledge is essential before we can decide which objects to introduce and how rapidly to introduce them. In the first learning session about birds and fish, for example, we should probably introduce only one or two examples of each, and in subsequent sessions simply familiarize the child with their characteristics in play. Once two or three similar examples of each have been presented, much activity should center on contrasting their features more specifically with each other again and again in play. Repeated comparisons between the wings, bills, feath-

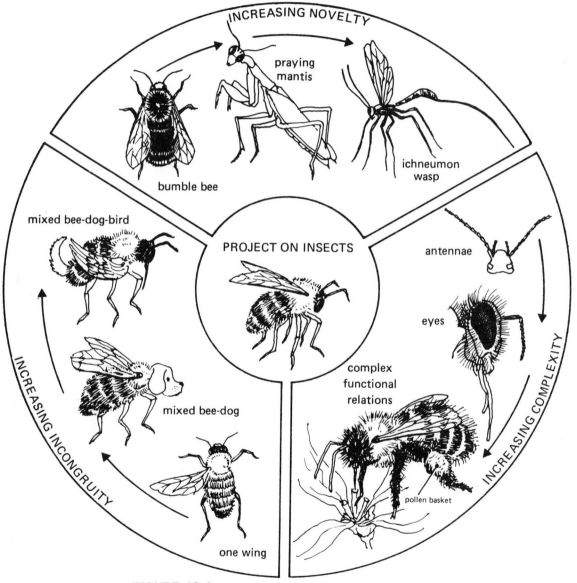

FIGURE 12–1
Intrinsic motivational methods. Children generally respond with more interest when the next step in a concept learning program is moderately *novel, complex, or incongruous, assuming each of the other conditions is equal.*

ers, and feet of the birds with the fins, mouths, gills, and scales of the fish, together with contrasts between how the various features work, will help to establish clearly in mind the different characteristics of the two types of creatures. As the child becomes familiar with these examples, and consistently distinguishes them from one another and from other animals, more examples less similar in form (pelicans and flamingoes versus eels and flounder) can be introduced, one or two at a time. Play with these objects follows the pattern already established.

Presumably, the younger and less experienced the child, the less rapidly he can absorb new complex items of learning. When the child's ability is in question, at any age, it is wise to err on the side of caution and introduce only one new example or talk about only one additional feature at a time, ensuring that the child is thoroughly familiar with it before introducing another or a more complex version of the first.

Ambiguity and Incongruity

When parts do not fit together properly, or objects do not function according to expectations, things appear incongruous to us. *Structural incongruities* are common in the drawings of younger school age children—birds with feet and wings interchanged, horses with the webbed feet of ducks, and airplanes with sails instead of wings. *Functional incongruities* appear somewhat later in such forms as automobiles driven on water, motorboats run on land, or shovels used for eating. Still subtler incongruities appear in representations that run counter to actual roles, such as a baby directing traffic or a policeman riding in a baby carriage.

These are not always seen as incongruities by preschool children; fact and fantasy are interchangeable in their minds and a combination of the two is often central to their play. Their concept of reality is still in a formative stage. More important, they are seldom sufficiently familiar with the possible range of characteristics in a given subject to recognize an incongruous feature. By the time they reach age three or four, however, as children become familiar with many things, they can distinguish better between imagination and reality, and find humor in incongruous situations and mixed-up social roles that increases their pleasure in learning. They *know* people don't have tools for hands and shovels for feet, but may find it fun to imagine what such a person could do. Mixing things up also helps to reinforce their understanding of how things ought to be, and they get a fine sense of mastery out of realizing that they *can* tell when things are drawn wrong in a picture.

Much the same value can be derived from *ambiguity*—presenting animals and other objects in a vague form. This technique can be used profitably only with children who are well advanced in a program or with bright or older preschoolers. It is not successful with babies whose interest is not held by things they cannot see clearly. But ambiguity and incongruity bring pleasure to the child who can respond to them. He enjoys the detective role of identifying things that are not clearly defined—and the heightened sense of mastery that comes from success in solving problems. It cannot be stressed too much, however, that incongruity and ambiguity can be used successfully only when a substantial body of knowledge about a subject area has been established. Even the bright child who knows nothing of butterflies will see nothing odd in a butterfly drawn with six wings or without legs—except in seeing a type of creature he has never seen before.

Extrinsic Motivational Methods

Sensorimotor Play and Problem Solving Activities

Sensorimotor techniques are designed to encourage and take advantage of the child's natural desire to explore and handle objects. They fall into four categories:

1. Curiosity arousing objects that encourage movement, handling, and exploration
2. Problem situations that stimulate experimentation with means and ends (causes and results)
3. Construction play
4. Socio-dramatic play

These activites are typical free play activities of infants and young children, as we have discussed in Chapter 6 on "Play and Development". By encouraging children to engage in sensorimotor play in a structured learning situation, we are really teaching them essential concepts through their own natural activities.

Supporting play materials and props are invaluable in conducting play and problem-solving activities. Miscellaneous things to use in play like blocks, paper, trinkets, miniature replicas, boxes, cans, and jars of all sizes and shapes, with varied lids and stoppers, conveniently placed on shelves accessible to the teacher will help her to maintain interest through novelty in session after session. Special boxes for each child to keep examples, wall charts, chalkboards, and other props make it easier to organize the learning situation. And even though sensorimotor play and problem-solving are not ordinarily modes of adult functioning, if the teacher can relax sufficiently, she may find much enjoyment in this kind of play. Exploring objects and how they work is part of our interest in the world.

It is the caregiver's or teacher's task to introduce miniature figures and other learning toys into the child's play activites, and to study the specific kinds of play that each child prefers. When she has introduced a new plaything she should avoid falling into the passive role of observer. Unless she is actively involved, the child will probably play with the toy for a moment or two, explore it briefly, and then turn his attention to something else.

How can a child's interest in a new toy be sustained until he has had time to learn about it? It is often not enough for a teacher to merely repeat the basic teaching plan. She must vary her approach to capture the child's interest, incorporate the task into play activities that he enjoys, and take part in his play herself. In this manner, she fosters a kind of *incidental learning*, by drawing the child's attention to an object and its properties in a play form that holds his interest. Much of what the child learns results from guiding his attention back and forth between play and the characteristics of objects as examples of concepts we wish him to learn. As discussed earlier in the chapter, we define this technique as *extrinsically motivating,* since the child's interest in the examples is often first aroused by his recognition of an object's potential for play, rather than by its concept-relevant characteristics.

If a child is playing in his usual way, putting a toy tiger in a jar or lining up a row of blocks, when a toy turtle (or a picture) is introduced by the caregiver, the child often just places it too into the jar or sets it to "crawl" along the line of blocks. He will usually give the object a cursory examination, thus gaining some familiarity with the concept, but his interest first focuses mainly on how the object can be used in his ongoing play, not on the features (for example, the shell) defining the concept of "turtle" to which the teacher is drawing his attention. A basic advantage of this approach is that the sensorimotor play activities in themselves are intrinsically motivating, natural forms of expression for young children. Concept learning that involves examples of live creatures will of course excite and sustain interest better than pictures or inert materials. But concepts about the latter (tools, roads, clouds) are also important to learn, and even concepts about very lively creatures often need a little play to sustain learning in depth.

Play and problem solving activities in planned concept learning projects usually become secondary to actual learning—at least in the long run. Well designed sequential learning programs develop the children's interest in both the program materials (intrinsic motivation) and the learning itself, because of the variety of examples and the way concepts are graded in difficulty and familiarity. Play is a useful supplementary tool of motivation, but using it excessively may cause diversion and reduce the desire to learn.

The teacher must be careful not to let herself or the child be continually carried away by the play itself. For example, when an example of a concept has been effectively introduced, let the child follow his own course of play for a while. After giving the example attention for a brief period, first to its relevant characteristic, then usually simply as a play thing, the child will turn to something else. When this happens, don't let the play continue indefinitely but introduce the same or a similar example into another activity after a minute or two, repeating the process in a cycle of alternating play and attention to concepts for ten or fifteen minutes or more. It is best to terminate a session *before* the child shows many signs of tiring, which then leaves him enthusiastic to renew the activities at another time.

Sooner or later the child will use one of the teacher's "toys" or one of his own in a method similar to that used by the teacher. He will mention, for example, that the turtle is moving her legs or pulling them into her shell to avoid attack from another animal, as the teacher has done in drawing attention to the turtle's characteristics. In doing so, the child is both enriching his play and developing an interest in the concepts themselves. As his knowledge of a subject area increases, he will become as much involved in concept learning as he is in sensorimotor play. He is learning to learn. If the teacher proceeds at an easy pace in an informal relaxed manner, play interaction can be one of the best motivating systems to start and maintain children's interest in learning.

Let us now look more closely at the four categories of sensorimotor play and problem solving activities.

Object Curiosity: Exploratory Activities

The central learning experience of the infant relates very directly to the nature of objects. He is concerned with color, texture, shape; whether edges are irregular, smooth, or sharp; and he satisfies his curiosity by looking at objects, feeling and moving them, turning them about, mouthing them, and listening for sounds when they are struck or dropped. The younger the child, the more he responds to a new object simply by exploring it. In his first year, activities of the simplest sort (looking, mouthing, handling) occupy the infant and he continues to pursue them extensively with new objects over his second year. In fact, object curiosity is an important, if less dominant, facet of his activity throughout the preschool period. An object appearing in a new guise (putting a hat on a doll, a block on top of another), with a different form of motion, or with a newly discovered property (hole in the bottom of a tin cup) captivates even a four-year-old. What we are discussing is, of course, an intrinsic motivational system, but its end product for the child is often interest in prominent perceptual features (such as color or hard quality) or simply exploring and manipulating for their own sake, rather than in the specific feature defining the concept (such as roundness).

Although objects lend themselves to many uses, particularly if they are new to a child, the appeal of a single object is short-lived. To maintain interest in a concept (such as that of a bird or a turtle), teacher must alternately present a variety of toys (dolls, animal figures, blocks, scraps of cloth, etc.), and different examples of concepts for the child to explore. In this way, it is easy to renew his interest in a concept from time to time, because it seems fresh again and because he is ready to discover something new as a result of his experience with other objects. Each renewed contact during the play makes it possible to draw his attention to an additional characteristic (a bird's sharp beak or the fact that the turtle's head and legs both withdraw) or to renew interest in one presented earlier (perhaps the bird's wings or the turtle's shell) to sharpen awareness. Understanding of a concept in all its facets develops gradually, and the processes cannot be pushed too rapidly or vigorously. Each child must make new connections and acquire understanding about things at his own rate.

Means-Ends Problem Solving Activities

In many ways, activities designed to achieve specific ends are extensions of simple manipulation of objects. But they differ in that in the means-ends activity the child becomes involved in *using* an object. His attention shifts from the properties of the object itself, (color, the fact that it moves), to *what it can do in relation to other things* (a bag holding marbles, a crayon marking paper) and he becomes aware of its potential for *achieving some goal objective*. The object becomes a *means* or *tool* to accomplish some *end* or *purpose*.

Interest in instrumental problem-solving appears during the latter part of the baby's first year as he or she begins to discover how one object does things in relations to others and how objects can be used to accomplish purposes. In

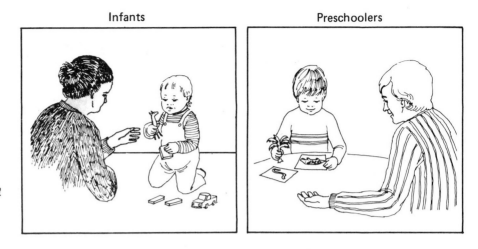

FIGURE 12-2
*Extrinsic
motivational
methods.
Using various
types of play and
problem solving
activities to
sustain children's
interest in concept
learning. Object
curiosity:
Exploratory play.*

the child's preschool years, instrumental problem solving attracts ever increasing interest because of its seemingly unlimited potential for performing complex operations.

The many things that can be done with objects form several basic patterns:

1. *Placing Objects (Targeting).* Perhaps the simplest one is placing or targeting objects— using one object to touch another object or position. In its more complicated forms it may include dropping an object into a container, trying to hit a round piece of paper on a table, or sliding an object across a table to hit another object. For four-year-olds, placing or targeting is meaningfully expressed in "Pin the Tail on the Donkey." All placement activities require a target object of some kind, such as a box opening, animal figure, boat, or piece of paper (with or without a bullseye), to aim at. For

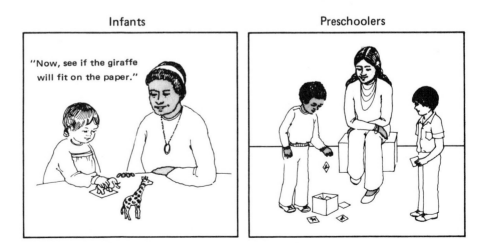

FIGURE 12-3
*Extrinsic
motivational
methods: Placing
or targeting play.*

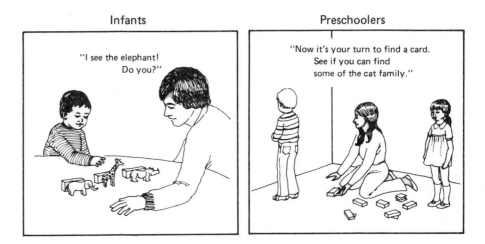

FIGURE 12-4
Extrinsic motivational methods: Search and find play.

example, the teacher may suggest to a baby under twelve months that he put the truck she has given him on top of a block, or she may ask a child of a year or more to place a small picture near a tree or to drop a toy grasshopper into an empty box on the table in front of him.

Targeting activities are increasingly useful for involving children in concept learning because children become increasingly interested in how objects can be placed in relation to one another, in finer and different ways. In all cases, the various examples of concepts under study (the short crayon in a length concept task) are used along with the miscellaneous play materials as objects to place in different positions or as missiles to aim or drop at specified targets. As the child develops targeting skill, smaller targets can be used (tiny squares of colored paper, small bullseyes), the distance between the child and the target increased and more complicated objects and targets

FIGURE 12-5
Extrinsic motivational methods: Container and contained, or "in and out" play.

FIGURE 12-6
Extrinsic motivational methods: Construction play.

brought into play: a three- or four-year-old can be asked to toss an animal figure over a wall of blocks on a table, to insert concept pictures into a narrow slot in a jar top, to throw a toy into a small box across the room, or to push a miniature car along a block roadway with a stick.

Challenge must be geared to the child's level of competence. What is fun for the infant (placing a car on a flat board) would be boring to a four-year-old; conversely, a year-old child could not drop a toy into a small jar from a height of eighteen inches—a task that delights many four-year-olds.

2. *Search and Find Activities.* The young child's interest in looking for hidden objects probably relates to his difficulty in understanding that objects continue to exist even though he cannot see them. During a baby's first four to six months, when a object disappears from sight it no longer exists

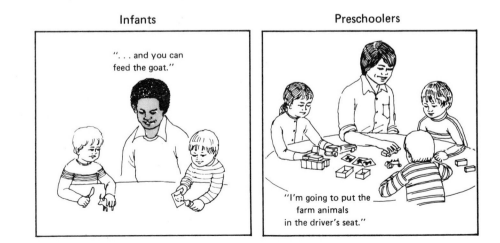

FIGURE 12-7
Extrinsic motivational methods: Sociodramatic play.

for him so he does not look for it. Over the next several months, he gradually acquires the ability to follow objects, and to keep track of them when they are partially, then totally hidden. As his object knowledge and memory span increases, he realizes that when an object, present a moment earlier, suddenly disappears, it is still around, and he begins to search for it *at the point where it disappeared.* During later infancy, he gains ability to keep track of an object and maintains his interest in searching for it over a wide area and for longer periods of time, even when it is hidden behind several barriers and he cannot actually see the object as it is being placed.

The teacher can use the child's fascination with disappearing objects by including "hunting and finding" games in the learning sessions. It is well to remember that objects need not always by completely hidden. Infants, and even older children, often prefer to see them peeping out from behind a block or a miniature tree. They also enjoy the sense of mastery that comes from occasionally "catching" the teacher (or other powerful adult figures) hiding things. Hiding places need not be complicated even with brighter four-year-olds; retrieving a toy hidden behind a wall of blocks or a wooden screen, in a box or under a piece of cloth gives the child continuing pleasure. Occasionally, with older preschoolers, the teacher may try hiding an object in some less obvious place, but this usually takes time, straying from the project goals too long. It is usually preferable to maintain interest by interspersing "search and find," other play, and problem-solving activities.

Hiding tasks are set up in much the same way as other learning tasks. At the beginning, and periodically during the session, the teacher shows the children how to hunt for a hidden object, and has them take turns hiding toys for one another. While hiding an object herself, a teacher can say, "Now, I want you to find the truck that has the cement mixer" or "the car that carries people to the hospital" or whatever identifying aspect or rule about the concept she is trying to teach. As with all play and problem-solving activities, a child's interest and attention will be divided between the play involved and the task of learning the program objectives.

3. The Container and the Contained. In some ways, putting toys in boxes and jars and taking them out is a variation of hunting and finding activities, and inspires just as much enthusiasm. Frequently it involves only the *partial* disappearance of objects because they are still partly visible through the open top of the container. If the container is transparent, a kind of double mystery exists in the fact that the object is visible but accessible only through the top of the jar. The main task consists of the teacher putting a toy in some container, mentioning its name, whether an example of a program concept (a giraffe as part of a project on mammals) or an ordinary toy, and asking the child to pull it out; or she may merely ask the child to put the toys in a container and leave him to pull them out automatically. Young children, especially those under three, frequently enjoy putting an object in a box and taking it out several times in a row, before they tire of the activity. If the object being inserted is an example of some program concept, drawing attention to concept rules (the length of the giraffe's neck, his horns, etc.) more than two or three times before a new task is started may become monotonous.

Construction Play

"Building" is a form of perceptual-motor activity vital to a young child's development. All open-ended construction without a fixed plan fits into this category; building involves new combinations, new organizations, sometimes with themes like houses, roads, or zoos made of miscellaneous or modular materials such as unit blocks. In free play with a variety of toys and modular materials, half the young child's activities will likely consist of arranging, rearranging, and building to see how things can fit together. Construction play is a highly effective means of developing children's combinatory (synthesizing) and inventive mental processes. Close to the heart of creative activity, it is among the highest forms of problem solving, from which new ways of doing things originate.

Children's natural curiosity about how one thing goes with another is a good base for planned learning activities. Presented with program examples with which to learn a concept, plus a collection of miscellaneous toys and blocks or other building materials, a child will usually first explore and handle the materials, then start building. Infants do little more than place one object on top of (or alongside) another, or touch (or bang) a second object with the first. But, with experience (about age two) children will begin to produce patterns, structures and themes.

The teacher's job in this situation is to give the child whatever item is the focus of the learning program, labeling it, from time to time, in the usual way, and letting the child use it as he sees fit in his building. If he is little inclined to build on his own, the teacher can easily let the play follow a problem-solving course if that is the form of play the child prefers, bringing in concepts as convenient. Since construction play adds variety to learning, it may be useful to get the child started by putting three or four blocks together, and demonstrating various concept rules as the construction continues.

Program concept toys, such as the giraffe in the illustration above, pieces of paper and cloth, trinkets, boxes, and other supportive play materials are used differently in construction play from problem-solving play. But they fit just as well. Trinkets and bits of cloth and paper add decoration to building structures, while animal figures, plants, vehicles, and other replicas, whether or not examples of program concepts, are woven into dramatic play with the building structures. Their various characteristics are thus quite easy to demonstrate in the course of such play, as in placing (and telling about) the giraffe so he can use his long neck and legs to help him peer into a high window, or use his long legs to run across an open field (a flat surface of blocks), or placing a toy tree to give shade from its branches and leaves. When boxes and blocks are among the items used to teach various size (length, width, height, area) and shape concepts, they of course fit quite naturally into the construction itself, making it easy to draw attention to relevant features or rules (edge, length) as they are used in building. In any case, a child need not use building materials or toys systematically, blocks for making buildings, or toy animals *as* animals in imagined activities. He will respond to the program stimuli more freely if they are incorporated into his own way of arranging things, however disorganized his structures may appear.

Children under two, or less-developed older children, may simply move objects around or pile them together in a haphazard fashion with little apparent regard for form or idea. Older preschoolers, on the other hand, may set up complicated patterns built around special themes. For example, a child may decide to design a zoo, an airport, or some other community facility. He may spend ten minutes or more—as long as a session lasts—building cages for animals, roads and garages for vehicles, or houses and offices for people. As long as the teacher does not disrupt the play activity, or intrude in it too strongly, she can easily introduce 10 to 20 examples of program concepts in the course of a session, naming them, their parts and what they do as often as is appropriate. She can comment on the place an object has in play (alligator in a pond), its features (powerful tail) functions (swim and steer with) or its relation to other toys (eats fish). Each suggestion gives the child another opportunity to play with a program toy in the course of which he increases his knowledge about the concept rules it represents. As the play progresses over a series of sessions he will more and more bring the program learning materials into the play on his own.

The boundaries between simple construction play and exploratory play are often indistinguishable, especially with infants under 18 months. The significant thing is to ensure that the child is allowed and encouraged to play *actively*, while the teacher maintains the child's interest in learning by presenting specific concept and supportive play materials regularly and in different ways.

Sociodramatic Play

Themes are an extension of construction play with the addition of social content—using objects in human action and dramatic form. Since construction and sociodramatic play often combine naturally, there is no necessity to distinguish between them; instead the increased diversity created by this natural alliance should keep the child's interest fresh. The preschooler who is building a complex structure with blocks or tinker toys may enjoy having cars move in and around it, and human figures located at strategic points. The social and construction play of infants and slower learning preschoolers consists of little more than manipulating and arranging blocks and figures in crude piles and patterns, but it is nonetheless a good context for learning and will evolve more rapidly with encouragement.

If several children are encouraged to work together, the buildings and social organizations often become more elaborate and interest is prolonged. One child can work on each section of a building project, while others manipulate toy figures in social roles suggested by the type of building and community setting. Thus one child builds a hospital wall, a second a parking lot, a third moves a toy figure through the door as a patient and fourth gives a shot or takes a blood sample from the patient when she arrives. In this way, co-operative play is encouraged, and the children's own form of play is used to maintain their interest in learning. Sociodramatic and construction play serve best as a motivating context for learning a series of concepts systematically in a planned project when the project concepts (concepts about illness and medicine) are developed in construction and dramatic play around a related theme (in this case about hospitals).

The feature of dramatic play that most arouses children's interest is *animation*. Children like to pretend that toy animals move and make noises; that truck motors buzz and roar; and dump trucks empty loads of cargo. Still more dramatic is their tendency to personify airplanes, boats, or any other toys representing objects in the activities of people in everyday life. These dramatizations resemble animated cartoon figures; but for younger age groups, particularly infants, actions and events should be simple. At the beginning of a program, even three- and four-year-olds may introduce only parts of a few themes in play (a plane flying, a street corner, a tree growing) but will not connect them unless the children are quite imaginative. They will, however, enjoy following the teacher's lead, imitating her actions and introducing variations (a plane lowering wheels to land, a store on the corner, a pond near the tree) as their imaginations and play skills gradually expand. As they progress they often become better able, in conjunction with fellow learners and the teacher, to stick to a single, elaborate theme in play with the concept characteristics of the objects (such as the scaly skin and other characteristics of fish and reptiles) that the teacher wants them to learn.

Any number of simple activities can be developed into narrative themes. It is not necessary to use the toys in a way that they are ordinarily used in real life, such as having a tow truck tow another vehicle or a cement truck appear to make cement. Following their interest in dramatic play, animation, and using almost anything as symbols, children accept very easily—and in fact will invent many ideas of their own—the idea of a trinket taking a swim, a red piece of paper (in a color learning project) milking a cow or a flat stone (in a project on flatness) visiting a friend or riding a car. Such symbolic or imaginery actions may be used either simply for dramatic play with any play object (as in the instance of the trinket swimming) or for the purpose of incorporating examples of relevant concepts into the play (as in the other two cases). True to life action themes are used, from time to time, however, to help the child learn real functions, and naturally are used when they form part of the immediate objectives of a learning program.

The less developed the child, the simpler and briefer the actions and themes used in dramatic play. Simple physical movements, such as jumping and hopping with animal and human figures, or social and physical routines such as feeding and being fed, or going to sleep, will easily capture his attention. For older or more advanced children, complicated social role play can be pursued for many minutes at a time. Complex themes can embrace as many as three or four aspects, to represent several people in a group setting with a variety of interactions and social roles. For example, one toy truck may be a "doctor", another a "nurse" and the third an "infant". The fourth could be the "father" or "mother" who holds the "infant" while it is tended by the "nurse" and "doctor".

Not all teachers have sufficient imaginative ability to be at ease with social dramatization. To be most effective, a teacher should use the form of sensorimotor play with which she is most at ease and which she can best adapt to the preferences of the children she is teaching. Some teachers, for example, enjoy manipulative play and problem-solving activities, or building play, while others prefer to work with story-telling themes and dramatization. Usually a teacher prefers, or can adapt to, more than one orientation and actually uses them in combination, varying the supporting toys and actions to suit the current form. For the most part, children are generally quite adaptive, enjoying whatever system a caregiver enjoys and uses best.

Teachers who are fascinated by story-telling and dramatic processes may tend to be carried away and dominate the activity. While imaginative dramatic activity may sustain the interest of a group of children for extensive periods, children sometimes remain too passive and may not learn rapidly or thoroughly. A more productive approach involves giving specific roles to each child in turn, pausing from time to time to give a timid or reflective child a chance to participate. Thus each child might dramatize one or another of the concept rules, such as (in a shape learning project) one child making an angular shaped piece of paper pick mushrooms, the next having a straight cut strip of paper gather wood for a fire and a third suggesting that a curved piece cook the mushrooms. Even if his activity bears little relation to the social theme (brings in a dramatization about flying in the picnic play), it is better to allow the child to complete it unless his interest lags, he strays too long from the original theme, or he actively disrupts the ongoing play. Some children, particularly boys, are often culturally more oriented to things and tasks than to social activity, and some children have never heard stories at all. It will take them time but be worth the effort for them to learn to engage themselves in story-telling play.

Again, the choice of play should be at least partially adapted to the interests and learning styles of the children in the program. In general, it is advisable to vary the play, moving from exploration to construction, to problem solving, to story-telling, keeping in mind that the central theme of guided learning is not play for its own sake (which is the place of free play) but the development of knowledge around the program theme, using play as a naturally productive motivating system.

Social Reinforcement

From the earliest days of life every child is exposed to attention, care, and instruction by other human beings to socialize him as a person concerned for and responsive to human care and attention. Everything he does is somehow related to how others perceive and value him. This is the basic social framework in which children develop, one we use to motivate children in a learning program. As he develops, the child's interests are affected by the reactions of significant adults (a caregiver, parent, older sibling or schoolmate) to the methods of play and learning he uses. In general, the teacher's actions in relating to and praising him are extrinsic to his acquisition of learning but intrinsic to his social development.

There are, in general, two emotional directions in which a teacher can express interest in a child—positively or negatively. But she can also ignore him or remain neutral and, by either attitude, provoke him to attention-seeking behavior. Persistent ignoring of children by caregivers (or parents) is a form of neglect or emotional rejection, which may lead the neglected child to resort to rebellion or destructive acts; he may break or throw toys, hurt another child, or make a great deal of noise to violate the teacher's values and irritate her.

Since most children are used to attention and actively seek it, the teacher must be careful to give it in constructive forms. She should encourage the child positively, so that he will perform and learn, and through conscious approval and warmth develop a stronger and less hostile personality in the child. If the teacher's attention centers on misbehaviors, the ignored or neglected child soon sees them as attention-getting devices. If, on the other hand, she consistently supports positive actions, minimizing her reactions to negative actions, he is more likely to give his attention and interest to things in the program that he is expected to learn. Skillful diplomacy is essential to resolving the rivalrous interaction between authority and child that sometimes arises out of a child's misbehavior, and which is so disruptive to the learning situation.

The kind of social attention or reinforcement we give a child can be divided into two basic forms: first, approval only when he performs correctly, such as picking the card with the same number of toys pictured as the teacher asks for (number learning project) or hanging a toy monkey by his tail in play to illustrate a characteristic (learning project on monkeys); second, approval of an action regardless of the quality of performance (such as smiling or saying "that's fine" or "that's a good try" even when he picks the incorrect card or doesn't recognize the tail of a monkey). In the first instance we are rewarding him for accuracy according to the teacher's definition, while in the second we are rewarding him for effort. Both forms of reinforcement can be used regularly but of the two, encouragement of effort is the more important. We want the child to do *something,* to perform, to keep trying, and we must be prepared to give whatever encouragement he needs in a warm and supportive manner— not excessively, nor with exaggeration, but enough to show warmth toward him and interest in his efforts. Tension, hostility and lack of response in the teacher breed similar attitudes in the children. How we structure the learning task, and the children's interest in the forms of play, may provide sufficient reinforcement to enable them to learn all we can teach them. But there is always a place in the learning situation for occasional praise of a constructive performance, whether or not it succeeds.

Social Reinforcement in Small Groups

If the teacher is the only person who gives praise, relations become too teacher- and authority-centered, which can lead to problems of dependency in the child. Learning in a small group has distinct advantages, because it provides a setting in which the children interact naturally and provide social reinforcement to one another. Encourage children to work together from the start and expand their interaction gradually as their social relations become more sophisticated. The aim should be a *joint inquiry approach* that combines an emphasis on autonomy with the social reinforcement of group relations and casts the teacher in the role of a general catalyst (see Chapter 13).

Competition

In any group learning program, competition is built into the activities. The resultant motivation is both useful and inevitable, as long as it is reasonably controlled. If each child receives his full share of attention and encouragement, and is given only tasks at his level, the emphasis falls not on the products but on the *processes* of learning and the satisfactions they bring. Very obvious forms of competition that stress accomplishments, such as seeing which child has learned the most concepts (types of boats) or rules (characteristics about a type of boat), awarding prizes, or displaying only the better drawings on the wall, are better minimized, while making opportunities for effort and participation freely available. The collaborative or joint inquiry approach (Chapters 10 and 13), taking turns together for all to learn, and encouraging children to help one another discourage unhealthy and extreme forms of competition.

In all activities the ultimate purpose is to develop in the child curiosity, the joy of learning, and problem solving for useful purposes. Standards are concerned with progress in relation to the child's own past performances and his interest in solving problems for some valid human purpose, *not* how many more boats or functions of a boat one child knows than another. Children's learning is advanced by working to help them try more, through encouragement and making the learning play interesting; and to help them improve their problem solving strategies, through showing them how to pick apart the examples and see how things are connected and work (observe the examples of boats more carefully to find the *critical* feature—the sails, propellors, motor, etc.; see *how* they fit on the boat—on a pole, called the mast, on a stick at the back, and inside; and how they work—wind blows sails which pushes the boat, and the motor turns the propellor which turns in water to push the boat). Knowing that another child knows more may "push" a child a bit, but it certainly also makes him feel bad, particularly if a teacher emphasizes it, fostering relations of superior to inferior ("who's best"), and causes many children to try less or even withdraw from learning—to give up. In any case, children learn nothing *directly* to improve their own skills from knowing that others have learned more.

A similar situation applies with regard to the case of material tokens as incentives to learning. Marks, gold stars, or other decals, if used at all, serve better as bench marks of progress, or as a record of efforts, rather than as scores with which to compare children against standards or with one another, as they may distract the child from developing an interest in the learning process. Such devices are better *not* displayed in a comparative framework through which slower children see themselves hopelessly outclassed by their brighter associates.

If material tokens are awarded, competitive comparisons between children may be reduced by periodcially withdrawing the current series and introducing a new one. This might be done when one of the children has earned, say, ten tokens. Comparisons can be further minimized by having the children keep their tokens in personal "treasure boxes" rather than on display on wall charts for all to see.

The accumulation of incentives (tokens) becomes more intrinsically related to the learning process when the tokens collected are, in fact, examples (exemplars) of concepts the child is learning. This furnishes him with a direct and visible record of his achievement, in the form, for example, of a set of card pictures (of different foods if that is the concept being taught) he can also use for review in his play alone or with another child. These can be collected in "treasure boxes" as described in Chapter 11. By arranging for the children to play together with one another's cards in turn, each child both reviews examples on his own cards he has already learned and gains the chance to learn any examples in his partner's card set that he has not yet learned.

Since children tend to learn at unequal rates, it will decrease any overtones of unpleasant competition by matching children for the review play roughly according to the number of token examples they have accumulated. Even so, it is wise to remove the earlier portions learned (tokens acquired) to reduce unhealthy competition. This and many other methods of reinforcement are actually a form of feedback, providing a knowledge of results that a performance is correct. In this sense, a token incentive system which utilizes stimulus objects (concept examples) can be extremely useful if employed with proper safeguards.

Corrective and Informational Feedback

One purpose in expressing social approval of a correct action is to show the child that he is learning and understanding a rule correctly. Social reinforcement and feedback are often confused. On the one hand, we give the child social reinforcement—support and encouragement to perform, to help him *want* to engage in an activity and to learn. On the other hand, we give him feedback—an assessment of the correctness of a particular response or action.

Generally speaking, it is desirable to place more stress on the child's effort than on the accuracy of the result and to minimize verbal criticism of incorrect performance. This tends to avoid discouragement and injury to the young child's ego. Children are not necessarily more fragile than adults, but their dependent status and lack of general knowledge gives them fewer defenses against criticism. In addition, most of us find it difficult to offer critical comment in an easy, matter-of-fact manner, and load our comments with implications of failure. Most of us have been reared in traditional ways of being "told what to do," and we tend to use the same overdirective manner when we work with children. Because overdirectiveness can be damaging to young children's personalities and learning, wherever possible try to provide informational feedback through alternative means.

One major form of corrective feedback involves showing a child how to do the same or a similar task a second or even a third time. If he points to the rudder, for example, when asked to find the sails of a boat, simply say "That's fine", then play with or encourage him to play with something else. Ask him to pretend the boat is sailing, something you *know* he can do, then later *you* point out the sails in play, and perhaps also the rudder soon after to help him keep them straight. Draw attention to the sails and rudder clearly in the course of playing with the toy boats (or pictures), several times if he has seemed confused or uncertain, before asking him again to find the sails or the rudder in one or another example. It is often desirable to extend this process over a number of days to make sure he knows. With this technique we are *re-presenting* the learning problem, in the basic perceptual-motor mode to which youngsters are most easily adapted, in a positive manner, and at a pace that ensures he will learn the rules comfortably, without a sense of failure. Comments should, of course, accompany the demonstrations, but they should be positive, simple, and brief, like, "Here's the sail" or "I'm going to turn the rudder to make the boat turn".

When a child picks out an eagle and a sparrow from a set of toys on the table and puts them in the same box at the teacher's request, it is evident that he is learning about the general class we call birds, and praise for this kind of correct performance is useful. However, problems arise if verbal praise is not selective; used too often, it becomes monotonous and irrelevant, or it may provide such emotional dependence in a child that he will do almost anything to earn praise, even to repeating the same limited response again and again. Also, it may stifle a child's efforts to learn and solve problems on his own or curtail the development of his desire to work and to learn things specific to the program. It is wiser to use praise moderately, expressing one's general satisfaction more often through warmth and enjoyment of the program activities and the child. One can find no more effective method of giving him the reinforcement he needs.

There are other reasons for avoiding lavish praise. Learning programs that are specifically designed to develop inquiry strategies and creative tendencies in the child, necessarily demand that more emphasis be placed on encouraging the *inquiring and creative processes* themselves. Programs designed to teach strategies of problem solving, for example, are concerned with the child figuring and working out *different* means to get around a barrier (for instance, a partition) to reach a goal (such as an interesting toy or trinket). Here we show more interest in his efforts to try out more than one way, such as climbing over, pushing the partition aside, or even asking a playmate on the other side to hand the goal object to him, than we do in his actual achievement of the goal. Similarly, in a project on painting or drawing, the emphasis is on using different techniques as much or more than on the final product. In both cases it is continuing interest we show in the child's experimentation more than actual approval of any specific actions. We pay attention and offer encouragement in a general way (smiling, saying occasionally, "You're doing fine" or "It's interesting") and when he asks, agree that he's doing well or that a line he has just drawn or his new approach to the problem is useful. This is essential if the child is to be stimulated to make new combinations, to search for alternatives, and to give original responses, rather than to be rewarded for learning a "right" way and a "wrong" way. Even though it is also important to praise the child's correct solutions from time to time, it is more constructive in the long run to show general interest in his efforts to inquire and seek alternatives. It is quite possible to encourage the child to explore and try out alternatives (as in fact the play activity contexts are designed to do), while helping the child to arrive at solutions, create good art works, and even learn important scientific concepts.

But how can we cope with wrong responses in a program made up of preferred alternatives, that is when it is important that a child learn scientific concepts like number or size, and not simply try out different methods? Although in advanced stages, as the child begins to really generalize about number, he may often be able to look around and find his own examples of three or four things (point to three chairs or four children in the corner), he must after all learn to count correctly as well as to experiment with number concepts. What do we do if a child keeps giving many more wrong than correct responses?

Most teachers will find it difficult not to correct wrong responses, at least some of the time. If it must be done, a simple, matter-of-fact definition of a desired label or the pointing out of an appropriate object, is preferable to saying, "That is wrong". In addition to repeating demonstrations with clusters of three and four objects, using different materials and various forms of play ("Let's give the bear three pennies," "Can the puppet count four leaves?"), when the child makes incorrect choices (picks four when asked for three animals), one can occasionally say "you found four animals" in an easy and positive tone, and then go on to further play and other examples. In this way, criticism of the child is avoided, yet the actual number is labeled correctly by the caregiver. The point is not to discourage effort and experimentation or emphasize failure, but to provide the child with the information that we would like him to learn. The child seldom misses an idea or performs an incorrect action deliberately; he does so simply because he does not understand. To have him understand we must give him emotional support as well as the desired information. Children are sensitive to failure and frequently have difficulty understanding because they have been criticized so much or treated so negatively that they become discouraged by even the slightest tone of criticism in a teacher's voice. For this reason, even labeling a child's wrong choice correctly to give him the correct information is better used sparingly, and not at all with obviously sensitive children.

On the whole, it is more productive to generally overlook incorrect actions, or regard them as expressions of useful hypotheses the child is exploring. This enables the teacher to move on to another demonstration with the same or a similar task, leaving the child free of any suggestion of failure. The child is given accurate information in a form that he can easily absorb—through physical demonstrations accompanied by language, rather than through abstract statements alone. His general exploratory styles are not rejected nor are his efforts to solve problems in his own way. Saying to a child "That is wrong", or "You should have picked a different one", does not tell him *why* he is wrong; it tells him only that he has done wrong, and makes him feel badly about it. Even saying "You should have picked the car instead of the truck" or making a specific statement without pointing out the correct relationship, does not give him adequate information. What he needs is constant encouragement to try out his own and other ideas.

13 Learning in Small Groups

Watching one another

Teaching children in small groups combines the best of two worlds; it provides the motivational framework of the group and the economy of teaching more than one child at a time. The size of small groups permits ease of control, flexible methods of regulation, personalized attention, and individualized programming, even with infants who are too young to pursue a complex learning activity for any length of time on their own.

The value of the social group as a setting for guided learning activity lies in the power of a group of peers to motivate children to engage in similar activity. A group provides a social framework with which each child can identify and use as a guide to determine his or her actions. Because a little girl sees a group of children as a world with her own characterisitics and interests, she wants to share in what they are doing. The group process provides a common basis for sharing experience that makes for enjoyment in playing and learning together. The values of the children and teachers may be either co-operative or competitive, but the underlying basis for interest is the group identity process. How much the teacher attempts to build co-operative as well as competitive relations, however, will influence how well the child comes to understand the value of pooling intellectual resources to solve problems—the basis for knowledge of herself as a social being.

Group Size

Because small groups are socially inviting to children and serve to reduce the costly process of day care and schools, they provide an effective setting in which to guide children in planned learning programs. Size is an important consideration in determining the quality of the learning and social relations that both children and teacher will enjoy. It takes at least two children to constitute a group of sorts; working together in pairs is not only ideal for infants under two, but can be a continuing useful experience throughout the preschool years. When three or more children are involved, the amount of attention an adult can give to each child and the program immediately becomes diluted, and the form of relations change. There are now three different children with their three different sets of needs, ways of doing things, and individual learning materials, instead of just two of each; and they relate to one another and the teacher in different combination of twos, threes and fours, instead of just twos and threes.

There is, on the other hand, more of a definite sense of "groupness" when at least three or four children participate, and the economics of day care usually require that every adult supervise at least four or five (and, too often, more) children. Apparently, it is the very fact that one can never quite keep track of the multiple materials, activities, and relations of more than oneself and one other person that magnifies this sense of group identity. With three or more children, moreover, a pooling of interests tends to become the group norm or standard, in contrast to the give and take of compromise between two individuals. The shifting relations between different members and, especially, both the greater difficulty of always guiding each child individually and the obvious advantage of showing the enlarged group examples of concepts together, develop greater awareness in the children that they are learning together, as a group.

There is a *maximum group size* in which young children can learn well. It is difficult to define this in exact numbers but, for children under five, for example, a group containing between five and eight children is large if maximum learning experiences are to be realized. Much depends on the skill of the adult and the children's interest in learning, attention spans, and freedom from tensions and behavioral problems. The teacher's personality is no less important than his formal training and skill in interpersonal management. Teachers differ in the amount of noise and wriggling they can tolerate, for example, and both noise and wriggling increase with the number of children. Also important are the complexity and clarity of the learning program and how well the children are matched in ability. In general, a pair of infants under twelve months, two to three children aged one to two years, two to four children aged two to three, and two to six children aged three to five make ideal groups to work with. Skilled and flexible caregivers, working with well designed programs and children with balanced interests and abilities, can often teach adequately, if not always as comfortably, in groups with larger numbers—even as many as four or five infants at a time (who may not see themselves as a "group," however).

Groups that grow beyond a certain size lose their sense of intimacy and informality because of the increased amount of attention to social regulation required, and the sheer number of relations involved. The increased numbers of children not only mean increased numbers and combinations of different needs and other characteristics; the chances of noise, friction, and conflict multiply with the combinations. Because each child *could* provoke each other child in a group, there are two possibilities of disturbances with a group of two children, but six with three children and as many as twenty with five children. Thus as groups grow in size it becomes increasingly necessary for teachers to limit these possibilities by controlling more tightly such things as keeping children in their places, and the amount they talk, move, and play with one another, lest there be no group and no learning at all.

It is thus *possible* to supervise the activities of larger groups of children. Some day care programs and preschools do this, but at some cost; the cost of stressing social rules, neglecting the children's individual needs and teaching to the group as a whole, regardless of their different problems and rates of learning. Usually what happens is that groups of more than eight or ten children are broken into subgroups of four to six children for different learning activities, or the children are simply supervised in free play most of the time. Both large group teaching arrangements and constant free play deprive the preschooler of the kind of learning that combines the teacher as an intellectual and social model and guide to learning with the peer group as a similar model and guide to cooperation in learning. In the large group the teacher becomes preoccupied with discipline (or the confusion is too great for the children to attend) and the concepts are necessarily watered down to give little of anything to anybody, because the range of understanding and the difficulties of attending are so great. In constant free play, children may be individually guided in planned concept learning activities, but if the numbers are large the frequency of individual attention is diminished proportionally, and in any case the value of the group experience is lost.

Methods of Teaching Children in Small Groups

The methods employed for guiding children's learning in pairs or small groups are essentially the same as those used for individual tutoring. The adult demonstrates the rules in the program, co-ordinating his actions with what he says and analyzing and interrelating the significant features of each problem. Similarly, he interacts freely with the children in play, encouraging and nonintrusively guiding their experimentation within a framework of searching for alternatives and monitoring their progress. The chief difference here is that he

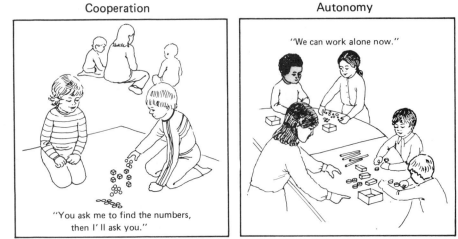

FIGURE 13-1
Advantages of
group process (peer
interaction)
teaching methods:
Social learning
competence.

relates to the children as a group as well as individuals, and the children inter-act with, and learn from, one another as well as the adult. The caregiver at times calls for the simultaneous attention of the children, showing and telling them in a simple demonstration (in a project on mammals) how a giraffe lopes along; at others he points out where the hooves are to a particular child or engages her in play; and different children are encouraged to play with and show one another about animals and use the play materials.

Teaching in groups does not require absolute quiet or other strict rules, unless the adult is unskilled or uncomfortable with the children, in which case rules don't usually help much; only experience does. Usually, a flexible set of rules, concerning such matters as aggression and the amount of movement and noise permitted, can be established early in a series of sessions with little diffi-culty.

The chief basis for exercising control over children is actually their strong interest in learning through play, their pleasure in being a member of a learning group, and their growing excitement over learning itself. If these experiences fail to maintain their interest, only the strictest type of control will prevent the children from becoming restless and mischievous, which in any case is a sign of failure to accomplish the central purpose of teaching, getting children inter-ested in learning. Without interest they will learn little and will fail to develop the sort of independence that causes children to seek new concepts on their own, with or without the aid of an adult. When disciplinary problems become chronic or children fail to become excited over the play and learning, it is time to review one's techniques. Am I going too fast? Are the concepts too advanced or poorly illustrated? Am I fitting them into the play and allowing the children to experiment enough? These and similar questions will help to zero in on the problem.

Not all problems of management can be blamed on the teaching methods, however. Management becomes a big problem in groups containing two or three children with attentional or behavioral problems. Even a single child who has to be the center of attention, who expresses her conflicts by rebelling or

Examples of Others

Insights from Other's Mistakes

FIGURE 13-1
continued
*Additional sources
of concept learning
and cognitive
skills.*

bothering others, or even a child who simply hasn't been exposed much to teaching before can easily be a constant source of disruption to constructive group play and learning. When a difficult child or children fail to settle down after a few sessions it is usually wise to continue without them, and work with them individually on something closer to their interests on other occasions as time permits. Such efforts will sometimes improve things enough for the disruptive children to be able to return to the same or another group later on.

Culture may also make a difference. Not all cultures place the same emphasis on achievement and learning, particularly on learning abstract ideas about number, classification, and similar concepts in formal ways. For most children from every culture, the play oriented approach recommended develops a keen interest in learning. Others may need more individual play and learning sessions to enable them to make more use of their own culturally natural approaches to learning and problem solving, and to develop in their own way. It may also be feasible to form special learning groups for children from similar cultures. When approached as a way of reinforcing their own cultural identity, making special use of their own background concepts and style, such as the cooperative approach that Hispanic children, for example, are accustomed to, this practice will do much to maintain this interest in learning. One must be careful, however, that such a practice does not become a device to relegate culturally different children to an inferior learning environment. Teacher attitudes count for much. The problem can be minimized by working with children in different combinations, sometimes in culturally homogeneous small groups for certain activities especially when teachers from the same culture are available, sometimes in culturally mixed groups.

Variation among children and cultures, among teachers, and from one day to the next is of course to be expected. Each problem can be faced as it comes and can be solved in some constructive way, as long as the atmosphere is one where learning and play can thrive comfortably side by side.

Aside from problems of management, the key problem of teaching in groups is how to furnish enough individual attention. Usually, the solution is to

Teaching Skills

"Here are 4 pennies, and here are 5: now **you** put 4 of these pennies in the box."

Longer Attention Span and Motivation

"We want to count some more ourselves, teacher."

FIGURE 13-1 continued
Additional sources of concept learning and cognitive skills.

shift attention from one child to another, or from pair to pair, always keeping an eye on the group as a whole. Therein lies the advantage of small groups. Though children must wait their turn, because there are few children they need not wait long. All the learning activity and play of the teacher or any child, moreover, is easily visible to every child in the group, because the few children can comfortably gather round one common area for activity. Thus the short waits and small loss in individual attention is well balanced by the opportunity and interest children experience in being together, and in repeated review as each child takes a turn.

Equally significant is the opportunity that small groups provide for children to relate to, play with and learn from one another. This opportunity is dependent upon the teacher's ability to get the children to work with each other as well as with the teacher. Teachers often expect that most information about a concept will come from the teacher. After all, he knows the program and the children do not. He may well work flexibly, giving each child in turn plenty of opportunity to play and to demonstrate toys moving at different speeds and directions, as well as showing and guiding them himself. Otherwise his only concern for how they behave toward one another is that they wait their turn and not interfere with each other. If one child tries to help another, to show her neighbor how to move a stick horizontally, when the neighbor is mistakenly moving it vertically, the teacher may say "Please wait your turn," or at best ignore the effort and move to the next child.

Yet, in point of fact, even infants can learn a great deal from their peers. The example above provides one illustration of the type of assistance children can provide. Others include:

1. The way in which a new learner approaches a problem, and the "mistakes" he makes, can reveal insights to another child that even the skilled adult is unlikely to think of. (For example, one child trying to roll a square block may make another aware of how the even curve of a cylinder makes the smooth, continuous rolling movement of a wheel possible.)

2. A child's size and direct and often awkward methods of manipulation are similar to those of the other children.

3. The mere fact of children experimenting *with* and demonstrating *for each other,* as well as the teacher, is an added source of learning; working in this manner with each other also involves them more *actively* in learning because they are *teaching* as well as learning, which is one of the better methods of mastering ideas.

4. Children are usually at least as eager to work with each other as they are with an adult. Moreover, children not only are able to learn much about concepts in a program through working together, but they are also gaining experience in an important type of social learning—how to cooperate.

Promoting Learning and Cooperation between Children

What techniques can be employed to foster learning and co-operation between children as well as between teacher and child? The essential way is to set up tasks for them to work on jointly.

Limitations of the Teacher-Child Interaction Model for Teaching Children in Groups

The teaching-learning model so far discussed is centered on the interactions between the teacher and the children, singly or as a group, with the teacher responding to each child's initiatives as well as making her own. Such a model works well for tutoring children singly. The stress on having *both* teacher and child initiating activity diminishes the imbalance inherent in a relationship between unequals, between competent adults and children who have only just begun to develop. It also teaches children to actively experiment and to seek to learn, as well as how to cooperate (at least with adults). Used with a group, however, this model says nothing about how children ought to relate to each other; if applied literally, there would theoretically be no communication at all among any of the children, an obviously absurd situation.

In actual fact, when all the interactions in a group are between the teacher and the child, relations among the children tend to become competitive. When the activity centers on a series of turns for the teacher's attention, the relation with the teacher becomes a highly valued experience, a prize. Unless handled carefully, the usually interesting activities of one's playmates lose their charm when faced with the attraction of playing with an encouraging and competent adult. Even the child's own play may lose its attraction and the atmosphere become weighted with anticipation to take one's turn. Each child's neighbor becomes a rival for the favors of the teacher.

There are a number of things a leader can do to cut down this source of competition. Ease and flexibility in handling the children, responding informally and briefly to the children's initiatives without always waiting for a formal turn, will ease some of the pressure. Emphasizing the *process* of play and learning, rather than accomplishment or performance in turns (finding an example at the teacher's request) will also help. Avoid rushing from turn to turn, but break off "turns" from time to time and let the children experiment on their own for a few minutes at a time. Further demonstrations and examples (new learning materials) can still be slipped in at odd moments, to show or guide a child who needs more help, without asking the others to watch. Keep it low-keyed and informal at certain periods. Then for a period renew the group demonstration and again ask each child to perform in order to stimulate the children's active involvement in mastering rules (by getting the opportunity to *show* how to make a car go in a circle in response to an inquiry).

It is also valuable to have the group as a whole inqure about how the rules under study work. Involve them in working together to figure out a learning problem like moving a heavy box to another side of a barrier, getting a pile of sand onto a shelf or discovering how an insect moves—whatever the current problem is. Using the word "we" frequently when talking about the tasks and the play, and asking each child to perform for the purpose of solving the problem or to contribute to the *group's* understanding, will go far toward modifying the intensity of competition. It will help each child feel he or she is part of the group and has something to contribute, substituting group feelings for competitive feelings.

Good teaching styles, flexibility, and a group approach are not enough alone, however, to compensate for lack of attention to relations between children. Some teachers allow children to solve problems together, but many teachers actually discourage cooperation, because they somehow feel each child must work out the concepts alone. In this they are following the individual achievement ethic that is so much a part of the American industrial society and the entire school system. Yet there is no difficulty in encouraging cooperation in learning while still getting good evidence on each child's developing ability through asking each child to demonstrate a rule. It is also evident that preschool children cannot strive long or productively for abstractly defined group goals without the teacher encouraging them in some practical method of cooperation.

In a curious way, on the other hand, a competitive framework can sometimes give older preschool children (especially four year olds) a heightened sense of group identity, but not the kind that teachers usually enjoy. If the rivalry is not too intense, the teacher relates easily, and he ensures that each child really understands the rules as they go along, all may enjoy both the play and the learning and gain a sense of achievement, despite the moderately competitive but zestful atmosphere. Children who are slower can be given more time on other occasions, separately from the entire group, and faster children can move ahead in ways we shall describe in Chapter 14.

Sometimes problems do not get solved. For example, one child falls behind or is naturally more mistrustful and challenging of authority; the program may become difficult at some point or the teacher may fail to interact or personalize well. Given an over-directing teacher, children often band together, led by a child skilled in social manipulation, and begin to rebel against all the teacher's demands. Relations between the teacher and the peer group become polarized so that virtually all the children's actions are colored by the motive to challenge the teacher's authority by challenging his requests and goals.

Difficulties may also arise when a teacher who does interact and involve each child well takes over a group from an overdirective teacher or vice versa. The first type of change usually leads to a period of turmoil as the children, suddenly released from tight discipline, feel free to challenge everything, and have now to learn to take some responsibility for their own learning. The second case usually leads to rebellion as the children chafe against this sudden restraint on their opportunities to express themselves. In either case it may take some time for both children and teachers to readjust to the new situation before they establish an adequate working relation. In the second case, it may never develop because groups do not relinquish willingly freedoms they have once enjoyed.

Peer Cooperative Interaction Model for Teaching in Groups

Given the limitations of an exlusive focus on teacher-child interactions in a group setting, an alternative framework that also encourages co-operation between peers may offer many advantages. But what form should it take and how would it vary with the children's developmental level? The key to developing co-operative peer relations is to encourage children to collaborate on tasks, sometimes supervised directly by the teacher and sometimes working on assigned tasks independently of the teacher. A comparison of the exclusive teacher-child interaction form with the dual model of teacher-child and child-child interaction is shown in Figure 13–2.

Both diagrams show a teacher and five children grouped around a semicircular table. The circular arrangement and inset position of the teacher places children at an equal distance from him to provide equal opportunity for teacher-child interaction, yet this arrangement also places each child within working range of every other.

As the double arrows in both diagrams show, three basic forms of interaction are available in the adult and peer cooperation model, compared with two forms in the exclusive teacher-child model (when the teacher's demonstrations performed for the group as a whole are included). The additional form is cooperation between children, preferably working in pairs, on tasks set up by the teacher or caregiver, until the children become skilled enough to set up their

FIGURE 13–2
Comparison of teacher-child centered with combined teacher-child and peer-interactive framework of small group processes.

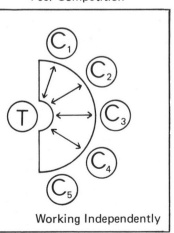

Teacher-Child Collaboration
Peer Competition

Working Independently

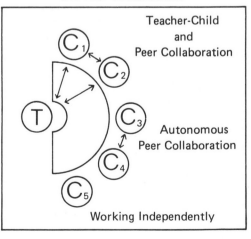

Combined Teacher-Child
and Peer Collaboration

Teacher-Child
and
Peer Collaboration

Autonomous
Peer Collaboration

Working Independently

own. With this method the teacher usually interacts with the children in pairs, in order to develop a working relation between children, as well as between himself and the children. When guiding a pair of children, for example, he asks each to show the other something soft and something hard, as well as pointing out for them and asking them to find examples of hard and soft things for him in the usual way in the course of play. Then at certain periods he asks the two children to work independently, finding and arranging soft and hard things together, while he works on a concept with another pair of children, as seen in the diagram on the right. Where a group has an uneven number of children, as in the group of five shown, the pairs can be arranged in different ways with children taking turns working alone or with the teacher individually from time to time. The result is a very different kind of social group and set of values, one in which all members relate to, and cooperate with, one another rather than with the leader alone. Leader-follower relations between children appear in many ways, and cooperation and competition between sub-groups are valued as highly as both individual competition and loose cooperation in the group as a whole. Relations become more fluid, complex, and varied, allowing opportunity for a wider variety of social skills to be learned.

With this system, the teacher will need to arrange tasks that encourage the children to collaborate, as well as tasks that they can work on independently in pairs, as they gain experience.

Peer collaboration in preschool children will vary according to the complexity of interaction and type of task. These may be outlined as follows:

I. *Complexity of Interaction.*
    A. *Parallel Play.* Children play in proximity to one another, working separately at different tasks and occasionally observing each other's actions.
    B. *One-way Exchange.*
        1. *Non-functional.* One child offers another a toy or other object, without regard to its utility for the second child's task or any effort to work at the same task.
        2. *Functional.* One child offers an object to be used as a tool to a second child, but in a non-specific way and still with no effort to participate jointly in the task.
    C. *Joint Operations.*
        1. *Uncoordinated Contributions.* Each of two children works on some part or phase of a task, but in separate areas or at different times, and without co-ordinating their actions. For the first time, they have a task in common.
        2. *Coordinated contributions.* Although working at different times or in a separate area, one child occasionally offers aid to another, or takes account of the other child's movements and what he or she does. Working at a common task.
        3. *Complex interaction.* Two children exchange ideas, mutual aid, and tools at every phase, from planning through execution to evaluation (if any) and subsequent use in play and display. Language as well as perceptual-motor exchange is essential at this level.
II. *Task Variations.*
    A. *Level of Abstraction.* This type of variation influences the complexity of interaction the child employs. Tasks vary in abstraction from the con-

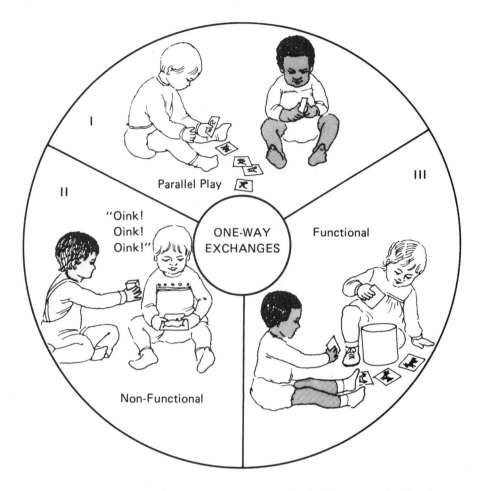

FIGURE 13-3
Stages in the development of complexity of interaction in learning tasks.

crete of perceptual-motor movement to the highly generalized rule operations using verbal and mathematical languages, the latter becoming increasingly important with development but seldom very abstracted from immediate events during the preschool period.

B. *Type of Social Rules*
 1. *Leader-follower.* A child leads one or more other children in defining task operations and goals. In the case of teaching activity, one child acts as teacher and the other child, or children, as his pupils.
 2. *Equalitarian.* Each child works on some part of the task without regard to status differences or role definitions. Mutual interchange in working on problems occurs, although one or another child may, through competence, be able to exercise more initiative and perform more complex actions than the others.
 3. *Differentiated roles.* There is a division of labor based on either interest or ability or both to perform different components of a task. The roles may be either *functionally* defined (to work with different features or functions of the task) or *socially* defined (to work with different social or occupational roles of people in socio-dramatic play).

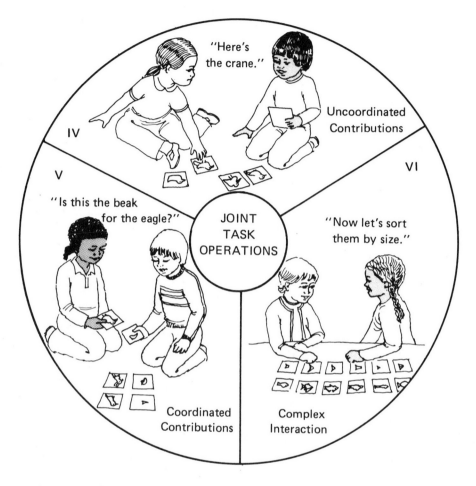

FIGURE 13-3
continued

C. *Types of Activity.* These encompass all the varieties of problem-solving and construction activities, types of knowledge (both physical and social), and language systems of which preschool children are capable.

Guiding the Development of Interaction

The complexity of the collaboration tasks that teachers set up will necessarily vary with the age and experience of the children. In general, children under two can be engaged in cooperative activities, if we accept the definition of parallel play and one-way exchanges as early forms of interaction. Infants usually enjoy playing alongside one another, and will generally offer and accept occasional toys from one another. This type of activity sets the stage for the more complicated working relations that develop as children learn more rules of social exchange and how to coordinate task activity.

It may require more teacher guidance to arrange cooperation at this level than at later phases of development with experienced collaborators. The role of the teacher is to place two infants side by side to work at similar learning tasks, stating with a tone of encouragement that they are "working together". Initially, and from time to time, he may want to comment on how well they are working together and occasionally ask each (in turn) to help the other. He will usually need to make specific suggestions on *how* to help, such as for one to hand the other a particular piece of a puzzle, to place a round shape or to help find (and point to) one of the features on a flower, according to the nature of the learning task in progress. Care must be taken that neither infant interprets another infant's efforts to cooperate as intrusions, a reaction that can be minimized by good timing (encouraging cooperation during a pause in activity) and arrangement of materials (so each child has room), being quick to help as needed (showing the infant when to place the piece of puzzle offered), and providing ample attention to both parties in turn. As in the ordinary interactions between teacher and child, each pair will need renewed guidance and *demonstrations* with the various materials as well as continuing suggestions on how to work together.

By the time children reach age two (and sometimes earlier if they have had experience in playing constructively with others), many children are ready for simple tasks that require joint operations. At the earlier level, there was little need to worry about whether an infant receiving help reciprocated in any way, other than acknowledging the co-operative act by receiving and perhaps using the toy. The main task centered on helping the child who received some odd puzzle piece or any other example to make use of it. The task was seldom difficult since the typical small infant puzzle has only edge pieces, and in concept learning tasks examples of shape, size, or other concepts are easy to use at almost any time.

But as children develop, each child begins to notice more details of what other children are doing, and observe how they react to the toy offered or the help given. At first the receiving child is capable of doing little more than trying to place the puzzle pieces (or say the shape is "round"), and may occasionally further acknowledge the joint relationships by looking (usually unsuccessfully) for another piece of the puzzle that fits close by (or look for a second round shape, etc.). On the other hand, she may simply perform a reciprocal action of her own (give another puzzle piece in return) when the other child does something for her. Thus there is usually not much success at first in fitting her actions to those of the other child, but there *is* more of a follow-through in effort at the same task.

As children start to show a few signs of persisting in these limited exchanges, the teacher can encourage them to work together more closely, encouraging them to follow up each other's exchanges. For a while this will work better with building blocks or in sociodramatic play, where children can work at separate parts of a physical or social structure, yet sustain a common activity. Occasional suggestions of where and what part to add (a block, tunnel) or what role to play (salesperson, baby sitter) will help. Cooperation is at first likely to be less successful in learning detailed information about general information concept categories (horses, flowers, boats) or dimensions of size, shape, and so on.

As the children progress in social concepts and language, they will begin to coordinate their actions with the materials more logically and consistently on a learning task; for example, fitting a series of puzzle pieces more or less in turn, or searching together for a series of square shapes or animals with wings.

When this development appears, a teacher can encourage two children to play and work continuously at learning with one another in a more systematic fashion. At this stage, the rule learning itself will be more complex; it will involve, for example, complicated puzzles, identifying several features of an information concept (the parts of a horse and their functions), or arranging several objects according to height. As concepts become more complex, and abilities develop to work in more complex ways children take longer to make use of the increasing possibilities for analyzing and sorting materials. Thus the pairs of children can be left to work independently for increasingly longer periods, depending on the skill with which the program is designed and the ingenuity of the teacher.

Guiding the Development of Task and Role Differentiation

The social organization of children's relations in pair collaboration can follow one of three forms: leader-follower, equalitarian, and differentiated roles, as indicated in the outline. So far we have indicated largely an equalitarian, interactive basis for social roles, in which each child shares in all aspects of a task. Children begin to divide up activites into different types of tasks and social roles (differentiated roles in the outline) partly through their experience in sociodramatic play. As their interests and understanding broaden, they will themselves invent and assume different social roles and tasks according to the type of situation and materials at hand. Starting with a gas station, for example, all the children may simply call themselves workers and pump gas; with time, one may be called the manager, another a mechanic, while the other workers also decide to repair tires and polish cars as well as pump gas.

There is nevertheless plenty of room in sociodramatic play for the teacher to introduce new themes for setting activites (office, kitchen, street construction, grocery store) to encourage task and role differentiation. In addition to participating actively in the play and learning tasks himself, he can also make the play more varied, persistent, and enticing for the children by making suggestions for new parts for the children to play ("I'm asking this plumber to fix my water faucet," or "When is the letter carrier coming?").

Differentiation of roles will also tend to arise spontaneously in any activity context, simply because children have different skills and interests. The moment we encourage autonomous play and rule experimentation, each child will logically perform according to what she knows and likes to do. Good teaching, therefore, involves awareness of what each child knows and likes and the ability to select tasks according to what they need to learn, as well as according to what they already know, so that every child develops a variety of competencies as well as perfects existing skills. (Note that this practice also follows the principle discussed in the previous chapter, that learning programs should be moderately novel, combining the new with the old, to effectively motivate children.)

For example, if one child is inclined to fiddle with parts of objects (the sail of a boat), while another likes to make things work (sail a boat) the teacher can first suggest an arrangement that will encourage them to work together, but in different jobs. This will get them started playing together, each doing what she likes and knows. For example, he can suggest that one child pull all boats out of the docks (using a box or block structure as the "dock"), after repairing their parts, while the other can sail them out of the harbor and back to the docks.

Then, to get them learning new roles, at some point he could ask them each to try the other's job, simply explaining, for instance, that dockworkers, repair people, and sailors have to know how to do one another's jobs.

One of the easiest methods to structure children's collaboration—which is better adapted than occupational role play for most concept learning programs—is to have them alternate in taking the roles of teacher and pupil. This form, moreover, is one that children adapt to eagerly, because it is a model of activity they confront every day. The task is set up so that one child introduces the materials (pictures of tools, replicas, or real tools), performs the demonstrations and guides the other child, who plays the pupil and tries to copy the teacher's actions or otherwise follows her instructions. (The idea of imitating and experimenting with rules rather than merely copying procedures literally may be communicated to older, well-developed preschoolers.)

When there is a series of items to be reviewed (tools, letters of the alphabet, words, numerals, colors, shapes, according to the program) the children will readily be able to pursue independent learning for some time. The "teacher" can, for example, ask her "pupil" to "show me the tool that can nail boards together," or "turn a screw," giving each child a turn, but skipping around rather than using a set order. As they become more skilled, the children will probably learn that the "teacher" should alternate demonstrations with inquiries (asking the pupil to perform) and miscellaneous play activity, using both the learning materials and the supportive play materials. But in any case, interactive teacher-child role play of this kind is not only excellent for reviewing examples to ensure mastery; it provides a cooperative play activity with differentiated social roles, and one that will last 10 minutes or so at a time with the more advanced and responsible pairs, to allow the caregiver to work intensively with other pairs of children who may need more help.

In the early stages of a learning project, before children have learned more than two or three items, this independent pair play will naturally lose interest for them after two or three minutes. This will mean the teacher will have to skip around more often among the pairs, taking less time for interactive play with any pair. It is often wiser during this introductory period to spend more time working with them as a group until at least one or two pairs of children have mastered four or five examples. On the other hand, starting the pair cooperation early, even if only under the direct supervision of the teacher as she teaches the first examples, establishes a cooperating framework and teaches children how to cooperate from the beginning. This lays the groundwork for the later more elaborate teacher-pupil play, and helps children work better independently for longer periods.

It is best to suggest a switch in roles periodically, either during each session, or for alternate sessions, so that all children gain experience in both roles. It is sometimes more difficult to induce a child to relinquish her leadership role as teacher than to induce one to leave the role of pupil and become a teacher. Almost everyone wants to be "teacher" but not everyone wants to be a "child" (pupil). But since everyone gets as many turns as everyone else, most children soon come to expect to alternate, and enjoy playing both roles. After all, the pupil role gives them a chance to demonstrate their competence, which is fun in an individually paced, sequenced learning program that assures continuously expanding mastery. In this regard, it is important to assign children in pairs roughly according to their rates of learning (see Chapter 14), shifting the pair combinations around if one member gets too far ahead. If that happens, the child who is substantially behind may begin to feel some sense of failure as she fails to know, for example, the uses and names of as many tools as her partner.

Although teacher-pupil role play is excellent for both reinforcing learning and teaching cooperation in children after the age of two, it does not entirely replace the need for children to learn to collaborate on tasks on a more equalitarian basis. A certain part of the pair play, both when interacting with the teacher and when working independently, needs to stress simple cooperation, as described earlier. Each child explores and works with the concept material with her partner, looking for different textures, feeling them and sorting them, working on a puzzle or sorting pictures of flowers together, as the guided learning sequence calls for. No one is designated leader.

As the children develop and become experienced in co-operating, three or more pairs of three-to-five-year-olds can be kept busily and happily occupied for half an hour or more at a time, using either the equalitarian or the teacher-pupil type of cooperation at different times. As many as two or three pairs of older infants can be similarly engaged for shorter periods. If a group of children are divided into pairs from the start, they will form a smooth working arrangement of collaborating subgroups; if this practice is followed over a series of sessions, they will come to anticipate and expect to work together. During some periods, the teaching approach may consist of moving from pair to pair quite quickly, showing each pair some new aspect of a learning task or offering guidance as they experiment in play. At certain points, it may be advantageous to interrupt briefly the "pair play" in order to demonstrate a problem to the group as a whole, particularly if all pairs are currently learning the same rule. At these times, emphasis can be placed on joint inquiry, drawing the group together in a common endeavor, much as one would do when working with the children individually in a small group. Continual stress on "groupness" in every context, including between pairs, will reinforce a spirit of co-operation, minimize invidiously competitive trends, and allow the children to concentrate their attention on solving problems.

If interest and learning flourishes, one or another, sometimes all, pairs can be given tasks to work on independently for a few minutes or more at a time, even though some children may not always be concentrating on the learning itself. The temporary loss of learning focus in some pairs will probably be more than compensated in the long run by the acquisition of skill in co-operation and autonomous learning. There is plenty of opportunity for learning to occur, moreover, during the teacher's demonstrations.

One of the advantages of pair collaboration for teachers is that it becomes easier to combine group supervision with individual attention. There is no group to fall apart socially while the teacher is trying to divide his attention between six individual learners. He is able to move at a more leisurely pace among three pairs, because the two other pairs are generally occupied. It is also easier to attend to the needs of three pairs of learners than it is to attend to six different learners in turn. Since both members of a pair are working on the same problem, what the teacher says to one child will often aid the other. This is less easy to do when there are three or more children involved. Also, the first child's attention can be held while one deals with the special problems of the second; this is more difficult in a larger group, where each child must wait longer for her turn and work alone while the problems of several other children in turn are being attended to.

Here lies a basic value of peer interactive learning. Once the children become a little experienced in working on tasks together, the teacher is relieved of the constant burden of attending to many needs at once and can work intensively with those who most need help. Because *children usually enjoy working together* more than on their own, so their span of concentration is increased and the teacher is free for longer periods to give individual attention to those who need it. The teacher's free time is further multiplied because pair collaboration occupies two children at a time.

Uses and Problems of Team Competition

A special characteristic of peer collaboration in subgroups is the structure it provides for combining the processes of co-operation and competition. Collaborating in subgroups supplies children with a sense of "belonging" while, at the same time, offering them the opportunity to compete—but in pairs, not individually. The several pairs (or other subgroupings) can become teams that compete against one another in games or in working on problems. There need not be any exact scoring system, a procedure that involves counting skills and social rules too advanced for most preschoolers, nor even a prize. Concrete rewards (prizes) and point scoring may add incentive, but they can also backfire by diverting interest away from the play and learning activities themselves. The use of scoring systems to monitor and provide feedback for children's learning (as opposed to grading) is discusseed in Chapter 14 on strategies.

In fact, objective standards and rules of competition (scoring, timing, prizes) are seldom required at all to achieve some of the advantages of competition without the disadvantages. Competition in any form will tend to turn some of the children's energy away from the desired goal of developing curiosity about the nature of things. It is nevertheless important to give children experience in one of the basic forms of community living, but through experience provided in a way that will strengthen their personalities without inducing anxiety or undermining their interest in learning. One way to do this is to organize children in cooperating pairs, as usual, then ask them "to see which pair can work the best," "the hardest," or "the longest." These goals should be stated with enthusiasm, but left deliberately vague to involve them in competition without bringing in any objective basis for comparison ("see which pair knows the most tools") that would stress winning and losing.

The arrangement can be repeated from time to time according to the results obtained. If it seems to make little difference, shift the focus away from learning, or arouse too much rivalry among the children, it can easily be dropped. If, on the other hand, children appear to respond enthusiastically and cooperate and learn better, competition could be continued occasionally.

At the end of a few minutes, the teacher can then inform each pair in turn, or all pairs together, that they have "won", since "everyone has finished," or "worked so well," or "so long," as the case may be. While it adds interest for each pair to hold up the examples each has covered, have them do it in such a way (for instance, a few feet apart) so that few direct comparisons are made.

Since many times the different pairs are working with different examples, or even different concepts (one on size and another shape) or necessarily create different things (pieces of clay sculpture, Leggo buildings) there is often no sense of failure for any pair. Each pair is made to feel that it has worked well to learn to create something through cooperating with a teammate.

If one or two pairs have *worked* more consistently than the others, regardless of what they have accomplished, it may involve children more to compliment them—but without making negative remarks about the others, which may be discouraging. Children who neither work well nor accomplish much may be kept apart from competitive "team" play, getting their guided learning activity separately at another time. Shifting pairs around from time to time will, however, prevent any particular rivalries from becoming too intense.

Thus the really significant aspect of the "team" experience for young children is, in the end, that of co-operatively working in, and belonging to, separate groups, each pair contributing something *different*, (different examples of concepts, of drawings, buildings), thus providing for its members a sense of combined purpose, participation, and accomplishment. Obviously this is not "competition" in the sense that the competitive institutions of the business world might define it, but it is far more important for each young child to have positive social learning experiences and a sense of competence in reaching goals, than for a few children to learn how to cut their neighbor's throat at the expense of those who lose.

The socio-emotional experience of losing should probably be deferred until a later age, when a child's cognitive development has attained the level of complexity necessary for understanding the intricate social rules involved. Among other things, a more abstract and relativist sense of time and situation is required for the child to realize that the loss is temporary, and that further efforts at skill development can bring later opportunities to compete effectively. There are plenty of simple frustrations for little children in the ordinary process of daily living, through learning to share toys, take turns, and adapt to schedules, without impressing the rules of stringent competition upon them.

The Size of Collaborating Subgroups

In some instances it may be feasible for children to work together in threes, or occasionally in fours, thus releasing the teacher for even longer periods to work with one or two others on special problems that take more time. This apparent advantage may prove illusory with preschool children, and especially infants, because relations are not the same in threes and fours as they are in pairs. Even four-year-olds seldom have sufficient cognitive development to apply the social and task rules of games in a group without direction, so the collaboration of four quickly reduces to two pairs, each interacting on some aspect of a task. Conflict may also arise because the social definition of collaboration was not made in pairs. For similar reasons, continuous teacher direction is more often required to maintain the task collaboration of children working in threes. Otherwise, two of the three soon "pair off," leaving the third a resigned observer or disturbing intruder. Unless very specific behaviors or different roles can be defined for each member of the trio, more co-operative relations and productive learning will occur in pairs.

Collaborative pair arrangements do not solve everything, of course. Children have their "ups and downs" from problems at home, other conflicts, and illness. In addition, groups will almost always include children with chronic social adaptation problems and learning difficulties. Special methods may be needed to attend to periodic conflicts and individual differences, anticipating that some days will go better than others. Yet the potential for resolving many problems of personal conflict and group discipline through casting learning in a framework of cooperation makes a peer collaborative approach invaluable for teaching in small groups.

14 Strategies for Stimulating Development

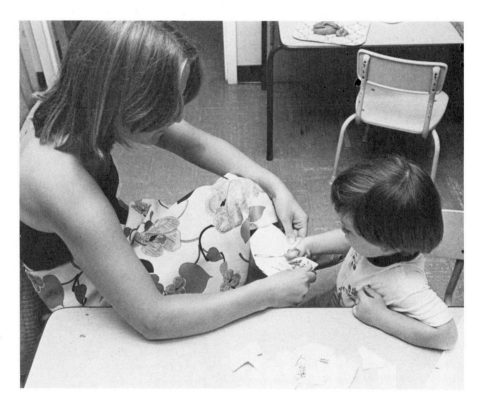

Checking progress

The strategic (long range) problems of early developmental stimulation are no more difficult to solve than the tactical problems of guiding learning in a single session. Both are based on principles of motivation and cognitive learning intrinsic to the action mode of early development. What, then, is special or unique to guiding children's learning over a period of time?

There are at least four major problems of teaching which, though they also appear in single sessions, are more evident in long-term learning. These are:

328

I. *Planning a developmental learning sequence,* from the simple to the complex, and matching children to programs.

II. *Monitoring and pacing* presentations (stimulation) to match each child's rate of learning.

III. *Ensuring children maintain developmental progress* instead of learning isolated facts or merely enjoying the play.

IV. *Adapting* teaching methods to learning and personality styles.

There are naturally other considerations, such as the problems of sustaining the motivation of both teacher and child over many weeks, especially in a program with many details.

Planning programs, monitoring development, and maintaining progress are the primary problems to consider in discussing teaching strategies. Techniques for solving the fourth problem, adapting teaching methods to children's styles, are so much a part of the methods employed for solving the other three problems that solutions to the fourth problem will be discussed while considering the first three.

The first problem starts with choosing or designing a learning program suited to the developmental levels of the children for whom the program is intended. The problem is one of finding programs whose concept sequences fit both the general and specific abilities of the children. Ideal concept sequences are graded in complexity so that the number and intricacy of rules match the rates of learning that can be expected. They are graded not only so that rules about the particular characteristics (about animals, for instance, that animals have legs and walk, have mouths and eat) are taught before complex relations (animals eat plants whose growth is partly dependent on animal excrement for fertilizer); but also so that concepts are not introduced too fast or too slowly for the children's abilities. Programs also need to allow for not only the children's familiarity with the particular concepts in question, but also the children's general competencies, such as their attention span, their ability to understand language, the extent of their general information, and the complexity of relations they can grasp. The efficiency of a program is governed by the fidelity with which sequences are organized in terms of such criteria; easy sequences are boring and difficult sequences are defeating, both producing little progress.

The second step in planning learning programs is to prepare teachers to teach a given program. Teachers cannot usually be expected to construct programs without released time, and special training or guidance in program development. Nevertheless, success in teaching is closely tied to understanding how a program is structured, because what one teaches must be matched to each child's level throughout the program. We must therefore consider the dimensions of programs in the process of choosing programs, diagnosing children's competencies, and organizing learning groups. I shall take up these problems first as a necessary basis for discussing the other long-term aspects of teaching and learning. The discussion will be presented within a broad framework of general considerations for curriculum organization and application.

I. Problems of Sequential Complexity:
Matching Children to Programs

Although the sequence in a prepared program will usually be mapped in considerable detail, it can never be like the track for a train to follow without choice. Even the analogy of a train underestimates the importance of decisions such as pace and timing.

A program will usually specify an age range (older infant, 18 months to 2 years or younger preschool, 2½ to 3½ years) for which the program is suitable. Age alone, however, is at best a crude marker of ability and readiness. Children of a given age vary widely in learning characteristics in complex, difficult-to-measure ways, and curriculum programs too often contain little information about the children for whom they are designed. Children are often skilled in different ways. One two-year-old, for example, may be fairly skilled at working puzzles and form boards, but hardly able to use more than two word phrases to express himself. Another two-year-old may be able to talk about activities in long sentences, yet hardly be able to work a puzzle. A program designed to teach problem solving on detour problems might merely say "suitable for two-year-olds". But if the program offered no further information on competencies required and both two-year-olds appeared generally oriented toward constructive learning in play, how would the teacher know that only the first child is probably ready for such a program—because both puzzle skills and detour problems draw heavily on spatial concepts? What, then, can a teacher do to increase the chances of choosing a suitable program for the children?

There are at least two main aspects of this selection problem: (1) to find a proper match for each child, and (2) to assemble a set of youngsters whose cognitive levels are not too divergent to learn together as a group. The economics of schools and day care typically offer less than one teacher per child, but fortunately there are also motivational benefits for children who learn in small groups (Chapter 13). Yet it is difficult to individualize learning, even in a small group of children, if they diverge widely in their quickness of understanding early in the program. We shall address ourselves first to the problem of the individual match.

Evaluating
Children
Individually

Judging a Child's General Developmental Readiness Level

Familiarity with the children in the group and a good background in child development, including knowledge of cultural norms for cognitive development, will help in evaluating readiness. Knowing the children may not include detailed knowledge of their ability, however, and a good background in child development tells little about any particular child. Too often it provides stereotyped ideas about general readiness that stress age at the expense of many other factors. Because children vary in many particular types of ability, such as number, spatial, language and other concepts, as well as in general ability and their curiosity about learning, readiness is difficult to assess. Is detailed psychological ability and achievement testing needed, then, to decide about readiness and programs? Few day care centers or preschools have access to this depth of analysis.

Diagnosis of Specific Program Concept Readiness

Some published learning programs adopt a different strategy. They contain diagnostic measures designed to assess each child's concept progress at each phase of the program. The value of this approach lies in the information it provides about particular competencies that are needed to meet the learning demands in the program. Whatever the child's general language, problem solving, and other abilities, they are considered, if not irrelevant, at least not needed to judge the child's likelihood of success. Any child who initially demonstrates beginning knowledge of the *program specific concepts* is ready to start in this type of program at the beginning level. Such programs may include preliminary diagnostic tests easy for teachers to use. For instance, a child who was able to pick out the bigger of two pictured toys three out of five times in a series might be considered ready to start a program on learning concepts of length, width, and area. Because such programs are often carefully sequenced, moreover, such an initial assessment is supposed to indicate that the child will progress through the program at a reasonably satisfactory rate.

Such an approach should be followed with caution, however, since the profile of a child's general abilities *is* relevant, even if we are often ignorant of *how* it contributes to the child's readiness and progress. We know, for example, that bright (higher IQ) children generally learn faster and better than intellectually undeveloped children of the same age. General ability (IQ) tests are poor and often misleading measures to use, however, because they provide only a vague, global measure of intellectual ability and are often culturally biased. For example, two two-year-olds might score at the same average (100 IQ) level, but this same score would be made up of very different language, perceptual, motor, memory, and spatial skills for each child, differences which the overall IQ scores would tell nothing about.

But while general IQ scores have limited value for teachers, many cognitive ability tests give information about fine and gross motor skills, and spatial, numerical, language, and other important competencies, quite useful for judging a child's readiness to undertake a program in some area. Children from different cultures may have varying skills and abilities and are probably not equally skilled at test taking. But specific ability or competence measures, in contrast to the vague notions of "general intelligence" which IQ tests try to measure, are concerned with assessing readiness for particular types of programs and ways of learning; these areas are chosen because they are generally useful in order to cope with the mainstream of contemporary industrial society. An increasing number of such measures, moreover, are being developed to fairly test children from different cultural backgrounds.

Unless a child's readiness is assessed on these types of broad skills, as well as in terms of the specific program concepts, not enough information may be obtained about his learning potential. A child may, in fact, be under- or overprepared when he enters a program, because certain underlying abilities, which were not apparent in the narrow, concept-based original diagnoses are, in fact, necessary. In the example cited earlier, a child may successfully pick the bigger of two pictured toys several times without understanding much about size *concepts*. He may have simply been exposed to a few common picturebook examples which he has learned by rote. Spatial ability tests, on the other hand, would assess size and other spatial abilities (orientation, position, distance) with various examples under different conditions, giving a more complex picture of the child's ability to learn spatial concepts *abstractly*. A method of diagnosing and monitoring concept development will subsequently be described in the section on the pacing of sequential learning.

Matching Children to Program Complexity Gradients

One consideration for deciding a child's readiness for a program is its gradient of complexity (or difficulty). This refers to the rate at which the material in a program becomes more complex, a very important determinant of which children are likely to be successful in following a program. This means in a learning program on insects, for example, how many new insects and their parts and habits are to be learned per week. Evaluations of readiness for a program often give too little thought to the child's expected learning rate over the entire program. This problem is illustrated in general terms in Figure 14–1. In this discussion ability refers, not to general IQ, but to a child's estimated skill for some more specific type of learning (verbal, spatial), whether measured formally by ability tests or informally based on a caregiver's familarity with a child.

It will be observed that the same amount of material is included in each gradient, namely, the equivalent of 10 concept units, but different lengths of time are involved; three, six and 10 weeks, for the rapid, moderate, and slow-paced programs respectively. There would be greater detail and elaboration of activities with more examples and branching for the moderate and slow gradients compared with the fast gradient. Thus in our example of the program on insects, when the program takes up bees, for instance, children in each of the three gradients would learn about them, not only at different speeds, but also in somewhat different ways. The slower group would need more examples of bees and take more time to observe them and talk about thin legs, antennae, eyes, fuzzy covering and so on (pictures, replicas, and live bees in hives). They might also spend several sessions with a different type of bees (such as wasps), while the moderate and especially the rapid group might well be comparing wasps, honey bees, and other types of bees all at the same time. The rapid group, and to some extent the moderate group, would probably also be able to discuss the habits and social life of the bees in more abstract terms, such as how they can locate the hive from miles away from any direction, and how the queen lays eggs, others work, and still others (drones) mate with the queen.

In principle, the greater the elaboration and the slower the pace, the less prior ability required to, and the younger the child who can, master a set of concepts. In practice there are limits, since at critical points along the way a child must move to new rules at different levels of understanding, as in shifting from learning about the individual features of bees and what they do to learning about the complex relations between bees and plants. No realistic amount of illustration and elaboration at a simpler stage of a program, can prepare children who require more *general* concept experience to jump to a new level. We must not forget that cognitive development is a process of acquiring complex hierarchies of general rules at increasing levels of abstraction, as well as learning many sets of particular rules. A child may need experience with many common things, such as people, clothes, weather, plants, soil, water, and sun to gradually begin to think about complex relations among things in the environment. It takes more than one program to make such a jump in general ability level.

Unfortunately, few early education programs are designed with more than a single gradient for an age group; it is mostly a question of deciding who fits the single gradient. One can only ask if the program avoids big jumps in ability level and if it is designed for children of average ability. This is a concept that can be misleading. "Average" may mean average middle-class, but if the children in a day care center are average middle-class when a program under consideration is designed for a much broader population defintition of "average ability," the program may not be right for the children. In any case, if an

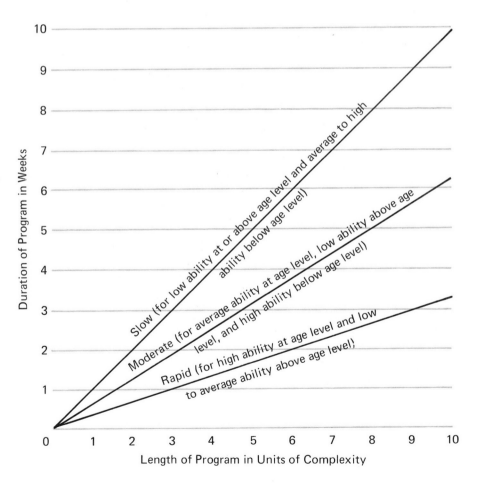

FIGURE 14–1
Three program gradients for combinations of age level and ability.

initial check indicates that the pace of a program is likely to match the learning rate of one age or the ability level of the group, the teacher can then make adjustments for age and ability similar to those indicated for the *Moderate Gradient* in Figure 14–1. That is, the teacher can include some younger children of high ability and some older children of lower ability, to work alongside children of the right program age who have average ability for the verbal logical concepts an insect learning program, for example, might require. It is probably well to err on the side of caution and only include children a *little* younger (less than six months difference, for example) who, by test reports and teacher judgment, are clearly brighter than average for their age for the type of abilities demanded in the program.

Whatever the program instructions state, moreover, and even when a program includes pretests to measure readiness to learn the program concepts, advance study of the later portions of a program, coupled with knowledge of the children's skills, can help the teacher decide whether a particular child is likely to make progress. As I have suggested, there are several things to look for in judging the pace and complexity of a program, such as the size of the steps and the variety of examples and practice provided.

Matching Children's Levels in Groups

In order to learn comfortably in the same group, children need equal ability to learn the subject matter. Not only must the type of abilities of each child match the level and gradient of a program, but children's ability levels and learning rates must also fit together as a group. Even though each child may initially be close enough to the program level in the important area(s) of competence, the total spread of ability in the group may be too wide for the children to progress very long at close to the same rate. While the children's difference in ability may grow narrower, aided by good teaching in a common learning experience, they may also widen. Higher ability often enables children to learn faster and become more interested in learning. The result is an accumulating advantage which pulls them farther and farther ahead of slower learning children who, though learning steadily, may fall relatively farther and farther behind.

If the initial differences between children are not too great and learning rates remain comparable, two groups of two or three children each can alternate their activities between independent, peer-interactive learning and teacher-guided learning (as discussed in Chapter 13). If, on the other hand, the groups turn out to be more different in ability and learning rates than expected they may soon diverge too widely. At some point it may no longer be wise to share any program learning activities in common. There is no point in teaching everybody more about bumble bees, for example, when one subgroup of two children already understands thoroughly at the level expected, and are bored and ready to learn another topic.

The teaching problem may remain manageable if only one child advances more rapidly, since he or she can be placed in a regular assistant teaching role (assuming an adequate personality style) to maintain relations with the group. This solution is feasible when the group is neither too large nor too mischievous to work alone some of the time. A single, slower-learning child can sometimes also be handled if the extra attention such a child demands from the teacher does not seriously diminish attention to the other children. If three distinct learning levels appear, the ordinary problems of supervising young children are further compounded.

There are a number of things caregivers and teachers can do to assemble small learning groups sufficiently compatible to interact and progress together. First, as we have indicated, is to check the range and clustering of abilities among the children available, according to either test reports or the teacher's own judgment. Second, is to select children for a program who are likely to enjoy playing and learning together and can do so without too much conflict and disturbance. Easy relations can do much to compensate for differences in ability. Sometimes two children are too close, however, to work with others in a group. And some friendship pairs are better discouraged because the relationship is not constructive for either child, as in the case where one child continually dominates another who accepts it without resisting.

Personality patterns, despite their complexity, are useful to take into account in forming workable social groups, following the principles described in chapters 5 and 9. There is, however, commonly a limited number of children in any play room from which to form learning groups. Actually, if children can be matched well enough on the two main points, ability and compatibility, the rest will generally follow, regardless of personality nuances and age differences. Young children are highly adaptive; initial conflicts and styles, whether hyperactive or apathetic in direction, are usually modified in the course of involvement in play and learning. Under the guidance of a competent and personable adult most children easily learn to cooperate.

There is an advantage in taking the time to study the children before beginning to set down on paper the comparisons systematically. This can be done for both ability grouping and associational patterns. If there are, for example, fifteen children available altogether in a total playroom group, *write down their names in order of your estimate of their ability,* from one (the most intellectually developed) to 15 (the least developed in understanding). Keep in mind the ability or abilities required in relation to the type of program, and make use of all the diagnostic information available. In this way, three groups of five children can be formed from your list which, if your initial judgments are accurate and the children maintain their relative differences, will represent three distinct levels or ranges of learning ability or abilities.

Associational patterns are perhaps better recorded by a type of *sociometric* measurement, where a diagram is drawn, on the basis of teacher observations, to show which children play together compatibly. For the specialized purpose of forming small guided learning play groups it is probably enough to focus on the single idea of the teacher's (perhaps combined with parent's) judgment of compatible association. If time is available, more detailed personality matching can be undertaken, using the assessment system described in Chapter 5. The problem will involve making three groups in which each of the five children will interrelate more positively than negatively with every other child in the group. That is, each child *will get along most of the time* without quarreling, even if he doesn't necessarily like any other child strongly. One of the diagrams may be represented as in Figure 14–2. Each child is represented by a

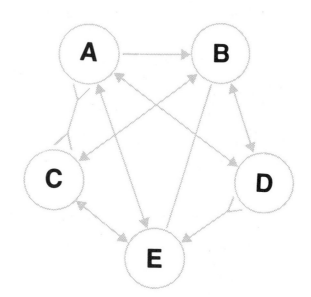

FIGURE 14–2
*Sociometric
compatibility
patterns for a five
child learning
group.*

circle in the diagram and interrelations between two children, which are, *on the whole,* more positive than negative, are represented by double arrows. A group of such compatible children would be expected to get along well as a whole with a minimum of conflict and disruption, as well as to be able to work together in pairs in various combinations. A *single, one way arrow* (A ———→B) would indicate that child A related constructively to his mate (B) but that child B, though not creating disputes, did not cooperate well with child A. A *linē with no arrows* (B ——— E) would indicate relations between two children were generally neutral in both directions, that is, though neither child was aggressive toward the other, they did not try to cooperate with each other either. Both of these types of relations might work well enough when the children were all playing and learning together, but neither type of pair relation would be very satisfactory if they were assigned to work together independently, because of their difficulty in cooperating. *Double reverse arrows* (A>———<C) would indicate that the relations between child A and child C were generally more negative than positive, suggesting the likelihood of social conflict unless one of the children was eliminated from the group or the two children were kept somewhat apart, not placed side by side. If they were asked to cooperate on a learning task alone, they would probably disturb the other children constantly, take up a lot of the caregiver's time, and get little done. A *single reversed arrow,* despite a positive arrow in the other direction (D>———→E), suggests that child D is fond of child E, but that child E may, for example, pick on child D, and thus be a source of disturbance. As in the other cases, if they don't have to be put together to cooperate in a learning pair, they may be able to get along well enough when the whole group is together.

Compromises will be inevitable. No group of 15 children will yield three perfectly matched groups of five children each. Sometimes considerable "juggling" becomes necessary. There is also the question of reconciling the three ability groups with the relationship groupings. One way to handle things might be to try to assemble three groups whose members were either alike or only one step removed in ability, and who were all positive or neutral in terms of their associational patterns. If, for example, the 15 children were all rated for ability in problem solving (for that type of learning project) as either slow, moderate or fast, then under this arrangement, the children might be found to form three learning groups, one fast, one slow and one moderate. Because it is unlikely there would be exactly five of each type, however, particularly where more than one ability is involved, one or two children could be placed in the next higher or lower group as needed to make five for each group, *as long as slow and fast children (on any ability important for the program) are not placed together.* In some cases there might well be a high proportion (nine out of the fifteen) who fit the moderate category in which case there would be two moderate groups with the other six children forming a separate group if all were either fast or slow, or combining with the other nine children to form three groups, two tending to be fast and slow, respectively, and the third in between.

These arrangements by *ability* would be made by taking account of *relations* at the same time. There are always choices. The problem with respect to group *relations* is simply to *avoid placing children together who don't get along.* Thus in the example above, there is likely to be a choice as to which of the moderates is placed in the fast group and which of the moderates goes with the slower group. In many cases, some of the fast or slow children could easily be placed in a "faster" or "slower" moderate group as needed. In this manner many combinations are possible.

The fact that balanced grouping may occasionally be difficult to work out will not necessarily cause serious difficulties; small groups permit adequate individualization within a fair range of ability levels and personality differences. Careful analysis in grouping at the beginning is mainly to start with the best arrangement possible and gain insight into factors influencing learning in groups. The teacher should anticipate occasional movements of children between groups when children's relations and learning abilities change or don't work out as originally expected, as we shall discuss later in the chapter. Planning ahead, flexibility, and continuous reassessment (monitoring) will go far toward resolving problems as they arise.

There is also the alternative of completely individualizing the teacher-child learning process, by having each teacher or caregiver circulate among the children each day to teach them one at a time. Teaching children in pairs or small groups would then be done only as groups of children spontaneously got together or perhaps occasionally in response to informal teacher suggestions for a special demonstration. Some teachers can manage to guide an entire group of five or six children effectively on a totally separated, individualized basis in the time they would have available for the group. They move around among the children in the course of ordinary free play activities. This method makes it possible to accommodate a very wide range of ability levels. Complete individualization, however, loses the motivational, social, and cognitive learning advantages of group processes, and, unless, the teacher takes each child to a quiet room—which takes time—it is harder for the children to concentrate. It is thus likely to take longer and to yield less actual guided learning time than combining individualized teaching with group and peer interaction methods.

II. Monitoring Developmental Learning: Pacing and Regulating the Course of Sequential Learning

Once an individual child or a group is selected for a learning program, the teaching role divides itself naturally into two areas of concern. The first of these, the tactics for teaching a play session, has been discussed at length in previous chapters. The second area concerns the problem of long-range strategy, the problem of teaching children in an orderly sequence over a series of sessions. If the concepts and tasks do not follow a logical path from session to session, but progress irregularly in difficulty, it will be harder for children to learn smoothly and consistently, and there will be too much confusion from skipping around, boredom because the same concepts tend to get repeated, and frustration when things suddenly become more difficult. Although some of the sessions may even be highly interesting for the children, they are less likely to develop any deep interest in learning from such a scattered approach.

Sequential learning activities consist, almost by definition, of a prepared program that schedules tasks to be followed over a series of sessions. There are a number of easily overlooked procedures to use in sequential learning programs to insure a comparatively smooth and continuing advancement in understanding for each child.

Learning is an individual, not a group, process, as almost every teacher knows but finds difficult to practice. While learning typically occurs through interaction between people in pairs and groups, it is inextricably bound up with the development of particular minds of particular persons. Caught up in the economics of teaching more than one child at a time, it is easy for teachers to measure their success by the *average progress* of the group as a whole rather than of the children as individuals. Among the procedures essential for promoting each child's development is to continuously monitor his progress in learning.

Individualized Monitoring and Recordkeeping

But what exactly does individualized monitoring mean and how is it carried out? In its simplest form, monitoring consists of little more than observing regularly each child's activities in the program sessions to see that he or she is interested and appears to be learning. At a more sophisticated level, this mental tracking is broken down into a few component dimensions of motivation and learning. It entails watching to see that the child's interest and concentration seldom fall below a point where they interfere with learning. At the core of this process is ensuring that the child learns without too many plateaus (periods of zero progress) or setbacks (periods of confusion over concepts, apparent forgetting or emotional conflict).

Keeping a *mental* track of multiple processes in a group is seldom sufficient. There are too many processes on which a teacher must concentrate to keep the activities going smoothly, such as settling disputes, making the rounds to give individual attention, organizing tasks for children to work at in pairs, and making sure each concept is well illustrated through play. Especially later in a program, when material becomes more complex and children often progress more rapidly, keeping mental records on more than two or three children is extremely demanding, making it easy to overlook details. Over a series of sessions a child's small difficulties may pass unnoticed by a teacher until they have become major learning difficulties and the child has become definitely confused. As an example of this problem, a teacher may assume a child is ready to learn to label another object in a series (an item of clothing), or to tackle the opposite pole of a dimensional concept ("small"), since he or she seems to have compared objects successfully in terms of one end of the pole ("large"). There is, however, a distinction between *learning* (familiarity with) and *mastering* a rule, which can be missed when trying to keep the progress of several children in mind. It is easy for a teacher to believe that three out of five children are ready to take the next step, such as learning "small," failing to notice or forgetting the occasional hesitations of one of them.

Methods of Keeping Records

Some form of regular but simple recording can help to prevent errors from arising. Taking occasional notes on the development of individual children is haphazard, and videotaping is far too cumbersome, time consuming and expensive to be worth the effort. And, though it provides a permanent record and useful feedback, television (or film) does not furnish a clear record of any child's progress and problems in learning; even after playing back an entire session's activities, the teacher is still without the brief summary, which can be scanned quickly, that only written records can provide.

The value of videotaping (and, to a lesser extent, audiotaping) lies not in making cumulative records, but in the opportunity it provides to "re-create" and review a session as it actually happened. The teacher is able to evaluate her own performance as if she were an outside observer free from teaching responsibilities. Segments of sessions can be reviewed and compared repeatedly at any time by the teacher, alone, or in discussion with colleagues to explore problems objectively in depth.

Television (or film) records do *not*, however, supply a faithful account of every event that occurs. There is, first, some loss of clarity through reduction of the scene to the size of a TV screen and, second, usually some loss due to the high pitch and poor articulation of young children's speech. Cameras take pictures and tape recorders record sound from a particular angle and distance, moreover; *not every event is visible*. There are too many hand, head and body movements and facial expressions, often of several children and the teacher facing in different directions or observing one another, for the camera to catch. TV (and film) are also after all flat pictures, even though moving ones, that don't show things in depth, and even different lighting and color change one's impressions. Finally, what we see is limited by the fact that we cannot possibly see everything, as well as by the fact that we always see according to how we interpret things from our likes and understanding. While any observation is subject to some of these limitations, people often expect more of the technology of the camera.

Videotaping is best as an instrument for training and occasional monitoring of teaching and learning problems. Although costly, it is particularly useful for recording one or two sessions during a period when a teacher is facing problems that he or she cannot identify clearly or solve, in order to call on the aid of others, including parents, to identify sources of difficulty and suggest alternative methods.

Video recording cannot, therefore, be a substitute for a running, written record. A few notes on each child's behavior, written as soon after each session as possible, can accomplish several purposes; they provide a continuous record for repeated review and comparison of each child's progress; they can be scanned quickly in detail; they can be used to identify problems common to the group, or subgroups, and problems of recurring difficulty for any child. Keeping a log helps fix in mind key observations on achievements, learning styles and motivations, which might go unnoticed or be quickly forgotten among many competing demands. The record itself, of course, helps insure against forgetting.

The principle object of a written record is to *sharpen teacher awareness* and keep a permanent record of the *most important events* of learning processes and progress. It should be a systematic but selective account, analyzing how and what the children are learning. It is not even necessary to comment on every teaching session, except at the beginning of a program and during other periods when new concepts are introduced or special problems arise. Too frequent or too detailed record-keeping will inflate the amount of material and discourage frequent review. Although brief notations on critical events as they occur are obviously invaluable, it is more useful to spend time looking over the trends than simply writing the records. Using a simple checkoff system, combined with keeping a few notes weekly, will make it easier to spot each child's problems and keep a picture of his or her long run progress.

Dimensions of Monitoring Records

However clear and logically ordered a program may be, children always differ in the way they learn. Each child has his own history that has shaped his mind with different skills, interests, and ways of doing things. A running record, therefore, ought to note especially *how* each child learns as well as *what* he learns, so that the teacher can individualize her teaching strategy to maximize the child's ease of learning. There are, fortunately, similarities between children, but even so, some children may learn best when no more than a single example is presented at a time, others when two or even three are used in the same session because they get the general idea quickly, and still others may like the teacher to always say the rule as she is giving the examples.

There is no foolproof method of recording and analysis, but there are techniques that will simplify the recording process, and still provide useful information and contribute to a teacher's excitement in each child's learning. Records can be as brief as a running checklist or as elaborate as narrative case histories. Major dimensions to keep track of are

(a) the program presented—the series of concepts, materials, and methods employed

(b) the child's progress in learning—his speed, how well he remembers and his depth and scope of understanding

(c) the pattern and development of his responses—including both his motivations and his prevailing styles of play and learning

(d) the social relations among the children and between the teacher and the children.

What this means in practice will be described below.

Such a comprehensive record system is not as difficult to maintain in practice as may appear at first. Once a simple system is set up to record only the degree of detail that a caregiver or teacher can manage, a little practice will make record keeping an interesting and useful routine. In addition, monitoring is more likely to improve teaching skills than to interfere with them, because it focuses attention on the learning and motivational essentials in guiding learning, while the actual recording of observations is done after a session is terminated. The teacher, therefore, can devote herself completely to teaching and enjoying the play with the children; knowing she may want to record a few details after the session serves to enhance her awareness of, and memory for, what is happening. A few notes should be taken as soon after each session as possible, while the recollections are fresh.

In many schools and day care settings, the limited teacher-child ratios and technical help ordinarily available make only the simplest check-off system feasible. In some centers, the caregiver's packed daily schedule allows little time for preparing the program each day and note taking must usually wait for a break in the program, such as naptime. Too often both preparation and record keeping come at the expense of her own coffee breaks and lunch period. Notwithstanding its value, it is essential that record keeping does not become a tedious extra demand in an already too-busy day. For this reason, we shall present two systems of monitoring: (1) a basically simple method for tracking the children's progress, which inexperienced teachers (and parents) can manage alone with minimum practice and supervision; and (2) a comprehensive system of continuous recording and analysis, which can be used by experienced teachers or by minimally trained staff and parents, who are provided with technical help from supervisors and given enough released time to prepare their programs and keep better records. In between the two extremes there are dozens of combinations possible to suit the needs of different teachers and centers.

Simple Monitoring

The first system is made up of several parts or stages: first, simply to identify and list the variety of learning activities to be used in a program; second, to make a convenient wall chart (or record book), listing the learning activities down one side of the chart (or page) and the names of all children in the group (or playroom) across the top; third, to make a record for each child each time he participates in each learning activity; fourth, to make weekly or periodic graphs of the number of learning sessions each child attends for the period; and, fifth, to use this information to increase the number or modify the propor-

FIGURE 14–3. Weekly record chart of guided learning activities

Dates _____ to _____

Types of Rules and Materials[a]	Children					Number of Sessions Per Week				
	A	B	C	D	E	A	B	C	D	E
Structured Problem Solving										
Dimensions										
Shapes:										
geometric (form boards, shape sorting boxes, etc.)										
irregular (puzzles)										
Color:										
(sorting, naming sets)[b]										
Size:										
Volume (stacking, nesting toys)										
Area (size gradient puzzles)										
Length (sorting sets, puzzles)										
Number:										
(puzzles, stacking-sorting sets)										
Other:										
Means-End—Construction										
Boxes:										
(puzzles, surprise boxes, button-lever boxes)										
Connecting Devices:										
(beads—snap, stringing; chains, trains)										
Assembly Toys										

a Typical activities; recording system may be used with alternative lists and prepared programs.
b Materials are often designed to teach more than one rule (e.g. color and shape); one may record either primary focus of an activity or two foci.

FIGURE 14-3. Weekly record chart of guided learning activities

Dates _____ to _____

Types of Rules and Materials[a]	Children					Number of Sessions Per Week				
	A	B	C	D	E	A	B	C	D	E
Open-ended Activities[c]										
Construction-Creative										
Modular–Three Dimensional: Blocks, tinker toys, open-ended assembly toys										
Modular–Two Dimensional Shape & color mosaics, collage (variable shape & color)										
Free Form Three-Dimensional (clay, play dough, wet sand, papier maché)										
Two-Dimensional (drawing, easel and finger painting, chalk, etc.)										
Sociodramatic[c] Miniature replicas (people, animals, vehicles, furniture, tools, etc.)										
Representational Rules Language-Pictorial (books, pictures, magazine picture—usually with comment, story, or poem)										
Natural Science Observation-discussion (plants, fish, insects, etc.)										
Gross Motor Activities[c] (climbing, bicycling, swimming, skating, etc.)										

c Activities recorded only when a definite plan for guiding is involved and should *not* replace periods of independent activity with these materials during free play periods.

FIGURE 14-4. Three methods of summarizing guided learning activity rates by number and types of activities
(Invented figures)

a. *Mean number of sessions per child for different phases of the program—Toddler group*

Guided learning activities	Phase I			Phase II			Phase III			(15–24 months) Program Mean
	Wk. 1	Wk. 2	Mean	Wk. 3	Wk. 4	Mean	Wk. 5	Wk. 6	Mean	
Structured Problem Solving Means End—Construction										
Boxes (puzzles, surprise boxes, lever boxes, etc.)	5	5	5	5.2	4.8	5.0	4.3	3.5	3.9	4.6
Connecting Devices (beads—snap, stringing, chains, etc.)	3.8	4.0	3.9	3.9	4.1	4.0	3.8	3.9	3.9	3.9
Assembly Toys	2.1	1.7	1.9	2.5	2.8	2.7	6.2	5.4	5.3	3.5
TOTALS	10.9	10.7	10.8	11.6	11.7	11.7	14.3	12.8	13.1	
MEANS	3.6	3.6	3.6	3.9	3.9	3.9	4.8	4.3	4.5	4.0

b. *Mean number of sessions per child per week (girls and boys) for all major types of cognitive rules—first month of program*

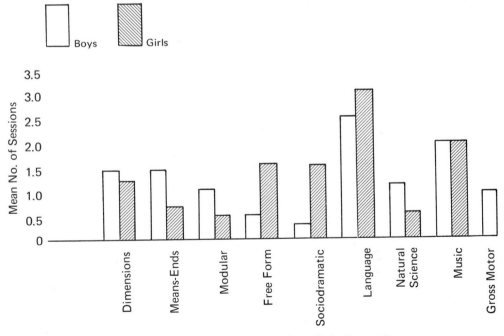

c. *Comparison of mean activity rates of three children in natural science sessions—first 12 weeks of program*

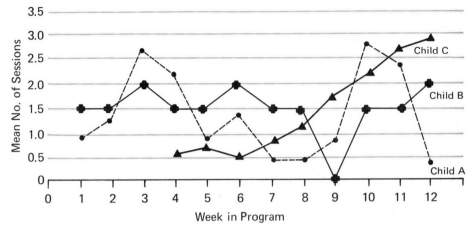

tions or types of guided play learning experience for each child as appears desirable.

This recording method is quite simple once a chart is made and tried out. The chart can be prepared with graph paper or by drawing a grid on large drill cardboard (or newsprint, construction paper, etc.) as illustrated in Figure 14–3. In this example, there are five children in the play group and a detailed list of various perceptual-motor, cognitive, social, and language play activities used in the program are listed vertically down the left side of the chart. The list of activities and materials indicated is by no means exhaustive and the recording system is readily adaptable to other types of concept learning activities. The list may also be considerably shortened by omitting all the particular concepts and simply making a check for a child when he gets a session in any of the main types (structural problem solving, means and ends, and construction). Or there might simply be a project on shape concept learning for example, which would of course greatly simplify the recording. On the other hand, prepared programs may be used or a teacher may prefer to record according to types of materials used, such as (1) puzzles, stacking toys, etc., (2) construction toys, (3) stories—and so on; the list can be as brief or as comprehensive and organized as desired.

In any case, the items listed in Figure 14–3 represent a balanced set of common activities, grouped according to the types of cognitive rules intrinsic to the nature of the materials, as discussed in Chapter 7. Structural problem solving thus grows out of the form boards, puzzles, color materials, and so on that are *designed* to teach the shape and other concepts indicated. Additional ideas for setting up programs can be found in Chapter 7, from prepared programs in early education texts,* or from the teacher's own experience, perhaps starting with an inventory of the materials available.

---

* The companion volume to this text, *Curriculum and Assessment Guides for Infant and Child Care,* contains extensive curriculum plans.

Another brief method of recording is to write a letter for the day of the week (i.e., M, T, W, Th, or F) under each child's name, opposite the appropriate activity. There should be enough space for a letter to be repeated if a particular activity is offered more than once in a day. At the top of the page the dates and the week in the program series (Week 1, Week 2) are recorded, in order to evaluate cumulatively the results of a program over a period of weeks. Alternatively, dates instead of days of the week can be recorded, with the month and period dates indicated at the top of the chart.

Teachers may also find it useful to record the time of day, or at least the initials of the particular teacher, which may give some idea of the preferences of both children and teachers for one another and the kind of activities they enjoy. Since more detailed information on a child's motivation, progress, and styles takes time, methods for recording them will be described in the more comprehensive recording system.

Analysis

Once a few weekly charts are completed, the teacher can begin to make an analysis of the long-term effects of her program. In the last column of Figure 14–3 there is a space for recording the total number of sessions a child has per week, but additional comparisons of long-range trends among children and activities are also useful aids for planning programs.

More detailed summaries are shown in Figure 14–4. These give information on individuals and subgroups of children for different types of programs over periods of different length. In the first section (a) there is a comparison of the mean (average) activity rates for a group of children over three phases of a seven week program for three means-ends–construction activities in structured problem solving. This table simply lists the various numerical frequencies and averages under the appropriate headings along the top and down the left side. The weekly mean and total number of sessions per child, as well as the program average and totals, are also shown. It will be noted that the frequency of working with box problems tended to decline while guided play with assembly toys gradually rose, perhaps because activity was shifting to more complex types of tasks as the children progressed. Activity with connecting devices, on the other hand, remained fairly constant, indicating (one could assume) a constant, moderate level of interest in these activities, which vary little in complexity.

In the middle section (b) of Figure 14–4, there is a bar graph which shows, plotted against a vertical scale on the left, the contrast between groups. In this example, we can see that girls were offered more free form, sociodramatic, and language activities, while boys were offered more dimensions, means-end, modular, natural science, and gross motor activities. The pattern of difference would suggest bias toward traditional sex role–typed experiences in the program. The teachers are choosing the activities in which they guide the children, in other words, in terms of what they believe are the different "natural" interests of girls and boys, perhaps unconsciously, without trying to see that both sexes get experience in *all* types of activities.

Such discriminatory trends usually arise, not only from the teachers' own unconscious biases, however, but also from the tendency of children to follow cultural practices originating in the home and elsewhere in the community, including those shown on television. Teachers and caregivers are likely to select the program activities which children appear to enjoy most, which thus perpetuates the biases. Similar biases appear when caregivers offer more books and language activities to children from verbal, better-educated families who are used to books and language play, thus overlooking the language developmental needs of the children who need *more* language stimulation. Again, the need for careful program planning in terms of the needs of individual children is indicated. Graphs are useful for drawing attention to such differences in a program, which can then be altered accordingly to correct biases of this kind.

In the third section (c) of Figure 14–4, there is a curve graph showing the contrasting average numbers of sessions per week plotted against a vertical column on the left. Curves are particularly useful for revealing contrasting changes in a program over time. We can see, in our example, that child A shows a marked fluctuation in the mean number of sessions he received; child B shows an even, moderate record—except for a severe drop for one week (when it is known he was absent); and child C had no sessions until the fourth week (when he enrolled in day care), then showed a steady rise to a very high level by the twelfth week. Monitoring the pattern of individual participation in this way can heighten the teacher's awareness of the children's patterns to seek the sources of difficulty and enable her to design programs accordingly.

In this instance, the teacher may not have realized the extent to which child A's variability was due to periods of depressions from conflicts at home; that child B was just "going through the motions" regularly but with little involvement; and child C was developing an unusually strong interest which might be dissipated without special thought and attention. Caregivers and teachers often fail to follow through with a project when a child becomes apathetic or depressed, or even moderately uninvolved. On the other hand, if a child becomes highly enthusiastic, as child C apparently did, asking for more and more project sessions, teachers may not automatically take advantage of his developing interest to plan the more challenging, complex program he probably needs.

The advantage of taking the time to plot such curves is that they dramatically point up how the program is actually working in practice, thus stimulating teachers to think about *why* one's child's interest fluctuates, another's is indifferent and a third rises so rapidly, then *do* something about it. Teachers would usually realize that they must look into the home life of child A and perhaps also give more special attention during her down periods; that the teaching methods or relations with the teachers or the other children in the project group may need some change for child B to get him more involved; and that a more advanced program might be useful for child C to further his specialized natural science interests. It may help to use the various diagnostic and sociometric methods of analysis discussed in Chapters 5 and 13, as well as analyzing the program learning and play methods (Chapters 10 and 12), especially for child B, to help in working out a constructive course of action.

Comprehensive Monitoring

The second and more comprehensive monitoring system makes use of all the major dimensions of cognitive learning and personality functioning I have defined above, and brings in several functions not used or analyzed with the brief monitoring systems. A plan for recording, as shown in Figure 14–5, consists of a brief *daily record* and a *weekly (or period) summary* for each child, which together can provide a reasonably complete picture of a child's development.

A more expanded format, providing room for detailed recording of single and weekly program sessions, but omitting the sections on learning styles and social styles, is shown in Figure 14–6. Although both of these record sheets are schematic, and would probably require more space for actual use, a brief sample record of a day care worker's notes for teaching concepts of *fish* and spatial concepts to a child are entered in the form. (Age is not important here, but the sample is for a child of about two.) The space available for recording learning and social styles will ordinarily need to be similarly expanded to accommodate notes on observations, even if style notes for every session are not needed. Items for each of three major categories (examples of concepts presented and the child's learning and social styles) can be entered in the appropriate rows. Provision can be made for noting the child's styles of behavior, and for brief comments on the sessions, as shown on the form in Figure 14–6 for concepts and learning progress. The weekly or period summary (depending on the frequency of sessions) repeats the same format as the single session record (not shown in Figure 14–6), but in an expanded form—again including a brief checklist of key items, and space for more comment as the need arises, time permits, and program objectives suggest.*

It is in the nature of sequential learning programs that material to be learned is presented in steps, *defined by specific rules.* These are first of all relatively concrete *unit* rules about concepts, based on highly visible features, such as the rules that chairs have backs, seats, and legs. These rules about concept characteristics are closely related to concepts about functions, which are rules for what things do (spoon holds food for eating, crayon makes marks for drawing). Although these action rules are not seen until the object is used, they are relatively concrete, seen in single, often dramatic actions that attract attention and are thus among the rules infants come to understand first. Similar concepts about action involve process rules like move, lift, and crawl. Concepts about other relatively concrete characteristics of objects, mainly color and form, are similarly made up of highly visible features, the redness or greyness, for example, of color and the roundness, or angularity, of shape.

As concepts become more complex the rules tend to get more abstract and less immediately visible. Among these are general concepts for classifying things at several levels in hierarchies, such as classifying pants and skirts as clothes, which involve rules about their features (cylindrical, holes to fit legs and waists) and functions (cover lower part of body, warmth, fashion). Clothes and jewelry can then, for example, be classified as personal adornments or wearing apparel, in a second level of the hierarchy. There are many combinations of such multi-level hierarchies. There are also many other concepts with their accompanying rules (such as object permanence, conservation, dimen-

---

* The program concepts shown in Figures 14–5 and 14–6 and illustrated in Figure 14–6 are typical of programs developed by the author in a number of investigations and designed for use in this book. A comprehensive set of curricula on concepts of knowledge, problem solving, and language is contained in *Curriculum and Assessment Guide for Infant and Child Care.*

Program ______________ Child ______________

Teacher(s) ______________ Period (Dates): ______ to ______ Birth Date ______________

Types of Concepts	Session 1		Session 2		Session 3		Session 4		Session 5		Period Summary	
	Stimuli	LP*	Stimuli	LP	Stimuli	LP	Stimuli	LP	Stimuli	LP	Program Stimuli	LP
Units												
(Objects, features, functions, actions, processes, etc.)												
Comments												
Complex Concepts	Stimuli	LP	Stimuli	LP	Stimuli	LP	Stimuli	LP	Stimuli	LP	Program Stimuli	LP
(Dimensions, relations, classes, levels, seriation, conservation, etc.)												
Comments												
Learning Styles	Rating	Comments	Rating	Comments	Rating	Comments	Rating	Comments	Rating	Comments	Rating	Comments
1. Attentive												
2. Persistent												
3. Initiates learning												
4. Analytic												
5. Integrative												
6. Free from anxiety												
Social Styles	Rating	Comments	Rating	Comments	Rating	Comments	Rating	Comments	Rating	Comments	Rating	Comments
1. Active-passive												
2. Cooperative (peers)												
3. Competitive (peers)												
4. Responsive to teacher												
5. Warmth												

*Learning Progress

Note: Ratings on *Learning Progress* and *Learning* and *Social Styles:* 1 = Mastery or very high; 2 = High; 3 = Moderate; 4 = Low; 5 = Little or none.

FIGURE 14–5. *Recording scheme for monitoring sequential learning*

Program _____

Teacher(s) _____

Child _____

Period (Dates): _____ to _____   Birth Date _____

Types of Concepts	Session[a] Concepts and Rules Examples—Materials	Session[a] Learning Progress[b]	Session 2 Concepts and Rules Examples—Materials	Session 2 Learning Progress[b]	Session 3 Concepts and Rules Examples—Materials	Session 3 Learning Progress[b]
Units (Objects, features, functions, actions, processes, etc.)	Characteristics of fish; goldfish - mouth; fins - eating; swimming (aquarium, picture)	3 (said "fish") 2 (mouth) 4 (vague on fins)	fish - repeat; also eyes, seeing	2 (said "goldfish" today) 2 (mouth and fins)	fish - repeat goldfish, pictured - long and thin side fins - balance	2 for all except side fins (5)
Comments	picture not very clear		better pictures found	child able to see side fins now.	difficult to show how side fins keep fish upright - must make a paper model.	
Complex Concepts (Dimensions, relations, classes, levels, seriation, conservation, etc.)	in - out - placing two small toys in and out of box and jar.	3 (hesitates with "out")	in - out repeat more examples of objects and containers.	— (no errors)	in - out - repeat also using things in cupboard. on - off - placing small objects on and off table and a table.	2 (set back - too soon to bring in a new concept) 4 (new concept)
Comments	in and out are easy to work with - lot of clear examples - small material a child can handle.				off - seems to be quite unfamiliar idea "on" not as exact as being contained in "something" - must go slow here.	

[a] Weekly Summaries follow same form.

[b] Ratings on *Learning Progress:* 1 = Mastery or very high; 2 = High; 3 = Moderate; 4 = Low; 5 = Little or none.

FIGURE 14-6. *Recording scheme for monitoring sequential learning*

sions of increasing size and weight) as are described in Chapter 1 and Appendix A,*—many extending beyond the complexity levels of young children.

The recording scheme provides space for listing both *small rule steps* (units) and *large rule steps* (complex conceptual relations). The child must acquire experience in manipulating the rules with these concrete concepts, (such as permanence, object characteristics and functions), before he can become acutely aware of relational patterns and make the mental integrations involved in complex rules about dimensions, classification, etc. The latter are rules whose mastery requires larger cognitive "leaps" for infants and children.

It is neither necessary nor useful to record every detail about all the rules presented and all the child's reactions. In any single session, when any new concept (length) or rule ("short," after learning "long" and "not-long") is introduced, it is enough to note the types of examples employed to demonstrate the rules (pencils, sticks of different lengths), and the significant steps a child makes in learning (chooses the different short and long sticks, then later chooses among boards). There is no need to record the details of the extensive review which takes up much of the time in every session to ensure each child masters the concepts. When time and staff resources are limited it may be enough to chart each child's progress largely through weekly or periodic summaries alone. They can include all the new concepts, materials, and methods and the significant learning events of the period. A note or two, jotted down soon after the important sessions to minimize forgetting, coupled with a check-off of rules covered, can later be written up for the period summary.

Learning and Social Styles

The other two processes to be monitored, the child's learning and social styles, point up specific ways in which a child is getting along. The several dimensions listed in Figures 14–5 and 14–6 can give clues to account for one child's success and another child's difficulties. Moreover, unless a child is experiencing consistent success or failure, there are likely to be areas of both difficulty and strength needing attention for every child.

One child, for example, who is making indifferent progress in learning may, nevertheless, generally rate high (1 or 2 on the scales) in all learning styles except attention and persistence, in which he varies a great deal (shifting from 1 or 2 some days down to 4 or 5 on others). (See bottom of Figures 14–5 and 14–6 for rating scale values.) On the other hand, he may be typically low (4 or 5) in his social styles, except for competitiveness, where he is unusually high (1, much of the time). Further inspection of this child's records over two or three time periods might indicate that upswings in attention and persistence occurred mainly on days when he worked alone with the teacher, or on days when a particular child with whom he was exceptionally competitive was absent. The child's learning difficulties would appear in this case to pivot around problems of competitiveness, insecurity, and social skills, problems which interfere with his attention to learning whenever he has to relate to his peers in a learning situation.

If his scores on the other dimensions of his learning style were also consistently high whenever he *did* perform, the caregiver would have additional evi-

*These topics are also discussed more completely in *Curriculum and Assessment Guidesfor Infant and Child Care*.

dence to support this interpretation. This would be indicated, for example, by the fact that whenever he *does* perform, he is relatively consistent in perceiving important dimensions and details (analyzes), generally relates objects and ideas to one another meaningfully (integrates), shows little anxiety, and initiates learning quite often. Only when in a setting with peers does his attention and persistence falter.

One evident remedial course to follow with such a child is to continue to ensure plenty of personalized attention, the caregiver being careful not to jeopardize her relations with the other children through slighting them. One way is to give him some special time alone or show special interest in his problem solving during free play periods. Showing the child that he can cooperate in a group and still have his share of attention and opportunities to participate will further his social development. The caregiver can accomplish this by praising any small efforts he makes to cooperate with another child; assigning very specific small tasks for cooperating, like simply handing the other child an example; letting him take a teaching role from time to time (giving demonstrations for the other children); encouraging all children to praise one another; and above all the caregiver herself maintaining a warm and flexible play atmosphere. Many problems can be solved through such methods, though it often takes time. A climate of friendliness and cooperation is important to foster social development and cognitive curiosity and learning in all children.

Other combinations of problems may be evident. Another child may be adequate in social relations and attentiveness but low in analytic abilities, leading her to overlook significant rules, such as that insects have eyes, thus reducing the quality of her generalizations (integration), in this case that insects can see. By keeping a record of important characteristics, a profile of each child's major strengths and weaknesses will soon emerge and a course of action to suit each one's needs can be formulated. If no initial assessment has been made, the child's styles will usually become evident in a few days or more of record keeping.

| Frequency of Ratings | Daily Records: Short-Term Trends |

Daily ratings on the children's styles give a convenient cumulative record of the children's patterns of functioning in running detail. Sometimes small, gradual changes occur, which only become noticeable when looking back over a series of ratings plotted in curves as illustrated in Figure 14–7. Such plots can be particularly useful for revealing how a child's characteristics are interrelated. Thus, in the example shown, apparently small changes in socio-emotional functioning (anxiousness) are often preceded by important declines in the child's ability to put things together (integrative competence).

Teachers need record only as often and in as much detail as they can comfortably manage, however. Guided learning, though important, must not occur at the expense of independent play and care for other needs. The real issue here is the adequacy of staff ratios for the provision of the kind of quality care and education needed to foster children's development in group care. Without staff ratios adequate for teachers to spend planned time periods, free of caregiving responsibilities, to do such things as prepare programs and chart

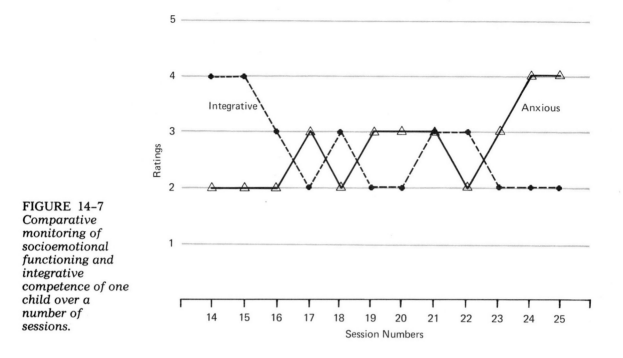

FIGURE 14–7
Comparative monitoring of socioemotional functioning and integrative competence of one child over a number of sessions.

the children's socio-emotional and cognitive progress (either for diagnositc monitoring or for progress in a learning project), the standard of care will soon deteriorate to a custodial (baby-sitting) level, despite the best of intentions. The value of conciseness in keeping daily records need not lead the teacher to overlook important information about styles or points about methods to help a child learn with more depth. Too little detail can result in leaving out mention of small problems in a child who is apparently making adequate progress. Yet, such small problems as a tendency to race through play or to get confused when more than one example is presented at a time, even using familiar material, may indicate anxiousness over learning or problems of abstracting (interrelating). More careful consideration in the early stages could prevent them from becoming big problems later on. It is ironic that the "problem child" is the one likely to be given the most attention and space in the records.

Periodic Summaries: The Cumulative Aspects of Guidance and Monitoring

Periodic summaries give the teacher information about a child's overall progress, enabling him or her to spot trends in development and problems with learning. The long-term trends in development, those that occur through the cumulative effects of learning a series of concepts and repeated exposure to strategies of problem solving, can only appear with time. Perspectives can be further sharpened by summarizing the number and type of cognitive units and complex relations a child has mastered over, say, five periods on a separate sheet. In this way, a single chart listing the main learning developments of all children in a group can be made up, without losing the major focus on each child's progress in relation to his *own* cumulative learning.

Recordings can become tedious and meaningless unless purposes and perspectives are remembered and records demonstrate their value to the teacher. Records will serve their intended purpose if the teacher keeps in mind two sets of perspectives; first, maintaining a balance between each child's daily and long-term rates of progress and, second, relating the individual child's progress to the development of the group as a whole. Again, records are only useful when changes and new developments are the major entries; unnecessary detail and redundancy will merely make the task of charting long-term learning patterns or searching for the roots of emerging problems a major sorting task.

Diagnostic and Achievement Measures

These are designed specifically to show the amount and quality of progress at selected stages during a program. They are usually constructed to show the child's cumulative progress to a specified level, such as when he can count to four or group things in terms of short and long, but not count to five or arrange things along a scale of three sizes (big, middle-sized and little). Since most programs are sequentially designed, so a child cannot reach a more advanced stage without understanding the concepts presented in the earlier stages, these records tell exactly how far he has progressed and how far he has to go in the program.

Program achievement measures also provide the basis for calculating rates of learning (see below) but are less useful for providing the individualized picture of learning patterns and problems that only ratings and personal commentary can give. A combination of sequential, program achievement measures and individualized recording techniques is therefore desirable.

Rates of Learning

It is useful to keep track of *rates of learning* for two reasons:

(1). *Young children typically learn at faster rates in sequenced rule-learning programs as the program proceeds.* The initial period in a program is often taken up with understanding key foundation rules that underpin an area of knowledge. Once these basic rules are understood, through the child becoming familiar with their major characteristics, subsequent learning consists of the easier task of applying variations of them to other examples. For instance, in a program about furniture, once children clearly understand such rules as that chairs have seats (for sitting), tables have flat, hard surfaces (for placing objects), and beds have soft, long surfaces (for lying down), in each case they can, with increasing speed, come to recognize many examples of chairs, tables, and beds, since they have learned the basic rules for recognizing furniture. They may occasionally become temporarily confused, for example, between chairs and stools or between beds and couches, but the new distinguishing rules (that chairs but not stools have backs, and couches but not beds have backs along one long side), are quickly learned because the basic rules have given them a foundation from which to make comparisons and build on the new rule variations.

(2). *A group usually contains children who learn at different rates,* as previously mentioned in this chapter. If children begin to diverge widely from one another in their speed of learning, a teacher may have to either switch a child to another program or break up the learning group. One of these solutions may eventually be necessary in any case, but quite often detailed recording of the children's rates and styles may help a teacher to anticipate the problem. With detailed records available to look over, he can easily spot any slight tendencies for gaps between rates of learning to widen. Then, before any gaps become too wide, he can take steps to keep the gap from widening too much, like giving a slower child more examples, more play alone, or a special picture book that illustrates the program concepts vividly. Unless a child has run into special difficulties, such as upsets at home, extended absences through illness, or perhaps is really in a program too advanced for his or her abilities in this area than originally realized, these extra measures will often do the trick to help the children follow a program at close to the same pace.

The *calculation of rates of learning* may be based simply on the number of units (or complex relations) learned in any period divided by the number of sessions in the same period, similar to the method of calculation shown earlier in Figure 14–4. Thus if a little girl were to learn 17 units in 10 sessions during a later phase of a program, her rate of learning would be 1.7 units per session, compared to only .8 units per session during the beginning period of the program, if she learned only 8 units over the first 10 sessions. This method of calculation can be applied separately to each set of units, simple or complex, contained in a program, to show each child's progress in different parts and phases of a program. The teacher can then monitor in detail all types of learning, as well as the social and learning styles, and identify problems in specific areas as they begin to arise.

Not all units will be learned at the same rate, even under ideal conditions. Small and simple units, such as the features and functions of a rocking chair (curved rockers on the legs to rock on), are the elements that make up complex concepts, like furniture, which require the child to learn to both bring together and sort out the various rules that distinguish straight chairs, arm chairs, and rocking chairs from other types of furniture. Well-designed sequential learning programs necessarily take account of the fact that many simple units, such as the features (a wheel), functions (a wheel rolls) and relations between things (a wheel rolls on the floor) will be learned in the same period that is sufficient for only a very few complex interrelated rules to be learned (a wheel is attached to a car through an axle, which is attached to the car, so that the car can carry passengers; or that cars have wheels to travel on the ground and boats have smooth, hollow hulls so they can travel through the water).

Learning rates in each of the categories should thus proceed at different rates with a certain consistency, according to the complexity of the material and phase of the program. These differences among categories enable a teacher to spot learning difficulties. He can for example tell whether any slowing down or acceleration in a child's rate of learning is to be expected because she must now deal with complex concepts (slowing her down) or, having mastered some new complex concepts, is now moving to a phase where she is learning more examples involving only simple new rules (thus normally enabling her to accelerate). On the other hand, if the child slows down during an easy phase, the teacher knows there must be other causes, such as a decline in the quality of his methods or new emotional difficulties.

III. Maintaining Developmental Progression

Two of the important teaching techniques to bring about continued progress in learning are *constant review* and *flexibiltiy of approach.*

Constant Review

Repeated exposure to the same ideas while varying the approach can make the difference between thorough mastery and complex development on the one hand, and superficial familiarity and uneven development on the other. Reviewing is perhaps one of the easiest things to try when a child begins to become confused or otherwise shows problems in learning. Simply going over the same concepts using different materials, examples, methods, and play activities can often gradually lead to dawning awareness. The variations in approach will keep up the interest (continuing novelty), while also illuminating the concepts through showing them in different perspectives.

Reviewing requires attention at two levels, one for systematically covering new and recent material, and the other for going back over material presented earlier in a program. The first ensures initial and continuing mastery and must be systematically incorporated into the routines of sequential instruction. The second is in part usually built into programs through their sequential, cumulative designs; later, more complex rules are built on the earlier, simpler units and relations and thus are incorporated in the latter at later phases of a program. For example, learning rules for classifying fruit and vegetables as food (a second level in hierarchical classification) necessarily involves continued review with object concepts such as cabbage and potatoes and apples and bananas in order to group them as vegetables and fruits. If new examples of object concepts were to be introduced, on the other hand, such as kohlrabi and papaya, review of the earlier examples may also be desirable, to prevent forgetting and enlarge the child's cognitive range of the classification rule. To a certain extent, detailed information and skills need to be reviewed and retained only to the extent they are useful for activity, as for example in the case of math or language skills, but well-grounded competence in an area of knowledge nevertheless requires considerable cumulative review.

Fortunately, once learned, a certain amount of knowledge and skills are more or less regularly reviewed in the activities of every day life. Thus many of the content details learned early in a program can be forgotten except as they are intrinsic to the later rules and tasks encountered.

Reviewing may also be built into sequential learning programs in the form of alternative sequences for children of different ability levels, as we have discussed earlier. The slower developing programs or those with extra branches for less skilled children differ mainly in the variety of examples they include along the way. Basically, this means more review of the rules, as in showing a child meadows of different sizes (through a trip and pictures) to add to the examples of area measurement (squares of paper, boards) he has already been shown.

Flexibility in Guidance

If a child fails to progress, a teacher may assume that both the teaching methods and her own attitudes are partly at fault. Whatever tensions, insecurities, and mental gaps a child brings to the learning situation from home or elsewhere, changes in teaching technique and emotional atmosphere will nearly always encourage him to further effort and help him to understand. A self-analytic and flexible approach will prevent a teacher from falling into the psychological trap of simply blaming the child, and encourage the teacher to analyze and search for sources of difficulty in more complex and productive ways. Learning is a complex process, the product of many things, in which the attitude of the child ("She just doesn't want to learn") is only one of many factors. Others are the match of the material to the child's level, the style of the teacher, moods, attitudes of other children, cognitive learning styles (analytic—does he pay attention to detail? integrative—does he look for relations between things?) and so on. Flexibility and readiness to vary method and style must inevitably fall largely upon the adult, who has obvious advantages in general knowledge and personality development, in specific teaching skills, and in social control, especially with younger children. Where one approach doesn't work another probably will.

Teachers are also people with their own tensions, mood swings, personal preferences, and styles, which work differently with different children and types of learning. One teacher's characteristic quickness and sense of fun is probably great with most children, but an occasional timid or highly serious child may find the style threatening. Another teacher's easy and flexible approach may be equally successful with all except an active, demanding child who wants more challenge. Many teaching problems can be solved by keeping this fact in mind, always automatically assuming the teacher's styles and methods may be contributing sources of difficulty. One's own actions and attitudes should be central to any analysis of the learning environment and experimentation with methods.

One method of analyzing the teacher's approach as a source of difficulty for the children's learning is to make behavioral ratings on a teacher during a few guided learning sessions. A simple set of ratings for assessing a teacher's effectiveness in three categories important for learning, namely, cognitive stimulation, use of language, and socio-emotional approach is shown in Figure 14–8. Each of the characteristics is described in terms of a teacher's actual way of doing things over the course of a typical five to twenty minute session. These ratings can of course be used at any time as a monitoring technique to evaluate teaching problems or to note changes. They are intended to help teachers see their own strengths and weaknesses to promote change, not to make invidious comparisons between colleagues. Ratings on videotaped performances, again, permit the teacher himself to make and discuss his own ratings with others.

FIGURE 14–8. Teacher observation record of quality of a guided play session

---

Name of Adult_____Date of Observation_____

Names of Children_____Group_____

Cognitive Stimulation

1. Teaches general rules about concepts (not procedures or rote learning) through varieties of examples.   *Rating*_____

2. Matches complexity of play material with the level of understanding of children.
                                                      *Rating*_____

3. Provides variety of play material.
                                                      *Rating*_____

4. Uses variety of methods of play (creative and imaginative in playing with children).
                                                      *Rating*_____

5. Regularly demonstrates learning tasks and concepts in terms of specific features and relationships (e.g., parts of a triangle).
                                                      *Rating*_____

6. Uses dramatic approach, role-playing during play sessions.   *Rating*_____

Remarks: _____
_____

Language Stimulation

1. Matches complexity of language with level of understanding.
                                                      *Rating*_____

2. Uses variety in language expression.
                                                      *Rating*_____

3. Uses language concretely (repeats nouns and concrete verbs frequently, labels objects, etc.) and avoids using abstract terms.   *Rating*_____

4. Times language description to the specifics of demonstration activities.   *Rating*_____

Remarks: _____
_____

Socioemotional Approach

1. Interacts: maintains a good balance between own and child's initiative.   *Rating*_____

2. Maintains a friendly and cooperative atmosphere (encourages children to take turns, waits for each child in the group).   *Rating*_____

3. Praises children with words and gestures according to need.   *Rating*_____

4. Demonstrates enthusiasm in play sessions.
                                                      *Rating*_____

5. Demonstrates perceptiveness toward children's moods and styles (e.g., depressed, withdrawn, tense).   *Rating*_____

Remarks: _____
_____

Rating Guide: 7. Extremely like.   3. Moderately unlike.
                  6. Much like.   2. Much unlike.
                  5. Moderately like.   1. Not at all like.
                  4. Neutral: sometimes like, sometimes unlike.

Flexibility of approach means more than flexibility of style and method. The children themselves may need to be moved around to different learning groups and programs from time to time because of changes in their rates of learning or intent, as described earlier. Where two or three teachers work closely together as a team, planning together and consulting one another frequently, it is easier to observe such emerging changes in the children and shift the children around as needed for short and long periods.

When children's progress is watched closely, it is usually apparent early in a program that some children are progressing more rapidly than others. Sometimes this may appear, not as differences in progress but as restlessness and conflict. Part of the difficulty may be that the teacher is presenting the things to be learned to the children only *as a group*. Unless both fast and slow children are allowed to progress according to their ability, the teacher is, in effect, forcing them all to adapt to an average, common rate.

Learning in common at average rates can, however, be a useful approach for certain purposes and periods of learning, particularly when groups are small and differences between backgrounds and abilities are not great. There are programs generally designed to provide a multiplicity of examples and small tasks to illustrate the rules for each of a series of broad cognitive concepts. Each of these broad concepts is in effect a general level that the child goes through as a stage. Because of the number of details to be grasped at any level or stage, some children can benefit from experimenting with a greater variety of examples, others from learning a greater number of variations in the general rule for that level (size applied to vertical as well as horizontal surface areas) and others will master the general rule of the level more thoroughly if they experiment more slowly with a limited set of examples and materials, picking up more rule variations later on. By arranging for children to explore the various tasks at each level in these different ways, as described earlier in this chapter and in Chapter 13, all members of a group can work in this manner for some time at about the same *general* level of ability and stage of a program. Each child or subgroup can work independently part of the time and come together as a larger group to work out a particular example all need to know or simply to review material in play activities for the fun of learning in a group. These variations in the particulars of learning make it feasible to combine the psychological advantages of teaching in small group with task adaptation to individual abilities.

Bibliography for Part IV

Almy, M. *Ways of studying children.* New York: Horace Mann Lincoln Institute of School Experimentation, 1959.

Berlyne, D. E. *Conflict, arousal and curiosity.* New York: McGraw-Hill, 1960.

Blank, M. A methodology for fostering abstract thinking in deprived children. In A. J. Biemiller (Ed.), *Problems in the teaching of young children.* Toronto: Ontario Institute for Studies in Education, *Monograph Series* No. 9, 1–26, 1970.

Blank, M., Rose, S., & Berlin, L. *The language of learning: The preschool years.* New York: Grune & Stratton, 1978.

Campbell, D. T., & Gruen, W. Progression from simple to complex as a molar law of learning. *Journal of Genetic Psychology,* 1958, *59,* 237–244.

Church, J. Techniques for the differential study of cognition in early childhood. In J. Hellmuth (Ed.), *Cognitive studies,* (Vol. 1). New York: Brunner/Mazel, 1970, 1–23.

Day, M. C., & Parker, R. K. (Eds.). *The preschool in action* (2nd ed.). Boston: Allyn and Bacon, 1977.

Drabman, R. S., & Hammer, D. Using incentives in early childhood education. In H. L. Hom, Jr., & P. A. Robinson (Eds.), *Psychological processes in early education.* New York: Academic Press, 1977, 133–156.

Elkind, D. *Child development and education: A Piagetian perspective.* New York: Oxford University Press, 1976.

Elkind, D. Problem solving in infancy and early childhood. In J. Eliot (Ed.), *Human development and cognitive processes.* New York: Holt, Rinehart, and Winston, 1971, 518–525.

Evans, E. D. *Contemporary influences in early childhood education* (2nd ed.). New York: Holt, Rinehart, and Winston, 1975.

Fiske, D. W., & Maddi, S. R. *The functions of varied experience.* Homewood, Ill.: The Dorsey Press, 1961.

Fowler, W. Concept learning in early childhood. *Young children,* 1965, *21,* 81–91.

Fowler, W. The effect of early stimulation in the emergence of cognitive processes. In R. D. Hess & R. M. Bear (Eds.), *Early education.* Chicago: Aldine, 1968, 9–36.

Fowler, W. The effect of early stimulation: The problem of focus in developmental stimulation. *Merrill-Palmer Quarterly,* 1969, *15,* 157–170.

Fowler, W. A developmental learning strategy for early reading in a laboratory nursery school. *Interchange,* 1971, *2,* 106–125.

Fowler, W. On the value of both play and structure in early education. *Young children,* 1971, *27,* 24–36.

Fowler, W., & Leithwood, K. Cognition and movement: Theoretical, pedagogical and measurement considerations. *Perceptual and motor skills,* 1971, *32,* 523–532.

Freeberg, N. E., & Payne, D. T. Parental influence on cognitive development in early childhood. *Child development,* 1967, *38,* 65–87.

Friedlander, B. Z., Sterritt, G. M., & Kirk, G. E. *Assessment and intervention,* Vol. 3: *Exceptional infant.* New York: Brunner/Mazel, 1975.

Gordon, I. J. An instructional theory approach to the analysis of selected early childhood programs. In I. J. Gordon (Ed.), *Early childhood education, Yearbook of the National Society for the Study of Education,* Part 2, 1972, *71,* 203–228.

Harvey, O. J. *Experience, structure and adaptability.* New York: Springer, 1966.

Havighurst, R. J. *Developmental tasks and education* (2nd ed.). New York: Longmans, Green, 1952.

Hertzig, M. E. Aspects of cognition and cognitive style in young children of differing social and ethnic backgrounds. In J. Hellmuth (Ed.), *Cognitive studies,* Vol. 2: *Deficits in cognition.* New York: Brunner/Mazel, 1971, 149–170.

Hess, R. D., & Croft, D. *Teachers of young children* (2nd ed.). Boston: Houghton Mifflin, 1975.

Hess, R. D., & Croft, D. *An activities handbook for teachers of young children* (2nd ed.). Boston: Houghton Mifflin, 1975.

Howe, M. *Learning in infants and young children.* Stanford, Calif.: Stanford University Press, 1975.

Hunt, J. McV. The psychological basis for using pre-school enrichment as an antidote for cultural deprivation. In J. Hellmuth (Ed.), *Disadvantaged child* (Vol. 1). New York: Brunner/Mazel, 1967, 255–299.

Hunt, J. McV. The epigenesis of intrinsic motivation and the fostering of early cognitive development. In J. McV. Hunt (Ed.), *The challenge of incompetence and poverty*. Urbana, Ill.: University of Illinois Press, 1969, 94–111.

Hunt, J. McV., Mohandessi, K., Ghodesi, M., & Akiyama, M. The psychological development of orphanage-reared infants: Interventions with outcomes (Tehran). *Genetic Psychology Monographs*, 1976, *94*, 177–226.

Inhelder, R., & Matalon, B. The study of problem solving and thinking. In P. H. Mussen (Ed.), *Handbook of research methods in child development*. New York: John Wiley & Sons, 1960, 421–455.

Kamii, C., & De Vries, R. *Piaget, children, and number*. Englewood Cliffs, N.J.: Prentice-Hall, 1976.

Kamii, C., & De Vries, R. *Physical knowledge in preschool education: Implications of Piaget's theory*. Englewood Cliffs, N.J.: Prentice-Hall, 1978.

Knobloch, H., & Pasamanick, B. (Eds.). *Gesell and Amatruda's developmental diagnosis: The evaluation and management of normal and abnormal neuropsychologic development in infancy and early childhood* (3rd ed.). Hagerstown, Maryland: Medical Department, Harper & Row, 1974.

Kogan, N. *Cognitive styles in infancy and early childhood*. New York: John Wiley & Sons, 1976.

Kohlberg, L. Early education: A cognitive-development view. In S. Chess & A. Thomas (Eds.), *Annual progress in child psychiatry and child development*. New York: Brunner/Mazel, 1969, 72–124.

Lambie, D. Z., Bond, J. T., & Weikart, D. P. *Home teaching with mothers and infants: The Ypsilanti-Carnegie infant education project—an experiment* (Monograph 4). Ypsilanti, Mich.: High/Scope Foundation, 1974.

Leithwood, K. A., & Fowler, W. Complex motor learning in four-year-olds. *Child development*, 1971, *42*, 781–792.

Lewis, M. (Ed.). *Origins of intelligence: Infancy and early childhood*. New York: Plenum, 1976.

McCarthy, D. Language development in children. In L. Carmichael (Ed.), *Manual of child psychology* (2nd ed.). New York: John Wiley & Sons, 1954, 492–630.

McGraw, M. B. *Growth: A study of Johnny and Jimmy*. New York: Appleton-Century, 1935.

Montessori, M. *The absorbent mind*. New York: Holt, Rinehart, and Winston, 1967.

Montessori, M. *From childhood to adolescence*. New York: Schocken Books, 1976.

Mueller, E., Bleier, M., Krakow, J., Hegedus, K., & Cournoyer, P. The development of peer verbal interaction among two-year-old boys. *Child development*, 1977, *48*, 284–287.

Painter, G. *Teach your baby*. New York: Simon and Schuster, 1971.

Palmer, F. H. Has compensatory education failed? In M. L. Hanes, I. J. Gordon and W. F. Breivogel (Eds.), *Update: The first ten years of life*. Gainesville, Fla.: Division of Continuing Education, University of Florida, 1976.

Pitcher, E. C., Lasher, M. C., Feinberg, S. C., & Brown, L. A. *Helping young children learn* (2nd ed.). Columbus, Ohio: Charles E. Merrill, 1974.

Ryan, T. J., & Moffitt, A. R. Evaluation of preschool programs. *Canadian psychologist*, 1974, *15*, 205–219.

Schickedanz, J. A., Stewart, I. S., & White D. *Strategies for teaching young children*. Englewood Cliffs, N.J.: Prentice-Hall, 1977.

Sigel, I. E. The development of classificatory skills in young children: A training program. In W. W. Hartup (Ed.), *The young child: Review of research* (Vol. 2). Washington, D.C.: National Association for the Education of Young Children, 1972, 92–111.

Soar, R. S., & Soar, R. M. An empirical analysis of selected follow-through programs: An example of a process approach to evaluation. In I. J. Gordon (Ed.), *Early childhood education, Yearbook of the National Society for the Study in Education*, 1972, *71*, Part II, 229–260.

Spodek, B. *Teaching in the early years* (2nd ed.). Englewood Cliffs, N.J.: Prentice-Hall, 1978.

Uzgiris, I. C., & Hunt, J. McV. *Assessment in infancy: Ordinal scales of psychological development*. Urbana, Ill.: University of Illinois Press, 1975.

Vance, R. *Teaching the prekindergarten child: Instructional design and curriculum*. Monterey, Calif.: Brooks/Cole, 1973.

Weikart, D. P., Rogers, L., Adcock, C., & McClelland, D. *The cognitively oriented curriculum: A framework for preschool teachers*. Washington, D.C.: National Association for the Education of Young Children, 1971.

White, B. L., Held, R., & Castle, P. *Experience in early human development: I. Observations on the development of visually directed reaching; II. Plasticity of sensorimotor development in the human infant. In J. Hellmuth (Ed.), *The exceptional infant* (Vol. 1). New York: Brunner/Mazel, 1967, 267–334.

White, R. W. Motivation reconsidered: The concept of competence. *Psychological review,* 1959, *66,* 297–333.

Wohlwill, J. T. The place of structural experience in early cognitive development. *Interchange,* 1970, *1,* 1–12.

Zigler, E., & Butterfield, E. C. Motivational aspects of changes in IQ test performance of culturally deprived nursery school children. *Child development,* 1968, *39,* 1–14.

APPENDIX

The Environment, the Child, and Principles of Early Care and Education

The principles of early care and education discussed in Appendix A are an elaboration of those outlined in Chapter 1. Principles for rearing children necessarily arise from two sources, the nature of the environment and the nature of children. What and how we teach children must be directed toward guiding them to understand and get along in both the physical and social worlds in order to serve their needs and enjoy life. But how we educate and care for them is also necessarily based on the biology of their development, starting with what they know and can do at birth and what and how they can learn to know and do during development. The organization of these principles thus follows essentially the same form presented in the outline in Chapter 1. There are ten conditions that define ten major characteristics of the world or environment which have basic implications for human development. Each of the ten conditions is described separately in conjunction with the child's potential competence regarding that environmental condition during early development. Several teaching-caregiving principles applicable to realizing the child's potential for that condition are then listed and discussed in detail. For clarity the discussion of principles usually includes a few suggested methods and illustrations of how the principles can be applied.

Condition I: Resources

Nature of the World (The Environment)

The environment is made up of material things that provide the physical basis for life. People, plants, and animals use and relate to the material resources and one another, in complicated ways, to survive.

People use minerals and other natural resources and cultivate plants and animals for many purposes. To supply basic needs they use such products as vegetables, meat, and dairy products for food; cotton, wool, and leather for clothes; wood, coal, and oil for heat and light; and wood, stone, and metal for housing. They use these same and many other resources to make tools, machinery, books, television, and other complex structures to expand control over the environment, leading to

363

1. expansion of societies in size and complexity
2. increase in the size of populations supported
3. multiplication of social needs and desires, including consumer needs, aesthetic tastes and intellectual ideas
4. constant increase in the complexity and problems of living

Survival, adaptation, and expansion of environmental control all require physical energy and increasingly complicated perceptual-motor and intellectual skills to obtain and cultivate the resources.

Characteristics of the Child During Early Development

At birth the infant is entirely undeveloped, physically and mentally, and totally dependent on others for fulfillment of such basic needs as hunger, thirst, warmth, and even of movement. Most babies are basically healthy and reasonably adaptable to differences in the way they are cared for (differences and irregularities in feeding schedules, room temperature levels, or type and amount of handling). Infants are, however, essentially weak, limited in understanding, and reflexive and poorly coordinated in using their bodies and their senses (seeing, touching, etc.).

Over the course of early development children can grow in strength and health and learn many fundamental skills needed to cope in meeting their own needs from the environment. By the time they reach school age, they can coordinate the use of their vision and other senses with the fine and large movements of their body systems with skill enough to take care of personal needs (dressing, toileting, moving about the neighborhood freely, and performing similar routine tasks.)

Teaching and Caregiving Principles

1. Providing care adequate to fulfill the child's basic developing needs in a cycle of daily routines.

The care needs to be adequate in both quality and quantity. The child needs, for example, to eat well and often enough, and needs nutritious food to foster growth and health. There should also be a balance between the caregiver's work demands to accomplish the caregiving tasks with ease and dispatch and provide personalized care to match the child's feelings (such as for independence) and accustomed ways (fast or slow). A cycle of daily routines, in which the time, place, and manner of caring for children is established with regularity and flexibility will contribute toward adapting the child to the care goals, yet maintaining some individualization of the care.

The form and scope of care naturally changes as the child develops. Early in infancy feeding an infant, moving her around, preparing her for sleep, and dressing, bathing and changing her, take up a good part of the infant's waking day. As she develops, the frequency of eating, changing, and related activities diminishes, the intervals for sleep and active play become longer and the type of attention demanded of the caregiver shifts more and more from direct physical care (feeding from a bottle) to general guidance and supervision (showing how to cut meat, providing an example, and maintaining order with preschoolers at a lunch table).

2. Guiding infants and young children in learning concepts and skills needed to cope with the environment autonomously (independently).

If children are not to remain dependent on others for care, they must be given the opportunity to learn how to care for themselves. To do this, they will need to learn many perceptual-motor and related cognitive skills. Daily encounters between caregiver and child in various routines provide repeated opportunities to guide children's learning. Eating and other basic care routines provide opportunities for teaching concepts and skills of caring for oneself, generally useful sensory and motor control, and other general concepts, such as spatial relations (teaching how things fit together as a part of dressing). Special learning projects are useful for helping children to learn other important concepts and skills (number concepts or roller skating).

3. Providing opportunities for exercise to develop strength and health.

The value of moving the whole body system vigorously every day is well known. Exercise develops and strengthens the muscles used, which is especially important in the growing child to promote development. Moving the whole body rapidly and long enough to cause the blood to flow rapidly and to get out of breath at least once a day develops a strong heart and lungs and good general health. Skills alone cannot substitute for total bodily strength and health.

The playground and indoor gross motor play area are obviously the places to encourage exercise for the whole body system. The availability of age-appropriate playground equipment and active play periods is all that is needed for many children to run, ride, and climb around actively for at least some part of each day. Many others, however, because they have been overprotected, are in poor health, or have been too often encouraged to play quietly, don't enjoy or know how to play actively. These children need more encouragement and sometimes special guidance in how to move independently in various activities with speed, strength, and confidence. Even before the preschooler is capable of complicated gymnastic or running activity, toddlers will benefit from encouragement to walk rapidly or ride a spring rocking horse vigorously, and crawlers from occasional encouragement to crawl across the floor quickly.

4. Providing experience in self-directed perceptual motor play to develop mastery and autonomy (independence) in a broad variety of fine and gross motor activities.

Guidance teaches children many specialized concepts and techniques they might otherwise never discover, but play on their own provides opportunities to practice skills and develop strength that insure mastery, autonomy, and enjoyment in activities. Play with other children provides further sources of interest and stimulation to practice old skills and learn new ones. Provide playtimes, play areas, and materials suitable for both small muscle control engaging the fingers and hands (puzzles, pegboards) and large muscle control engaging the whole body (as described above). The greater the variety of materials provided and play encouraged, the more skills are extended to other areas and the more the child's abilities become generalized. This extension of skill in turn develops greater autonomy in the child to solve problems on his or her own.

Condition II: Social Life

Nature of the World (The Environment)

Human survival depends mainly on two things, work to obtain resources from the environment to supply basic needs and the organization of activity in social groups to pool the work load. Work requires the persistence of effort of autonomous and competent individuals. Social organization is dependent on cooperation between persons to enable them to work and play together amicably. People are therefore social beings who live and work together primarily for purposes of adapting to their environment in more efficient ways. Living in groups to organize activity has brought about the need for cooperation and regulation of work, family life, and other social activities. Different groups of people have over many generations worked out their own ways of adaptation, work, and social life which they pass down in their particular culture from one generation to the next.

Living in social groups has also led to the growth of many additional needs, not directly related to problems of human survival or environmental adaptation, but nevertheless very important to social life. These social needs appears in specialized forms of social activity, such as social rituals (eating meals together), play, recreation, art, literature, and music, which each culture has developed in its own forms.

The development of children to become autonomous (independent) but cooperating members of their society is in large part dependent on the type of social rules, tasks, and relations and the quality of socioemotional experience provided during early life. This process of socialization takes place through adult-guided and peer experiences in different types of:

1. Work tasks and roles
   a. For the individual
   b. For group practices
   c. For family and sex roles
2. Social rules and achievement standards (morality, ethics and social values).
3. Play, recreation, sports and aesthetic activity.

Characteristics of the Child During Early Development

Infants are as dependent on others to supply their emotional needs and for social development as they are for their basic physical needs and mental development. Initially the emotional patterns of babies are simple and immediate, with little social awareness or feeling. They respond mainly with distress or pleasure in reaction to frustration or satisfaction of hunger, comfort, and other primary needs, the intensity of feeling depending on the degree of frustration or satisfaction.

Socialization begins immediately, however. The way in which the infant is handled emotionally and the types of tasks and rules he is taught for doing things, following the practices of his culture, soon begin to shape how the infant feels and reacts to things in more complicated ways. He develops feelings and expectations for the ways he wants to be treated and for ways of doing things. For example, he comes to expect his bottle at certain times, his diapers changed when he is wet, and to be cuddled in a certain way and may show anger or irritation when rituals are varied. By six months or so he often exhibits preferences for who cares for him and may become anxious or uncertain when his closest caregivers leave the room. He is becoming socialized. Gradually, through the various care routines and other social learning activities with adults and other children, the child will learn more and more complicated emotions (e.g., jealousy, intellectual curiosity, desire to share) and rules for independent striving, cooperation, and competing in work, play and various sport and art activites. The form and extent of this social learning and emotional development will depend on the type and quality of his socialization.

Teaching—
Caregiving
Principles

1. Providing emotionally supportive care and guidance
to develop positive self concepts and feelings towards
others.

The quality of later emotional life is rooted in how the child is cared for emotionally from earliest infancy. Positive feelings, trust, and respect toward himself (self esteem) and toward others, as well as the capacity for friendships and love, grow from the way the infant and child are treated in everyday life, when caregivers are sensitive to each child's feelings and personality style; are open, warm and friendly, communicating trust and respect; provide affection and praise, through gesture and words freely and spontaneously; recognize effort as much as success in doing things; avoid criticism and hostility in enforcing rules; and show the child how to do something more often than criticising errors.

2. Fostering positive attitudes and ways of relating
among children (peer relations) and between children
and adults (authority relations) in play, care routines,
learning, and work tasks, maintaining a balance
between each child's autonomy (independence) and
cooperation between people.

A. Autonomy (Independence).   In every activity, exercise care so that the child is actively involved rather than passively watching, waiting, or automatically following the lead of the adult or another child. From earliest infancy care and instruction can be presented so that the child is given opportunities for making decisions and taking responsibility for performing parts of the daily routines and actively experimenting with examples in play learning sessions, according to his or her abilities. In an eating routine, for example, the ten month old can be encouraged to experiment in using a spoon, not simply be fed. Similarly, in a shape learning project, the child needs opportunities to try to match triangles and other shapes himself, not merely watch the teacher demonstrate all the examples. Development depends on expanding the child's awareness of his own responsibility for care and learning, through constantly increasing the amount of his autonomy with development.

B. Cooperation. Opportunities for children to exercise initiative and autonomy should ordinarily be presented in a *cooperative framework*. This takes two basic forms:

(1) Leader-follower (authority) relations. The dependency of children in early life means that much of the child's activity must be planned, prepared for, and regulated by adults. Necessarily the relationship involves cooperation between unequals. But the way in which the adult exercises control to furnish care can still be *interactive*, encouraging initiative in the child as well as in the adult. One way the child learns to cooperate is through having a caregiver lead the child's initiatives into useful contributions toward accomplishing the task at hand. In the examples above, teaching cooperation in feeding or learning shapes might be accomplished by the caregiver and child *taking turns* in using the spoon (or each using a spoon) and matching shapes, *not* having the caregiver or the child do all the feeding or all the matching—that is of course until the child has acquired sufficient skill and sense of responsibility to do the job alone. Good teaching and caring for young children steers a course between doing it all for the child and letting him do it all, by encouraging his independent efforts but channeling them into constructive actions to get the task done.

(2) Peer relations. Children quite naturally interact in play and other activities. The problem for caregivers is to insure that this natural experimentation proceeds constructively by:

a. Providing adequate play space and a variety of toys.
b. Guiding children to constructively work and play together by suggesting roles and demonstrating actions each child can perform to share in both play and work tasks (working on each end of a jigsaw puzzle, taking turns matching colors, one child sweeping while another holds the dustpan).
c. Ensuring that each child gets his turns in leadership roles and that no child dominates or falls into passive roles (just watching, taking directions, or copying) too often.

3. Teaching children to work alone and in groups to develop good work attitudes and competence.

Children learn work skills and attitudes through regular experience in performing *useful tasks* contributing to the daily life of their social groups at home, day care, and elsewhere. They need to learn to take routine *individual responsibil-*

ity for their own personal care in appropriate social ways of eating, dressing, toileting, etc., and in such other assigned individual tasks as cleaning up a private play area and carrying messages. They also need to learn to work cooperatively with other children and adults in groups to develop *social responsibility* in sharing tasks which benefit an entire group, and when the work load is too large for a single person (preparing a meal or a playroom activity, cleaning up).

To develop strong, positive attitudes toward work and the ability to persist in striving to overcome obstacles, work tasks will need to be:

a. Regularly scheduled routines of caring for personal needs and work activities for children in groups in day care, school, or the family.
b. Guided with interest in and respect for both the worth of the task and the effort of the child.
c. Supervised according to the child's competence and sense of responsibility.
d. As often as possible as part of cooperative activity in a group, in which all children take some definite part in planning, working, and evaluting according to their developmental level.
e. Graded in difficulty according to the child's competence and work habits.

4. Encouraging achievement standards in activity and fair play in social relations through fostering care for work and play and consideration for others.

Standards are a matter of concern for *quality,* whether for well-made materials, well-performed tasks or for consideration toward others in relationships. Children will come to care about standards if they are:

a. Shown (by example and guidance) how to respect and care for their own things and other people's things.
b. Shown the details of things well made (e.g., comparing the features of a well designed toy tow truck or goat with stamped out plastic ones).
c. Shown respect when they are guided in play, building things and relating to others; shown as much interest in their *effort* to do well as in the quality of the result.
d. Talked with about quality (as language develops), helping them to evaluate their own performance (did he take turns with the swing?).

5. Fostering awareness and appreciation of differences between cultures, ethnic groups, families, sexes, and individuals. Avoiding cultural, ethnic, sexual, and individual stereotyping.

The importance of developing sensitivity to group and individual differences is difficult to overestimate. The world is made up of many people and groups who differ in all sorts of ways yet need to live in harmony. They differ both individually and as groups in what they eat, the clothes they wear, their facial characteristics, skin, hair and eye color, how tall or fat they are, what they like and do, and of course boys and girls differ physically. Background and personality differences in any day care center or school are substantial, particularly in cosmopolitan urban areas, and the separate needs and interests of boys and girls can never be ignored. Like most developmental goals, learning to value differences begins early in life. Awareness of cultural and other differences comes about best through experiencing differences first hand. The place to start, then, is with the differences found between families and their children enrolled in the day care center. Some of the ways that will contribute to valuing differences include:

a. Making sure that references to differences in characteristics between individuals and groups are generally presented as interesting, alternative ways of doing things. Avoid implying that one individual is better or worse than another.

b. Directing criticism at the specific behaviors of individual children ("he hit someone"), not on the weaknesses of "character" of the whole child ("he's an aggressive child"), nor on the behavior as characteristic of a social group (the fact that he is a boy, an Italian, or that his family always does things that way). Even if certain negative trends are sometimes characteristic, centering attention on them furthers negative social images (stereotypes) at the expense of valuing positive features in more rounded, real-life pictures of individuals, who are always complicated.

c. Developing projects on cultural learning to support parents in fostering children's awareness and pride in cultural identity. Periodic *theme* projects (see Chapter 7) on different cultures represented in the center will give children both knowledge and a sense of worth of their own and other cultural groups. Home visits by the day care staff will sharpen staff awareness and interest, reinforce children's learning, and involve parents, encouraging closer relations with the day care staff and cultural and other contributions to the program.

d. Promoting varied play for both girls and boys to ensure rounded development for all. Avoid sexual stereotyping, as for example involving girls in playing mainly with dolls, in domestic play, and in art activities while providing boys with mechanical and construction toys, problem solving materials, and rough physical play.

6. Developing aesthetic interests, skills and values (see
also Condition VIII, Abstraction)

Concepts of beauty and opportunities for personal, creative expression are greatly undermined in contemporary society by the control of popular culture by commercial organization through the mass media, especially television, radio and the movies. It becomes particularly important accordingly to build creative activities into the daily life of the day care centers and schools to establish strong artistic interests in early childhood. Among things to emphasize are:

    a. Opportunities for play with a variety of creative materials, such as drawing, painting, collage, clay, and blocks and other construction materials.

    b. Extensive and varied musical and dance experiences through listening to good classical, folk, jazz, and other records (not just as background music), live performances, and rhythm and dance activities.

    c. Plenty of poetry reading and recitation, and story reading and telling activities, involving children in poetry recitation and story telling as they move into the preschool period.

    d. Regular projects in which specific aesthetic areas are explored systematically in detail over a series of sessions (poetry reading and rhyming play; drawing animals or fruit, using real examples; listening to and talking about a particular record, such as "Peter and the Wolf" by Prokofiev).

    e. Working with parents to encourage aesthetic activities for children in the home, and utilizing parent skills and interests where available (inviting a parent who plays an instrument, tells stories, draws, or makes things to perform or work with the children).

    f. Encouraging specialized appreciation or skills (drawing or music) by looking for signs of repeated interest in a particular activity and providing special guidance and opportunities for development (including preliminary instruction in playing an instrument when parent interest and background is strong). (See Condition X, Quantity).

Condition III: Concreteness

Nature of the World

The environment is real and concrete, made up of all kinds of materials in space, which have a variety of properties, such as color, form, texture, and state (liquid, solid and gaseous). Even live animals and plants have a material basis (bodies, trunks, leaves, etc.). Movement and other processes of change similarly involve alterations in physical characteristics of things (movement involves shifting the position of something and freezing involves changing water to ice).

Characteristics of the Child During Early Development

Young children learn primarily by direct experience with the surface characteristics of the material world through their senses (vision, hearing, touch, smell, taste, and balance) and their own movements. Starting with no knowledge, infants must first learn all about the surface features of the environment by experiencing them directly before they can develop an organized picture of how things work. They respond to the physical properties of color, form, temperature, movement, etc., through seeing and doing things (using sensory and motor processes) through which they gradually build up a detailed familiarity with what can be seen and done in the environment. Only as language and more abstract mental strategies are acquired can children begin to learn and organize knowledge more abstractly.

Teaching-
Caregiving
Principles

1. Providing extensive sensory and motor experience
with materials to develop direct knowledge of the nature
of things.

Children need to be presented objects and activities that strike their vision, hearing and other senses in order to learn all the surface qualities of the environment. They need:

a. Experience with objects of all kinds to learn about shape, color, pattern, movement, space and other visible characteristics.
b. Experience with different types and intensities of light, sound, smell, taste, texture, weight, solidity, and other environmental characteristics.
c. Initially to be moved around physically or have different materials brought to them until they become mobile, but in any case to be taken to or have materials placed where they can have access to them throughout early childhood. Children's limited knowledge will not lead them to the necessary experiences without adults arranging for them.

2. Providing guidance and experience in actively
exploring and manipulating materials to develop
sensorimotor coding skills and problem solving
strategies to cope directly with the environment.

It is not enough to make materials available to infants to learn about environmental characteristics. They must also learn effective ways of exploring and using them in order to understand and cope with the environment in concrete terms. They need:

a. Many small objects with different characteristics that can be actively explored and easily handled.
b. Different lights, sounds, melodies, textures, etc., made available in forms that they can easily respond to and explore without fear or injury. For example, sounds should not be too loud or sudden, nor lights too bright, sudden, or quickly flashing, until they become used to them. Things to taste or smell should not be unpleasant (too bitter, burning, acid, salty or sweet) and, of course, not poisonous.
c. The environment arranged to make access easy and the various objects, sounds, tastes, and other environmental stimuli frequently placed close at hand, within easy reach of their hands, eyes and other senses, as appropriate and according to age. Things to taste will need to be offered in containers in liquid or at least soluble form (that is, one that will dissolve in the mouth). As they develop, children can be encouraged to seek different materials on their own.
d. Guidance and play experience with many different and gradually more complex sensorimotor tasks to develop perceptual and action coding and problem solving strategies. Children need tasks that teach them to work senses and actions together (to touch what they see and look for what they hear). They will need other tasks to teach them to follow things that

move and search for disappearing objects. They will need still others that encourage them to use and coordinate their hands, bodies and other objects as tools to get and do things in increasingly complicated ways (to ride tricycles, load and pull wagons, draw with crayons, etc.).

Condition IV: Regularity

Nature of the World (The Environment)

There are many underlying regularities in the physical world, seldom directly visible under the frequent surface clutter of shapes, colors, and materials in the concrete physical environment; for example, objects have relative stability, ordinarily for long periods. They continue to exist whether we can see them or not.

Similarities

Regularities are determined first by similarities in some characteristics between objects and events, regardless of how they are separated in space or time or how they may differ in other respects. For example, two balls may both be round, though located in different places; and one can be a large, red rubber ball and the other a small, white golf ball. Stirring cake batter is also similar to stirring water, though done in different containers, with different substances, at different speeds, and can be done in opposite directions. Things similar in all respects are identical, though even identical objects usually differ in small, almost invisible ways (specks on "identical" blocks). Among the characteristics in which things may be similar are features (color, shape, and content characteristics, such as having a nose or a wheel, etc.), state (gas, liquid, solid), type of material (wood, metal), dimensions (size, number), functions (stir, sweep), and relations of cause and effect (push, pull).

Spatial arrangements (Patterns)

Regularities become visible in proportion as the important characteristics of objects are designed or arranged to stand out in terms of such patterns of organization and continuity as:

1. Their *figure-ground* relations (how things stand out against their background).
2. How they are *clustered* or grouped (one set of marbles bunched together, while others are scattered).
3. How they *stick out* or protrude (an angle or sharp point).
4. How objects or patterns *repeat* themselves (parallel lines).

Organization

Regularities also arise through how things are formed into complex structures (building), tools (pencils, machines), networks (pond environments), systems (factory systems) and many different levels of abstract classes, which form ladders of generalization, such as that in Figure A–1.

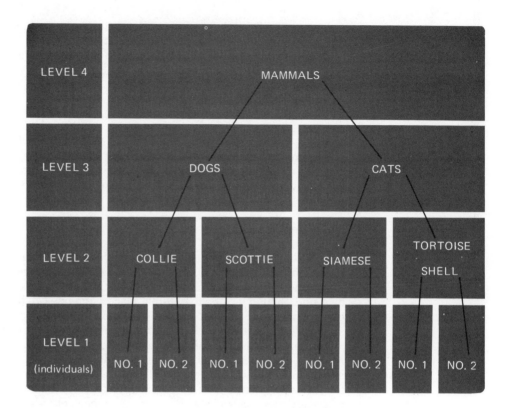

FIGURE A-1

Objects may be grouped in different ways to make alternative combinations of classes with different numbers of levels. In Figure A–1, dogs and cats, along with horses, deer and other four legged animals may be classed as quadrupeds, while humans and chimpanzees are bipeds with two feet; or the animals might be grouped simply by size or weight.

Characteristics of the Child During Early Development

At birth, infants have no objective knowledge of environmental regularity. They can see individual figure-ground relations, forms, colors, and movements, and can hear differences between sounds, but they know little about how these all relate in regular patterns. Having no experience with repeated events and similarities, infants have no idea of patterns, no memory, and no understanding that objects have a continuous existence (object identity). Reappearance of the same object is a new event.

The child's knowledge of regularities and the development of memory builds up during early development essentially through repetition. Repeated experience with the same people and objects that regularly disappear and reappear establishes the idea of the permanence of objects, enabling a little girl to reorganize and remember objects as familiar. Constant exposure to clothes, toys, food, and other objects that vary in small ways but are similar in others gradually enables her to notice how colors, shapes, tastes, uses and other regularities cut across particular objects. Similar experiences repeated in daily and weekly routines establish regularities of processes over time and expand memory. It is not repetition alone, of course, that develops awareness of regularity and memory. It is the total pattern of how the child's experience is repeatedly selected and organized to draw attention to similarities, patterns and organizations of things and events, in ever-expanding ways, that determines the quality of her recognition and understanding of general regularities.

Teaching-
Caregiving
Principles

1. Providing cognitively oriented care and instruction; explaining things because there are regularities that can be understood.

Caregiving approaches and procedures that are rational instill confidence in the child that things can be explained in terms of consistencies and causes and effects (means that produce ends). Consistency in routines is an important basis of rational care.

2. Teaching general rules about regularities instead of collections of unrelated facts.

Facts that are fitted together in a meaningful way will be better understood. This means that items and strategies used for teaching concepts and problem solving are offered as *examples* of rules to be understood (regularities), not as facts to be memorized and procedures to be slavishly followed.

3. Drawing attention to similarities between environmental characteristics through matching objects and processes which have similar features, functions, or other characteristics. (Used in connection with principle of discriminating differences listed below under Condition IX, Variety).

For example, the teacher places two things (or more at later stages) which are similar in color, shape, or function, but different in other ways, side by side. Ongoing processes can also be compared, for example, two girls walking compared with two girls running or balls rolling with balls dropping. Among other ways in which objects and processes can be matched are by comparing things by their relational characteristics, for example, by showing how two toys are similar in being bigger than two other toys, two lights brighter than two others, two sounds louder than two others, or two cars similar in moving faster than two others.

4. Arranging the features illustrating a concept to be learned so that they stand out clearly for the child to see.

This means that the significant features of each example are prominent and clearly visible; objects are presented on a smooth surface of plain contrasting color; and examples are presented in clusters, rows or other spatial arrangements that make them stand out in relation to one another.

It is not always feasible in busy care routines to arrange such ideal viewing conditions. Doing such things as pausing to point out carefully a particular item for the child to touch (a button) or holding up something to see (holding up a spoon full of squash) will usually work about as well.

5. Teaching knowledge systematically to help the child
to build up gradually and cumulatively an organized and
comprehensive picture of the world (the structure of
knowledge). (See also Condition VI, Complexity).

    a. Showing how objects can disappear and reappear, partially and totally, gradually from more angles, an increasing variety of hiding places, and eventually without the child seeing you hide it.

    b. Drawing attention to the parts of simple but gradually more complex objects (separate features, functions, and materials of which they are made), showing their purpose and position in relation to the whole object.

    c. Guiding children in taking apart and putting together jigsaw puzzles and simple assembly toys, using creative materials, and performing common household task items, (making beds, setting the table, dressing-undressing), drawing attention to part-whole relations and functions. Vary complexity according to child's progress.

    d. Grouping and interrelating things according to their characteristics (colors, geometric shapes like squares and rectangles), dimensions (arranging blocks or sticks in a row according to size or length), functions (tools like hammers for fastening nails or chairs for sitting) and other common ways of classifying (plants, animals, food, fruit, clothes, vehicles). Teach the child to search for important, and whenever possible, visible features that distinguish functions and features of different groupings (classes), such as the wheels, steering wheel, and engine of vehicles and the food-holding space and raised edges of dishes.

Beginning at the simplest levels of abstraction, gradually work up to more complex levels: start off with similarities between two, then three or more objects; then group two and later more examples of single classes of things (fruit, then fruit and vegetables) and eventually two or more classification levels and complex systems—but usually not until the late preschool period (over three).*

6. Providing hiding, discussing, and related activities to
develop memory of regularities of objects and events

    a. Hiding interesting objects for the infant to search for in more and more difficult and distant places and at increasingly longer intervals (from seconds to weeks).

* A complete chart of sequences and suggested ages for teaching logical classification are contained in a "Knowledge Curriculum" in *Curriculum and Assessment Guides for Infant and Child Care.*

    b. Asking the child to pick out a familiar object (and later newly introduced objects and pictures) that is later placed in a group of objects he or she has never seen; gradually increase the distance and time between seeing and identifying, but also increase the number of objects from which to choose (up to 15 or 20) and the similarities between the sample and the other objects.

    c. Playing games of trying to describe characteristics of hidden objects and pictures, again after increasingly longer intervals, and checking the children's descriptions (perhaps through tape recording) with the originals.

    d. Encouraging discussions of excursions and other past events, particularly where they can be compared with some record of the events (a return trip, teacher's written notes, tape recordings, photographs, or newspaper account).

Condition V: Change (Processes)

The Nature of the World (The Environment)

Change is as much a part of the environment as regularity. Basic to the processes involved in change are such dimensions as:

1. *Causality*—everything is caused by something acting on something else (often conditions in a chain of events). For example, the heat of the sun warms the ground, which, along with water and soil, causes seeds to grow.
2. *Form and functions*—various means can produce the same or different ends (one can pull or push a wagon or a toy car).
3. *Time and rate*—change takes place over time at different rates of speed (moving something or boiling water fast or slowly).
4. *Sequence*—things tend to happen in a certain order; sequences can be reversed when events are not causally linked (one can leave and return to the playroom).

Change can take several forms, such as:

1. *Movement*—from place to place
2. *Alteration in the structure* of objects or materials, such as
   a. *Reorganization*—rearrangement without changes in function (simply moving things around).
   b. *Modification*—the addition, subtraction, or alteration of parts (adding, removing, or reshaping arms of a clay figure).
   c. *Development*—construction and invention (making buildings with blocks).
   d. *Destruction*—damage causing change in function (losing a wheel of a toy car).

All forms of change may be found at each of the following levels of organization of matter in the environment:

1. *Mechanical*—physical change which does not affect the material of which something is made (changing parts without changing the material itself).

2. *Chemical*—changes in molecular composition (cooking dough to become cake, burning things).
3. *Biological*—changes in live plants and animals (growing).
4. *Social*—changes in an individual's or a group's way of doing things, in habits or customs.

Characteristics of the Child During Early Development

At birth, the infant can respond to change (stimulation) only in terms of a few automatic and poorly coordinated reflexes (sucking, looking, grasping, jerky arm and leg movements), which become more adaptive with experience. Gradually, according to the quality of experience they encounter, children learn to understand that change occurs in regular ways according to rules. They learn that things move in predictable ways, that certain events (means) cause others (ends) in predictable sequences. Children learn to use these and other rules to manipulate changes in the environment more or less automatically in increasingly complex chains of events (changing clothes, going to the store or building a block structure).

The infant's first concepts of time are acquired through the cycles of activity in care routines that stablize the infant's needs in regular time cycles. Signs of developing awareness of time are seen in the simple anticipatory movements made at two to four months in response to caregiver preparations for care (such as sucking movements made at the sight and sounds of the bottle being prepared for feeding). The gradual expansion of the scope of the child's activities and their linkage with clock and calendar time in social rituals expands the child's awareness of time concepts.

Teaching— Caregiving Principles

1. Teaching rules for how change occurs by helping the child to cope with and master the environment in daily routines and learning activities.

Actively involve the child in various tasks. Children begin to learn about change above all through working with something *they* can *do* with the environment, as a process of finding different *means* to satisfy personal needs and accomplish their own goals. Daily schedules and routines are one of the best means of teaching change concepts to infants because they experience change in relation to their closest needs. Schedules that are flexible, smooth, and varied in small ways from time to time develop the best awareness of time and change concepts. When infants are only passively involved in care routines, they are slow to develop a sense of change as a process of means producing ends and thus of how to bring about the changes they wish in order to fulfill their needs and desires. In the same way, encourage children to work out for themselves many of the problems encountered in play, such as where to find a block or a yellow crayon, how to roll a truck down a ramp, or when to find space to build. Guidance is important for learning concepts, but active experimentation is vital for mastery of change and other concepts.

2. Teaching causality, predictability; relations between means and ends, form and functions; sequence and other concepts of change as the child develops.

Show how different forms of change (movement, alterations) are found at each of the successive levels of complexity (mechanical, chemical).* Concepts of change to be taught include:

a. *Means and ends.* Demonstrating how means are related to ends (goals) and are necessary to achieve them (retrieving or moving objects with hands, tools, boxes, vehicles).

b. *Form and function.* Showing how common objects and tools are designed with features shaped to produce specific ends (seat and back of chair, knife edge, egg beater, etc.).

c. *Causality.* Drawing attention to events that are *not* directly produced by the child (or any one) to develop awareness of causes independent of the child's own actions (papers blowing by the wind, objects falling from gravity, things burning by fire, objects getting wet, plants growing).

d. *Predictability.* Guiding children in repeating similar actions to show how change involves regularities that make prediction possible; encouraging the child to say what will happen before he (or the teacher) performs the repeated action.

e. *Sequence.* Showing how parts of a task often follow a certain order because each successive event must follow or depends on the accomplishment of the earlier one (combing hair before putting on hat).

f. *Time and rate.* Helping the child to become aware of time and speed by starting different activities at the same instant. Draw attention to how the activities go at different rates, thus taking different amounts of time (two balls rolling or toy cars moving at different speeds). Show how size and complexity affect time and speed (pouring water through a small pipe and a big pipe; putting away two blocks versus ten blocks).

3. Showing how change involves the appearance of
new arrangements and forms.

Helping the child become aware that change is the way new things appear by:

a. Making comparisons between arrangements before and after change has occurred. For example, *reversing* the direction of change in simple tasks (building a tower with blocks, then taking it down; placing objects in and out of a box) and routines (drawing attention to how a sock can be put on, then removed). Comparing differences with two sets of objects, in which one set is left unchanged (seeds, cooking ingredients).

b. Showing how completely new forms often emerge from changing things (transformations). There are many ways of teaching this concept in day care, such as mixing ingredients to make cookies or a cake; growing plants from seeds and chickens from eggs; mixing water with mud or paint powder; and demonstrating with creative and constructive materials (clay, blocks).

* A detailed chart of examples and suggested ages for teaching forms and levels is presented in the "Knowledge Curriculum" in *Curriculum and Assessment Guides for Infant and Child Care.*

4. Teaching creative skills through providing
opportunities for experimentation and guidance in
creative play with different types of materials.

Creativity is a part of social life because much of human activity is directed
toward making changes that create new forms. Guiding the various types of
creative play outlined in Condition II, Social Life involves especially:

a. Emphasizing that creating involves making *new* forms (figures from clay,
   designs from collage). The child needs to be encouraged and occasionally
   shown how to try out different techniques with the same materials such
   as using a different size crayon, using shading or thick and thin lines, and
   drawing different objects in different colors, sizes, and from different
   angles. Avoid telling the child what to do—make suggestions and encourage experimentation.

b. Introducing plenty of creative materials for experimentation. Variety
   helps the child understand the endless possibilities for creating new
   forms according to the material used, such as shaping crude roads and
   houses from wet sand compared with building more even and complicated roads and buildings from blocks.

c. Showing differences between materials that perform very specific tasks
   (a piece of clothing or furniture) and those that can be used to make
   things (pencils, building bricks, paints). But also show how seemingly
   ordinary things can also be used to create in different ways, such as
   making toy boats, hats, houses, collages, from paper.

d. Guiding children to look for different ways of doing things in ordinary
   play and work tasks similarly develops inventive and creative approaches toward change. For example, making a temporary shoelace to
   substitute for a broken one from a piece of string.

5. Developing an increasingly objective sense of time
through (1) maintaining routines and activity cycles and
(2) gradually introducing the preschool child to the
measurement of chronological and calendar time.

Variation in routines and schedules is important to give children a sense of how
much change is a part of life, even their most routine experiences. But without
some consistency in schedules, the child will be retarded in learning change as
an orderly process that people can regulate. Moreover, it is especially through
a controlled flow of routine experiences, repeated daily in much the same way
and at the same pace, that the infant first learns about *time.* Eating a meal,
tying on a bib, putting on shoes and socks each take about the same relative
length of time, day after day. And it is the *difference* between how long each of
these separate events (putting on socks compared to putting on and tying
shoes) takes that establishes in a highly personal way the infant's first mastery
of time concepts. Both time, and sequence as a chain of events, are learned first
through the predictability of events in these routine cycles which vary in rate,
time, and order in consistent ways.

Teaching objective measures of *clock* and *calendar time,* as the child
moves out of infancy (age two or more), is a matter first of using the common

terms in the daily routines. Use such expressions as "it will only take," or "in five minutes," to tell the child how long it will take to wash her hands, to prepare a snack, pick up the toys, go outside. Try to give reasonably accurate estimates to develop an accurate sense of clock time. Place a big clock in the play room and point to the hands, numerals, and distances between numerals from time to time to tell the hour or show how many minutes before (or after) something happens. Do this casually without pressuring the child, and prefer-rably when he or she is looking forward to something with excitement (an excursion, a turn with a toy, a birthday cake, a snack). Because telling time is complicated, it is usually learned only over a period of years, through repeated, small experiences. Learning to count and read numerals will help in learning to tell time, but clock experiences will also help in learning numbers and numer-als.

Daily and weekly time can be similarly developed through telling about what happened yesterday, the day before, last week, tomorrow, and so on. But calendar time is also measured of course in terms of days and months with names, such as Monday and Tuesday, and September and October. These too will become familiar to the preschooler more rapidly if they are used regularly by caregivers. If a big calendar is placed on the wall and the day of the week, dates, and names of the months are referred to from time to time in interesting ways, many older preschoolers will gradually become quite familiar with those terms in preparation for school. Like clocks, calendars are also useful in learn-ing counting and numerals.

6. Keeping in mind that both short term and long term changes are characteristic of children's development.

The child's mind and personality never stay still, but are constantly developing, accumulating more knowledge and skills (more color names, new words) and acquiring new forms of skill (walking, talking, sense of independence), the variety and scope of these developments depending partly on the quality of his or her experiences. Basic to fostering developmental change in the most con-structive ways are:

a. Keeping perspectives in mind by thinking about long-range goals for de-velopment (a cooperative but self-reliant and self-supporting adult with a variety of definite interests and skills), and how short-range experiences affect these future outcomes (opportunities to cooperate and take respon-sibility in tasks each day).

b. Planning regularly and anticipating the short and long-term conse-quences of events, routines, and teaching efforts for the child's develop-ment. For example, making provision in advance for children to enjoy a few play experiences with older children under supervised conditions as a means of developing readiness and easing social adaptation to a coming promotion to the next older age group.

c. Keeping track of the daily, weekly, and monthly experiences and signs of development in order to check systematically how well things are going and see what might be done better or differently. Recording the efforts and methods that are used to promote understanding of number concepts, for instance, and looking for signs of the child's efforts to walk or budding interest in counting to consider which methods seem to work.

d. Acquiring knowledge of the characteristic ways of children at different phases of development, such as sensorimotor manipulation during infancy and the periods of learning to walk, speak in sentences, cooperate in group games, etc. Knowledge of these phases will need to be applied flexibly, recognizing that the timing of phases is to an important degree dependent on the quality of caregiving and stimulation, not only currently but *cumulatively* over the span of the child's life history.

Condition VI: Complexity

Nature of the World
(The Environment)

There is an infinite complexity of details and relationships in the world which extend over vast areas of space and can be traced both backwards and forwards in time (history). There are limitless irregularities in perceptual detail, such as the many variations in shades of color and the countless little differences in shapes, patterns, size, and material, which are usually mixed together in the ordinary environment. At the same time regularities which underly these perceptual mixtures are themselves complex. There are, for example, many potential degrees of size and loudness or examples and ways of classifying fruit, boats, or anything else. All of this complexity and the systems, networks and hierarchies into which the environment is and can be organized are difficult for the human mind to understand.

Characteristics of
the Child During
Early Development

The most prominent general characteristic of the infant mind is its simplicity and lack of differentiation. The actions of infants tend to be uncontrolled and poorly organized, moving directly and quickly in response to movement or sharp contrasts between color or form patterns. Infants lack the knowledge and skill to use complex chains of highly selected and coordinated actions in interaction with ongoing complex environmental systems.

Even the infant has considerable potential for complexity, however, such as dealing with many stimuli, employing objects as tools, discriminating different examples of a type of object, and learning language. When the environment is adequately simplified and ordered the child gradually acquires the concepts necessary to deal with the complexity of the world.

Teaching—
Caregiving
Principles

1. Guiding children's learning systematically to build up an organized, general body of knowledge adequate for coping with the complexity of the environment.

The problem of guiding learning through the sequence of stages needed to acquire a general framework of concepts during early development has been outlined under principle 5 of Condition IV, Regularity. Following this general sequence helps the child to construct order out of the apparently complex chaos in the world.

2. Using *techniques to simplify and order concepts*
presented for learning in order to ease learning of
complex material and foster cumulative progression and
mastery of a complex body of knowledge.

The task of steering a child through the complicated maze of perceptual irregularity and potential for regularity may be greatly aided by using the following
techniques:

A. Limiting the number of elements in a learning session.   Too many examples,
objects, or details presented at any one moment is confusing to an infant. Typically, present no more than 1 or 2 items at the beginning of a program and from
4 to 10 (depending on age and skill) later on. The total number of items brought
into play in any learning session should *usually* be limited to about 8 to 10 for
infants and 20 to 25 for preschoolers.

B. Matching the complexity of the learning materials and concepts presented to
the child's level of understanding.   Both the general level of understanding and
the specific competence in the particular area of learning must be taken into
account. Thus what an infant understands generally about cause and effect, for
example, needs to be considered when presenting a project to learn about the
functions of garden tools, as much as the child's knowledge of gardens and
tools. The problem of matching is especially important at the beginning of a
program, because the child's familiarity or unfamiliarity with the particular
program materials makes it easy to overestimate or underestimate the actual
level of general competence and readiness for a program. A teacher's unfamiliarity with a particular program may also cloud his or her judgments on this
point. Experimentation with several types and levels of materials may be necessary to arrive at a good diagnosis of the child's competence.

C. Balancing presentation of the novel (new) and the familiar.   Learning is
above all mastering the unfamiliar. Whether new rules or simply new examples
are involved, too many *new* items in a learning session will tend to overwhelm
the child. No more than one or two new items should be introduced in any task
or trial and usually only a few over the course of any fifteen to twenty minute
session. Use as few as one or two to as many as nine or ten, depending on the
difficulty of the material and the age and learning rate of the child. Care must
be exercised at every point, however, that mastery is not sacrificed for speed.
This approach encourages a review of previous material to build mastery and
confidence, and a rapid learning of the novel items through comparison with
the familiar ones. Even at the start of a program, such as one on size concepts,
it is usually easy to use some familiar examples the child already knows in a
general way (big blocks and balls versus small blocks and balls) as a basis for
comparing the new examples involving size in a more exact way, such as
length (crayons, rods) or width (boards, paper).

D. Repetition and review.   The importance of repetition and review cannot be
overestimated. Fortunately these procedures are partly fulfilled by the fact that
the increasingly complex concepts that appear as a program progresses almost

automatically involve reviewing previously learned simple material. Learning about area and learning to speak in sentences, for example, necessarily include continuing to use the corresponding length and width concepts and word concepts that would come first in size concept learning and learning to talk.

Nevertheless, a certain amount of learning in many concept areas uses a lot of examples or concepts that are not closely connected. Learning color names or new words (especially nouns for infants) is fairly arbitrary, needing lots of practice before the child can remember them consistently. The problem is how to continue to review regularly all the items in an increasingly large pool of learned items at the later stages of a program. One method is to review a sample of the previous colors, words, etc., in turn each day on a systematic basis, so that none are forgotten. Actually, the problem is not difficult, since many things like colors and words are encountered frequently in the children's everyday experiences and with enough review become part of their basic vocabulary.

Although initial learning is slightly different from later recall processes, repetition is a key in both phrases. Gauge the amount of repetition individually, by when the child is able to discriminate the item among several other similar items at least two out of every three trials. The range for the number of repetitions required is likely to vary from two or three exposures among quick learners in later program and review phases to as many as 20 or more clear exposures of new items to slower learners at any phase except review.

E. Examples. Every new concept needs to be accompanied by several examples. It takes more than one example of a new concept for a child to understand the concept as a general idea, rather than merely as an individual fact to be learned by rote. Examples vary in small details but share in common the critical features defining the concept. Thus in learning rules about length, for instance, the child needs to see examples in which objects of the same length vary in width, color, texture and form; this helps him to grasp the idea of length as a general, abstract rule and to treat the other features as irrelevant to the concept. The number of examples needed to insure mastery depends on the child's competence and the complexity of the concept. At least three to five examples is a recommended range for most new concepts.

F. Pacing. Regulating the rate of teaching new concepts is a key element for teaching children individually, to insure that all children are progressing, not just the group average. Pacing means introducing as many examples as *each* child needs to learn and remember just which features define each concept. It means insuring that each child learns a concept before he or she is faced with a new one, which inevitably requires a teacher to adapt to different speeds and styles in learning. Individual pacing can be a difficult problem in large play and class room settings with poor teacher-child ratios.

G. Sequencing. In order to individually pace the rate of presenting concepts to children, learning programs need to be ordered in difficulty from the simple to the complex. It is difficult to know what pace *is* fast or slow unless one knows which are the simple and which are the complex steps in a series. As illustrated earlier, concepts of area, for example, require an understanding of the dimensions of length and width separately before the child can understand how both are used to measure area. In the same way, children need to be offered simple examples, containing little confusing, irrelevant detail (triangles against a plain background) before they are exposed to complicated examples with lots of detail (triangles set in intricate designs or patterns).

The number of steps and examples in a program will influence the difficulty of the learning program, determining how fast the child can progress. Learning about the characteristics of both goats and pigs at the same time omits a sometimes needed step of familiarizing the child with goats or pigs separately, before expecting him or her to classify them at the same time. Similarly, some children will need a lot more examples of various shades of green or purple than others before recognizing shades of color accurately.

H. Immediacy (Quickness of response).   Closely linked to problems of pacing is the problem of holding attention, a critical problem with young children. Little children can and need to be taught to wait and take turns, but too much waiting breeds passivity and conformity. Unnecessary delays can be avoided through careful, advanced preparation and thorough mastery of the skills involved in the procedures and ideas of a program. Familiarity with the characteristics of the children is also essential to conducting a learning session successfully. Only with adequate knowledge of both program and children can a teacher respond flexibly and quickly enough with the variety of examples required to hold the interest and advance the progress of every child in the group. The heart of the process is, when time is limited, to be able to move yourself quickly without rushing the child; this can only be done comfortably through experience and preparation.

I. Brevity.   If an example is not grasped in a few seconds, aided by a few well-chosen and well-timed words, dragging out a demonstration usually only muddles the situation and often stifles interest. Prolonging the example tends to make the process an empty ritual, pedantic and overcontrolling, and frequently generates boredom, resentment and rebellion. Demonstrations need to be simple, clear, and above all short. Good explanations are correspondingly quick and concise. Early development is not the period when children can work over an idea in the face of confusion or pressure. They lack the abstract mental equipment to work it through in a detached, objective fashion over a period of time. Turning to play, adding another example after a pause, or even teaching a new concept are better strategies than prolonging an unsuccessful demonstration.

Condition VII: Problems

Nature of the World (The Environment)   Conflict is inherent in the nature of things. Change in itself is a result of conflict between environmental circumstances, such as between water flow and natural barriers (which produce rivers) or between growth and decay.

Problems and conflict are built into the efforts of people to survive, adapt, and expand social and cultural life in a changing world. All actions and tasks, from the simplest to the most complex, present problems that demand mental as much as physical effort to solve.

Characteristics of the Child During Early Development

Young children lack objective awareness of the nature of conflict and problems. They do, however, continually meet conflict in satisfying their personal needs, and through this and other experiences with everyday problems, they gradually develop an understanding of conflict and competence in rules for problem solving. Their inability to distinguish between their own needs and the objective world makes physical experimentation with physical and social processes in play a predominant expression of early mental activity and a primary means for learning to cope with personal conflicts in rational form. Children's progress in this area may be enhanced by incorporating the principles of care given below into day care, home, or nursery school experience.

Teaching— Caregiving Principles

1. Using a problem-solving approach to child care and education through presenting care tasks and concept learning activities as problems to be solved through experimentation and effort.

This means drawing the child's attention to differences which are in conflict and to ways change comes about as a result of conflicts needing resolution. Activity is approached as an active inquiry, trying to figure out what the parts of problems are (analysis) and how to resolve them through seeking and experimenting with alternative means (new syntheses). Even the simplest acts of eating, like using a fork, involve figuring out what part to hold, how to hold it, where the business end is and how to use it—to spear or to shovel—to get some food. The child can come to understand conflict and uncertainty as the norm, but can also come to expect that tasks can be accomplished through active effort on problems to realize goals.

2. Providing extensive self-directed experience in problem solving through free play.

Experience in free play is a highly important means of teaching children knowledge and problem-solving rules needed for physical and social adaptation. They need opportunities to think out their thoughts in action: to explore and experiment; to work with alternative means and ends; to make their own creative constructions to solve problems, and to dramatize their concerns and conflicts about problems.

3. Using problem-oriented social and object play techniques in conducting concept-learning activities.

It is easier to engage children's interest when the objects used for learning are presented in the context of play activity through:

a. Encouraging children to handle and explore objects frequently to maintain their interest and further their understanding.

b. Presenting learning materials in company with a variety of supportive play materials (blocks, boxes and toy figures) suitable for different forms of manipulative play.

c. Teaching in a relaxed and informal manner that encourages the child to play freely with the materials while learning.

d. Interacting with the child, alternating between teaching (demonstrating and asking the child to discriminate concepts) and encouraging the child to use the materials in play as he or she chooses.

e. Making learning activities more interesting through presenting tasks in such characteristic types of play as:

(1) Object play. Using search and find and object placement activities, placing examples of concepts to be learned, such as different pictures of animals in a program about animals, in and around various supportive play objects, screens and containers for the child to locate. Little children love to hunt and find and target things, especially when the objects are right in front of them (often visible) and the placement target is difficult to miss. Children quickly pick up the idea of "hiding" the learning examples in all kinds of ways to teach or simply to lead the teacher in play. The difficulty of the tasks will of course vary with age.

(2) Sociodramatic play activities. In this type of play, the caregiver (or child) pretends that the learning object is "alive", moving it around in a variety of social activities like "going to work", "visiting a friend" (which is another toy), or doing some activity, such as "washing dishes," "fishing," or "driving a car." In each case, the name of the object is an example of a concept being learned, like (for color) "red is swimming" or "orange is hopping."

(3) Creative play. Learning materials may also be used with building blocks, bricks, and other creative materials in creative activities. As the child constructs with the building materials or shapes with clay, for example, examples of the concepts to be learned can be brought into the play by the caregiver or child to form part of the construction.

In each of these activities, there is a kind of *incidental learning;* that is, learning is incidental to the play. The child's interest is maintained by teaching concepts through the different problem and dramatic play situations. The process is one of playing with objects, while, from time-to-time, drawing attention to a concept. As learning progresses, however, most children become as interested in learning concepts as they are in the play.

4. Teaching the child means-ends and other strategies
(rules) for solving problems.

The rules for solving problems apply at every level of development, from the simplest to the most complex, and in every type of activity, from language and math to athletics and dance. The chief means of ensuring developmental appropriateness is by selecting problems at the child's level, working chiefly on sensorimotor tasks for young babies, for example, and only gradually introducing problems with language after the first year.

Special attention needs to be given to important rules for problem solving as distinct from learning concept rules (knowledge). (See also Condition V, Change.) Among several important strategies for working effectively on problems are:

A. Relating means to ends. Perhaps the most basic strategy for figuring out problems is maintaining awareness of means and ends. Looking for means to bring about ends is the first rule of all activity. The question is always what ingredients and tools will produce what changes or desired goals, such as water to make seeds grow or a wrench to turn a nut.

B. Analysis. Any object or task is made up of parts. Unfamiliar problems require attention to details, such as the parts of a jig saw puzzle or a complicated new toy. For children to master what to them are the complicated routines of ordinary living, like dressing and setting the table, we need to draw their attention to the important details of each task, such as the fact and use of the handle and bristles of a broom in learning to sweep the floor. Constant analysis not only helps the child learn each task but develops an effective general strategy for solving all problems.

C. Synthesis. The parts of every object and task fit together into patterns. The child needs guidance in how parts fit together to make the whole (engine in front of a car, doors hinged on the side) and how parts relate to other objects as means to perform a task (bristles push the dirt on the floor, and we hold the handle with our hands). Synthesis is also the basis for creative activity, in which we put things together in *new* ways, as when inventing something, painting a picture or designing a building. Working with open-ended types of play materials like blocks, paints and collage gives experience in creative synthesizing.

D. Coordination. Many tasks can only be performed by keeping track of and interrelating two or more component activities simultaneously over a period of time. Experience in handling two or more small blocks; putting two and gradually more things into a basket at the same time (using one hand or two); and holding a box with one hand while opening the lid with another are all illustrations of simple infant tasks teaching coordination.

E. Seeking alternatives. Flexibility teaches the child to expect that encountering obstacles is normal to solving problems and that problems can often be overcome by several means (using crayon instead of pencil), by detours (going around a chair) or with the aid of tools (placing a chair to reach a shelf). Looking for alternative ways of doing things helps the child to become more efficient. Encouraging children to seek substitute goals (fruit instead of candy, sharing a toy or playing with another toy when one child is playing with a desired toy) similarly teaches him to be adaptive in solving problems.

F. Encouraging both reflectiveness and trial and error experimentation. It is difficult to solve problems solely in one's head—especially for the young child who lacks the abstract skills needed for complex reasoning. But it is also difficult to work out problems without thinking about how something works. Children need to be encouraged to think about what they are doing by asking them key questions about parts and relations—thus getting them to form an idea (hypothesis) about a task (how a puzzle piece fits, how a toy truck rolls) *before* they act. But some young children (particularly timid or withdrawn children) need to be encouraged to engage in more trial and error activity, through providing demonstrations and suggestions for specific action (trying out a puzzle piece, rolling a toy car). Both processes, *reflecting* on a problem and *trying out* alternatives, complement one another in reaching solutions. Together they embrace the two most important pillars of strategy, theory and practice, for coping with life's problems.

Condition VIII: Abstraction

Nature of the World (The Environment)

Many regularities in the environment are obvious only because we have acquired knowledge about them through years of experience. Dimensions of length, width, area and volume, for example, are abstractions requiring comparisons between things that may not even be present. They also ignore numerous small differences in shape, color, texture, and other aspects. Biological groupings of plants, animals, and other classifications are similarly based on selecting certain critical features (wings of birds versus leglessness of snakes), to the exclusion of a host of irrelevant details of color, shape, and size present in individual examples. The problem of grasping these abstract regularities is compounded by inconsistencies, overlap, the use of multiple criteria (houses have floors, walls, rooms, etc.) and the invisibility of many criteria (blood circulation, which is one of several criteria defining mammals).

Understanding regularities that transcend direct perceptual experience (what we can see and touch) demands that we make *mental constructions* of the world that both include many different examples, whether present, absent, or imaginary, and exclude unimportant and indeed often interfering details. To this end, language, which so easily embraces the imaginary and which defines the regularities while eliminating the trivia, is an invaluable aid to forming these mental constructions. Thus, the words "toy" and "push" for example, define the essence of *any* object or *any* action of the type named, regardless of how the particular toy looks or the particular pushing movement is executed. The human mind is capable of mastering a wide variety of complex language and aesthetic systems—ranging from pictorial and diagrammatic codes to complex verbal and mathematical systems. The foundations of abstract meaning and all symbolic codes can be well established during early development.

Characteristics of the Child During Early Development

Although for the most part mental processes work directly on the environment with the senses and actions during early development, the child is also capable of learning language early in life. In the first few months the infant learns the sound (phonological) rules for language, followed soon after by understanding and speaking words and sentences. By three years of age or earlier, depending on the quality of language stimulation, he or she can master many of the complex rules of language such as articles and subject-predicate relations ("a jet flies" as opposed to "the jet lands") that are critical to comprehending abstract regularities of the environment. The following principles are important in teaching the various abstract codes such as language, music, math and aesthetics to the young child.

Teaching—
Caregiving
Principles

1. Teaching the abstractness of regularities through guiding the child to select the essential aspects of regularities and ignore irrelevant detail and local conditions. (See also Condition IV, Regularity, and Condition VI, Complexity.)

It is as important to lead the child toward abstract regularities as it is to guide concrete perceptual-motor experiences with the environment. Young children can understand little that is not related to direct action, and must learn to abstract in order to understand environmental regularities. That is, they need to deal with the environment *selectively,* seeing how things go together on the basis of certain characteristics, even though they are different in other ways and are not physically together. Thus two trees may be tall in relation to other trees, even though one is a maple and the other is pine and the two are miles apart; and two children who are brother and sister may resemble one another and share the same parents, but are of course of different sexes and probably are different in many features and personality characteristics. If young children are always anchored in all the details of how things look, sound, and feel, they will be hampered in solving problems in school and later in work, which require thought in terms of abstract dimensions and groupings (classification). *Abstraction* is at the heart of learning the regularities we have outlined above under Condition IV. Simplifying and graduating concepts in difficulty (as outlined in Condition VI) will greatly assist children in learning to abstract.

Children can only learn to understand complex regularities through *gradually* building up their ideas in increasingly abstract forms. The process is one of aiding the child to see how our modern scientific understanding of the world is organized into many levels of abstraction, based on increasingly selective and intricate networks of features and functions, from cars, trucks, boats, and planes, to vehicles, stores, factories, transportation systems, communities, and systems in general. The techniques of simplifying and grading concepts involve a gradual *distancing* of the child in space and time from particulars to broader abstract classifications of things. For example, as children learn that apples and bananas are both fruit, they learn to see that both fruits generally share the fact of sweetness and growing on trees. But such particulars as shape, texture, skin, and taste, which had been useful criteria for telling difference between the two species of fruit, are now ignored. Effective teaching of abstract principles thus necessarily requires reducing the amount of concretization and simplification with the degree of abstractness of the concept as the child's mental processes develop. However, each new step still demands *direct* manipulation of selected and well-arranged examples to further the process of abstracting more generalized regularities. Thus direct comparisons of apples with bananas (and with other species of fruit) are still necessary, even though the particular features the child is guided to search for in identifying that the examples are fruit (as opposed to vegetables or meat, for example) become more selective (and less visible).

2. Teaching symbolic codes (picture, language, math, aesthetic,) as tools for abstracting regularities and thinking abstractly.

Symbolic codes are an essential key to developing the child's abilities to understand regularities and to think abstractly. Because of the way symbols like pictures, words, and numbers summarize information and can be manipulated, they are essential tools enabling us to deal with the environment indirectly in abstract forms. Codes help us to reflect on things and work out problems in our heads, without always having to experiment or take immediate action to work out a problem. Like any other concepts, codes of all types can be taught profitably from early infancy through daily routines, play, and planned learning activities, simplifying and ordering in difficulty the various coding concepts. The nature of the various codes, the roles they play in abstracting, and how they can be learned may be summarized as follows:

A. Pictures.   Pictures code the world on a flat surface through the use of shading, size variation, perspective, and other devices. Extensive daily exposure to pictures offers unlimited possibilities for learning many things about the environment difficult or impossible for the child to see at first hand. For example, the insides of things (machinery, the human body, bodies of water), not ordinarily visible in real life, may be shown in pictures. Miniaturization and ease of storage, access, and manipulation are additional advantages.

First, select clear, photo-like illustrations of simple, usually single objects (against a uniform, contrasting color background) common to the infants' daily experience. The infant can learn two-dimensional picture coding more easily if drawings or photographs (particularly colored ones) are compared with the same or very similar real objects. A few weeks (or less) of viewing for 6- to 12-month olds will teach them to enjoy and understand basic rules for recognizing things in pictures, opening up infinite possibilities for learning.

Their rapid and complicated movements and their frequent use of complex scenes make most films and television difficult for infants to understand, however. Even good documentaries about animals usually present themes and situations far too complicated for infants to grasp. Simple, graduated series of pictures or photographs can easily be assembled. Television and film equipment are both expensive and more complicated for day care centers to operate. Commercial films and TV tapes are too often violent or presented with considerable sexual and other social stereotypes. For example, the women are too often presented only as mothers in the homes and few people of different ethnic backgrounds are included. There is a need for well-made documentaries, both graduated for age and less stereotyped in form, presenting everyday concepts about actual children in simple play activities in urban settings. "Sesame Street" and a few similar children's programs are exceptions. But even they are too complicated for infants. They also tend to project a kind of fast-paced, almost competitive atmosphere, and emphasize monsters and other bizarre figures who appear to be stupid, quick, or bright in stereotyped ways. More emphasis is needed on gentleness, kindness, and cooperation, as well as a slower, more varied, and thoughtful picture of people and situations.

B. Verbal language. Language is unquestionably *the* essential code for the child to acquire in order to represent and manipulate abstract regularities. Words and sentences do not ressemble objects and events at all, making them initially more difficult to learn than picture codes. However, because language symbols are independent in form, as well as completely removable from the environment in space and time, they are very flexible in representing abstract and totally imaginary ideas. Language is therefore a critical tool for developing abstract, conceptual thinking in the child.

The infant can only learn the names of objects (nouns), descriptions of actions and functions of objects (mainly verbs), relations between things (prepositions) and descriptions of things (adjectives) through *hearing the labels used in relation to the objects and events referred to.* One needs to say the key word or phrase *at the moment when the infant's attention is centered* on the event in question, until he or she is spontaneously using words and short phrases.

Words that stand for common objects (nouns) are learned most easily, followed by words for frequently occurring actions (verbs), like waving "bye bye," "kiss," "drink," "eat," and "push." Babies respond best, naturally, to the names of favorite toys and to actions serving their needs (drink, eat), but any small object the baby can handle and any simple, concrete action performed dramatically is readily learned. Terms relating one things to another (prepositions like "on" or "in"), characteristics of things (adjectives like colors, shapes, or size), pronouns (I, you, me) and other parts of speech will gradually appear after the infant understands nouns and verbs and has begun to say a few individual words.

It is unnecessary to stick to only a few words (10 or less) or to use only nouns and verbs during the period before or just after the infant has begun to talk (which may come as early as 7 to 9 months or as late as 18 months or more, depending on the quality of adult language stimulation). As long as a few of the early words are repeated several times daily until they are part of the child's talking vocabulary, the bulk of the key words caregivers stress are nouns and verbs, and effective techniques are used, the infant is likely to progress rapidly. Even in the early stages, variety is also important. The child needs different examples of things each label refers to (several toy cars and real cars, or milk and juice in different containers), and in different situations to help generalize the use of each new word. A rich vocabulary from the beginning, moreover, even if children learn only a few words initially, makes them aware of the scope of language. They also need the natural context of simple phrases and sentences spoken with ease, naturalness, and varied expression to enrich the development of sound and sentence structures. In this way, children develop language in a conceptually rich manner.

C. Bilingualism. Learning two or even three or four languages fluently during early childhood is a common experience in places like middle Europe where people from different cultures marry and mix together frequently. Several languages can sometimes be as easily or more easily learned later in life, because a person's general intellectual abilities are more developed. However, when conditions are favorable, it is often easier and more advantageous to learn two (or more) languages during early development. Mastery is usually more thorough, fluent, "natural," and without accent.

Learning two languages early in life is often easier because the child's freedom from social and work responsibilities allows him or her many hours to devote to play and learning. The comparative lack of organization of mental structures and corresponding goal commitments is responsible for a responsiveness and play-oriented informality that is peculiarly well suited to experimenting with and absorbing the increase in sounds, words, and rules involved in multiple language learning. For both these reasons it is easier to devise several different natural communication settings of the kind that are so appropriate for learning languages, which are above all tools for talking about the events of everyday life.

While processes of learning two or three languages are much the same as learning only one, it helps children to realize the separateness of each language, and to learn them accurately and appropriately, when they learn them from separate sources. Hearing only Spanish at home and English in day care, or French from father, German from mother and English in school will minimize confusion in his mind. Learning more than one language from early infancy may delay speech development by a few months, but to the extent that the sources are kept distinct in the early periods and that the quality and frequency of stimulation for each language is good, progress will be consistent in each of the separate languages. Once the child has grasped the idea that there are separate languages and has mastered each one fairly well, understanding and talking freely in each one in sentences, it becomes less important to keep the sources separate. Eventually the child will be able to switch back and forth with any person at any time assuming the child continues to use each language from time to time. As long as good relations are established with the adults and other children involved, the sources are kept separate, and the new language experience of good quality is maintained long enough to develop mastery, new languages can be started by children at almost any age.

Learning two or more languages in childhood is not only sometimes necessary to help the child communicate, learn, and get along adequately with his family, playmates, and caregivers. The process also seems to broaden the mental abilities of children. The experience of learning words from two languages to stand for the same thing, and two sets of grammatical rules, appears to develop more complex and flexible mental processes that are more creative and adaptive to different ways of doing things. Bilingual children then become more skilled in figuring out all types of problems because they are used to having to find different ways of saying the same thing. They also may think abstractly more easily because of having to master and switch back and forth between two abstract codes, and being able to draw on two codes when searching for ideas.

D. Mathematics codes. The main learning task for infants to stimulate mathematical coding and thinking is to acquire familiarity with the dimensional regularities of the environment (size, length, shape, number, and the ideas of more and less) more and more abstractly. Combining the learning of general rules about regularities with solid mastery of the verbal code will prepare the groundwork for the child to master the specialized number, measurement, and calculation coding systems of arithmetic, algebra, or geometry later on.

About the age of two, the child can start to learn to count on the basis of one-to-one correspondence (as well as by rote) and to identify the number of objects in a group or set. Much of the activity for learning math concepts should consist of making direct comparisons of dimensions of line (length, width, height and depth), area, and volume, leading up to more abstract manipulation of measurement in terms of a unit system (with generalized units of inches or centimeters, quarts or liters, and pounds or kilograms, which can be used as standard units and for measuring anything without having to make direct comparisons). Putting together and taking apart groups (sets) of objects (addition, subtraction, multiplication, and division) similarly leads toward the abstract manipulation of numbers in calculating.

Simplifying and ordering math coding and concept learning activities are obviously as important as for teaching any other concepts. Indeed, because mathematic concepts and codes are relatively more abstract than other concepts, simplifying is especially important.

E. Aesthetic codes.   The development of skills in most aesthetic codes occurs as a logical extension of development in various basic skills and coding processes. Thus dance (and athletics) is founded on skill in gross sensorimotor movements, painting relates fine perceptual-motor skills to pictorial coding, and poetic and literary competence build on language skills. Music, on the other hand, follows a relatively independent origin in its specialized refinement of sound patterns in musical tones and melodies. Each aesthetic code demands its own kind of specialized activity, nevertheless, which, together with extensive experience, is essential for learning how to interpret and create meaningfully and with emotional expression.

The development of any aesthetic competence depends upon the quality of adult guidance and the extent of opportunity during development to experiment through play in the area concerned (music, drawing, play with clay for sculpture). Although qualified art or music teachers (or even partially skilled adults) are too seldom available, an open atmosphere for experimenting, stimulated by the example of much good poetry, painting, and music, will contribute much toward a good general aesthetic appreciation in young children. Every day care center can ensure that, from infancy on, good literature and poetry are read or recited regularly, good quality, live music or records are played daily, dancing is available regularly, and paper and crayons (and clay, collage, paints) are offered daily, and can encourage parents to stimulate their children in the development of artistic taste and talent.

Activities can be simplified and graded in difficulty in these areas through using appealing nursery rhymes, children's poetry, songs, and dance, and pictures (as described earlier) that are both simple and artistically pleasing (balanced in design and color). Adult music, dance, and painting (though not poetry or literature) will often arouse considerable interest in young children and serve as good examples for their own efforts to sing, dance, or paint and draw. Because of the melodic appeal of music, regular routines of listening to symphonic records will often become favored activities for infants, leading them to select and play their own choices of music by the time they reach preschool. When specialized art and music teachers trained in early education are available, aesthetic skills can be developed in more specialized ways.

Condition IX: Variety

Nature of the World (The Environment)

The world is filled with many different types of things at many levels of abstraction. There is variety in the past, in the present world, and in the many things constantly being formed through natural change, evolution, and human invention of objects, activities, and ideas. In every category and process at each level, down to the simplest concept or rule, there are endless examples, types, and combinations of things.

Characteristics of the Child During Early Development

Just as little children are limited in the complexity of what they know, so they are limited in the variety of their knowledge. Children's limited physical and mental skills make them dependent on others and restrict their ability to move about to explore the world; restrict their access to the tremendous body of information stored in books and other abstract materials; and limit their ability to understand the variety of abstract ideas that people have created.

Children's development of a rich and varied body of knowledge comes about in many ways. It is formed through exposure to variations in personal experience with different caregivers and playmates and different materials, activities, and types of environments. But it is made possible principally through the development of a varied repertoire of concepts and skills in problem solving, abstract reasoning, and language that enable children to seek and create variety on their own. By the end of the preschool period, the children can observe and understand variety meaningfully, how things are varied by type; (eating and cooking utensils, evergreen and deciduous trees); can grasp new ideas easily through talking with others; can learn about many strange things through pictures, television, movies, and (for early readers) through reading in books; and can create new and varied forms and concepts with creative materials or even ordinary objects.

Teaching— Caregiving Principles

1. Providing experience in discriminating and understanding differences in environmental characteristics through presenting objects and processes with contrasting features. (Used closely with principle of teaching similarities listed under Condition IV, Regularity)

Differences between things are the root of variety in the world. Children need exposure to the many, many ways in which the environment varies. Organized experience in how things vary also helps them to develop a more systematic understanding of differences as well as similarities in abstract regularities. The child must learn, for example, not only that things can be similar in size (or shapes, color, loudness) but that they may vary in size and in other ways.

Teaching about differences usually begins with displaying extremes of difference (polar contrasts) side by side to make them obvious, by bringing together a very large and very small dog or two obviously different colors. As children catch on to the idea of differences in size (or color, taste), shades of difference can be introduced, showing, for example, two, then three and four dogs and other things that are only slightly different in size. Differences between things with markedly contrasting functions (brooms and soap) and between contrasting processes (push or pull) are similarly learned more easily, usually, than those with less different functions (pencils and pens) and with less different processes (pushing and sliding). More shades of difference can of course be introduced to preschoolers than to infants. Much of this activity is conveniently interspersed with showing similarities between objects in their various features, as described for regularity. Variety and regularity are two aspects of the nature of things which can be constantly alternated for emphasis in teaching situations.

2. Developing awareness of the extent of variety in the world through exposing the child to many different concepts and areas of knowledge.

It is important to develop awareness of diversity by covering many different concepts and topics in the types of objects, pictures, and books shown to the child. Frequent excursions to many different settings and activities, such as different types of stores and forms of transportation; different sections of the city—new and old, business and residential, rich and poor, waterfront areas; different natural environments—the woods, lakes, mountains; and different cultural settings, are all valuable to this end. Excursions can begin as early as the infant's first year, pointing out the objects, activities, and people in simple ways. Neighborhood walks will often turn up many local events of interest, such as snow removal, street repair, and building construction.

3. Using a wide variety of examples for each new concept to enrich the child's grasp of ideas.

For each concept, a wide variety of examples will enrich the child's knowledge through broadening understanding. Furniture and houses from many regions, cultures, and climates, for example, can be looked at in pictures, if not first-hand. This approach helps to develop an adaptive as opposed to a rigidly abstract mind, as an approach confined to a few fixed types of examples would tend to do. (See also Condition VI, Complexity).

4. Selecting generally important topics and skills in various areas of knowledge in order to develop a representative variety of knowledge.

An occasional inventory of each child's development is helpful to determine whether he or she is being adequately exposed to all major categories of knowledge, skills and cultural activity. Children need familiarity with milieux and cultures other than their own, city and country environments, indoor and outdoor activities, rugged physical play involving the whole body as well as fine perceptual-motor skills, samples from at least the main bodies of knowledge of the physical and social environment, verbal and numerical coding, and continuing experience in music, dance, drawing-painting, and poetry. Early development is beyond everything a period of *general education* to establish a broad foundation needed to work imaginatively in areas of later concentration.

Condition X: Quantity

Nature of the World (The Environment)

The physical and social worlds are full of numberless things. Although they can be grouped into many types and combinations, they are too numerous to estimate, let alone inventory. Even the number of types of things, when one considers the countless alternative groupings that can be made, is endless, while adding up the examples and features, from the most microscopic to the most astronomical, leads to infinity.

Characteristics of the Child During Early Development

As with complexity, abstraction, and variety, the amount of the infant's knowledge is limited. Even through the preschool era, children under the best of circumstances will hardly have begun to tap the quantity of information that can be known.

Over the period of early childhood, an extraordinary number of concepts about the world can nevertheless become familiar and learned to varying degrees, at certain concrete and partially abstract levels. To take one index, by the time the child is five years of age, he or she can have acquired a vocabulary of several thousand words, each one representing a different concept.

Teaching—Caregiving Principles

1. *Quantity.* Presenting lots of information for the child to learn because there is so much to learn.

The child need not grow up in a physical environment unnecessarily restricted in the number of things to explore nor in a social environment that does not actively encourage learning many different things. The problem of realizing adequate development is as much one of learning quantities of concepts as it is of learning a representative variety of concepts, partly because an adequate variety necessarily requires many concepts. It is in any case an advantage to acquire early a foundation of a large body of information as well as a large variety of concepts. Because much knowledge is cumulative, learning many things early in life provides a good basis to build knowledge in any direction faster and further later on.

2. *Intensity.* Engaging the child regularly each day in guided learning without sacrificing periods of self-directed play and recreation.

A necessary part of ensuring quantity is *intensity*. Attention to planned learning activities can be a continuing daily experience throughout childhood, if the child is to absorb even in small part and in some depth all there is to know. This does not mean seriousness at the expense of play and enjoyment. Learning is best when it is integrated with the joy of understanding and mastery in experimental play, but in any case a day that includes systematic attention to learning leaves many hours for other types of enjoyment and recreation.

3. *Selectivity.* Choosing what is important to learn since we can't learn everything.

Since we cannot begin to learn all there is to know in the longest lifetime of the most intensive effort, it is obvious that the principle of quantity must be tempered by the principle of *selectivity.* It would be unwise to push a lot of miscellaneous facts at the child. Learning programs will always need to be carefully chosen and organized as to representativeness, value, utility, and above all the balanced cognitive developmental needs of each child.

Lots of miscellaneous ideas will of course be picked up spontaneously by children in the course of daily experiences in shopping, neighborhood play, illnesses, visits, trips, and various unplanned events. This is all to the good since they add to the store of the child's personal understanding of life. But when children attend a group care program for many hours daily months on end, it becomes important to select programs and materials with obvious value.

4. *Specialization.* Encouraging each child to develop specialized types of competence according to his or her emerging interests and skills.

A variety of knowledge and skills in major areas needs to be balanced by opportunities to *specialize,* to acquire a great deal of knowledge and skill in certain areas. Education that is limited to learning something about everything, or even only all important things, leaves the child with superficial general knowledge of the world and no real skills in anything. "A Jack of all trades is master at none."

It may seem silly to think of children beginning to specialize so early in life, but the seeds for later serious interests are often planted during infancy. That is why it is as important to expose children to many areas so early—music, creative activities, motor skills, and many fundamental concepts about people and things. Without variety, they will have no opportunity to develop any interest and skill at all in the neglected areas. But as a child develops, there are usually also certain areas, often following the interests of parents, older siblings, or a favorite caregiver, in which the child begins to show more persistent interest on his or her own. Special encouragement and extra time and guidance in those activities helps the child to master them better, whether they be painting, watching things grow, or playing with numbers and numerals. Not all children will become highly skilled or develop lasting interests from such early specialized encouragement, of course, but the possibilities should not be lost from want of attention. Special competence in *some* activity, moreover, adds to each child's pleasure and gives him or her a special place in the eyes of other children and adults. Many different special interests in a day care or school group lend diversity and excitement, enhancing the development of all, as long as children's overall development is not allowed to lag.

APPENDIX

Diagnostic-Development Monitoring System

(For Children 6 Months to 6 Years Old and their Caregivers)

Instructions

So much of the care and education of school age children is organized in terms of groups that many specific aspects of the development of the individual child are often left unattended. Records usually consist of grades for achievements in school learning tasks, but less often embrace processes of socioemotional and cognitive functioning that may affect school achievement and basic development in important ways. On the other hand, when attention is individualized, as is more usual in nursery schools and day care, there is not always a regular record kept of each child's progress in either learning or personality development.

At a time when group care and preschools are becoming more widely established for early development including infancy, it is important that the measures we introduce to assess children's progress do not neglect the processes of how children think and interrelate. A process orientation toward the assessment of each child's styles of development provides insight into how, and thus why, the child does what he or she does, which a record of achievements alone does not provide. This method gives teachers a means of reorienting children toward alternative modes of problem solving and social functioning where their current modes are ineffective or lead to conflict, or of strengthening present styles in those areas where children's ways seem productive and creative.

With some training, assessment of a child can be successfully carried out in the home.

Description of the Methods

This developmental monitoring plan is an instrument, for periodically assessing young children's characteristic ways of doing things, in aspects of personality and cognitive processes considered significant for coping and development. Similarly, adults' skills in facilitating such characteristics are assessed using a comparable instrument for caregivers. Processes are classified in eight categories: cognitive style, motivations, object relations, social relations with adults, social relations with peers, representational rules, locomotor skills, and the child's physical state. Each of the six psychological domains encompasses several characteristics, while the child's locomotor skills and physical state are each defined by two. The categories and their characteristics are listed as column headings on the scoring sheets (Diagnostic-Developmental Monitoring Form for Children/Caregivers). Each of the characteristics is defined in the accompanying guide in terms of positive (+) through neutral (0) to negative (−) extremes for the trait in question. When ratings are scored on the more refined seven point scale, the most positive definition is rated as 7 and the most negative definition is rated as 1. A guide defining the characteristics and the values for ratings at all points along the two different scales that can be used is included.

The scales* have been used extensively in a five year study on day care conducted by the author. The scales were found particularly useful for jointly monitoring the styles of caregivers and the clusters of children for whose development they assumed special responsibility. Each caregiver was asked to look after the week-to-week development of certain children in the group without necessarily tending to all of their daily care. In this way there was always some adult who kept track of all aspects of a child's development, since all children were divided equally among the caregivers. Usually, children were matched with caregivers in terms of how well caregivers felt they got along with the child. Some part of each day would be spent by each caregiver in caring for and observing his or her special charges and talking informally with the other caregivers about how the children were progressing in various ways.

Each cluster of children and their special caregiver were also assessed every two or three weeks (sometimes more frequently) on these diagnostic scales to see how the children were getting along and how well the caregiver was fostering each child's development on the different characteristics. Each child's and caregiver's ratings were compared with previous assessments to give an insight into both the short and long term progress. Reliabilities in the ratings between observers generally ran between .50 and .71, and typically improved with increased use of the scales. The ratings and recommendations for change were discussed each time a child was rated. The entire process proved extremely helpful for staff in working out particular ways for handling the different children's needs. Over the course of several ratings, most caregivers tended to improve in the way they handled their special children and the children correspondingly showed better adaptation in important socioemotional and cognitive processes measured by the scales.

Use of the Rating Scales

These scales are designed to be employed in two major ways: (1) to provide a diagnostic profile of a child's current patterns of functioning; or to provide a diagnostic profile of a caregiver's skills in developing optimal functioning for children in his/her charge; (2) the diagnostic information then serves as a basis for writing a set of recommendations for child care and stimulation and for improving the child-rearing skills of the caregiver. Thus on the same scoring sheet the teacher, parent, or any caregiver will have available a picture of the child's or caregiver's modes of functioning and a behavioral prescription of what methods to employ to further the child's or the caregiver's development.

---

* Developed in collaboration with Nasim Khan. See Fowler, W. *Day care and its effects on early development: A study of group and home care in multi-ethnic, working-class families.* Toronto: Ontario Institute for Studies in Education, 1978.

The Rating Scales: Assessment-Guidance Forms

Ratings on Child Characteristics

The monitoring plan is most easily described through reference to the Assessment-Guidance Form for children, on which the ratings are recorded and recommendations are written. Across the top of the page are listed in columns the child's characteristics or traits of functioning on which he or she is to be rated, each set grouped under the appropriate category. The ratings for each trait are made on the vertical lines extending between the brief positive and negative descriptions of the extremes for the characteristics. More elaborate descriptions of positive (+) and negative (−) extremes are included at the end of this guide. It will again be noted that ratings may be made either in terms of a seven point scale or by a plus or minus system.

The set of ratings to be made in the vertical rating scales will, when complete, provide a detailed picture of how well a child functions on a variety of significant psychological characteristics.

It will be noted that each of the trait names (analytic, inquisitive, autonomous, etc.) represents a positive end of a psychological dimension. A high rating on autonomy for example, implies a great deal of self-reliance and ability to assert oneself in the presence of others; a low rating on this dimension implies dependency, passivity, and a general inability to cope on one's own, either alone or in activities with others, without considerable emotional support and/or cognitive guidance. In the same way, a low value on inquisitiveness would imply a dull, monotonous, and unimaginative approach, and a low rating on cooperativeness would imply a highly individualistic or competitive approach.

It is not necessary to rate the child on each characteristic. The activities in which a child is observed may not involve all of the different characteristics. Activities in the physical environment, whether verbal or perceptual-motor, may not, for example, involve social relations; conversely, the usual conversation or sociodramatic play in the verbal medium, if that is the only situation in which the child is observed, would preclude rating the child on object adaptation, though the child could be rated on constructiveness, productivity, and creativity.

It is evident that the accuracy of ratings will improve with knowledge of the child. Ratings made on a child known intimately, through daily contact in varied situations and milieux over many weeks, can yield more complete, valid, and reliable information than a few observations derived in the course of a day or two in a single setting. It is usually difficult, however, to spend the amount of time necessary to develop a systematic set of ratings. For this reason, ratings can be based on information derived from two sources: (1) firsthand observations by a single rater in as many types of situations as feasible and (2) discussions with other observers, such as day care teachers and supportive staff, and parents, relatives, baby sitters, and others, who through continuous daily or weekly contact may be able to provide more precise information on the child's behavior in other situations.

The amount of time necessary to develop a reasonably accurate set of ratings will of course depend on the clinical and observational skills of the observer. It will also depend on opportunity, the consistency and clarity of a given child's traits, and whether they are expressed in situations available for

Diagnostic-Development Monitoring Assessment Form for Children (1975)

William Fowler and Nasim Khan

Developmental record of ______________, ______________, __________, for the period ______ to ______ ______________________

Child's Name — Group — Age — Date — Date — Name of Adult(s)

____

Setting (home, day care, indoor, outdoor, free play, guided play, physical care, etc.)

Area	Dimension	7 (+)	1 (−)
Cognitive Styles	Analytic	Focuses on significant details	Overlooks significant details
	Integrative	Puts things together	Disorganized
	Reflective	Thinks before acting	Impulsive
	Flexible	Adaptive	Rigid
	Problem oriented	Perceptive of problems	Poor awareness of problems
	Complex	Likes complex things	Likes simple things only
Motivation	Inquisitive	Explores the unfamiliar	No interest in the unfamiliar
	Concentrative	Highly absorbed	Loses interest easily
	Attentive	Follows an activity	Scattered attention
	Persevering	Overcomes obstacles	Gives up easily
Object Relations	Adaptative	Likes things	Little interest in things
	Constructive	Uses material positively	Destructive
	Productive	Accomplishes things	Finishes no product
	Creative	Original combinations	Unimaginative combinations
Social Relations — With Adults	Cooperative	Interacts constructively	Very little constructive interaction
	Adaptive	Friendly and trustful	Withdrawn / Aggressive
	Autonomous	Shows initiative	Passive dependent / Attention demanding
	Empathetic	Sensitive to others' needs	No awareness of others' needs
Social Relations — With Peers	Cooperative	Interacts constructively	Very little constructive interaction
	Adaptive	Friendly and trustful	Withdrawn / Aggressive
	Autonomous	Shows initiative	Passive dependent / Attention demanding
	Empathetic	Sensitive to others' needs	No awareness of others' needs
Representation (Verbal)	Comprehension	Excellent understanding of language	Little understanding of language
	Production	Excellent speech/babbling	Little speech/babbling
	Pictorial	Excellent use of pictures	Little use of pictures
	Number	Excellent understanding of numbers	Little understanding of numbers
Locomotor Skills	Fine motor	Excellent use of fine muscles	Poor use of fine muscles
	Gross motor	Excellent use of large muscles	Poor use of large muscles
Physical State	Energy level	Functions at a high level of energy	Functions at a low level of energy
	Health	Maintains excellent health	Maintains poor health

Rating scale: 7; + 6; 5; 0 4; 3; − 2; 1

	Cognitive Styles	Motivation	Object Relations	Social Relations: With Adults	Social Relations: With Peers	Representation	Motor Skills	Physical State
Comments on child's patterns in different areas								
Summary of adult's strengths and problems								
Suggested methods for improving child's development and learning								

Reprinted by permission

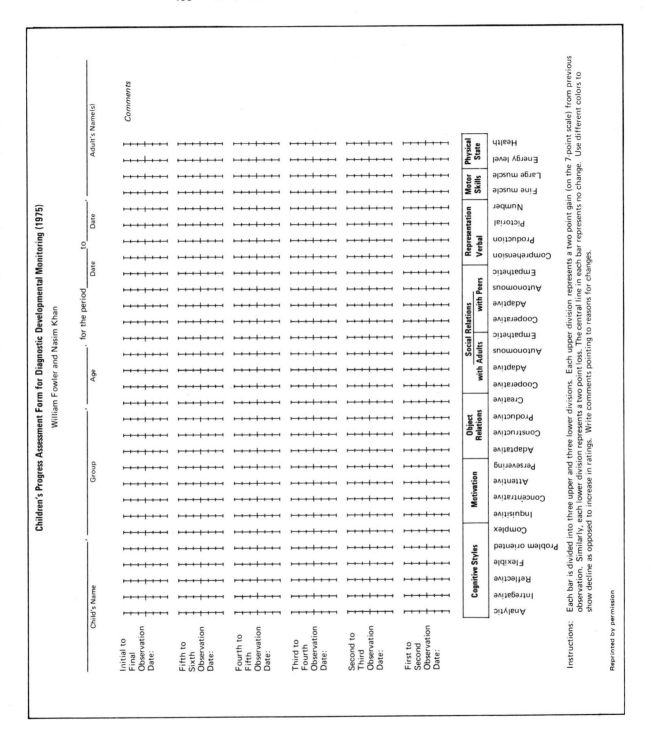

Children's Progress Assessment Form for Diagnostic Developmental Monitoring (1975)

William Fowler and Nasim Khan

Child's Name _____ Group _____ Age _____ , for the period _____ to _____ Date Date Adult's Name(s) _____

Comments

Initial to Final Observation Date:

Fifth to Sixth Observation Date:

Fourth to Fifth Observation Date:

Third to Fourth Observation Date:

Second to Third Observation Date:

First to Second Observation Date:

Column headings (bottom):

Cognitive Styles: Analytic, Integrative, Reflective, Flexible, Problem oriented, Complex

Motivation: Inquisitive, Concentrative, Attentive, Persevering

Object Relations: Adaptative, Constructive, Productive, Creative

Social Relations — with Adults: Cooperative, Adaptive, Autonomous, Empathetic

Social Relations — with Peers: Cooperative, Adaptive, Autonomous, Empathetic

Representation — Verbal: Comprehension, Production

Representation: Pictorial, Number

Motor Skills: Fine muscle, Large muscle

Physical State: Energy level, Health

Instructions: Each bar is divided into three upper and three lower divisions. Each upper division represents a two point gain (on the 7-point scale) from previous observation. Similarly, each lower division represents a two point loss. The central line in each bar represents no change. Use different colors to show decline as opposed to increase in ratings. Write comments pointing to reasons for changes.

Reprinted by permission

Diagnostic-Developmental Monitoring Assessment Form for Caregivers (1975)

William Fowler and Nasim Khan

Profile of _____, _____ for the period _____ to _____

Caregiver's Name   Group   Date   Date   Child(ren)'s Name(s)

Setting (home, day care, indoor, outdoor, free play, guided play, physical care, etc.)   Age(s)

Cognitive Styles	Motivation	Object Relations	Social Relations — With Adults	Social Relations — With Peers	Representation	Loco-motor Skills	Physical State

Encourages Child to:

Analytic, Integrative, Reflective, Flexible, Problem oriented, Complex | Inquisitive, Concentrative, Attentive, Persevering | Adaptive, Constructive, Productive, Creative | Cooperative, Adaptive, Autonomous, Empathetic | Cooperative, Adaptive, Autonomous, Empathetic | Verbal: Comprehension, Production, Pictorial, Number | Fine motor, Gross motor | Energy level, Health

Focus on significant details; Put things together; Think before acting; Adapt; Perceive problems; Like complex things; Explore the unfamiliar; Be highly absorbed; Follow an activity; Overcome obstacles; Like things; Use material positively; Accomplish many things; Original combinations; Interact constructively; Be friendly and trustful; Develop initiative; Be sensitive to others' needs; Excellent understanding of language; Excellent speech/babbling; Excellent use of pictures; Excellent understanding of numbers; Excellent use of fine muscles; Excellent use of large muscles; Function at a high level of energy; Maintain excellent health

Scale: 7 +6 5 4 3 −2 1

Leads Child to:

Overlook significant details; Be disorganized; Impulsiveness; Rigidity; Poor awareness of problems; Like simple things only; Lack of interest in the unfamiliar; Lose interest easily; Scattered attention; Giving up easily; Little interest in things; Destructiveness; Finishing no product; Unimaginative combinations; Very little constructive interaction; Withdrawing; Aggression; Passive dependence; Attention demanding; No awareness of others' needs; Very little constructive interaction; Withdrawing; Aggression; Passive dependence; Attention demanding; No awareness of others' needs; Little understanding of language; Little speech/babbling; Little use of pictures; Little understanding of numbers; Poor use of fine muscles; Poor use of large muscles; Function at a low level of energy; Maintain poor health

Cognitive Styles	Motivation	Object Relations	Social Relations — With Adults	Social Relations — With Peers	Representation	Motor Skills	Physical State

Comments on patterns in different areas

Summary of strengths and problems

Suggested methods for improving caregiving skills

Reprinted by permission

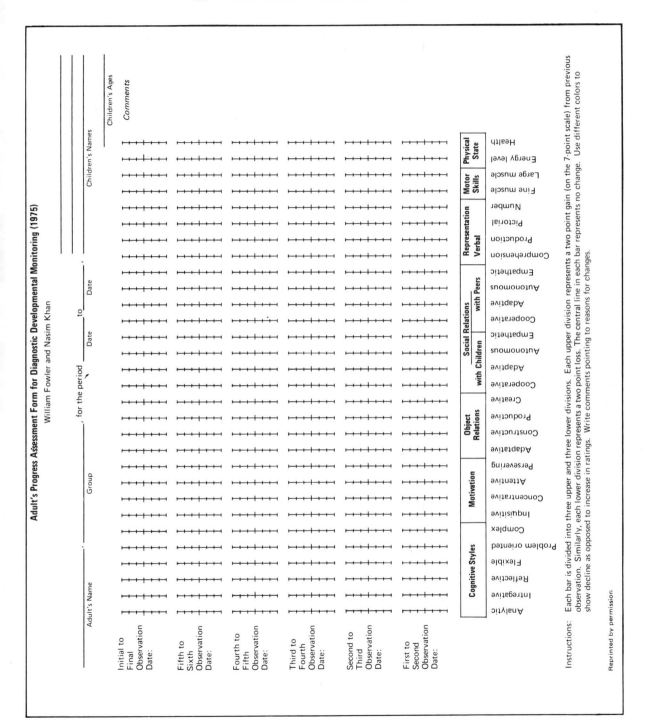

Adult's Progress Assessment Form for Diagnostic Developmental Monitoring (1975)

William Fowler and Nasim Khan

Instructions: Each bar is divided into three upper and three lower divisions. Each upper division represents a two point gain (on the 7-point scale) from previous observation. Similarly, each lower division represents a two point loss. The central line in each bar represents no change. Use different colors to show decline as opposed to increase in ratings. Write comments pointing to reasons for changes.

Reprinted by permission.

observation. It is in general more difficult to rate children who are average in many things than those who are high or low on numerous items. Usually, an observer who is unfamiliar with a child should expect to spend several sessions, distributed over two or three days and several distinct areas of activity, to complete an observation series. If a child is already quite familiar to the observer or information is available from informants (parents, teachers, students, etc.), the amount of time needed for observation should decline accordingly. Repeated experience with the use of this observational system, as well as experience with the age group and psychological observation generally, should shorten the time necessary to complete a series to an hour or so.

There is also no reason why the instrument should not be employed selectively. Repeated use with the same child as a method of monitoring critical areas and processes should enable important information to be assembled for communication to teachers weekly or even every other day or so in a few minutes' time on each occasion.

Ratings on Caregiver Characteristics

The Assessment-Guidance Form for Caregivers follows the same pattern as the children's Form. The observer evaluates the caregiver's behavior that encourages the development of positive characteristics or leads to negative characteristics. The physical, emotional, or verbal interactions of the parent, babysitter, or day care staff may be assessed on a seven point scale or by a plus or minus system in a similar manner as in the children's form.

The Rating Profile

Once the ratings are complete, a line may be drawn between ratings for each characteristic to plot a profile of the child's (or caregiver's) processes, to provide a visual picture of his or her strengths and weaknesses. If ratings are made in terms of the ($+$), (0) and ($-$) system, the plots may be placed at the center of the three respective levels (i.e., about opposite the 6, 4, and 2 points of the 7-point scale), thus yielding effectively a three-point scale plot. Where ratings have been omitted connecting lines should probably be omitted. Obviously, the more completely and consistently areas are covered, the more complete and consistent the profile will be.

Interpretative Summary by Categories

Below the rating profile is a set of spaces for describing in narrative terms the child's manner of functioning or the caregiver's level of fostering of such functioning. This method provides an opportunity to paint a qualitative picture, to single out those aspects of functioning that are most salient and explain the dynamics of how and why the child or the caregiver does what he or she does. This section is divided only into the major psychological categories to enable the description to be put together in a more meaningful way, utilizing the available ratings but adding further points about the subject's style that are specific to his or her personality. The space allocated for each category is limited in keeping with the intention of providing periodic, brief analyses of numerous children and caregivers in day care, rather than an extended analysis of each child or caregiver, once or twice a year. Where needed, further information can be added on the reverse side of the rating sheet.

General Summary of Child's/Caregiver's Styles and Problems

The final diagnostic section is a completely open space designed for a narrative summary or outline of how the child's or caregiver's ways work together to form his or her personality as a whole. In this description, for the child, the characteristics and how they are manifested from situation to situation would be emphasized. Consistencies, preferred areas of activity, and central problems would be pointed up to attempt to provide an overall understanding of the child's needs and the conditions in his life situation that have made and continue to make him act the way he does, both in positive and negative aspects. Thus conditions, attitudes, and styles in the home would be expected to be central to understanding a child and his history, but patterns in day care might in certain cases contribute to perpetuating both the strong and weak points of a child's personality. There is a strong assumption here that young children, while having the beginnings of definite styles of their own, are relatively open to change through understanding and the application of consistent ways of handling.

In the caregiver's form this summary outlines his or her strengths and weaknesses in interacting with children, but would not be expected to probe the caregiver's background and life situation with the same detail. It is assumed that awareness and discussion of problem areas would be enough to enable adults to make improvements or build on strengths.

Recommendations for Care and Stimulation

The section at the bottom of the work sheet is intended to serve as a guide for day care staff and teachers (or parents) on how to care for a child in day to day activities. Using the ratings and interpretive summaries, the rater can write a set of specific methods for working with the child or for improving the skills of the caregiver. The recommendation may be phrased in different ways, for example, one emphasizing immediate, practical techniques to deal with current problems and the other emphasizing long range considerations, which might or might not be feasible to entertain, but which in any case would take time and probably extended effort. Over-crowded home conditions, severe parental illness or death, conflict between parents and grandparents or between day care staff, unsatisfactory job conditions at home or day care, and dysfunctional parental personality styles would fall in the latter category.

A second set might divide into recommendations for teachers and recommendations for parents. These distinctions are useful, depending on the information available from home or day care and the means of implementing alternative approaches in the different settings. Other divisions might be useful, such as recommendations applying to socioemotional as against cognitive processes, or those specific to the several categories or characteristics. None of these are listed, however, to keep the form flexible since each child is likely to need his or her own combination of care methods.

The chief source of information for the recommendations is of course to be drawn from the ratings and interpretations. *The general principle to follow* is to define for teachers (or parents) the kind of experiences specially needed to improve characteristics where the child or caregiver is low (− on the plus or minus rating system or one and two on the seven-point scale). These are problem areas in which extra thought, attention, and perhaps a change in methods of care and stimulation are needed.

For those characteristics and areas in which the subject is average (left blank or marked 0 on the ± system and from three to five on the seven-point system), or above average (+ or six and seven, respectively) less immediate or significant attention is presumably required because these are already areas of relative strength, in which the child is functioning fairly well. These aspects should not be neglected, however, since most individuals can usually learn to cope better in processes in which they function in an average way, given a little guidance, particularly on traits rated on the low side of average (e.g., 3 on the 7-point scale).

In some cases, it is also important to take account of the special strengths of the individual (the areas scored + or 5 to 7), to insure that he or she continues to encounter conditions that will fortify these strong points to strengthen personality styles along already developing lines. A child who is already highly inquisitive or concentrates well, for example, needs materials, activities, and sufficient order and stimulation in his daily play environment to reinforce these positive trends. An adult who is skilled in arranging play environments for developing complexity needs to be encouraged by being assigned to tasks developing complexity.

It is, however, also true that children can have too much of a good thing. Thus a child high in social adaptiveness, cooperation, and flexibility may be too accommodating and conformist in relating to others, particularly if he or she is also low in autonomy, perseverance, and reflectiveness, characteristics that are essential for the development of his or her own cognitive and personal self system. Recommendations should be considered in the light of how the various traits are *balanced* in some constructive general system of intellectual and emotional coping.

How does one decide upon specific recommendations? Given the principle of providing experiences to help children become, for example, more analytic if they are diffuse or superficial in their approaches to problem solving, the task for adults is to draw attention to the details of objects in learning tasks, encouraging the children to search for relevant detail. The task is usually easier if a child is simply deficient in a single area (fails to perceive particulars or concentrate only when looking at pictures or when listening to statements of peers). A few special sessions of looking at pictures (or other work in a problem area) with friendly guidance in a setting free from distraction will often do wonders.

Working with a child is more difficult where the child is *generally* undeveloped in some process, such as in reflectiveness, perseverance, or object adaptiveness (interest in things). In these cases the child will need special experience and attentive guidance on the relevant characteristic in many types of situations—with toys, language, pictures, gross motor play, etc. Such children will need help in thinking and reflecting about what they are doing if they are generally low on reflectiveness (that is, impulsive) in many different activities. What is needed, in other words, is a *general* change in approach to play and problem solving activities in which the impulsive child is encouraged to take his or her time; helped to play in unpressured play situations (avoiding settings with competitive or quick-acting peers); and in which problems are explored with the child in a slow and thoughtful manner (talking quietly and asking questions about processes—how things work—as opposed to focusing on achievements or outcomes alone). There is, fortunately, usually *some* activity for almost every child in which he or she has some positive interest (object adaptiveness) and is therefore slightly less impulsive. It is often easiest to start guiding the child in new directions with such an area as a point of departure.

Quite often below-level functioning on some aspect of cognitive style or motivation is accompanied by problems in emotional functioning, which show up in specific ways in object relations (destructiveness or low productivity) or social relations (low autonomy—that is, dependency, passivity or apathy, or poor cooperativeness). In these circumstances the main direction of effort will need to be toward the child's modes of relating to others, particularly toward the significant figures in his or her life situation. Problems of insecurity, elements of rejection by parents, separation anxiety from or emotional dependency on adults are not always even the major source of emotional difficulty. But they are a common source of difficulty that may affect the child's functioning and skill development in many areas. Recommendations for resolving problems like these will lay stress on the socioemotional aspects often implicated in many areas of functioning. Involving parents and day care staff in discussions of the child's needs for a little extra emotional support and attention, particularly at points of transition between activities, can usually go a long way toward improving a child's self-concept and thus his or her motivation and cognitive styles in many areas. More deep seated or pervasive emotional problems, rooted in family conflicts will, however, usually require professional consultation.

Another source of children's emotional difficulties can be traced to the failure of adults to guide children in knowledge of social rules of cooperation and autonomy, and related rules of object adaptiveness, and constructiveness toward materials, etc. Reared too permissively or restrictively, or neglected, the child may fail to learn and value these attitudes and modes of coping. The child may not be particularly insecure emotionally or hostile toward others, but may simply require definite and consistent redirection in ways of doing things. Concerted and consistent efforts on the part of all day care staff—and preferably coordinated with discussions with the family—will be necessary to develop such modes in children, particularly if the dysfunctional modes have become generalized and habitual.

The particular prescription for each child will thus depend on the nature of the problems and the child's strengths and weaknesses. Whatever they are, recommendations will follow from the particular pattern of functioning with which the child is rated on the assessment form. Wherever socioemotional characteristics show signs of difficulty, special attention will need to be devoted not only to these problems directly but to the manner in which they affect other characteristics of the child's behavior in a number of areas. Keep in mind that the aim of this diasnostic technique is not to make each child function in some theoretically ideal and similar way in every trait and area. Each child will necessarily develop his or her own set of styles of coping and achieving, arising from the particular set of experiences that cumulatively develop his or her own modes of living and striving. The purpose of this monitoring system is merely to resolve some of the difficulties and stimulate the child's strengths in the best manner possible.

Similar prescriptions for a caregiver can be developed on the basis of observed strengths and problems in working with children. An important dimension in the development of caregiving skills in adults is communication of the weaknesses. Written statements need to be supplemented with personal discussion. If possible, make self-evaluation via video-tape or film in conjunction with the observer's discussions.

Progress Assessment Forms

Summary graphs showing changes from initial to later observations are made on the Children's Progress Assessment Form or the Caregiver's Progress Assessment Form. Each vertical bar is divided in the middle by a wide horizontal line. The three narrower horizontal lines on the upper portion are used for marking increases in ratings compared to the previous rating. The lower portion of the vertical bar is used to show declines. A rise or decline of two points on the 7-point rating scale is represented by one interval between two of the narrow horizontal lines on the progress assessment form. Each interval also represents one value (+, 0, or −) on the 3 point plus-or-minus system of scoring. It can be helpful to use different colors to designate rise and decline.

Another way of evaluating changes is to use transparencies of individual diagnostic monitoring forms to study the overlay of two observations.

Scoring System for Diagnostic-Developmental Monitoring

Plus-Minus Rating System

+ above average, highly characteristic
− below average, not at all characteristic
0 within an average range
? uncertain or insufficient information
/ does not appear applicable

Seven-Point Scale Rating System

Plus statement (+)
7 highly characteristic or salient
6 quite characteristic or salient
5 somewhat characteristic or salient

Middle Level (0)
4 neither upper statement nor lower statement is characteristic or salient-or both apply equally (at different times)

Minus statement (−)

3 somewhat characteristic or salient
2 quite characteristic or salient
1 highly characteristic or salient

Score items on the basis of the average developmental levels culturally expected for his or her age.

Note: Both children's and adults' assessment forms follow the above scoring system. However, the ratings of adults' behavior evaluate the extent to which they encourage or discourage children in comparable characteristics described below.

Definitions of Categories and Characteristics

Cognitive Styles

(Modes of looking, manipulating, and thinking in the course of solving problems, and constructing or creating things and/or interrelating with others).

Analytic

+ child focuses on details, features of objects, objects in a field, isolated relations.
− child attends to no single feature or object, has global approach to objects or situations, overlooks even prominent features, objects, and relationships.

Integrative

+ child concentrates on putting things together; looks for patterns and organizations; has synthetic approach, tends to organize things.
− child has diffuse, scattered approach, disorganized, does not connect things.

Reflective

+ child deliberates before responding, tends to work out a problem mentally.
− child tends to act without thinking, comes to decisions prematurely, very quickly; impulsive.

Flexible

+ adaptive to changing circumstances; tries out different approaches when one does not work.
− rigid, gets upset over changing circumstances, fails to adapt or try different ways.

Problem Oriented

+ Perceptive of problems and conficts; oriented toward searching for and reaching solutions; enjoys working on problems.
− Little awareness of problems; glosses over or avoids problems; little interest in working at or solving problems.

Complexity

+ Seeks complex or difficult activities, tasks and forms of play; enjoys challenge.
− Prefers simple things; generally chooses materials and activities easy for his or her developmental level.

Motivation

(Strength and type of desire to achieve, solve problems and construct things and interrelate with others).

Inquisitiveness
+ actively explores and examines environment, concerned with how things work and curious about differences, discrepancies, and the novel; points inquiringly to objects, asks questions if he or she is able.
− disinterested, plays in dull repetitive fashion largely with familiar toys and routines; unexcited by change or the unfamiliar.

Concentration
+ centers attention on objects or tasks for long periods and is not easily distracted; becomes highly absorbed in task.
− easily loses interest; fleeting attention, constant shifting of attention from one activity to another.

Attentiveness
+ watches and follows a demonstration of a toy, picture or activity with alertness; responds readily to attempts to get his or her attention.
− difficult to capture and maintain attention; resists efforts to interest him or her in an activity or demonstration.

Perseverance
+ perseveres in the face of obstacles; tries hard to overcome obstacles, works until the task is completed well.
− gives up easily in the face of obstacles; purposeless random activity.

Object relations

(Orientation toward and modes of interrelating with things, including plants and animals, but excluding people).

Object Adaptation
+ child is positively oriented toward play with toys and activity with things generally; has definitely developed interests, but adapts reasonably to change and novel objects, whether or not he or she is curious about change, novelty, or how things work.
− child is timid, fearful, has little sustained interest in activities with toys or other materials; adapts poorly or is indifferent to change.

Constructiveness in Play
+ makes positive use of materials; sensitive to the nature of materials, cares that objects, plants, animals, etc., are used to good purpose.
− very careless or aggressively destructive in use of materials; frequently breaks or ruins materials.

Productive
+ produces large number of finished products or a highly differentiated single product.
− produces no products.

Creative
+ combines things in unusual, original, imaginative ways or creates new elements, not stereotyped.
− constantly reproduces highly familiar elements, makes only stereotyped combinations.

Social Relations

(Orientations toward and modes of interrelating with adults or peers)

Cooperative
+ actively seeks to work out problems in cooperation with others, is sensitive to needs and requests of others, shares, takes turns.
− is unable to work in cooperation with others; shows no initiative in proposing solutions; often found working alone; may be highly individualistic or competitive.

Socially Adaptive
+ child approaches another person with friendliness and trust; participates in group activities but also enjoys play alone.
− child is aloof withdrawn, is not happy among people or is persistently and strongly aggressive in work or play, often without provocation.

Autonomous
+ independent, shows initiative and self reliance in coping, alone or with others; can cope with unexpected frustrations.
− child either shows no initiative and is generally passive, pliable, or dependent on others; *or* frequently seeks attention of and clings to others.

Empathic
+ aware of, sensitive to, and identifies with psychological needs and states of others.
− shows little or no awareness of, sensitivity to, or identification with psychological needs and states of others.

Representational Rules

Verbal Comprehension
+ child has excellent comprehension of spoken language.
− child has very little understanding of language.

Verbal Production
+ child babbles a lot or verbalizes at a very high level, depending on age
− child shows very little babbling or speech.

Pictorial
+ shows great interest in pictures and their details.
− shows very little interest in pictures or picture books.

Number
+ shows high interest in numbers, enjoys counting and measuring (length, width, area); interested in numerals.
− Shows very little interest in number activities, counting (either rote or one-to-one correspondence), measuring, or in numerals.

Locomotor Skills

Fine motor
+ excellent skills in fine motor activities, such as manipulating tiny objects, placing pegs in holes, cutting with scissors, stringing beads.
− Poor skills in fine motor activities.

Gross motor
+ excellent skill in large muscle activities, such as running, climbing, bicycle riding, ball throwing.
− very little skill in large muscle activities.

Physical State

Energy Level
+ highly active, continues in activities for long time without apparent fatigue. (Real energy, not nervous energy, not hyperactivity.)
− highly passive, tires easily, lies around, requires an excessive amount of sleep

Health
+ subject to very few illnesses such as colds; recovers quickly from illness; no specific continuing infection (such as eczema or chronic nasal drip).
− chronically ill with several specific health problems, easily catches infections, recovery often prolonged.

A Toy Curriculum

Key Concepts (Cognitive Rules) Intrinsic to Various Toy* Designs and Suggested Ages (Months) to Begin Using Them

Closed Structure, Specific-Purpose Materials

I. Rigid Structures (Immovable Parts)

Materials	Concepts

Real Objects
- all sizes and shapes; common and uncommon (clothes, household items, tools, community articles)
—2 to 4 months

object constancy
object variety: general information of world
object characteristics: features and functions, material characteristics such as color, shape, substance, etc.
means-ends control: contingency/causality according to use, problem solving
spatial concepts
similarity-difference: object types (leads to classification later); discrimination and matching
object relations: part-whole; dimensions of size, brightness, weight, etc.
sociodramatic-symbolic

*Certain toys (e.g., clocks, appliances) are often introduced earlier than ages indicated, but simply for object recognition without conceptual elaboration. Nearly all activities involve motor coordination, largely fine motor, but a few gross motor tasks are illustrated.

Materials	Concepts
Replicas	
• miniature copies of objects, common and uncommon (animals, people, vehicles, plants, furniture, clothes, etc.) —6 to 12 months	same concepts as real objects representation of things in three dimensional codes
• occupational and family play materials and props —12 to 18 months	
Pictures and Drawings	
• children's books, photos, adult magazines, etc. —6 to 12 months	representation of things: two dimensionally coded forms, stylized and thus more abstract forms but with greater potential variety, and abstract two dimensional representations
• diagrams (more abstract) —24 to 36 months	
Miscellaneous Manipulable Small Objects	
• containers (boxes, jars, cans)	means-ends: problem solving, etc.
• screens, barriers	containment
• small hand-sized objects (cubes, sticks, trinkets, gadgets, replicas, etc.)	obstacle-detour retrieval search and find
• retrieval tools (sticks, rakes, chairs, etc.) —5 to 8 months	
Sensory Materials	
• cotton, sandpaper, sand, wood, metals, clay, etc. —12 to 18 months	sensory variety: touch texture, material characteristics: soft-hard, rough-smooth, etc.
Tools and Utensils	
• hammer and hammering board, screwdriver; knife, fork, spoon (used earlier) —18 to 24 months	means-ends control; variations, contingency/causality, problem-solving
Multiple Sets	
• sets of any small, similar (and later dissimilar) materials —30 to 36 months	object characteristics, variety, and relations spatial concepts means-ends control similarity-differences, leading to classification
Mazes	
• groove (used with stylus), pencil	means-ends problem solving
• child size (tunnels, wooden and hedge mazes) —24 to 36 months	tracking, sequence fine motor skills gross motor skills

Materials	Concepts
Climbing Apparatus	
• walking boards, jungle gym, bars, ladders; climbing logs, forms, etc.	management of body in spatial object structures
—12 to 18 months, with equipment scaled to size	gross motor modular and hierarchical manipulation principles and coding (balance, coordination, sequence, substitution, subroutines, organization, etc.)
	alternative means-ends
Tumbling Mats	
• mats, grass, sand	management of body in relation to gravity, alone or coordinating with others; similar modular and hierarchical coding principles
—18 to 30 months	

II. Movable Structures (Movable Parts)

Materials	Concepts
Mobiles	
• free moving	movement and gravity
—0 to 3 months	object constancy, variety, and characteristics (as in Section I)
• contingency	means-ends control, (as in Section I)
—0 to 6 months	visual-motor control
	object characteristics
Rattles	
• Rattles, bells, etc.	sound
—0 to 3 months	movement and gravity
	means-ends control (as in Section I)
	visual-motor control
Live Things	
• people, animals, plants	real life object characteristics
—2 to 4 months (beginning with people)	life (gradually leading to concepts of growth, development, live systems, and ecological, psychological, and social concepts)
	movement
Balls	
—4 to 6 months	roundness
	movement: bouncing, rolling
	means-ends variations
Pull Toys	
—5 to 8 months	means-ends control (as in Section I)
	movement: rolling
	wheels: roundness, rolling
	sociodramatic-symbolic

Materials	Concepts
Devices	
• jack-in-the-box	means-ends control: variable
• surprise boxes	alternatives
• variable lever doors	object constancy
• variable lock doors	surprise
—8 to 12 months	
Mobile Replicas	
• simple vehicles	sociodramatic-symbolic
—10 to 12 months	object constancy, variety, and
• operable construction vehicles	characteristics (see Section I)
• bendable figures	different means-ends activities
• operable furniture, utensils, and	structural-functional relations
appliances; doll houses	sociodramatic-symbolic: increasing
—18 to 24 months	complexity
	object variety and characteristics
	(see Section I)
	classification
	creative shaping (see Section V)
Sand and Earth	
• dry and wet sand	sociodramatic-symbolic
• earth (with various tools,	creative-free form (see Section V)
containers, replicas)	means-ends control (as above)
—10 to 14 months	characteristics of materials: leads to
	conservation of substance
	containment-space
Water Play	
• water and colored liquids (with	sociodramatic-symbolic
floating and sinking objects,	means-ends control (as in Section I)
containers, and sociodramatic	characteristics of materials: states of
replicas)	matter; floating, sinking, density
—12 to 18 months, with close	containment-space: leads to
supervision	conservation of volume
Puppets	
• hand puppets	sociodramatic-symbolic
—18 to 24 months	story line (narrative sequence)
Counting and Measuring Sets	
• multi-object sets of discrete small	number concepts: counting, seriation,
objects (similar and later	1 to 1 correspondence
dissimilar); commercial or home	(equivalence), reversibility;
prepared	addition, subtraction and other
—18 to 30 months	arithmetic operations; conservation
• multi-object sets varied by length	length concepts: measurement
(similar and later dissimilar)	(direct and indirect, i.e. unit),
—18 to 30 months	equivalence, reversibility,
	arithmetic operations, conservation

Materials	Concepts
Mobile tools	
• pliers, adjustable wrenches, vises, large sewing needles, etc.	means-ends control: variable alternatives
—24 to 30 months	
Automatic Devices	
• wind-up toys	independent causality systems
—18 to 24 months	variety of means-ends relations
• watches, clocks, motors, machines, lights, buzzers, etc.	structural-functional relations
—24 to 36 months	power, energy, fuel, electricity
Wheel Toys	
• walkers, crawlers, kiddy cars, wagons	gross motor skills: mobility in various structural-functional forms; balance, transportation, wheel, etc.
—6 to 12 months	
• trikes, bikes	complex mobility: balance, transportation, wheel, etc.
—18 to 30 months	sociodramatic-symbolic
Swinging, Balancing, Riding Equipment	
• swings; rocking and spring horses; rocking boats; see-saws (teeter-totters); circular rides (carousel, swinging rings)	management of body on moving objects (principally balance and postural adjustment to gravity and centrifugal force)
—8 to 18 months	alternatives; means-ends control of momentum, balance

III. Take Apart Structures (Detachable Parts)

Materials	Concepts
Put Together Forms	
• rings and pegs (ungraded)	means-ends control: contingency/causality, problem solving, analysis and synthesis
• rods and holed cubes	
• snap beads	
• stringing beads	concrete structure: part-whole relations
—8 to 12 months	sequence (ungraded)
Puzzles	
• jig saw	fitting and matching: by shape, size, color, etc.
• form boards (two dimensional) and shape sorting boxes (three dimensional)	equivalence: 1 to 1 correspondence
(all starting with one to two piece puzzles)	containment-space
—10 to 12 months	object characteristics (see Section !)
	similarities and differences (see Section I)
	means-ends relations: problem solving, etc.)

Materials	Concepts
Graded Series	
• materials varying in size, (length, area, volume):	seriation of quantity, various dimensions
—10 to 16 months	reversibility
• materials varying in weight (use uniformly colored and shaped materials initially)	sequence, transitivity similarities and differences (see Section I)
—18 to 24 months)	
Complex Structures	
• defined objects built by various connecting mechanisms: bolted or screwed together, having interlocking parts, etc. (vehicles, log cabins, dolls, houses, gas stations, people, etc.)	system organization: hierarchical part-whole relations means-ends, problem solving spatial relations: increasingly complex sequence and order object characteristics (see Section I)
—24 to 36 months	sociodramatic-symbolic
Science Kits	
• materials for mechanical, electrical, magnifying, chemical experiments, magnets, etc.	means-ends: variable control (see Section I); complex inquiry characteristics of materials:
—18 to 24 months, according to complexity	processes of different states and types of matter, according to purpose

Open Structure, Variable Product Materials

IV. Modular (Unit) Construction

Materials	Concepts
Cubes	
—6 to 8 months	means-ends
	fine motor skills
	spatial relations: position, balance, gravity, linear area, verticality, bridging, etc.
	creative construction (later): modular, variable structure
Unit Blocks	complex spatial relations: enclosure,
• table (small) blocks	curve, level, cantilever, arch,
—12 to 18 months	foundation, etc.
• floor (larger—$2\frac{1}{4}'' \times 2\frac{1}{4}'' \times 1\frac{1}{4}''$)	creative construction: as above, plus
• large, hollow blocks	design principles (balance,
—14 to 18 months (small)	composition, symmetry, etc.)
—24 to 30 months (large)	sociodramatic-symbolic
	fine motor skills (microspheric scale)
	gross motor (macrospheric scale): spatial relations
	creative construction

Materials	Concepts

Construction Materials with Specialized Mechanisms

- various shapes and connecting or interlocking mechanisms
- mechanical construction sets (Meccano or Erector sets, or others with bolt-screw construction)
- carpentry and various modular craft work projects such as metals or leather (linked to free-form shape cutting)

—30 to 36 months

alternative means-ends
connecting mechanisms: dovetail, glueing, nailing, screwing, snapping, insertion, multiple connections, etc.
spatial organizations: cylindrical, oblong, stick-like, angular, etc.
two and three dimensional space
creative construction
design principles: rhythm, symmetry, composition, etc.

Aesthetic Design Blocks

- various shaped and colored sets of blocks, tiles, mosaics, etc.

—24 to 30 months

design principles: two and three dimensional space
creative construction

V. Free Form (Shaping)

Materials	Concepts

Two Dimensional

- finger paints, crayons, drawing materials

—12 to 18 months

- easel painting, pencil drawing

—18 to 24 months

- collage (related to three-dimensional and modular materials)
- cutting and shaping

—30 to 36 months

- engraving

—36 to 48 months

creative shaping
  creation of forms in space, coding
  design principles (shape, color, structure, line, symmetry, etc.)
  alternative shaping processes: painting—broad, flowing control; drawing—refined line control, shading; collage—preshaping (cutting, tearing, selecting)
  cutting—removing: combining outlining and drawing
  engraving—removing: refined line control; depth
object characteristics; part-whole relations, etc.
characteristics of materials

Three Dimensional

- sculpting materials: clay, plasticene, play dough, wax; wet sand or mud using molds

—12 to 18 months

- carving materials: soap, soft stone, wood

—36 to 48 months

creative shaping: creation of forms in space; coding; design principles (color is less important with three-dimensional materials)
alternative shaping processes: sculpting, shaping, removing, cutting, shaping
characteristics of materials
object characteristics, part-whole relations, etc.

Materials	Concepts
Craft Materials • materials for pounding, denting, bending: metals, leather, wood —24 to 36 months • weaving, knitting, needlework materials (related to modular crafts) —36 to 48 months	alternative creative shaping and organizing processes: shaping through minor alterations in relatively solid materials shaping through interlocking fine-grained linear materials on a two-dimensional plane (weaving) design principles as for other media characteristics of materials object characteristics, part-whole relations, etc.

INDEX